Information Security Management

Information Security Management

Edited by **Fiona Hobbs**

New York

Published by Willford Press,
118-35 Queens Blvd., Suite 400,
Forest Hills, NY 11375, USA
www.willfordpress.com

Information Security Management
Edited by Fiona Hobbs

International Standard Book Number: 978-1-68285-153-1 (Hardback)

The publisher's policy is to use permanent paper from mills that operate a sustainable forestry policy. Furthermore, the publisher ensures that the text paper and cover boards used have met acceptable environmental accreditation standards.

Trademark Notice: Registered trademark of products or corporate names are used only for explanation and identification without intent to infringe.

Printed in the United States of America.

Contents

Preface VII

Chapter 1 **An activity theory analysis of boundary objects in cross-border information systems development for disaster management** 1
Nitesh Bharosa, JinKyu Lee, Marijn Janssen and H Raghav Rao

Chapter 2 **A multi-modal network architecture for knowledge discovery** 18
Craig M Vineyard, Stephen J Verzi, Michael L Bernard, Shawn E Taylor, Irene Dubicka and Thomas P Caudell

Chapter 3 **Police patrol districting method and simulation evaluation using agent-based model & GIS** 30
Yue Zhang and Donald E Brown

Chapter 4 **Predicting sentencing outcomes with centrality measures** 43
Carlo Morselli, Victor Hugo Masias, Fernando Crespo and Sigifredo Laengle

Chapter 5 **An "Estimate & Score Algorithm" for simultaneous parameter estimation and reconstruction of incomplete data on social networks** 52
Rachel A Hegemann, Erik A Lewis and Andrea L Bertozzi

Chapter 6 **Social and organizational influences on psychological hardiness: How leaders can increase stress resilience** 65
Paul T Bartone

Chapter 7 **A psychological perspective on virtual communities supporting terrorist & extremist ideologies as a tool for recruitment** 75
Lorraine Bowman-Grieve

Chapter 8 **Algorithmic criminology** 80
Richard Berk

Chapter 9 **Biologically-inspired analysis in the real world: computing, informatics, and ecologies of use** 94
Laura A McNamara

Chapter 10 **Evaluating text visualization for authorship analysis** 104
Victor Benjamin, Wingyan Chung, Ahmed Abbasi, Joshua Chuang, Catherine A Larson and Hsinchun Chen

Chapter 11   **Automatic detection of cyber-recruitment by violent extremists**   117
Jacob R Scanlon and Matthew S Gerber

Chapter 12   **CrimeFighter Investigator: Integrating synthesis and sense-making for
criminal network investigation**   127
Rasmus Rosenqvist Petersen and Uffe Kock Wiil

Chapter 13   **Emotion classification of social media posts for estimating people's reactions
to communicated alert messages during crises**   140
Joel Brynielsson, Fredrik Johansson, Carl Jonsson and Anders Westling

Chapter 14   **Anticipating complex network vulnerabilities through abstraction-based
analysis**   151
Richard Colbaugh and Kristin Glass

Chapter 15   **Factors influencing network risk judgments: a conceptual inquiry and
exploratory analysis**   162
Jennifer Cowley, Frank L. Greitzer and Bronwyn Woods

Chapter 16   **Acoustic environment identification using unsupervised learning**   178
Hafiz Malik and Hasan Mahmood

Chapter 17   **Security informatics research challenges for mitigating cyber friendly fire**   195
Thomas E Carroll, Frank L Greitzer and Adam D Roberts

Chapter 18   **Evasion-resistant network scan detection**   209
Richard E Harang and Peter Mell

Permissions

List of Contributors

Preface

Every book is a source of knowledge and this one is no exception. The idea that led to the conceptualization of this book was the fact that the world is advancing rapidly; which makes it crucial to document the progress in every field. I am aware that a lot of data is already available, yet, there is a lot more to learn. Hence, I accepted the responsibility of editing this book and contributing my knowledge to the community.

Information security has gained significance over the last decade. It is playing a crucial role in designing algorithms and data bases which are implemented for international security applications. This book aims to bridge the gap between the researches and practices in this field. Some of the topics included in this book are intelligence information sharing, enterprise risk management, infrastructure protection, etc. This text will serve as a useful reference for students, professionals and researchers.

While editing this book, I had multiple visions for it. Then I finally narrowed down to make every chapter a sole standing text explaining a particular topic, so that they can be used independently. However, the umbrella subject sinews them into a common theme. This makes the book a unique platform of knowledge.

I would like to give the major credit of this book to the experts from every corner of the world, who took the time to share their expertise with us. Also, I owe the completion of this book to the never-ending support of my family, who supported me throughout the project.

Editor

An activity theory analysis of boundary objects in cross-border information systems development for disaster management

Nitesh Bharosa[1], JinKyu Lee[2], Marijn Janssen[3] and H Raghav Rao[4,5*]

Abstract

One of the main challenges in cross-border disaster management is the development and use of information systems that cater the needs of heterogeneous relief agencies, policies, activities and cultures. Drawing upon activity theory, this paper examines cross-border information systems development for disaster management. We infuse the concept of boundary objects into activity theory by the characterization of the artifacts. This allows articulating how the socio-technical objects are meshed with the process of cross-border collaboration for systems development. Our longitudinal ethnographic field study on a cross-border flood management project, VIKING, revealed how the project was empowered and developed by four key boundary objects, i.e. the governance structure of the program, two information systems (a disaster management information system and an online collaboration portal), and recurring cross-border exercises as an evaluation and feedback mechanism. The selective institutionalizations of these key boundary objects helped the participants overcome various contradictions existed in the systems development. The study results also show that both goal-oriented actions and boundary objects can affect the outcomes of long-term large-scale disaster management systems development.

Keywords: Disaster management, Information systems development, Cross-border collaboration, Activity theory, Boundary objects

Background

Disaster management (DM) entails a range of complex interdependent activities involving many collaborating organizations. It is particularly so if the disaster affects multiple countries as we have seen in the 2004 Indian Ocean tsunami or multiple regions in a single country as has been seen in the floods of Oct-November 2011 in Thailand. Although information systems are often adopted to expand the scope of management in both private and public sectors, information system development (ISD) is by itself a complicated endeavor, especially in inter-organizational and international settings where organizations with different goals, existing technologies and cultural backgrounds have to collaborate [1-3]. DM organizations (DMOs) have attempted to leverage

information systems (IS) in an effort to effectively coordinate various disaster management efforts. Developing an IS to support complex cross-border DM activities, however, is an overwhelming task even for most capable government authorities for a number of reasons.

First, the development of such a disaster management information system (DMIS) requires cross-organizational collaboration between multiple autonomous organizations. These organizations often have incompatible responsibilities, procedures and objects [4], highlighting the diverse requirements for cross-organizational information sharing systems that must accommodate a wide range of information needs and flows [5]. Second, the relational ties between many DMOs are often temporary and weak as inter-organizational collaboration is not necessary in their day-to-day operations during non-disaster periods [5]. Most DMOs rarely need cross-organizational information sharing, and thus it is hard to keep them interested and committed to the development of a DMIS for occasional use. The special systems requirements for cross-

* Correspondence: mgmtrao@buffalo.edu
[4]Management Science and Systems, University at Buffalo, 325C Jacobs Mgmt Center, Amherst, NY 14260, USA
[5]Department of GSM, Sogang University, Seoul, Korea
Full list of author information is available at the end of the article

organizational and cross-border DMIS, such as reliability, interoperability, functionality, and accessibility, present yet another reason that makes it a daunting task. Accordingly, we conceptualize a cross-border DM ISD as a complex collaborative process in which many stakeholders conduct a wide range of activities centered around various socio-technical artifact (e.g., inter-organizational structure, shared systems development environment, communication channels, etc.), some of which may change as the development process evolves.

Due to the importance of effective disaster management, there are an increasing number of scholars picking up on the challenges of cross-organizational DM ISD e.g., [6-8]. While some contributions have been made on understanding cross-organizational ISD [9], studies on cross-border collaboration for DM ISD are scarce, with only a few exceptions e.g., [1,10]. This research aims to understand the nature of boundary objects that facilitate long term cross-border DM ISD process. For this purpose, a collaborative DM ISD project between Germany and the Netherlands, entitled Program VIKING, is investigated. Employing an ethnographic field study approach, this study identifies the collaborative activities and boundary objects that have made substantial positive effects on the cross-border DM ISD process. The field study was conducted using three data collection techniques: (1) semi-structured, face-to-face interviews, (2) participatory observations, and (3) document analysis. We draw on activity theory (AT) to frame the interactions among the activities, objects, and advances in the DM ISD.

In the next section, we discuss about activity theory and boundary objects that provide a theoretical foundation for our study of cross-border DM collaborations. Then we present our research design and methodology along with a brief introduction to the studied cross-border DM collaboration case. Next, the boundary objects that play a pivotal role in the success of the collaboration activity are identified. We conclude the paper with key research findings and discussions on the theoretical and practical implications of the findings.

Theoretical foundation
Activity theory
To understand the critical success factors for a cross-border ISD, the collaboration activities must be systematically specified, and the mechanisms through which the critical factors influence the collaboration must be articulated. Activity Theory (AT) [11,12] fits well with our research objectives. AT portrays a social system as a group of individuals engaging and interacting with their environment [13], which will result in output objects (a.k.a. artifacts) [14,15]. The number of interactions and resulting artifacts can increase as the social

system persists over time, while some of the artifacts can affect the future activities and structure of the system. AT underlines the role of emergent artifacts in relation to the activity system and can untangle human-object relationships to observe the unfolding of the activity system (e.g., cross-border DM ISD project group) over time. As such, AT provides us with a useful analytical framework to examine the activities and artifacts of a cross-border DM collaboration system that can facilitate and prolong the system.

AT defines a social system as an activity system that consists of various components, including the subject (i.e., agent or actors), objectives (i.e., purposes of actions), tools, rules, community, and division of labor [11]. A subject is a person or a group of people engaged in an activity. Acting as subjects, actors can take a set of collated or extended actions in order to achieve a goal (i.e., a desirable outcome at the individual action-level), which should collectively contribute to the system-level activity. An objective is the desired outcome [16] held by the subject and motivates the activity, giving it a specific direction [13]. Transforming the objective (e.g., reduction of flood damage) into an outcome (e.g., cross-border DM initiative, development of DMIS, effective disaster response) motivates the existence of an activity system. There can be a multiplicity of objectives that may be revised or evolve over time in a long-term DM project. Community refers to the group of subjects that share the objectives of an activity system. In the context of cross-border ISD collaboration for DM, a large number of DMOs and IS vendors/consultants from the participating countries will comprise the community of the activity system. The relationships between subject, objectives and community are mediated by tools, rules and division of labor. An activity achieves an objective via a development process that typically has multiple steps or phases [17]. A "tool" can be anything used in the development process, including both material tools (e.g., servers, workstations) and tools for thinking (e.g., online forums, pressure); "rules" cover both explicit and implicit norms, conventions and social relations within the community, while "division of labor" refers to the explicit and implicit organization of the community of an activity system as the subjects are involved in the transformation process [17]. In the cross-border DM context, the rules and division of labor include institutionalized business processes and (inter-)organizational structures (e.g., national incident management system) that can widely vary from one country to another as well as among different types of collaborating organizations (e.g., firefighters vs. law enforcement vs. domain experts/hazmat).

AT was initially adopted in the IS field to understand human-computer interaction [13,16], and has also proved to be valuable in analyzing complex processes such as cross-organizational data model development i.e., [18,19]. Shankar et al. [20] outline five fundamental principles of AT based on [11].

1. The prime unit of analysis is an activity system, where an activity system refers to a collective, artifact-mediated, and object-oriented system of actions, which exists in a network of related activity systems.
2. Every activity system is subject to multiple perspectives and beliefs (i.e., multi-voicedness). The division of labor in an activity system induces diverse positions for the diverse groups of actors involved in the activity. The division of labor is a primary component of any activity system, impressed with the rules and conventions.
3. The issues and capabilities of an activity system can only be analyzed by their own history (i.e., historicity). Thus, AT implicitly incorporates the structurational view of organizational transformation where human actions and institutional structures can mutually influence each other [21-23].
4. Contradictions are the sources of changes and developments. Contradictions amass structural tensions within and between activity systems.
5. An activity system can expand its capability (i.e., expansive transformations). Expansive transformation refers to a process through which an activity system expands its capability by redesigning its own structure and changing its actions in order to resolve a challenging contradiction. As suggested in the previous (4th) principle, activity systems generally enter lengthy phases of fundamental transformations when a contradiction cannot be resolved by existing structure and practice. Such fundamental transformation, if successful, will results in a reoriented activity system [24] with an expanded capability required in the new environment.

The principles stated above make AT appropriate for examining cross-border DM ISD characterized by collective actions, historicity, contradictions and expansive transformations.

Boundary objects

AT recognizes the influences of both existing structure (i.e., rules, community, and division of labor) and human agents (e.g., human subjects using instruments or initiating an expansive transformation) [11]. Furthermore, AT appreciates shared understanding (e.g., expansive learning by the community members) as a means to improve social structures [25,26]. In relation to shared understanding, it is essential to understand the concept and role of boundary objects in cross-border collaboration activities.

Boundary objects are referred to as conceptual or physical artifacts that reside in the interfaces among organizations [27]. From a functional perspective, a boundary object is an artifact shared by a community of subjects (e.g., DMOs in cross-border collaboration) that work together to reach their individual goals. Such an object can be a material thing, but it can also be less tangible or totally intangible (e.g., plans, common ideas) as long as it can be shared for manipulation and transformation by the participants of the activity. For an object to serve as a boundary object, it must be "both plastic enough to morph to local needs and constraints of the several parties employing them, yet robust enough to maintain a common identity across sites" p. 393 [28]. Boundary objects help interacting organizations facilitate cross-organizational communication and form an organizational identity [27], while they can also act as gatekeepers that selectively filter information between the organizations. Hussenot and Missionier [29] depict them as bearers of compromises that promote cooperation between the stakeholders (p.274). Therefore, boundary objects should be able to bear various meanings assigned by different organizations while serving as a common reference point to the members of multiple organizations when they engage in mutual practice [28].

IS researchers have recognized the potential of IS as a boundary object that can facilitate boundary spanning [30,31]. Accordingly, boundary objects may include physical product prototypes, design drawings, shared IT applications, standard business forms, or even shared abstract constructs such as product yield [32].

For a boundary object to emerge, a new joint field of practice must be produced [25]. For example, a shared information system can be a joint field of practice. However, not every IS becomes a boundary object in reality because human agents in some organizations may not see its local usefulness or the IS may fail to establish a common identity across all organizations [25]. The VIKING alliance was originally an outcome object (a.k.a. artifact), but it became a part of the structure and influenced the transformation process of ISD. Hence it served as a boundary object that developed a shared identity and functioned as a communication hub.

Research design & methodology

This study adopts a qualitative, ethnographic field study approach in order to identify important factors (e.g., conditions and actions) for successful development of cross-border DM ISD. We chose a qualitative research methodology to develop a comprehensive understanding from rich field data. Qualitative methodologies are more appropriate where the research question is exploratory in nature and exists within a broader sociological context, thus necessitates rich descriptions of the social environment [33]. Furthermore, such an approach allows the exploration of unforeseen relationships and offers better insights into the inter-dependencies among the factors captured in the study [34]. Research on the evolution of a partnership, the controversies and compromises between organizations across a national border requires data that is both rich in contextual information and deep in understanding [35]. The field study was conducted over a 9-month period, covering over 4 years of cross-border collaboration that developed a DMIS at the Dutch-German border, dubbed Program VIKING. This program is described in a later section in details. Both the process of the DM ISD and the use of the DMIS in a cross-border exercise were investigated.

This field study has employed three data collection techniques: (1) semi-structured, face-to-face interviews, (2) participatory observations, and (3) document analysis. A series of semi-structured face-to-face interviews [36] were conducted with representatives of the first responder and water management agencies, the lead IT developers, and technical and managerial staff of Program VIKING. The interview protocol contained questions concerning the project initiation (e.g., history, scope, leadership), the technological solutions developed and their development process (e.g., participants, negotiation, objectives, conflicts), and factors affecting the success of the project. In the formal interviews, subjects were asked a series of open-ended and unstructured questions, augmented by follow-up questions for clarification. This procedure allowed the respondents to elaborate on the issues and ask for clarifications from the interviewees to ensure a better understanding of the context and concepts in the study [37]. Informants also discussed their motivations for participation in the program, key milestones, and technical and non-technical challenges that they had encountered thus far. Formal interviews were conducted during a cross-border DM exercise (a.k.a. ROAR). Twelve formal interviews were completed with nine key informants; three of them were interviewed twice. All formal interviews were recorded and transcribed for data analyses.

In addition to the formal interviews, we observed the use of the DMISs developed by the VIKING alliance during the three-day ROAR exercise. Participatory observations allows researchers to collect rich data in a direct way [38] while distortion of the results can be reduced to a minimum through direct interaction with research objects [39]. In total, three days of training with approximately 500 participants from both nations was observed. At least one member of the research team observed each training run, and one member attended three full days of the ROAR exercise. The data collection

criteria that guided the interviews also guided the observations. In addition, the observations allowed us to conduct opportunity-based informal interviews with DMIS users. Thanks to the cooperation and support of the Program VIKING committee, we were allowed unrestricted access to the VIKING file sharing system that hosts internal documents generated during Program VIKING. We analyzed both Dutch and German documents to enrich our understanding of the program and to clarify our interpretations of the interview and observation data. Examples of documents include project meeting reports, software requirements specification and DM ISD schedules. The lists of interviewees and full document corpus are included in the Tables 1 and 2.

Analytical framework

The literature in the field of organization studies argues that organizations, collective activities, and organizational processes are all constructed through the relationship between agencies (i.e., subjects) and objects [30]. To better understand the relationships between agencies and objects, we must observe their entanglement over time. As Hussenot & Missionier [29] have demonstrated, boundary objects evolve over time. Although the transformation and nature of boundary objects have been researched in cross-organizational environments e.g., [27,40], previous contributions have not clarified the relationships among activities and boundary objects nor the implications of changes in boundary objects for the agencies that use them. This calls for more careful consideration of how the material and social objects become "entangled" in the process of collaboration. We propose an analytical framework (Figure 1) that augments previous studies by analysing boundary objects from an AT perspective.

The proposed framework suggests that boundary objects can be synthesized by an activity system, which

Table 1 The subjects of formal interviews – the primary affiliation and the role in Program VIKING

ID	Organization	Role
1	Wateboard Gelderland	Coordinator water board
2	Decis Lab	Project manager Exercise Integration
3	Geonovum	Project manager system development and maintenance
4	Province Gelderland	Program coordinator for the Netherlands
5	Fire department	(former) Chief of the regional Fire department
6	FLIWAS	Application developer
7	Justice department	Auditor
8	Police Academy	Coordinator control room
9	Busy to	Program VIKING evaluator

Table 2 Corpus of Analyzed Documents

- Notes of the steering committee meetings from 2004–2006
- Annual project plans from 2004–2009
- Internal reviews of the cross-border exercises (both in Dutch and German), including user satisfaction with the information sharing systems
- ICT architecture planning and development documentation
- Helpdesk log files of the ISs used during cross-border exercises
- Observation notes of IS use during exercises
- Cross-border exercise scenario and scripts
- Analysis and description of the available information systems for flood management in both countries
- Analysis and description of the necessary cross-border information flows
- User manuals for FLIWAS
- Maintenance reports of FLIWAS
- Service level agreements on FLIWAS and outsourcing plans for 2009
- The education and training program for VIKING
- Functional requirements of the FLIWAS components

can in turn be morphed into the system and act as expansive solutions for subsequent cross-border DM ISD collaboration. The framework embraces AT elements such as agencies (subjects), instruments (tools), artifacts (outcomes), and environments, while environments encompasses the concepts of rules, community, and division of duties. As an activity system starts (t0 in Figure 1), it continues to exist for an extended period of time, some artifacts of its actions become boundary objects (t1). Such boundary objects transform the structure and behaviors of the activity system (t2), helping the system achieve its goals (t3). This framework emphasizes the pivotal role of boundary objects and delineates the dynamics among the structure of an activity system, the actions of its actors, and its environments.

Our framework can be directly applied to a transforming cross-boundary collaboration system (i.e., cross-border

DM ISD program), captured over time. In such a system, the desires of the subject(s), instruments and actions in the given environment shape recursive transformation processes. Some, but not all, artifacts resulting from the subject's purposeful action (i.e., outcomes) at one point of time (t1) may become a part of the structure for actions at a subsequent time (t2). Such a structure would include subjects, instruments, and environments, while the environments encompass the concepts of rules, community, and division of duties. Whether an artifact becomes a part of the system structure or not depends on the attributes of the artifacts, thus we dub "a selective institutionalization process". We posit that the acceptability of these attributes to the various stakeholders in the system (i.e., community) is the key determinant of the selective institutionalization process. Artifacts that possess the characteristics of boundary objects, i.e., well accepted and shared by the stakeholders [32,41], are very likely to become a part of the activity system's structure and exert significant impacts on subsequent activities, especially when the community of the system includes a large number of stakeholders (e.g., cross-border DM ISD). Accordingly, we pay special attention to the selective institutionalization processes in Program VIKING, where some artifacts become formal boundary objects in the system. This will enable us to identify the conditions (e.g., existing rules, available instruments, imposed division of labor) and actions (i.e., creation, institutionalization, and utilization of the artifacts) that can help achieve a desirable state of the system. The focus on institutionalized artifacts will also suggest why the conditions and actions are important in view of the internal contradictions addressed via the boundary objects, and how the expansive learning and solutions that addressed the contradictions are implemented (e.g., the subject, object, instruments, action) [42]. We use the analysis framework as a guideline for our data encoding and analysis activities.

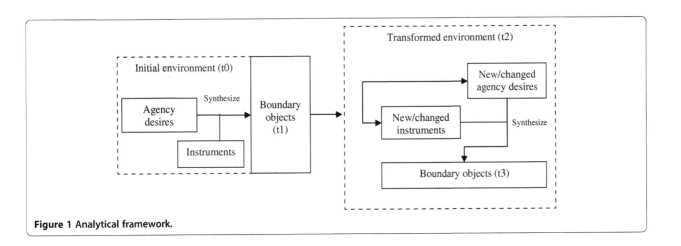

Figure 1 Analytical framework.

Coding scheme and analysis process

Collected interview data were coded using a coding scheme keyed to conventional terms used to specify the conceptual or physical objects in the program (e.g., Viking alliance, User group, Waterboard, FLIWAS, Viking Cockpit, ROAR, EU guidelines, program manager). Each instance of the objects was associated with an element of activity (i.e., actor, instrument, environment, and artifact) according to the analysis framework shown in (Figure 1) The association was recorded at instance level (i.e., each appearance in the data) because one object could be categorized into more than one element, depending on the context where the object was mentioned. For example, the Viking alliance was an artifact in the context of alliance formation activity, but it played a role of an actor, an instrument, and an environment in a later stage as it became a central part of the structure of Program VIKING.

We operationalized boundary objects as the objects mentioned by multiple data sources (i.e., interviewees from different organizations). With this operationalization,

we searched for the key boundary objects that once emerged as artifacts and later appear again as another element (e.g., actors, instruments, environment), assuming that they were the (enablers of) expansive solutions that significantly facilitated the cross-border DM ISD activity. Upon the identification of the expansive solutions, other objects and theoretical antecedents of collaboration factors were related to the solutions. This analysis was to clearly understand the conditions and actions that triggered (or were triggered by) the emergence of expansive solutions. As expected, some of the identified boundary objects had a large number of connections to other coded objects, suggesting that they played critical roles in Program VIKING. (Figure 2) is a visual representation of the concept coding scheme. The results of the analysis are described in details in the research findings section. While this research is designed as a qualitative study, this coding scheme confers some level of objectivity on the analysis procedure. The results of the interview data analysis were triangulated with the researchers' insights derived from observations of the IS use, discussions with users (DMOs)

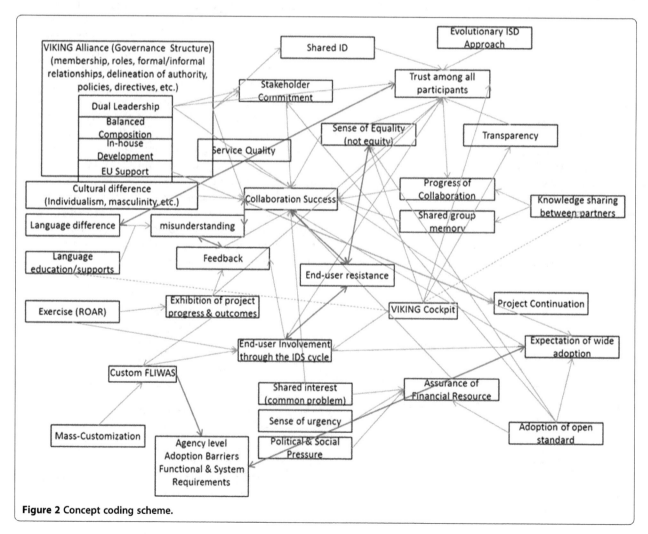

Figure 2 Concept coding scheme.

during the exercises and analyses of archival data, which enabled us to build a clear, in-depth understanding of the studied case from the compiled qualitative data [43].

Case background: program viking

In 1993 and 1995, the area surrounding Rijn River across the border of the Netherlands and Germany was affected by major floods. This area belongs to the Province of Gelderland, the Netherlands and the Province of Nordrhein-Westfalen, Germany. Both sides of the border together, this area has over 1.7 million inhabitants spread over 56 municipalities. During the floods, cattle and over 250,000 people had to be evacuated for 5–20 days. Fortunately, the dikes did hold the floods, but if they were destroyed, some parts of the area would have been submerged under 5 meters of water. This area is particularly prone to major floods as the Rijn River flows through Germany into the Netherlands before it meets the North Sea. A flood of the Rijn in one area may result in a flooding in another area as far as 40 kilometers away, which will not stop at the countries' border. In preparation for major floods, the local and regional governments in both countries have heightened dikes and stimulated development of information systems for flood management. After a myriad of agency specific, local and regional projects, an inspection of safety and flood management in the area called for integration and collaboration between Dutch and German counterparts in both water and disaster management. This led to the instantiation of Program VIKING. Program VIKING focuses on improving four aspects of flood and disaster management capability: (1) the operational processes, (2) the information sharing systems (architecture and maintenance), (3) cross-border collaboration between DMOs,

and (4) the education and training of multi-disciplinary DM teams.

There are some noticeable differences between the DM environments of the two countries (see Table 3). The differences can be understood on different levels, including the cultural, technological, and institutional levels. On a cultural level Hofstede's [44] study revealed that the Germans are generally more formal than the Dutch in their ways of interactions. On the technological level we found that the two countries use totally different sets of information systems for flood management. On the institutional level, the main difference between Germany and the Netherlands is the division of duties and jurisdictions. In Germany, municipalities have their own police, fire brigade and ambulance services, whereas in the Netherlands these DMOs are organized around 25 safety regions, each of which covers 10–20 municipalities.

As a result, various DMOs are coordinated by the mayor of the largest municipality in the safety region in the Netherlands, whereas in Germany the coordination is distributed over three levels: districts, regions and states. The province of Gelderland and the Regional Government (Bezirksregiering) of Düsseldorf have no direct operational role in this, and are primarily responsible for coordination with entities outside of their jurisdictions (e.g., the national disaster coordination center, foreign governments). With regard to the program's emphasis on improving information sharing systems, both countries have a common motive to support the program: to quickly exchange flood related information in a major flood. In the past, different municipalities and provinces were using different flood management systems and could not share information even within the

Table 3 Differences between two nations

Level	Aspect	The Netherlands	Germany
Cultural	Main language	Dutch	German
	Cultural differences	Small power distance, informal, flexible, modest, individualistic	Big power distance, formal, inflexible, strict, collectivistic-committed to institutional structure
Technological	Flood information systems	1. PoldEvac,	1. HZG,
		2. Hoogwater InformatieSysteem (HIS),	2. X-border GDI,
		3. Geautomatiseerd Draaiboek Hoogwater (GDH),	3. Deichinformationssystem,
		5. POIRE,	4. HOWISS,
		6. SHERPA	5. COBRA,
			6. DISMA
Institutional	Institutional structure	Decentralized relief agencies with high autonomy	Centralized relief agencies, moderate autonomy
	Government standards for IS development	NORA	INSPIRE
	Disaster classification and coordination structure	GRIP structure containing four levels, flood is immediately GRIP 4 (highest level)	Stuffe structure (1,2,3)

same country. The initial project budget for Program VIKING was 1.6 million Euros. Because the program is partly financed by European funds, the products of the project (e.g., reports, software) are available for government agencies of other EU countries. So far, Ireland, Scotland, England, Poland, Czechia, Slovakia and Hungary have expressed interest in the products.

Program VIKING has been a successful project, according to multiple evaluation reports from both Dutch and German sides. Every stakeholder the research team has interviewed also considered it a successful project. For example, one of the project managers noted that they could obtain continued commitment from the participating agencies and additional funding to extend the collaboration efforts after the original project term (~2006) because their cross-border collaboration and DM ISD were successful. The program managers also believed that the collaboration between the Netherlands and Germany had significantly improved since Program VIKING started.

Another indicator of the success is the prestigious National Safety Award bestowed upon Program VIKING in 2006. In addition, several countries including Slovakia and Romania have decided to adopt FLIWAS [45]. Therefore, at least as of the time this study was conducted, Program VIKING was viewed as a good exemplar of successful cross-border DM and DM ISD project.

Analysis results

To keep our research manageable, we demarcated the beginning of Program VIKING as the starting point of our analysis when the VIKING Alliance was first formed and took the leading position in the cross-border collaboration project. The alliance originally included only a small number of partners including the regional fire departments, the water boards, and some other organizations in the province of Gelderland, the Netherlands. On the German side, only one agency, Regional Government of Düsseldorf, participated in the initial alliance, resulting in an unbalanced alliance structure skewed toward the Netherlands. The Province of Gelderland was coordinating the Dutch partners, while the Region of Düsseldorf that recently took over the water management in Germany was representing various German municipalities and DMOs. The first project meetings clearly pointed out that a wider range of partnership that includes regional police departments, municipalities, and ambulance services is required in order to develop a more sustainable program and gain regional commitment for further collaboration. Some of the major contradictions in the initial Program VIKING structure existed between:

- The budget and work to be done (instrument vs. outcomes)

- Political/economic power and the wider range of stakeholders to be mobilized (instrument vs. community/rules)
- The potential partners to be included and the hierarchical structure of the organizations (stakeholders vs. community/division of duties)

The alliance responded to these challenges by actively lobbying high level officials (action) in the hierarchies of DMOs in both countries, in an effort to expand the alliance partnership (action-level goal). Although the action-level goal of the lobbying actions may not look relevant to the system-level objective (i.e., facilitating cross-border DM) of Program VIKING, it turned out to be an important step that helped the alliance build its capacity to cope with the pressure in the cross-border collaboration environment (e.g., different cultures, institutional rules, & technological preferences) and effectively utilize distributed organizational knowledge [46] to achieve intended outcomes in the subsequent actions, which eventually led to successful system-level activity of the program.

Program VIKING can be viewed as a social structure created by a cross-border DM initiative, and thus the pre-existing environments in the Netherlands and Germany, as well as the purposeful strategic decision making of the initiative, determined the initial fate of how the program was to be governed, operated, and concluded. Nevertheless, the program, as an evolving activity system, justified its existence and extended its lifespan by serving the needs of the DM communities in both countries. Our analytical framework identified four key boundary objects: the governance structure of the program (i.e., VIKING Alliance), two information systems (i.e., FLIWAS and VIKING Cockpit), and cross-border DM exercise (e.g., HAGAR, HELGA, and ROAR). These were once artifacts of Program VIKING's activities, but became parts of the program itself and played pivotal roles in the successful development and continuation of the program. Using the AT terms, Table 4 outlines the significant activities from which the key boundary objects emerged and resolved contradictions in Program VIKING. More detailed descriptions of the key boundary objects are presented in the following subsections.

Governance boundary object: cross-border governance structure

One of the first actions taken by the VIKING alliance was the installment of governance structure in itself. (Figure 3) illustrates the governance structure of Program VIKING. According to the project meeting notes, two requirements were initially set for this governance structure. The first requirement was that the representatives of the water management agencies should have a

Table 4 Analysis results of key activities

Activity / Contradictions to be resolved	Subject	Instruments	Environments (i.e., Community, Division of labor, Rule)	Outcome (Later became B.O.)
Transformation of cross-border governance structure (2001–2004)	Initial partners of VIKING Alliance	Project meetings (physical)	Dutch side: The Province of Gelderland and some regional agencies (e.g., fire depts., water boards, etc.)	New governance structure of VIKING Alliance (2004, February)
→Participation and resources to perform all expected collaboration activities		Lobbying	German side: The Region of Düsseldorf.	→Expanded & mandated participation
→Authority to mobilized all stakeholders			The Province of Gelderland coordinates other Dutch partners, while Region of Düsseldorf represents Water Mgmt. and (non-member) German agencies in the region.	→Symmetric distribution of authority and control across the border
			The roles of Police, municipalities, and ambulance services cannot be covered by the initial partners.	
			Agencies in one country must be controlled by a higher authority in the same country, but there was no clear hierarchy set for the Alliance.	
Development of IS for DM collaboration (2005, May-November)	Transformed VIKING Alliance (esp. steering committee)	Project meetings (physical) with the end-user groups and key stakeholders	An expanded set of alliance partners with incompatible ISs	FLIWAS (version 1 was first released in November 2005)
→Exceedingly fragmented ISs		Decentralized/unorganized info sharing	All partners in one country are now under the leadership of a single program manager in that country.	-First possibility of cross-boundary information sharing
→Need to support agencies in two countries/languages		EU Funding secured by the transparent governance structure		-Awareness of the potential of DMIS for effective flood management
→The deployment, access, and use of the IS must be easy for the large number of partners		ISD feasibility study		-VIKING Cockpit (first online release in June 2006)
Development of IS for ISD Collaboration (2006, January-June)	"	"	Increasing number of alliance partners (e.g, the Dutch National Ministry of Internal Affairs)	→Efficient cross-border info sharing, knowledge/project management for collaborative ISD
→Inadequacy of physical project meetings for the large stakeholders		+ Advanced knowledge/project management technologies	Prospect of extended funding by the European commission	Easy access to & evaluation of DM IS (FLIWAS online version)
→Inadequacy of decentralized information sharing among the large stakeholders		Existing Internet infrastructure		
→Need easier access to FLIWAS		FLIWAS (web-invoked light version)		
Institutionalization of regular field exercises (November 2005-May 2009)	"	"	Increasing number of alliance partners & other stakeholders (spectators, potential partners/adopters/investors)	Cross-border DM

Table 4 Analysis results of key activities *(Continued)*

→Need to evaluate the performance of cross-border DM collaboration, information sharing, and DMIS		Performance metrics	Exercises (HAGAR exercises in 2005, HELGA exercises in 2006 ROAR exercises in 2008)
	+	Independent consultants	→Demonstration of the successful progress & justification of the collaboration program
Need to demonstrate and promote the program for continued support	FLIWAS	Academic researchers	→Empirical test and improvement of collaborative DM IS (FLIWAS) & DM performance
	VIKING Cockpit	Exercise planning, advertisement, promotion	→Stronger sense of community/partnership
	Prospect of commercialization (consultation and software delivery) to other countries in Europe		

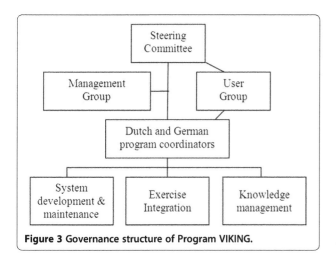

Figure 3 Governance structure of Program VIKING.

formal position in the governance structure. According to one of the informants, the motive behind this was "without the representation of the end-user group in the governance structure the program would not attain the necessary level of commitment of all the necessary partners. Moreover, we had to incorporate the end-users in our group meetings in order to understand their information needs". The second requirement for the cross-border governance structure was that it should equally distribute the authority and control between Dutch and German partners. Consequently, the alliance appointed two program managers, one for the Dutch partners and one for the German partners, to mediate the partners at the national level. One of the program managers stated that "we needed to have two program managers because we wanted to gain full commitment of all the agencies involved. It would be very difficult for a Dutch program coordinator to organize and lead German program teams… the [dual-head] leadership was also expected to better appreciate the cultural differences and promote the trust in the program, in addition to securing commitments, from the both sides".

The creation of governance structure for the VIKING alliance can be interpreted as a goal-oriented purposeful action, from the AT perspective. VIKING alliance was the subject of the action that formalized their structure (outcome) by using various instruments like requirement analyses and project meetings. This action and the resulting outcome addressed a contradiction between the alliance partners (subject) and the (absence of) rules and specification of duties to coordinate them. The design of this governance structure was influenced by the existing structure (e.g., the organizational hierarchies among the alliance partners, power structure in the cross-border context) and yet could influence the following actions as an added structural factor of Program VIKING. According to the analysis framework, this is because the outcome became a boundary object for the

stakeholders while it was transforming the structure to resolve the internal contradiction. In addition to developing a shared identity among the alliance partners-a necessary condition for a boundary object [41]-the dual-head leadership prevented potential conflicts emerging from cultural differences by separating control over the partners on each side of the border. The two program managers acted as spokespersons for partners in each country to ensure the internal consistency of the alliance within and across the border. The governance structure also assured commitments of key stakeholders by mandating their involvement in the governance structure. As a result, partners could understand their roles in cross-border DM operations and had a good overview of what was expected from them and from the other partners. In general, the governance structure promoted a high level of trust among the alliance partners by providing a sense of equality and transparency. Especially, the high level of transparency developed through the governance structure was critical for obtaining further EU funding for Program VIKING. Mandated participation of key stakeholders and dual-head leadership are two distinctive attributes of the self-evolved governance structure. In terms of authority, the appointed program managers were well known and experienced leaders in the DM community and provided with the legal authority to mobilize all alliance partners in each side of the border. As a result, the governance structure could successfully coordinate the roles, responsibilities and resources of the alliance partners without explicit rules and policies.

IS boundary object: information systems for collaborative disaster response

As one of the original focus areas of Program VIKING was cross-border information sharing, one deliverable expected from the program was an architecture that would interconnect existing ISs of various DMOs across the border. Nevertheless, development of a new IS was not planned in the project proposal. The steering committee conducted a study of the existing DMIS in both countries, in an effort to find the best way to integrate the ISs already in place. However, the analysis reports revealed that the existing IS not only lacked the functionality for flood management, but also were exceedingly fragmented with overlapping functionalities. Based on the analysis reports, the steering committee concluded that it would be more viable for the partners to develop an entirely new IS for cross-border DM, which was later named FLIWAS. The purpose of FLIWAS was to "ensure that all relief workers on both sides of the border have access to the same information systems and make decisions based on real-time data in a disaster situation." Thus, FLIWAS has strong a characteristic of decision support solutions with the capability to

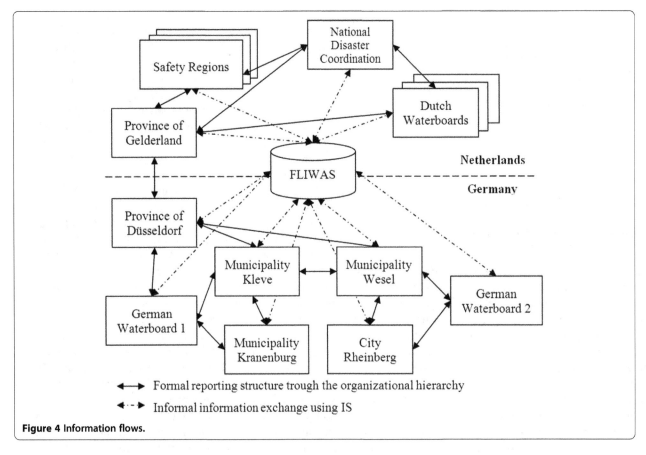

Figure 4 Information flows.

integrate data from heterogeneous sources and run simulations to predict possible flood scenarios. The FLIWAS design guidelines specify that: the application (1) must be multilingual (Dutch, German and English), (2) accessible on the web (invocation via a browser), (3) come in multiple versions (e.g., full vs. light, installable vs. online) with a modular-architecture, and (4) comply with open standards. Major functional modules developed to date include: flood visualization, flood level and risks prediction, evacuation scenario simulation, and emailing.

FLIWAS is designed to make use of existing measurement and flood forecast systems, flood warning plans, flood risk maps and disaster scenarios, as well as various geographical information systems (GIS) data [47]. Users can selectively install the modular components of FLIWAS to meet their specific needs, while their access to the different functions is controlled by a role based authentication system [47,48]. The system uses a client–server architecture, where an Internet browser or installed software agent can be used to access FLIWAS services running on a Linux-based server [45]. The GIS module is built on UMN-MapServer, and the databases can be built on PostgreSQL or Oracle [48,49]. (Figure 4) illustrates the FLIWAS-aided information flows between different Dutch and German DMOs.

As shown in the figure, only one formal communication channel existed between province of Gelderland and Region of Düsseldorf at the international level, which had to mediate all cross-border information flows from/to the waterboards and regional DMOs. Even within a country, not every DMO had a direct formal connection with every other DMO. FLIWAS enabled DMOs to bypass the clogged formal communication channel and instantly exchange information with each other, achieving a shared situational awareness of the status of dikes, water level, and pumps during a flood.

IS boundary object: information portal for collaborative project management

Similar to the case of FLIWAS, the initial proposal for Program VIKING did not include any plan to develop an IS for the collaborative program itself. In the early stages of the program, the alliance partners shared information with each other via physical group meetings and presentations, printed documents, and emails. However, as the number of partners steadily increased, these means of information sharing quickly turned inefficient, and issues such as document versioning, format compatibility and security started to gain priority on the meeting agendum. After multiple requests from partners for a shared document repository, the steering committee decided to initiate the development of a collaboration portal, which resulted in a new IS named VIKING Cockpit. VIKING Cockpit collects and provides access to all essential information of Program VIKING. There were three initial requirements for the VIKING cockpit. First, this cockpit should be able to store a large amount of data in various formats, ranging from geographical maps to meeting reports. Second, access to this portal should be secured as the stored data may contain sensitive information. Finally, the portal should be available in both Dutch and German. Later, another requirement was added to the list: the portal should be able to invoke FLIWAS. Consequently, the VIKING Cockpit now has a link to a light version of FLIWAS and thus can play the role of a DMIS during disaster, in addition to the role of a collaboration portal for the program during a non-disaster time.

FLIWAS and the VIKING cockpit are two major, but originally unplanned IS artifacts of Program VIKING. Development of FLIWAS was initiated by an expansive learning-a realization that the original plan of action (i.e., interconnecting existing ISs) was not a good solution, given the available economic, organizational, and technical resources (instruments), for the system level activity (i.e., facilitate cross-border DM). Similarly, the VIKING Cockpit was developed to better fulfill the alliance partners' managerial needs for the collaborative project, rather than for cross-border DM operations. Since both ISs are expansive solutions designed to solve eminent contradictions in the existing structure (e.g., the large number of stakeholders and their legacy systems incapable of effective information sharing), many alliance partners quickly accepted these solutions. For example, while FLIWAS was still in the beta stage, two out of three Dutch Waterboards had already adopted it to exchange information with their neighboring German Waterboards. Such proactive early adoptions accelerated the IS-led transformation of the cross-border DM communication structure, as the practice instated an efficient direct information sharing network across the two countries, in addition to the existing hierarchical and formal reporting channel [46]. The link to FLIWAS in the VIKING Cockpit further boosted the responders' adoption of both ISs and secured their places in the institutional structure. Even though many DMOs have not officially adopted FLIWAS yet, they still can try FLIWAS via VIKING Cockpit anytime anywhere, which has made the learning and feedback structure of Program VIKING radically easy and simple. The enforced involvement of key stakeholders and use of open standard in the IS development process also helped lower resistance to the ISs and cultivated the emergence of a common identity among the alliance partners as they engaged in a common set of practices (i.e., development, evaluation, and revision of the ISs) [25]. Note

that FLIWAS and VIKING Cockpit have gone through a cyclic process of evaluation and revision, through which the cross-border DM and DM ISD structures have also been transformed along the ISs.

Feedback boundary object: cross-border exercises

The other key boundary object that we have found is a series of large scale cross-border DM exercises. Three major exercises are: HAGAR (2005), HELGA (2006), and ROAR (2008). The explicit goals of the exercises were to improve (1) multi-agency collaboration between relief agencies on different echelons (strategic, tactical and operational levels) of response, (2) cross-border information sharing between the Dutch and German relief agencies, (3) information provisioning to the operational units during floods, and (4) developments of skills in using information systems for flood control. Apparently, the primary contradiction addressed by the exercises is the fact that cross-border DM structure, including the institutional rules, coordination plans, and operational procedures, cannot be examined under the normal condition due to the distributed DM responsibilities (division of duties). VIKING Alliance used its political and relational power in order to mobilize alliance partners and resources to conduct full-scale exercises, which provided the participants with chances to get acquainted with the cross-border DM structure, surrounding environments, and available ISs. ROAR had an additional objective to evaluate whether or not the newly developed DMIS (i.e., FLIWAS) were successful in meeting the requirements of the DMOs. One software developer stated that: "Even though we knew FLIWAS was not yet fully functional, we had to show our sponsors and users that FLIWAS was on a path to success, in order to build a foundation for survival of the program and prevent partners from exiting the alliance". Hence, ROAR was also used as a showcase and a test bed that allowed a large number of stakeholders to experience and evaluate the new DMIS.

The cross-border exercises made significant impacts on the collaborative DM activities in several ways. Since the exercises were recursive and large in scale, they became a widely recognized institutional mechanism for training and evaluation by mid-2007. Through the exercises, end-users of the newly developed FLIWAS could try the system in a simulated disaster environment, share their ideas with other end-users, and provide feedback to DMIS developers. In doing so, they could also improve their understanding of the roles and interdependencies of various DMOs in the larger context of cross-border DM operations. Thus, the institutionalized exercises became a knowledge creation and sharing mechanism, significantly improving the expansive learning capacity of Program VIKING. Cross-border

Table 5 Attributes and effects of key boundary objects

Key boundary object*	Attributes	Consequences (factors)
1. VIKING Alliance Governance Structure	•Expanded partnership	•Assured commitments of key stakeholders
	→Covers the full spectrum of necessary functions for collaborative DM & ISD.	•Improved understanding on the division of duties.
	•Mandated participation	•Prevented cultural conflicts
	→Institutionalized positions for key stakeholders (e.g., end-user groups) in the governance structure	•Ensured national-level consistency
	•Dual-head leadership	•Ensured political power to mobilize all alliance partners
	→Appoint an authoritative leader.	•Provided a sense of equality and transparency
	→Confer enough legal authority.	→Promote trust among partners
		→Secure further funding
2. Information Systems	•Convenient & secure access to all partners	•Created a new layer of direct communication links for DMOs.
A. FLIWAS	→Web-based	→Bypass hierarchical controls
B. VIKING Cockpit (Knowledge/Project Mgmt.)	•Modular multi-version	→Remove stove-piping
	→Flexible implementation options	→Remove bottleneck at the border
	•Multi-lingual	•Increase knowledge sharing/creation for ISD
	•Neutral design	•Lowered adoption barrier
	→Use open standards	•Interested other EU states
	→Independent of national DMO structure.	•Increased acceptance of IS
	•Mandated involvement of all key stakeholders	•Increased interoperability
3. Feedback mechanism (Cross-border DM Exercises)	•Large scale to involve the full spectrum of	•Improved individuals' understanding of cross-border DM operations.
	→Partners	•Provided a built-in feedback mechanism
	•Recurrent exercise	→Offer DMIS evaluation opportunities
	•Invite potential stakeholders	→Encourage expansive learning
		•Demonstrated the progress of the ISD
		→Showcase for FLIWAS to EU states
		→Revamp internal interests, involvement, and commitment
		→Keep EU/external supports

* Conditions for a key boundary object in the analysis framework: 1) developed as an expansive solution, meaning it is adaptable and scalable to changing stakeholder needs, and 2) become an influential part of the activity system structure.

exercises have also been great places to exhibit the progress of the project, as the exercise organizers invited not only the current alliance partners but also members of a wider community including media, academics, investors, and DM managers in other regions and countries. By demonstrating the progress of the exercise, the program could earn trust from its stakeholders and secure further involvements and commitments (e.g., partnership & budget) for the program activity. Table 5 summarizes the attributes and positive effects of the key boundary objects, which can answer not only "what" influenced the successful cross-border DM collaborative but also "how" and "why" those success factors were enacted in the particular social structure.

Conclusions

This research developed and applied an AT-based analytical framework to investigate key boundary objects in cross-border ISD for disaster management. We identified three types of boundaries objects that greatly contributed to the cross-border collaboration: 1) governance structure, 2) information systems and 3) recurring evaluation/feedback opportunities. The information systems category included two boundary objects: an easily accessible DMIS prototype and an online portal for project management. The selective institutionalizations of these key boundary objects helped the participants to overcome various contradictions existed in the socio-technical system of collaborative cross-border disaster management.

Specifically, the uncertainty about the collaboration project's future (i.e., lifespan), the limited information sharing capability in the DM community, and the wide geographic and functional dispersions of the collaboration partners were alleviated by the key boundary objects.

Provided the circumstances are similar, managers of cross-border DM projects are recommended to take a strategy that develops and institutionalizes the above mentioned key boundary objects. It is not the creation of boundary objects however, but the attributes possessed by those boundary objects that actually determine the fate of a project. For example, each participating country must have an authoritative and trusted representative in a trans-national governance structure, if the governance structure were to play a key role in the cross-border DM project. For an information system to be a key boundary object, it should allow all potential users convenient and secure access, flexible implementation options, and power to overcome the limitation in the existing DMO structure (e.g., formal reporting channels in the national incident management system). DM exercises can also be a key boundary object if they involve the full spectrum of stakeholders and offer evaluation and feedback opportunities in regular bases. The managers of cross-border DM projects are also expected to constantly monitor and analyze, using our analytical framework, the socio-technical structure of their project. They should look for structural contradictions and devise a solution that can be implemented with existing means and resources. If such a solution has the characteristics of boundary objects, the managers should promote the solution to be a more permanent part of the project structure even after the target contradictions are eliminated. Adding a clear and useful boundary objects will further improve cross-organizational interactions, commitments and appreciation of the project activities and outcomes.

This study also contributes to the academic community by developing a framework that analyzes the process through which material and social objects become interwoven in a cross-border DM collaboration system. This AT-based framework can help researchers identify important key boundary objects that can overcome the structural limitations and challenging conditions of large-scale DM collaboration projects. This research is, to our best knowledge, the first to employ AT for an investigation of cross-border DM ISD. The principles of AT (e.g., mediation by objects, historicity and expansion) make this theory suitable for studying a cross-border DM ISD context. By accounting for the time component (i.e., historicity) in AT, our analytical framework recognizes the possible feedback loop between pre-existing social structure and goal-oriented purposeful actions. Accordingly, the proposed analytical framework can suggest potential causal links between the success factors for cross-border DM collaboration and the attributes of key boundary objects

While this study examines a cross-border ISD in the DM domain, the findings can provide useful insights to researchers in other domains as well. Many private-sector companies seek to establish collaborative relationships for new opportunities or threats. When such a collaborative relationship spans across multiple cultures, legal jurisdictions, and an extended period of time, the key boundary objects identified in this paper can be developed to induce a similar positive influence in a new context. Our framework will be particularly useful when the system being analyzed is a complex and persistent social structure that involves a large number of stakeholders. This study is based on a single ethnographic study and presents only a partial view of cross-border DM ISD collaboration. Since we studied two countries in Western Europe, some cultural similarities might have affected our findings. Future research may examine relationships between cultural distance and collaboration success in cross-border DM ISD. Although our qualitative approach provides a deep understanding of the processes and issues in question, the findings require quantitative validation. Therefore, developing and validating a quantitatively testable model of cross-border DM ISD success will be the next step of this research stream. Of course, more qualitative studies in the cross-border DM ISD collaboration area will enrich the small pool of testable hypotheses.

Abbreviations
AT: Activity Theory; DM: Disaster management; DMIS: Disaster management information system; DMO: Disaster management organization; IS: Information systems; ISD: Information system development.

Competing interests
The authors declare that they have no competing interests.

Authors' contributions
All four authors equally contributed to this study. They were deeply involved in every step of the study including research design, literature review, data collection & analysis, paper write-up, and multiple cycles of internal revisions phases. All authors read and approved the final manuscript.

Authors' information
N Bharosa received his PhD from the Delft University of Technology where he currently works as a research associate. The topic of his PhD dissertation was netcentric information orchestration in public safety networks. His current research interests include standard business reporting, compliance by design and information quality assurance. His work has appeared in several conference proceedings and journals including Decision Support Systems, Information Systems Frontiers and the Journal of Cognition, Technology and Work.
J Lee is Associate Professor of Management Science and Information Systems in Spears School of Business and a faculty associate of the Center of Telecommunications and Network Security (CTANS) at Oklahoma State University. He holds a Ph.D. (2007) in Management (MIS) from University at Buffalo, Master of Information Systems from Griffith University, Australia, and B.B.A. from Yonsei University, Korea. His current research interests include inter-organizational information sharing, effective information security and privacy measures, and success of new information technology applications. J. Lee's research articles have appeared in leading academic journals and

conference proceedings such as DSS, CACM, ISJ, IEEE Transactions on SMC, ICIS, and HICSS. He has also served as a guest editor and associate editor for special issues of leading journals and conferences such as MIS Quarterly, Information Systems Frontiers, and ICIS. Some of his research and educational projects have been supported by NSF, NSA, and DoD.

M Janssen is director of the interdisciplinary Systems Engineering, Policy Analyses and Management (SEPAM) Master program, manager of the "IT and Business architecture" executive program and an associate professor within the Information and Communication Technology section of the Technology, Policy and Management Faculty of Delft University of Technology. His research interests are in the field of e-government, crises management, information coordination, intermediaries, brokers, orchestration and shared services. He is particularly interested in situations in which heterogeneous public and private organizations want to collaborate, in which information technology plays an enabling role and solutions are constrained by organizational realities and political wishes and there are various ways to proceed, all directions having its own implications. He is (associate) editor of various journals, edited several special issues, chaired various conferences and has published over 200 refereed publications.

HR Rao is SUNY Distinguished Service Professor in the School of Management and Adjunct Professor of Computer Science and Engineering at the University at Buffalo. He is also WCU visiting professor at the department of GSM, Sogang University, Korea. He holds Ph.D. (1987) degree from Krannert Graduate School, Purdue University, M.B.A. (1981) from University of Delhi, India, and B. Tech.(1979) from Indian Institute of Technology, India. His research interest includes Information and Decision Theory, e-Government and e-Commerce, Information Assurance, and Economics of Information. He serves as Co-Editor-in-Chief of Information Systems Frontiers, guest senior editor of MISQ and AE of IEEE SMC, DSS, ACM Trans on MIS, etc. Prof. Rao has published over 120 archival journal papers in MISQ, ISR, IEEE SMC, DSS, Management Science, etc. He has received best paper and best paper runner up awards from ISR, ICIS, AMCIS and other conferences.

Acknowledgements

The research of the 2nd and 4th authors has been supported by US National Science Foundation under grant # IIS-0809186. The research of the fourth author has also been funded in part by Sogang Business School's World Class University Project (R31-20002), funded by Korea Research Foundation as well as by the Sogang University Research Grant of 2011. The usual disclaimer applies. The authors appreciate the Dutch disaster management personnel who provided their valuable opinions and the ROAR organizers, Program VIKING, for their cooperation and support for our research.

Author details
[1]Delft University of Technology, Jaffalaan 5, 2628BX, Delft, The Netherlands. [2]Spears School of Business, Oklahoma State University, 317 North Hall, 700 N. Greenwood Ave, Tulsa, OK 74106, USA. [3]Delft University of Technology, Jaffalaan 5, 2628BX, Delft, The Netherlands. [4]Management Science and Systems, University at Buffalo, 325C Jacobs Mgmt Center, Amherst, NY 14260, USA. [5]Department of GSM, Sogang University, Seoul, Korea.

References
1. M Akmanligil, P Palvia, Strategies for global information systems development. Inf. Manage. 42, 45–59 (2004)
2. SR Urs, KS Raghavan, Vidyanidhi: Indian digital library of electronic theses. Commun. ACM 44, 88–89 (2001)
3. N Bharosa, J Lee, M Janssen, Challenges and obstacles in information sharing and coordination during multi-agency disaster response: propositions from field exercises. Inf. Syst. Front. 12, 49–65 (2010)
4. M Turoff, M Chumer, B Van De Walle, X Yao, The design of a dynamic emergency response management information system (DERMIS). J Inf Technology Theory and Application 5, 1–35 (2004)
5. J Fedorowicz, JL Gogan, Reinvention of interorganizational systems. Inf. Syst. Front. 12, 81–95 (2010)

6. A Sagun, D Bouchlaghem, CJ Anumba, A scenario-based study on information flow and collaboration patterns in disaster management. Disasters 33, 214–238 (2009)
7. J Fedorowicz, JL Gogan, CB Williams, A collaborative network for first responders: lessons from the CapWIN case. Gov. Inf. Q. 24, 785–807 (2007)
8. JJ Xu, H Chen, Fighting organized crimes: using shortest-path algorithms to identify associations in criminal networks. Decis. Support. Syst. 38, 473–487 (2004)
9. N Romano Jr., J Pick, N Roztocki, A motivational model for technology-supported cross-organizational and cross-border collaboration. Eur. J. Inf. Syst. 19, 117–133 (2010)
10. M Careem, C Silva, R Silva, L Raschid, S Weerawarana, Sahana: Overview of a disaster management system (In IEEE international conference on information and automation, Colombo, Sri Lanka, 2006), p. 361
11. Y Engeström, Activity theory and individual and social transformation, in Perspectives on activity theory, ed. by Y. Engeström, R. Miettinen, R.L. Punamäki (University Press, Cambridge, 1999), pp. 19–38
12. Y Engeström, Learning by expanding: An activity-theoretical approach to developmental research (Orienta-Konsultit, Helsinki, 1987)
13. B Nardi, Context and consciousness: Activity theory and human computer interaction (MIT Press, Cambridge, 1996)
14. LS Vygotsky, Mind in Society: The development of higher psychological processes (Harvard University Press, Cambridge, 1978)
15. Y Engeström, R Miettinen, RL Punamäki, Perspectives on activity theory (learning in doing: social, cognitive and computational perspectives), in, ed. by R.L. Punamäki (University Press, Cambridge, 1999)
16. OW Bertelsen, S Bodker, Activity theory, in HCI models theories, and frameworks: Toward a multidisciplinary science, ed. by JM Caroll (Morgan Kaufmann, 2003), pp. 291–324
17. K Kuutti, Activity theory as a potential framework for human computer interaction research, in Context and consciousness: Activity theory and human-computer interaction, ed. by BA Nardi (Massachussetts Institute of Technology, Cambridge, 1995), pp. 17–44
18. R Chen, R Sharman, N Chakravarti, HR Rao, SJ Upadhyaya, Emergency response information system interoperability: development of chemical incident response data model. J. Assoc. Inf. Syst. 9, 200–230 (2008)
19. R Chen, R Sharman, HR Rao, S Upadhyaya, An exploration of coordination in emergency response management. Commun. ACM 51, 66–73 (2008)
20. D Shankar, M Agrawal, HR Rao, Emergency response to mumbai terror attacks: An activity theory analysis, in Cyber security, cyber crime and cyber forensics: Applications and perspectives, ed. by R. Santanam, M. Sethumadhavan, M. Virendra (IGI Global, Hershey, PA, 2011), pp. 46–58
21. J Yates, WJ Orlikowski, Genres of organizational communication: a structurational approach to studying communication and media. Acad. Manage. Rev. 17, 299–326 (1992)
22. WJ Orlikowski, Using technology and constituting structures: a practice lens for studying technology in organizations. Organ. Sci. 11, 404–428 (2000)
23. WJ Orlikowski, The duality of technology: rethinking the concept of technology in organizations. Organ. Sci. 3, 398–427 (1992)
24. M Tushman, E Romanelli, BM Staw, Organizational evolution: A metamorphosis model of convergence and reorientation, in Research in organizational behavior, ed. by LL Cummings, BM Staw (JAI Press, Greenwich, 1985), pp. 171–222
25. N Levina, E Vaas, The emergence of boundary spanning competence in practice: implications for implementation and use of information systems. MIS Q. 29, 335–363 (2005)
26. Y Engestrom, Activity theory as a framework for analyzing and redesigning work. Ergonomics 43, 960–974 (2000)
27. U Gal, K Lyytinen, Y Yoo, The dynamics of IT boundary objects, information infrastructures, and organisational identities: the introduction of 3D modelling technologies into the architecture, engineering, and construction industry. Eur. J. Inf. Syst. 17, 290–304 (2008)
28. SL Star, JR Griesemer, Institutional ecology, 'translations' and boundary objects: amateurs and professionals in Berkeley's museum of vertebrate zoology, 1907–1939. Soc. Stud. Sci. 19, 387–420 (1989)
29. A Hussenot, S Missonier, A deeper understanding of evolution of the role of the object in organizational process: The concept of "mediation object". J. Organ. Chang. Manag. 23, 269–286 (2010)
30. PR Carlile, A pragmatic view of knowledge and boundaries: boundary objects in new product development. Organ. Sci. 13, 442–455 (2002)

31. R Lindgren, M Andersson, O Henfridsson, Multi-contextuality in boundary-spanning practices. Inf. Syst. J. **18**, 641–661 (2008)

32. N Levina, Collaborating on multiparty information systems development projects: a collective reflection-in-action view. Inf. Syst. Res. **16**, 109–130 (2005)

33. A Strauss, J Corbin, *Basics of qualitative research* (Sage, Newbury Park, 1990)

34. I Benbasat, D Goldstein, M Mead, The case research strategy in studies of information systems. MIS Q. **11**, 369–386 (1987)

35. AM Pettigrew, Longitudinal field research on change: theory and practice. Organ. Sci. **1**, 267–271 (1990)

36. RK Merton, M Fiske, PL Kendall, *The focused interview: A manual of problems and procedures*, 2nd edn. (Free Press, New York, 1990)

37. JP Spradley, *The ethnographic interview* (Holt, Rinehart & Winston, New York, 1979)

38. CJ McCall, JL Simmons, *Issues in participant observation: A text and reader* (Addison-Wesley Publishing Company, Reading, MA, 1969)

39. FR Kluchkohn, The participant observer technique in small communities. The America J Sociology **46**, 331–343 (1940)

40. EK Yakura, Charting time: timelines as temporal boundary objects. Acad. Manage. J. **45**, 956–970 (2002)

41. N Levina, E Vaast, The emergence of boundary spanning competence in practice: implications for implementation and use of information systems. MIS Q. **29**, 335–363 (2005)

42. R Chen, J Coles, J Lee, HR Rao, Emergency communication and system design: The case of Indian ocean tsunami, in *International conference on information and communication technologies and development (ICTD); Apr 17–19, 2009* (, Doha, Qatar, 2009), pp. 300–309

43. MC Lacity, MA Janson, understanding qualitative data: a framework of text analysis methods. J. Manag. Inf. Syst. **11**, 137–155 (1994)

44. G Hofstede, *Culture's consequences, comparing values, behaviors, institutions, and organizations across nations* (Sage Publications, Thousand Oaks CA, 2001).

45. J Vinke de Kruijf, The role of Dutch expertise in romanian water projects-case study 'pilot implementation FLIWAS in Banat region, Romania', in *Book the role of Dutch expertise in romanian water projects -case study 'pilot implementation FLIWAS in Banat region, Romania'* (Department of Water Engineering and Management/Twente Centre for Studies in Technology and Sustainable Development, 2011), p. 91

46. K Mahesh, JK Suresh, Knowledge criteria for organization design. J. Knowl. Manag. **13**, 41–51 (2009)

47. K De Gooijer, FLIWAS, the right information at the right place at the right time for the right persons to take the right decision, in *BALWOIS 2010; May 25–29 Ohrid, Republic of Macedonia* (2010)

48. EJ Langkamp, LR Wentholt, BE Pengel, C De Gooijer, J Flikweert, EJ Langkamp, LR Wentholt, BE Pengel, C De Gooijer, JJ Flikweert, in *Floods, from defence to management*, ed. by A. Van (Taylor & Francis Group, London, 2005), pp. 305–308

49. M Gretzschel, R Jüpner, M Grafe, R Leiner, *Application of flood management systems in germany* (The First European IAHR Congress, Edinburgh, UK, 2010)

2

A multi-modal network architecture for knowledge discovery

Craig M Vineyard[1*], Stephen J Verzi[1], Michael L Bernard[1], Shawn E Taylor[1], Irene Dubicka[1] and Thomas P Caudell[2]

Abstract

The collection and assessment of national security related information often involves an arduous process of detecting relevant associations between people, events, and locations—typically within very large data sets. The ability to more effectively perceive these connections could greatly aid in the process of knowledge discovery. This same process—pre-consciously collecting and associating multimodal information—naturally occurs in mammalian brains. With this in mind, this effort sought to draw upon the neuroscience community's understanding of the relevant areas of the brain that associate multi-modal information for long-term storage for the purpose of creating a more effective, and more automated, association mechanism for the analyst community. Using the biology and functionality of the hippocampus as an analogy for inspiration, we have developed an artificial neural network architecture to associate k-tuples (paired associates) of multimodal input records. The architecture is composed of coupled unimodal self-organizing neural modules that learn generalizations of unimodal components of the input record. Cross modal associations, stored as a higher-order tensor, are learned incrementally as these generalizations are formed. Graph algorithms are then applied to the tensor to extract multi-modal association networks formed during learning. Doing so yields a potential novel approach to data mining for intelligence-related knowledge discovery. This paper describes the neurobiology, architecture, and operational characteristics, as well as provides a simple intelligence-based example to illustrate the model's functionality.

Introduction

Currently, intelligence analysts are hampered by the need to sift through very large amounts of constantly changing data in order to forage for "nuggets" of information that may support or discredit an existing hypothesis. The collection and assessment of national security related information often involves an arduous process of "connecting the dots" within very large data sets. This process has proven to be extremely difficult, especially when analysts need to piece together information cues associated with various individuals, groups, events, and places, along with such items as communication and transportation logs [1]. The ability to more effectively perceive connections among events, locations, and people could greatly aid in the process of knowledge discovery.

Recent data mining and fusion tools have become much more effective in uncovering evidence of potential threats by sifting through Internet traffic, financial and communications records, as well as transcripts of audio streams for patterns of interest. While this type of capability is useful in understanding general patterns of behaviour, it is typically limited to one type of information domain (e.g. textual) and must rely on a large number of statistically related links to uncover relevant patterns. In addition, systems that utilize video sources to analyse video surveillance information to classify video footage are typically achieved without the ability to infer common relationships among related video events or actors.

Regardless of the information source, a significant problem faced by existing approaches is the immense difficulty in finding an information signal that is indicative of specific adversary behaviours and associating it with other meaningful signals in a vast expanse of noise. That is, current statistical database approaches, by themselves, are generally ill equipped to detect meaningful associations across a spectrum of information sources. Consequently, existing systems are generally considered poorly equipped to actively assist in the marshalling and assessment of multi-source information. Developing a

* Correspondence: cmviney@sandia.gov
[1]Sandia National Laboratories, Albuquerque, NM, USA
Full list of author information is available at the end of the article

system that assists analysts with knowledge discovery by helping to uncover associations, as well as help marshal evidence by assembling individual pieces of evidence into a single context, would be a great advancement to the analyst community. This is particularly true with the increasing need to more rapidly detect associations across various information modes for threat identification and determination in real-time, security-related contexts—for example, in situations involving time critical targets of national importance where rapid assessments must be made as to the type and degree of threat that may or may not exist.

In response to this need, an internally-funded effort sponsored by Sandia National Laboratories is seeking to advance the field of knowledge discovery by exploring both traditional statistics-based approaches as well as a neurologically-based, or "neuromorphic", approach to auto-associate information similar to the way a mammalian brain processes and associates multi-sourced information. This process of collecting and storing information naturally occurs in an awake mammalian brain. While a system that can fully auto-associate relevant, multi-modal information as described above is still in the future, we assert that an effort to replicate the associative processes of the brain to an appropriate degree, has the promise to greatly advance the process of knowledge discovery. This process would more effectively generate threat determinations in support of rapid decision-making in security-related contexts by filtering through a large corpus of multi-source/multi-mode information to uncover relevant associations.

The focus of this effort, termed the Augmented COgnition for Rapid Decision making (ACORD) capability, is to explore how to model relevant neurological processes in the brain that naturally associate information from different modalities for long-term storage as a memory episode. Recent advances in knowledge pertaining to the processes underlying associative memory have made it possible to model these processes at a level of fidelity that is applicable to knowledge discovery. This discussion will emphasize our neuromorphic approach underlying the ACORD capability.

Neurological underpinnings of the ACORD effort

The brain receives a variety of sensory input signals such as visual, auditory, and olfactory. Although each input stream does receive its share of focused individual processing, additional insight comes from the converged processing of all input modalities. Such an occurrence takes place within the Medial Temporal Lobe (MTL) region of the brain, and more specifically within the hippocampus. Beyond receiving a convergence of sensory inputs, the hippocampus is essentially involved in episodic memory formation. Rather than simply being a

mechanism for storing information, episodic memory associates information such as the spatial and temporal contexts of an event.

The episodic memory capability of the brain enables us to encode personal experiences as converged neural activations across cortical areas using diverse sensory modalities. In doing so, we are able to remember a large number of events including detailed sequences of events comprising experience as well as the temporal and spatial context of each event in the sequence [2]. One brain area, the hippocampus, is critically involved in remembering the spatial and temporal context of an event. The location of the hippocampus within the human brain may be seen in Figure 1. The MTL, where the hippocampus is located, is the recipient of inputs from widespread areas of the cortex and supports the ability to bind together cortical representations [2]. A key component of episodic memory is association of diverse types of information [3]. This capability allows humans to relate knowledge pertaining to elements of an event such as who, what, when, and where. In this paper we present an artificial neural network architecture that learns these types of association inspired by the hippocampus. We start with an overview of hippocampus biology; then explain the design of our neural network architecture; follow this with sample experimental results to motivate its use; then present a real world terrorist network scenario, and conclude with a discussion of the significance of our architecture and directions for future research.

Cortical inputs to MTL arrive from various sensory modalities, with different emphases depending upon the mammalian species. For instance, rats receive a significant olfactory influence whereas bats receive a strong auditory influence [4]. Nevertheless, across species, most of the neocortical inputs to the perirhinal cortex come from cortical areas which process unimodal sensory information about qualities of objects, called the "what" stream, and most of the neocortical inputs to the parahippocampal cortex come from cortical areas which process polymodal spatial information, called the "where" stream [4,2]. There are some connections between the two streams, however overall processing in each stream remains largely segregated until they converge within the hippocampus [5,6].

Extensive neuroscience research typically describes the anatomy of the hippocampus as consisting of a loop (see Figure 1) beginning with the dentate gyrus (DG), proceeding to CA3, followed by CA1 and propagating through the subiculum out to the input streams [7]. The hippocampus receives its inputs from the entorhinal cortex (EC) and passes its outputs back to the EC. The EC receives inputs from both perirhinal (dorsal) and parahippocampal (ventral) cortices. The perirhinal cortex is involved in object recognition, and the parahippocampal cortex is involved in recognizing scenes. The sub regions of the hippocampus and surrounding cortex, specifically related to the motivation for our neural model, will be addressed individually as follows (also see columns 1 and 2 in Table 1).

The DG receives the conjoined multimodal sensory signals from EC. Anatomically, DG consists of a large number of neurons with a relatively sparse neural activation code at any given instant. Effectively, this behaviour suggests that the DG creates non-overlapping sparse codes for unique events [8]. In this case an event consists of simultaneous neural activation leading into (afferent to) the hippocampus (specifically the DG in this case) within a short span of time. The sparse DG outputs serve as the input for CA3.

The CA3 region of the hippocampus consists of extensive recurrent connections. The CA3 region also receives direct input from the EC. The sparse encoding of the DG allows the CA3 to uniquely encode EC activation patterns as specific events within an episode as well as facilitating later semantic encoding. These neural processes enable CA3 to perform auto-association. Anatomically, the output of CA3 proceeds to CA1 and subiculum as the major output regions of the hippocampus [9]. While the exact functionality of the subiculum is largely unknown, CA1 functionality is typically identified as learning relational information for temporal sequences and connecting episodic encodings from CA3 with the original EC sensory activations. We have used some of these functional properties of the hippocampus as the basis for an artificial neural network architecture

for learning and forming associations. Table 1 depicts the relationship between these anatomical regions and the corresponding computational implementation, which we will describe next.

Computational architecture

In general, an association is a relationship between entities where they share some degree of commonality. For example, an individual is associated with his/her name, or two individuals may be associated with a common workplace. All entities are trivially related to themselves. The simplest non-trivial association is between two entities, but in general, k individual entities may be associated with one another. The question arises as to how relationships are learned and encoded as memory?

Numerous domain specific rules or heuristics may be utilized to discover commonality among entities based upon criteria such as distance metrics or shared feature counts. In contrast, our architecture inspired by the hippocampus builds relational codes by associating multiple modal specific entities with their mutual context, analogous to the dorsal and ventral partitioning in EC sensory input signals. In its simplest form, our approach associates what and where information based upon their shared frame of reference. For example, multiple people may be associated with the house in which they live.

In order to create associations, the network must first create representations (or neural codes) of the individual unimodal sensory perceptions of the entities. Prior to entering hippocampus, sensory signals pass through numerous layers of cortex. Throughout these layers a distributed representation for entities is gradually

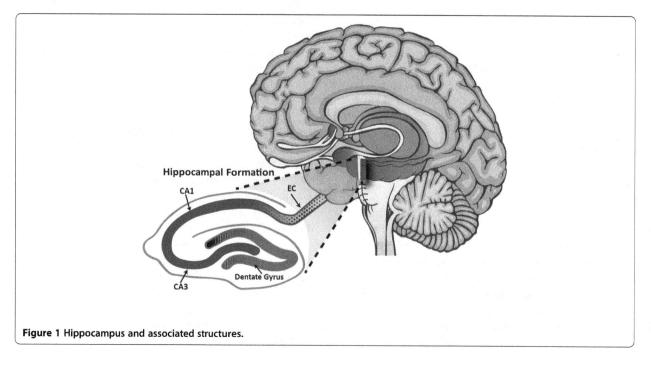

Figure 1 Hippocampus and associated structures.

Table 1 Relation between anatomical functionality and model representation

Associative brain anatomy	Function	Model representation
Hippocampal Formation	Associates and consolidates multi-modal, event related information into long term memory	Associative-ART
Entorhinal Cortex (EC)	Aggregates sensory inputs	Fuzzy-ART modules inputs
Dentate Gyrus (DG)	Provides sparse coding of dense neuron population to enable pattern separation	Fuzzy-ART modules
Cornu Ammonis Subarea (CA3)	Acts as the auto-association network within the hippocampus	Tensor mapfield

constructed. Eventually, within the hippocampus, the DG is believed to create unique sparse encodings for unique multimodal sensory perceptions allowing it to either learn new associations or recall existing ones. Through the use of self-organizing neural networks, our architecture performs similar operations. It can detect entities that it has previously experienced and therefore reinforce existing associations, or detect novel entities necessitating a new association encoding.

Our architecture, shown in Figure 2, addresses this capability by using fuzzy-Adaptive Resonance Theory (Fuzzy ART) artificial neural network modules. Developed by Carpenter and Grossberg, the ART family of neural networks are online, unsupervised (self organizing) neural networks, which are excellent at rapid category formation [10]. The Fuzzy-ART version used in our architecture operates upon real valued inputs. Given a vector of real valued numbers as input, Fuzzy ART performs pattern categorization through winner-take-all competition, yielding a unique category code as output. A single parameter (vigilance) regulates mathematically how similar inputs must be in order to be grouped within the same category. A vigilance parameter value of unity requires the inputs in the same group to be identical. Lowering the vigilance parameter towards zero allows for generalization such that similar, but not exactly identical, inputs may be grouped together. If no existing category is sufficiently close to capture an input, then Fuzzy ART automatically creates a new category code. In the neuro-physiology, DG creates nearly unique encoding for novel inputs. Fuzzy-ART creates and maintains representative categories for inputs. Repeated presentation of previous inputs activates the same categorical representation whereas novel inputs are represented by new category encodings. Categorical activations are the basis for learning associations in our architecture.

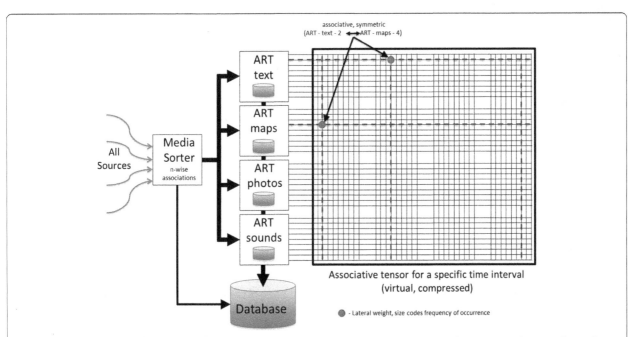

Figure 2 Associative ART architecture. A version of the architecture with four input modalities. The Media Sorter module accumulates a frame of informational entities that are presented to the modal channels represented in this diagram as boxes with ART labels. The Database module is a reference to the archiving of the learned relationships plus all ART based learned parameters. The Tensor is represented as a matrix showing learned relationships as red dots at the intersections of rows and columns indicating category nodes active in the current frame.

The DG encodings in the hippocampus propagate to the CA3 region that is believed to be heavily composed of recurrent connections supporting the formation of associations. In a sense, the CA3 acts like an association "mapfield" where the simultaneous arrival of signals at CA3 neurons from DG neurons representing mixed modal entities strengthens their ability to fire in the future. Similarly, in our architecture, the activations of category codes from k unimodal Fuzzy ART modules are connected in a fully connected mapfield containing synaptic weights encoding associations among k-tuples of inputs. This association map has the structure of a kth rank tensor with variable dimensions and will be henceforth referred to as the "tensor mapfield".

Existing ART based associative neural network architectures, such as ARTMAP [11] and LAPART [12], link two ART modules using a mapfield that effectively associate category outputs from the two ARTs together. This class of architecture connects an ART module to each axis of a matrix of synaptic weights-- the intersecting grid lines of which encode a connection between the two ART modules [11]. These models are usually used for supervised learning or function approximation applications that require unidirectional many-to-one associations from the first ART to the second (see Figure 1 in [11]).

Our architecture consists of an arbitrary number of unimodal Fuzzy ART modules symmetrically connected through an association tensor mapfield to encode arbitrary associations between unimodal entities (Figure 2). As with ARTMAP and LAPART, the output category layer of each unimodal module is connected to an axis of the tensor. Unlike these architectures, the category layers of each module are buffered and connected to a mirror axis (see the top axis in Figure 2) of the tensor, thus allowing associations between entities of the same modality. All tensor elements, which can be thought of as synapses between modalities, are initialized to zero prior to learning.

During training, the system receives a sequence of data records that can contain any mixture of modal data components. Upon entry into the system, the components of the record are placed in a queue from which each unimodal component is directed to the corresponding unimodal ART module sorted by its modal type. This module performs its categorization, activating the corresponding output node and its gridline in the tensor mapfield. For each grid intersection in the tensor where there exists at least two current activations, the tensor element (modelled synapse) is strengthened. In the version of this architecture described in this paper, the synapse strength as represented by the tensor element is immediately set to unity. After learning has occurred, the active node is mirrored and buffered for the remainder of the processing of the record, and the next modal data component is drawn from the queue and directed to the appropriate unimodal module. Through the processing of the sequence of data records, the tensor mapfield learns symmetric binary associations between pairs of unimodal module output representations.

Fuzzy ART has excellent learning properties for this type of application. Configured with its choice parameter set near zero and with the use of complement encoding on the input vector [10], this module exhibits single pass learning. That is, given a finite set of training patterns, the number of learned categories and all internal synaptic weights converges to their final values in one training epoch. A training epoch is the process of presenting each and every member of the training set to the module once and only once. During the second presentation of the training set, it is possible that individual patterns will change category membership, but this will cease in subsequent presentations. Scaling studies have shown that for higher dimensional input patterns, membership change is unlikely during the second presentation epoch. As mentioned above, the vigilance parameter for Fuzzy ART determines the ultimate number of categories learned during the first presentation. When this parameter is unity, the number of categories equals the number of unique training patterns, thus memorizing the training set. When this parameter is near zero, the number of categories will approach one, thus over generalizing over the training set. The choice of this parameter will strongly affect the dimensionality of the tensor mapfield.

Extension of trained ACORD system to scenario analysis

Once we have trained an ACORD system using k-tuples of domain-specific records, it can then be used with analyst direction to traverse the associations learned. Given a particular unimodal record of interest, such as the image of a person, vehicle or residence, or a name (text) of an individual or place, the ACORD system can help guide the analyst through the levels of transitive associations it represents. In this mode of operation there is no learning, thus when a record of a particular modality is presented to the system, it will activate the closest matching category (in its unimodal ART), which through the tensor (mapfield) will activate any (and all) matched categories of any modality which can then be traversed further in either depth or breadth first fashion. In this mode of ACORD operation, which we call re-resonance, the analyst provides feedback and direction to the reinforcement learning. This mode of operation is called re-resonance because the initial (unimodal) input record resonates with the best matching category in its modal ART, which is then allowed to generate a cascade of re-resonances determined by the associations learned in the tensor specific to the input record presented at the start of this operation. Note that this portion of the model has not been fully implemented, but we will explain its potential in the simple example described next and return to it in the future work section below.

Experiments

Initial association study

As an introduction to the associative capability of our Associative-ART architecture we have constructed an initial image association experiment with 20 unique inputs and 22 associations among the inputs. The parametric configuration we used for each Fuzzy-ART module is β set to 1 (fast learning), a choice parameter α of 0.01, and a vigilance of 0.99. The values selected for α and β are standard choices [10]. The vigilance value

specified can be lowered as desired to allow for greater generalization of information. However, we have selected a large value to ensure accurate entity identification in a domain as sensitive as intelligence analysis. As the base case, we have set k equal to two so that the associations are pairs. While ART is capable of processing any vectorized inputs, for this experiment we have presented our architecture with images of uniformly sized circled letters and numbers as shown in Figure 3. Each row in the figure portrays an associative pairing and the column depicts the individual input which was presented to the architecture.

Although this is a generic, fictitious example, it can be conceptually compared with the type of task presented to data analysts. These analysts are tasked with processing large quantities of information and forming

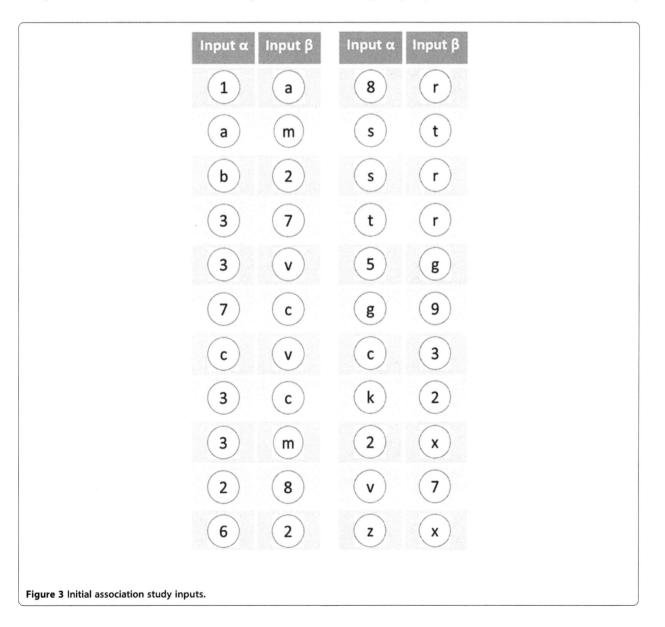

Figure 3 Initial association study inputs.

associations for a variety of reasons including but not limited to knowledge discovery, discovering groups and individuals of interest, and analyzing criminal or terrorist networks. Thus, for this initial example it may be understood that numbers are representative of people and letters representative of locations respectively. As such, people may be associated with other people or locations such as businesses and addresses. Likewise, locations may be associated with people for the same reasons just stated, or they may also be associated with other locations. Locations may be associated with other locations for a variety of reasons such as representing concepts like a business partnerships or geographic hierarchies such as cities within a subsuming state or country.

Association results

Upon processing the inputs shown in Figure 3, the tensor mapfield of our architecture has encoded all of the symmetric binary associations between inputs. For this initial study, the mapfield encodes the associations between pairs of images. The tensor mapfield may be queried in order to generate an equivalent, but often more visually intuitive, association graph. The graph of this example is illustrated in Figure 4. As portrayed by this figure, although simple pairings were presented to the architecture, the net result is a more sophisticated network, which may aid an analyst in comprehending the structure of criminal networks or identify connections previously unperceived. For instance, as may be seen in Figure 4 the resultant association network is disjoint and from the 22 input pairings 3 sub networks emerge. The topological layout shown is arbitrary, but the connectivity allows for potential knowledge discovery such as by means of transitive association path analysis. As an example, individuals '1' and '7' were never presented together in a single intelligence snippet[a], but by traversing the association graph they may be connected through a third party (individual '3') and two locations ('a' and 'm'). This example, although hypothetical, illustrates the extension of a trained ACORD system to analysis with analyst feedback to help the reinforcement learning of the most relevant transitive associations to the specific task at hand.

Degree centrality is a quantitative network analysis technique to assess the relative significance of a node within the network. Degree centrality is computed as the summation of edges incident with a node normalized by the number of nodes within the network [13]. The degree centralities for all of the nodes in this experiment are listed in Table 2 in decreasing order. This analytical technique quantitatively captures than individual '2' is the most connected entity within the association network, and conversely several other nodes such as individual '1' only have a single association. Information such as degree centrality can be used to help the analyst navigate very large trained ACORD association networks by focusing on nodes (or links) with a specific value (such as high degree centrality). Actual intelligence scenarios are typically much more complex yielding much more ambiguous association networks and requiring more sophisticated analysis techniques beyond the scope of this paper. However, as follows is a second scenario illustrating the associative capabilities of the ACORD architecture.

Benchmark comparison with K-means clustering

The K-means clustering algorithm is a widely used, popular unsupervised category formation methodology. It is an iterative method which strives to partition the given data into K clusters such that each data point is

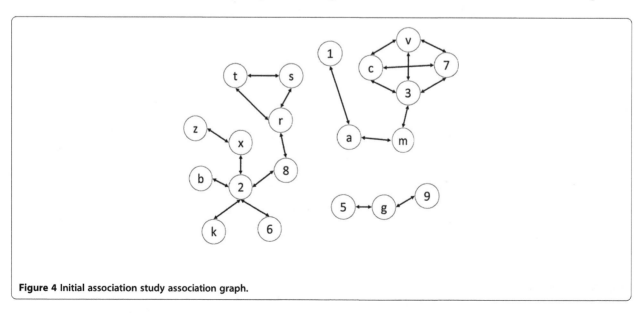

Figure 4 Initial association study association graph.

affiliated with the cluster with the closest mean [14]. We have analysed our initial association study using K-means clustering as a benchmark comparison.

The K-means algorithm requires that the desired number of clusters, K, must be specified *a priori* whereas our architecture does not. Consequently, we have performed a parameter sweep experimenting with K values from two to seven. This range was selected based upon knowing the structure of the associations in the example. The partition results that K-means comes up with can depend upon the randomized selection of initial cluster means. For this particular dataset, as K increased, the variability in the partitioning increased as well. With three clusters (K = 3), there are only two unique partitions. These two partitions are shown in Figure 5 with the ovals representing clusters. If clusters are perceived as connected sub-graphs, then our architecture identified three clusters as shown in Figure 4. One method of formally assessing the similarity between graphs is to compute the edit distance, which is the minimum cost to transform one graph to another. The edit distances between the result given by our architecture and the two partitions yielded by K-means (A and B of Figure 5 respectively) are 9 and 10. Considering the small size of the example, these are relatively high edit distances (approximately half of the nodes in the graphs had to be

modified) expressing the poor performance by the K-means algorithm.

The clusters K-means identifies are typically not connected sub-components of the overall graph, but rather consist of several disjoint groups. This disconnectedness brings into question the validity of the clusters K-means identified since inter-cluster components may have no apparent reason to be grouped together. Furthermore, by examining the individual nodes to try and identify any sort of semantic coherence within a cluster one may identify the same nodes are frequently located within different clusters. This is a consequence of K-means errantly misinterpreting repeated presentation of the same data element.

Real world network example

To analyse our architecture with a more realistic data set, we used an actual terrorist scenario. However, the events pertaining to the scenario were anonymized, stripping out the actual names, places, and events. These were replaced with generic descriptions (for example Villain1, Villain2). This scenario focuses upon the central character Villain1 and its known associations. The scenario was designed to investigate Villain1's known criminal network and reveal potential interconnections between Villain1 and criminals directly linked to a terrorist act. The intent was to embody traits associated with real terrorist networks as opposed to artificial network types that may or may not be realistic. While the scenario portrayed in this example is relatively simple compared to a complete scenario, it is able to demonstrate this architecture's ability to operate upon a much larger scenario.

The parametric configuration used for each Fuzzy-ART module is β set to 1 (fast learning), a choice parameter α of 0.01, and a vigilance of 0.99. The values selected for α and β are standard choices [10]. The vigilance value specified can be lowered as desired to allow for greater generalization of information. However, we have selected a large value to ensure accurate entity identification in a domain as sensitive as intelligence analysis.

As a more sophisticated example, rather than constraining the inputs to be simple pairs the k-tuple inputs varied in size from 2 to 4 entities being presented to the architecture simultaneously. Overall, this example was comprised of 179 tuples constructed from 189 unique inputs.

Real world network results

As noted with the previous example, the tensor mapfield yielded from processing the input tuples encodes the binary associations between inputs. Also, the tensor mapfield may be queried to generate an association

Table 2 Degree centrality measures for initial association experiment

Input	Degree centrality
2	0.263158
3	0.210526
r	0.157895
c	0.157895
v	0.157895
7	0.157895
x	0.105263
g	0.105263
t	0.105263
s	0.105263
8	0.105263
m	0.105263
a	0.105263
z	0.052632
k	0.052632
9	0.052632
5	0.052632
6	0.052632
b	0.052632
1	0.052632

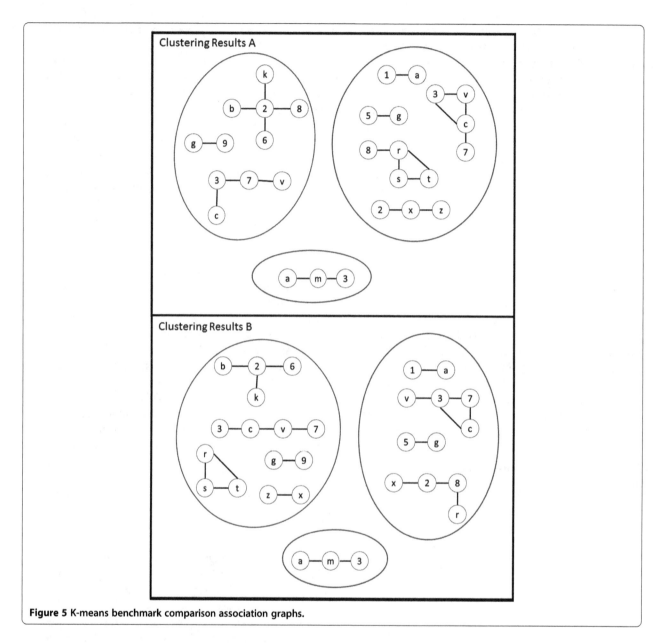

Figure 5 K-means benchmark comparison association graphs.

graph. The association graph of this real world example is captured in Figure 6. Just as the input tuples are more complicated both in terms of quantity and length in this real world example, the resulting association graph is much richer. In this case, the graph shown is nearly fully connected, but that is a consequence of the highly focused nature of the input data, whereas in a general intelligence scenario it is also possible that an analyst may receive a barrage of unrelated information. Despite the indecipherable appearance of this association graph, it provides a means for an analyst to investigate individual associations and facilitates a larger overall understanding of the mass quantity of information. For example, Figure 7 illustrates a subset of the overall scenario, focusing upon Villain1 and highlighting all of the interconnections between people, places, and events associated with the intelligence data. Not only does it allow for connections between crimes and specific individuals to be identified, but all the additional associations allow an analyst to attain a greater understanding of the overall scenario, such as perceiving the structure of the larger criminal network carrying out a specific event, as well as how the criminal network operates.

Conclusions and future work

In this paper we first presented an artificial neural network computational architecture with functionality inspired by the neural processes of hippocampus. Specifically, this architecture was based upon the DG and CA3 regions of hippocampus as a means to learn associations

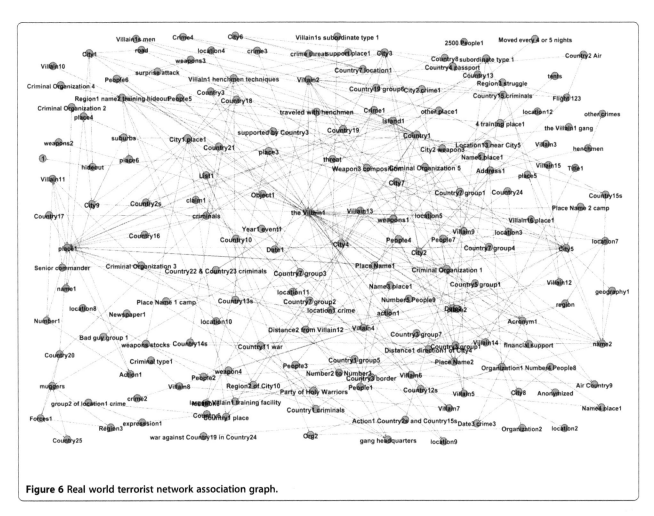

Figure 6 Real world terrorist network association graph.

among k-tuples of entities. It is a general architecture, as opposed to a domain specific solution, in the sense that it can handle any sort of input as long as the input can be represented as a numeric vector. Developing a general architecture enables it to be flexible enough so that it can be applied to an intelligence domain where it is a common practice to form association networks.

Second, we demonstrated the architecture first on an initial generic problem that shows the architecture's potential for representing non-explicit association networks. Then, we demonstrated the architecture's ability to process data from a real world terrorist network and construct the resulting associations. As a benchmark for comparison, we have compared our architecture with the well-known K-means clustering algorithm. We have shown that the resultant clusters identified by K-Means are unreliable and not well suited for this problem domain. Additionally, we have also shown degree centrality as one quantitative network assessment technique, however constructing association networks such as these potentially aid an intelligence analyst by allowing for further more sophisticated analysis such as transitivity, centrality, clustering, connectivity, and other network

metrics. Additionally, in regards to data mining, our approach provides a means of representation and structured presentation.

Future development of this architecture may include additional processing within the association field. Rather than simply recording a binary association value, additional metrics such as a frequency count, such as is used in Boosted ARTMAP [15], or a recency value may provide interesting enhancements. Incorporating a frequency count is one possibility to identify strength of association such that pairings repeatedly presented together are more strongly associated than items only presented once. Furthermore, the ability to represent non-symmetric associations would allow for directionality in yielded association networks. In our described architecture, presentation order is irrelevant. However if order does matter, a temporal marker could be utilized to assess how recently an association was formed. From this approach, various additional processing could be incorporated, such as the decay of associations over time. Another potential extension to ACORD would be to experiment with incorporating a supervised training mode. Presently, the architecture is an unsupervised online-learning neural network that is

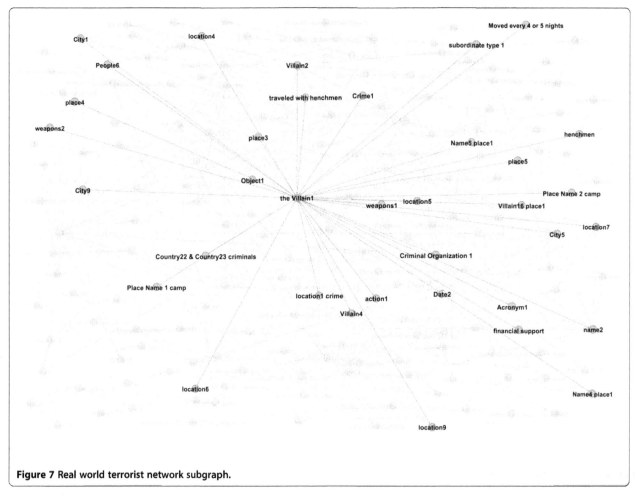

Figure 7 Real world terrorist network subgraph.

trained fully online. If meaningful insights are known about the specific problem domain, performance improvements may be possible by operating in a supervised learning mode. Depending upon the particular application, architecture modifications, such as those described above, could provide great potential for enhanced, further processing, as well as addressing episodic or sequential data. In addition, the resonance mode of operation has the potential to offer semi-automated (possibly even automated) generation of higher order associations, such as transitive chains. The integration of network metrics, such as degree centrality, into the process of generating higher order associations could help focus the analyst's effort on domain areas of metric interest.

Together, these advancements are intended to provide the national security community with a next-generation knowledge discovery system that associates relevant information across various source modalities. As with many efforts, our goal is to enable analysts to more effectively, and more timely, connect the dots to increase the probability of detecting 9/11-type of events before they are carried out. Not effectively connecting the dots has been seen as a failure of pre-9/11 analysis [16]. Our approach to this effort is to is better understand and model the pre-conscious,

associative mechanisms of the mammalian brain, albeit to much simpler degree, in support of rapid decision-making for security-related contexts. While our approach may be considered unconventional compared to most efforts, we believe replicating specific aspects of the brain has the potential to ultimately produce advancements in knowledge discovery that cannot be achieved through current means. We believe the neuromorphic advancements, along with advancements in more conventional, statistically based data filtering have already produced promising results. Ultimately, an appropriate mixture of neuromorphic and statistically based approaches should, in effect, shore up weaknesses in each approach to produce a knowledge discovery system that can more effectively associate relevant information.

Endnotes

[a] An intelligence snippet contains specific information concerning an event (or events) related to national or international law enforcement, and this information is presented to the ACORD system as a record (or k-tuple) of events.

Competing interests

The authors declare that they have no competing interests.

Authors' contributions

CMV is the technical lead and participated in the research and development of the model, and led the execution and analysis of experiments on the model. SJV helped in design and implementation of the proposed model. MLB is the project manager and participated in the sequence alignment. SET participated in the design of the study and performed the statistical analysis. ID provided background on hippocampal neuroanatomy and human factors engineering guidance on potential applications to all-source analytical tradecraft. TPC conceived of the study, and participated in its design and coordination. All authors read and approved the final manuscript.

Acknowledgements

We would like to thank Jonathan McClain for his work in developing essential statistical components of the ACORD capability, as well as Wendy Shaneyfelt for her work in structuring multi-model information used for testing the ACORD capability. This research was possible in part by LDRD program support from Sandia National Laboratories. Sandia National Laboratories is a multi-program laboratory managed and operated by Sandia Corporation, a wholly owned subsidiary of Lockheed Martin Corporation, for the U.S. Department of Energy's National Nuclear Security Administration under contract DE-AC04-94AL85000.

Author details

[1]Sandia National Laboratories, Albuquerque, NM, USA. [2]Department of Electrical and Computer Engineering, University of New Mexico, Albuquerque, NM, USA.

References

1. T. Quiggin, Connecting the Dots: President Obama, [http://globalbrief.ca/tomquiggin/2010/01/12/connecting-the-dots-president-obama/]
2. H. Eichenbaum, The hippocampus and declarative memory: cognitive mechanisms and neural codes. Behav Brain Res 127, 199–207 (2001)
3. N.J. Cohen, J. Ryan, C. Hunt, L. Romine, Hippocampal system and declarative (relational) memory: summarizing the data from functional neuroimaging studies. Hippocampus 9, 83–98 (1999)
4. R.D. Burwell, M.P. Witter, D.G. Amaral, Perirhinal and postrhinal cortices of the rat: a review of the neuroanatomical literature and comparison with findings from the monkey brain. Hippocampus 5, 390–408 (1995)
5. W.A. Suzuki, D.G. Amaral, Perirhinal and parahippocampal cortices of the macaque monkey: cortical afferents. J Comp Neurol 350, 497–533 (1994)
6. W. Suzuki, H. Eichenbaum, The neurophysiology of memory. Annals of the NY Academy of Sciences 911, 175–191 (2000)
7. D. Amaral, P. Lavenex, Ch3. Hippocampal Neuroanatomy, in The Hippocampus Book, ed. by P. Anderson, R. Morris, D. Amaral, T. Bliss, J. O'Keefe (Oxford University Press, New York, 2006). ISBN 978-0-19-51002703
8. S. Leutgeb et al., Independent codes for spatial and episodic memory in hippocampal neuronal ensembles. Science 309, 619–623 (2005)
9. H. Eichenbaum, N. Cohen, From Conditioning to Conscious Recollection: Memory Systems of the Brain (Oxford University Press, Oxford, 2001)
10. G.A. Carpenter, S. Grossberg, D.B. Rosen, FuzzyART: fast stable learning and categorization of analog patterns by an adaptive resonance system. Neural Netw 4, 759–771 (1991)
11. G.A. Carpenter, S. Grossberg, N. Markuzon, J.H. Reynold, D.B. Rosen, Fuzzy ARTMAP: a neural network architecture for incremental supervised learning of analog multidimensional maps. IEEE Trans Neural Netw 3, 698–713 (1992)
12. M.J. Healy, T.P. Caudell, Acquiring rule sets as a product of learning in the logical neural architecture LAPART. IEEE Trans Neural Netw 8, 461–474 (1997)
13. P. Bonacich, Power and Centrality: A Family of Measures. Am J Sociol 5, 1170–1182 (1987)
14. R.O. Duda, P. Hart, D. Stork, Pattern Classification (Wiley-Interscience, New York, 2001)
15. S.J. Verzi, G.H. Heileman, M. Georgiopoulos, Boosted ARTMAP: modifications to Fuzzy ARTMAP motivated by boosting theory. Neural Netw 19(4), 446–468 (2006)
16. 9/11Chair, Attack Was Preventable, [http://www.cbsnews.com/2100-18563_162-589137.html]

3

Police patrol districting method and simulation evaluation using agent-based model & GIS

Yue Zhang[*] and Donald E Brown

Abstract

Police patrols play an important role in public safety. The patrol district design is an important factor affecting the patrol performances, such as average response time and workload variation. The redistricting or redrawing police command boundaries can be described as partitioning a police jurisdiction into command districts with the constraints such as contiguity and compactness. The size of the possible sample space is large and the corresponding graph-partitioning problem is NP-complete. In our approach, the patrol districting plans generated by a parameterized redistricting procedure are evaluated using an agent-based simulation model we implemented in Java Repast in a geographic information system (GIS) environment. The relationship between districting parameters and response variables is studied and better districting plans can be generated. After in-depth evaluations of these plans, we perform a Pareto analysis of the outputs from the simulation to find the non-dominated set of plans on each of the objectives. This paper also includes a case study for the police department of Charlottesville, VA, USA. Simulation results show that patrol performance can be improved compared with the current districting solution.

Introduction

Police patrols play an important role in public service by responding to incidents, deterring and preventing crimes. It can give a sense of security to people who need protection and discourage those who may commit crimes in the absence of a patrol [1]. Police patrolling is an indispensable component and function of police departments [2]. The goals and objectives of police patrol include crime prevention, criminal apprehension, law enforcement, order maintenance, public services, and traffic enforcement [3]. However, since police resources are limited, there is an understandable interest in patrol strategies and operations that provide safety at minimum cost.

Typically, a city is partitioned into command districts or precincts. Each command district usually has a headquarters and a commanding officer to manage and supervise the police patrol operations. Each command district is further divided into several beats or sectors [4]. Police can effectively manage their operations through the design of the command districts and the choice of patrol strategies of the police units within those districts. There are three major types of patrol strategies for patrol officers: active

patrol, random patrol, and directed patrol. In active patrol, patrol officers should use every opportunity to discover, detect, observe, and interdict the unusual event. Random patrol means patrol routes should be random and varied so that the patrol behaviors will not be predicted by potential criminals. In directed patrol, patrol officers pay more efforts to hotspots of crime so they can respond quickly and reduce the crimes in hotspots. In practice, patrol officers may choose one strategy or combine them to accommodate the specific conditions in their area [3]. Another important patrol principle is beat integrity. Patrol officer is expected to remain within assigned patrol district. Beat integrity can be absolute or relative, depending on the number of patrol units assigned and the size of the patrol district and the activity within the area [3]. For absolute beat integrity, patrol officers should remain in the assigned patrol district at all times. In relative beat integrity, patrol officers remain largely within the patrol area and leave it only for good reason, such as back up another officer or respond to a call for service (CFS) incident in another patrol district [3]. When there is a CFS incident, many police departments use the principle that "the nearest police car responds to the call", which belongs to the case of relative beat integrity.

*Correspondence: yz5yf@virginia.edu
Predictive Technology Laboratory, Department of Systems and Information Engineering, University of Virginia, Charlottesville, Virginia, USA

Police patrol district design or region design is one of the important resource allocation strategies of police department. The deployment of patrol force through designated patrol districts is a standard management method to enhance the deterrent capability of uniformed patrol force [3]. Better districting plans can lead to lower response times, officers' familiarization with their assigned area, more efficient utilization of personnel, equalized distribution of workload, uniform police visibility, enhanced officer safety, balanced police response to calls and officer accountability [3]. For small and medium-sized cities, patrol district design determines the patrol boundaries for each patrol unit, for example, police car. For large cities, patrol region design usually starts from higher level of resource allocation. Larger patrol districts for several patrol units are determined first then these districts are further divided for each patrol unit. Patrol districts should be designed in a rational and systematic manner [3]. Several factors need to be considered when designing patrol districts: 1) the size of the area to be patrolled should not exceed the limit that a single officer can cover, depending on types of the area (urban, suburban or rural), 2) natural or man-made barriers, (e.g., rivers, railroad tracks, interstate highways, valleys), 3) workload indicators (e.g., CFS, criminal incidents, traffic patterns), 4) significant area characteristics (e.g., local neighbor hoods, major shopping centers) [3]. Different cities have different CFS and crime pattern. CFS incidents or crime events are more likely to happen in some area than other areas. So, the police patrol resources should be spatially allocated based on the characteristics of cities. The size, shape, demographics, and geography of the patrol district is a major determinant of the effectiveness of patrol operations and is the focus of this paper.

Police patrol district design

As noted previously the design of police patrol districts can significantly impact the effectiveness of police operations. Typically two major questions constitute the essential elements of patrol design: 1) What areas define each district and 2) What resources should be assigned to each area [5]? This paper concerns the first question and clearly the answer to this question determines the expected performance of the police on a number of performance metrics. The next subsection highlights these metrics. Subsection "Operations research and GIS methods" provides background to previous work in this area and the remaining two subsection show the districting problem reduces the graph selection and then how simulation can be employed to help design districts.

Performance measurements and related problems

There are two common performance measures used for police district design: the average response time and the variation of workload [4]. Quick response to citizen calls for service can 1) improve the chances of catching the offender at the scene or nearby 2) increase the changes of identify and locate witnesses, 3) provide immediate gathering of physical evidence, 4) provide immediate lifesaving first aid, 5) enhances the reputation of police department, 6) creates citizen satisfaction with the police [5,6]. The spatial distribution and allocation of police cars to districts affect both performance measures. In a 1971 study of the New York Police Department more than half of all dispatches were inter-sector dispatches (between districts). Usually, the nearest police car responds to the CFS incident so it may cross the patrol boundaries to respond. The average response time for these inter-sector responses was approximately 40% greater than that for intra-sector responses and the average travel distance was about 53% greater [7]. This large proportion of inter-sector cases indicates that the district design may not be efficient with regard to the first measure, response time.

Our own interviews with members of the Charlottesville, VA Police Department have shown that the response times do not vary much between or within districts. This is because Charlottesville is small city (approximately 7 miles in diameter) with a population of about 40,000. However, these interviews did reveal large variations in the workloads of officers in different districts. This shows a lack of efficiency with respect to the second objective: variation in workload.

Approaches to police district design
Manual methods
Historically, the geographic patrolling boundaries were drawn by hand based on police department's knowledge and experience of the total area and the availability of the police resources [2,8]. Police department also considered the natural boundaries, such as the hills or rivers, the locations of hotspots of crime as well as the administrative boundaries, such as neighborhoods and communities [9]. The limitation of the hand drawn boundaries is that the human is limited in the number of options they can consider and in their formal evaluation of the alternatives. Each alternative represents a different possibility in terms of workload and response times, but assessing these by hand can be very time consuming. The assessment is particularly difficult since both workload and response times are stochastic. This inability to measure the efficiency of the districting alternatives means that manual methods are not appropriate and good computer-based methods are required in order to create district that can positively impact high-level decision making by the police [2,9].

Operations research and GIS methods
According to [9], the first OR application was to use p-Median clustering as in [8] to minimize the total weighted

travel distance to service the expected calls. In 1979, Aly and Litwhiler used an interchange heuristic method to allocate police briefing stations to districts [10]. In 2002, a simulated annealing approach was used by Amico et al., to search for a good partitioning of the police command districts by assessing the average response time and variation of workload of police officers with a simulation called PCAM [4]. GIS methods can be also used in police district design. In 2010 [9] used GIS methods with a maximal covering formulation to determine optimal police patrol areas. This approach produced good alternatives for police districts design. However, the criteria for evaluation were based on static calculation of distances, weights of incidents, and queuing model statistics. Police patrols are highly dynamic activities. It is difficult to use static approaches to find effective answers for most police. Instead, simulation methods (as discussed in Subsection "Evaluation of districting plans using simulation") of police patrol can provide more useful evaluations.

Problem complexity
Computational complexity
A convenient formulation for the police district design problem is as the aggregation of smaller geographic units into larger units that form the districts. This problem has a rich history in mathematics and operations research. This problem reduces to the graph-partition problem with the constraints of contiguity and compactness. One example of graph-partitioning is the political redistricting problem. The census blocks are partitioned into districts such that each district has equal population. There are two constraints on the problem solution: contiguity and compactness. The polygons within each district must be spatially contiguous so that all members of district can connect with one another without leaving the district. Compactness provides for shorter travel times between members of the district. Evaluation of compactness depends on the distance metric used. For Euclidean distance a circle is the most compact shape, while for Manhattan distance a square is most compact. The graph partitioning problem has been shown to be NP-hard [11].

Another formulation for districting uses graph theory. In this formulation, the regions or geographic units as nodes and the adjacency between regions as edges connect the nodes. For each node, there is a weight representing attributes of the region, for example, population. The objective of districting is to maximize or minimize the function of the weights between different districts. For example, we could use the absolute difference as the function and minimize the difference in population between districts. For the police districts we want to minimize the difference in forecasted activity between districts since

this will minimize the difference in travel or response time. We could also minimize the difference in workload between districts. This formulation of the districting problem can be reduced to the problem of "Cut into Connected Components of Bounded Weight", which is also NP-hard [12].

As with all optimization problems we can employ either exact or heuristic methods [11]. Exact methods systematically exam districting plans explicitly or implicitly. Since the problem is NP-hard, we can use explicit methods only for small districting problems that have limited practical applications. Heuristic methods, such as, simulated annealing, genetic algorithms, and stochastic gradient ascent can find local optima for the districting problem. These local optima can provide good operating solutions for police departments. The approach described in this paper in Section "Approach to police patrol districting" is a heuristic.

Evaluation complexity
The police patrol district design problem has greater complexity than the computational issues mentioned in Subsection "Computational complexity". Consider the graph-theoretic formulation of the districting problem. In this formulation some function of the region weights is used as the optimization criterion. For example, the sum of the absolute difference in populations between all pairs of regions can be used. In the police districting problem the evaluation is more complicated than a simple sum of average differences. To evaluate the response time we need to compute the travel times for the incidents within each district that require police attention. The locations and times of these incidents are stochastic and must be modeled by an empirical distributions based on current incident data. Further the travel times depend on the characteristics of the road networks in the regions and the environment conditions, e.g., weather and traffic congestion. None of these factors can be conveniently modeled by single variable functions of the region weights.

The workload metric has similar complexities. Since the actual workload depends on travel times, the complexities described above hold for workload. Additionally the types of incidents and their spatial distribution within and across the districts affect workload. The type of incident is also stochastic and cannot be calculated by single variable functions typical of districting problems.

The complex evaluation need for districting requires an approach that can produce accurate estimates of response time and workload for different districting designs. The next section describes our approach to the districting problem including a discussion of our evaluation methodology using simulation that is contained in Section "Evaluation of districting plans using simulation".

Approach to police patrol districting

The approach we have developed for the police districting problem begins by generating alternative districting plans. Subsection "Generation of alternative districting plans" gives details of the parameterized algorithm to generate the alternative plans. To evaluate these alternatives we have developed an agent-based simulation. We use the simulation to measure district performance using two metrics: average response time and workload. The simulation we use reveals important complexities in the choice of districting plans. More details on our simulation and its use for evaluating districting plans are contained in Subsection "Evaluation of districting plans using simulation". Because the simulation provides high fidelity evaluation of response times and workloads using data from actual CFS it is a time intensive process. So rather than evaluate all potential districting plans using the simulation we first evaluate some plans generated by randomizing the districting parameters. Then, the relationship between districting parameters and final performance measurements is studied and better districting plans can be generated. The iterative experiment-analysis-learning process can efficiently find better districting plans than random search method. We provide additional discussion of this screening step in Subsection "Relation between parameters and response variables".

Generation of alternative districting plans

The generation of districting plans is based on atomic geographical units. There are some existing geographical units such as police beats or census blocks. Usually, these geographical units consider administrative boundaries, important roads, or some natural boundaries (mountains, rivers). The redistricting procedure can start from these units and re-group them into several districts. When developing districting plans for large areas containing hundreds of such geographical units, police beats or census blocks are good choices for atomic units. However, some cities only have 20 or 30 census blocks. Police beats or census blocks are not small enough for optimal patrol boundaries. In such case, grid network can be used instead. The city can be divided into several hundreds of grids and they are small enough to be atomic units. Clearly, more atomic units represent more possible districting plans. Such representation is more suitable for systematic and scientific study of districting problem. The output districting plans based on grid boundaries can be adjusted according to existing boundaries such as important roads, administrative boundaries and natural boundaries.

The main idea of our districting algorithm is similar to the Constraint-Based Polygonal Spatial Clustering (CPSC) algorithm developed by [13]. The two main steps of the algorithm are 1) select seed polygons (one atomic geographical unit) and 2) select the polygon in neighborhood to be added to the existing cluster until all units are assigned to districts. The major difference of our redistricting algorithm is the selection of seed for each district. Rather than totally randomizing the locations of the seeds, we locate the seeds on several concentric circles over the urban region (see Figure 1). The underlying intuition is that there is a general trend that downtown area of city has more population than suburbs. So the CFS incidents and crime events are also more likely to happen in central region of city. In the concentric circles model, central region of city has more seeds than suburbs and the patrol districts in downtown area tend to be small, which may facilities quick response and reduce workload variation. When selecting the seeds, the minimum distance between these seeds should be greater than a threshold to allow space for the districts to grow. Then, each seed alternates in acquiring adjacent atomic units until a stopping criterion is reached. The stopping criterion is that the sum of CFS probabilities of units in the district is greater than a user selected bound.

During the growing process, the districts or existing cluster of polygons select one adjacent unit to develop. If there are several alternatives, it chooses the one that can maximize the compactness score. Some randomness can be added to this procedure. The difference between random growth and compact growth can be seen in Figure 2. The district can randomly choose one adjacent unit to

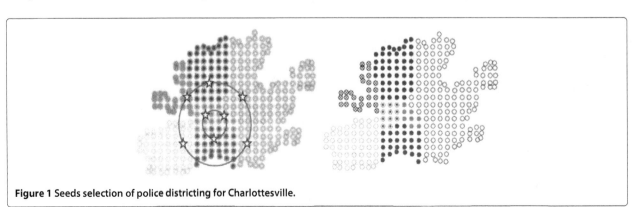

Figure 1 Seeds selection of police districting for Charlottesville.

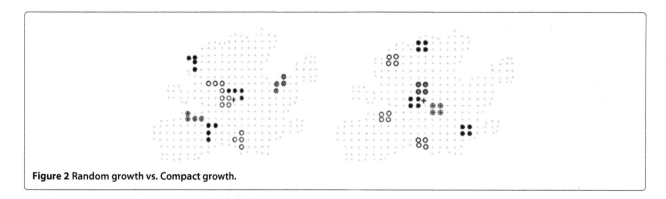

Figure 2 Random growth vs. Compact growth.

develop. After a number of iterations of development, all districts stop growing because the stopping condition is met or because there are no more adjacent units for growth. Usually, there are still some unassigned units in the peripheral region of the city. They are assigned to the adjacent districts based on compactness principle. Then, the districting plan is adjusted to balance the CFS probabilities in each district and smooth the boundary between districts.

The locations of the seeds for districts determine the framework and basic structure of the districting plans. The relevant parameters for starting the growing process are: 1) the center of the concentric circles, 2) the number of circles, 3) the radius of each circle, 4) the number of seeds on each circle. Additional parameters determine the course of district growth. Examples are: 5) the stopping criterion, 6) the number of growth iterations, 7) growth randomness vs. compactness, 8) the number of iterations that balance the CFS probability between districts, 9) the number of iterations that smooth the boundary between districts. Therefore, a districting plan can be described and represented by a set of districting parameters. Once a districting plan is generated, some measurements can be quickly calculated without detailed simulation evaluation, such as compactness of plans and the variation of CFS probability of all districts. These intermediate measurements of districting plans can be used to select top proportion of plans for further simulation evaluation.

Relation between parameters and response variables

Without prior knowledge about how districting parameters affect final response variables, we randomize these parameters to generate some plans, quickly calculate the intermediate measurements, and take some time to get final responses through simulation evaluation. Then we build statistical models to study the relation between them, especially how districting parameters and intermediate measurements affect the final performance variables. The districting parameters can be adjusted to generate more plans that may have better performances. Since it is time intensive to use simulation to evaluate these plans,

they can be ranked by the combined weighted score of the intermediate metrics. The weights are adjusted based on the relation between intermediate variables and final performance variables.

Evaluation of districting plans using simulation

Because the assessment of response times and workloads requires the incorporation of multiple factors that interact in complex ways we cannot use closed form expressions. Also, field experiments in the law enforcement and safety management are clearly not feasible because of the risks and costs, not to mention, the public relations problems [14]. This means that evaluation of the police patrol districting plans requires a high fidelity simulation. A feature key needed in this simulation is the ability to accurately represent behaviors of the police in response to calls-for-service. Agent-based simulations afford the ability to effectively represent these behaviors.

Agent-based simulations capture of the behaviors of objects in an environment, such as police patrols in city, through the use of decision rules. These decision rules govern the interactions between objects in the simulation. For example, when a police car object interacts with a road object the rules specify the rate of transition to the next road object. These rules can also represent static properties of the object, for example the speed limit, and the dynamic properties of the environment, such as weather, construction, and traffic conditions. Other example rules used in our simulation include:

- The nearest police car to a new CFS responds to that CFS;
- The responding police car takes the shortest path to the location of the CFS;
- If a police car is servicing a CFS then it is no longer available to respond to a new CFS;
- If the nearest available police car is in a different district it will cross the district boundary and respond to the CFS.

The interactions between multiple objects governed by the rule sets in the simulation produce emergent behaviors or properties that cannot be predicted before running the simulations. For our purposes the most important emergent properties are the response times to CFS and police workloads. These properties are the metrics that allow us to score the effectiveness of different patrol districting plans. Neither of these properties can be accurately anticipated a priori using only a districting plan and the numbers of CFS within the districts. As we indicated in Subsection "Evaluation complexity" if we could simply develop districting plans that equalize the expected CFS in each district then our problem reduces to the graph-partitioning problem. Although graph-partitioning is NP-hard; nonetheless, there are available heuristics than can be applied.

Instead the police districting problem has evaluation complexity (see Subsection "Evaluation complexity") in addition to the computational complexity of the graph-partitioning problem. In fact, when we use our high fidelity simulation to evaluate police districting plans that minimize the difference in CFS between districts they actually do worse than some other plans. The same is true for workload. The ability to discover these emerging properties is an important feature of the agent-based simulation we built and a critical requirement in the assessment of competing districting plans.

We implemented the simulation using Java Repast. Java Repast is an open source, agent-based modeling and simulation platform [15]. It uses object-oriented model and has a source library of classes for creating and running agent-based simulations and for displaying and collecting data from these simulations. Geographic data, such as the data expressed in shapefiles, can be imported into the Java Repast model. Using these geographic data the behaviors and movements of the agents can be controlled according to rule sets that exploit these data. For example, the shapefile data layer on secondary roads can have attributes that provide speed limits in different segments of this layer.

We built our police patrol simulation model as an extension to Malleson's RepastCity prototype [16]. The inputs to our simulation model consist of the shapefiles of the city, the patrol district plan, the police patrol allocation plan and a data set of CFS times, locations, and severity (this last attribute determines the distribution of the service time for the CFS). The shapefiles for the city include primary and secondary roads, major highways, and obstacles or impediments (e.g., construction or road work).

In order to simulate the time and spatial pattern of actual CFS and maintain the randomness of the city environment, the time between incidents and the locations are randomly chosen based on the distribution of actual CFS. Rather than use a bootstrap approach which would resample from actual CFS, we instead use an empirical fit of the distributions of the CFS in space and time. We then chose CFS values based on random draws according to these distributions.

Police cars are on patrol in their districts until they are dispatched by a CFS. Their patrol routes are randomly chosen from the network of roads in their assigned districts. An incoming CFS will generate the dispatch of the nearest police car and that car will follow the shortest route to the location of the CFS. In following this route it will use the maximum safe speed for the route which is greater than or equal to the speed limit on the route.

After the police car reaches the CFS location, the police car will remain at that location for the service time of that CFS. We obtain this service time as random draw from the service time distribution for the type and severity of the particular CFS. The service time distributions are empirical distributions found from the data set of actual CFS. When the service time ends the police car returns to its patrol route and again becomes available for dispatch to the next CFS.

We run the simulation for chosen number of runs or for a selected amount of simulation time. For each CFS in a run we record

- The time and location of the CFS;
- The identity of responding police car;
- The time of dispatch for the responding police car;
- The time of arrival at the CFS location for the responding police car;
- The time of departure from the CFS by the responding car (i.e., the time of arrival plus the service time);
- The travel distance of the responding car.

Using these data we can calculate the average response time and workload for each run and, hence, for each districting plan.

Case study and preliminary result

To illustrate the use of our approach to police patrol districting we used data from the Charlottesville, VA, USA police department. Charlottesville is a city with a diameter of about 7 miles and a population of about 40,000. However, this population increases during most of the year by another 26,000 due the presence of a major university. The population lives in multi-dwelling buildings, as well as, detached townhouses, apartments, and homes. There are more densely populated buildings near the university and the downtown. There are also commercial areas and some light industrial parks.

The current police patrol district of Charlottesville was designed more than 20 years ago. There are 8 patrol districts and in most of cases, one police car is assigned to patrol each district. The police managers and commanders want to draw district boundaries to incorporate census block groups. These block groups are too large to serve as the atomic geographic units in our district growing algorithm (see Section "Approach to police patrol districting"). There are 37 block groups in Charlottesville. To create more useful atomic geographic units we decomposed the city into 323 grids. Figure 3 shows the locations of historical CFS incidents for several years, including 317,548 events. Many incidents happened at same places so each red point may represent many CFS events. To have a better view of the CFS density distribution in the city region, these historical incidents were spatially projected into the grid network. Based on the counts of CFS incidents, the CFS probability was calculated for each grid. The CFS distribution across these grids is shown in Figure 4.

As noted in Section "Approach to police patrol districting" our approach begins by generating thousands of plans using randomized districting parameters. Due to size of the city and number of districts, two circles are used to generate the seeds. For large cities, seeds can be located on

several circles, depending on the size of city and the number police cars. For cities with general shape of rectangular, ellipses can be used to generate seeds instead of circles. Then, these randomly generated plans were ranked by the weighted sum of two normalized intermediate measurements: standard deviation of CFS probabilities among districts and compactness score. Without prior information about the relevant importance of the two intermediate measurements of districting plans, they were considered equally important with the weights [0.5, 0.5]. Then, the top proportion of the ranked plans was evaluated using simulation model and final performance measurements were obtained. Due to the randomness of the districting algorithm, some combinations of parameter settings cannot generate compact districting plans. Furthermore, we cannot use simulation to evaluate too many districting plans due to the evaluation complexity of the problem, especially at the beginning phase of the experiment. In this case study, top 5% of the randomly generated districting plans were evaluated. More plans can be evaluated

Figure 3 Locations of historical CFS incidents.

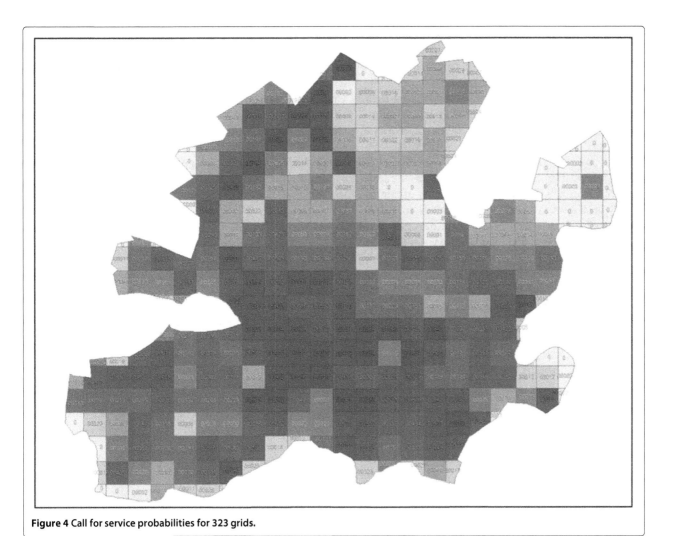

Figure 4 Call for service probabilities for 323 grids.

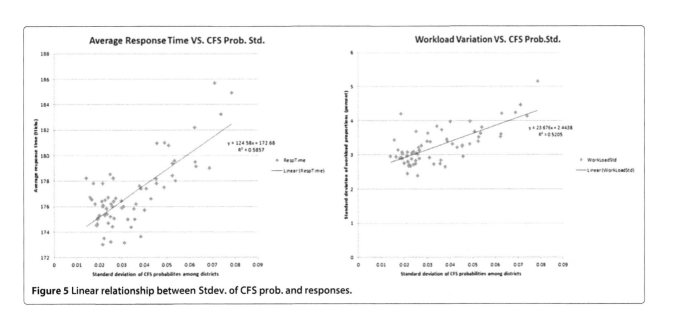

Figure 5 Linear relationship between Stdev. of CFS prob. and responses.

if more computational resources can be used. Based on result from statistical analysis, the center of the concentric circles, the radius of the outer circle are significant to average response time. For workload variation, the significant districting parameters are number of seeds on each circle, the center of the concentric circles and the number of iterations of balancing the CFS probabilities of districts. For the intermediate measurements, the variation of CFS probabilities is more important for both response variables. Its linear relationship to both responses can be seen in Figure 5. It can be seen that lower variation of cumulative CFS probabilities among districts leads to better performances for both responses. So, in the next iteration of ranking randomly generated plans, more weight can be given to standard deviation of CFS probabilities. Then, the relationship between responses and each districting parameter was analyzed individually and they were adjusted in the steepest decent direction to responses and another batch of thousands of plans was generated. The weights for two intermediate measurements became [0.4, 0.6] tentatively for compactness and standard deviation of CFS probabilities among districts. After ranking them

by the weighted sum, the top 5% plans were evaluated in-depth by simulation model. For each of the selected districting plans we ran the simulation for 450000 ticks (simulation time units) and 50 minutes of actual time. Under parallel running in current computing resources (13 batches on 3 PCs), the actual evaluation time for a districting plan can be reduced to 5 minutes. This length of time ensured the convergence of the simulation to a steady state, which can be seen in Figure 6.

Output analysis

While we put more effort into analysis of the performance metrics, average response time and workload, we also wanted to visualize the simulation. This allowed us and our police colleagues to visually assess and validate the behavior of the simulation. We showed the simulation to members of the police and they confirmed its behavior was consistent with that of their patrols. A static view of the simulation is shown in Figure 7. A dynamic view of the simulation can be seen in Additional file 1 or web link: http://www.youtube.com/watch?v=23ghFNAvdP4.

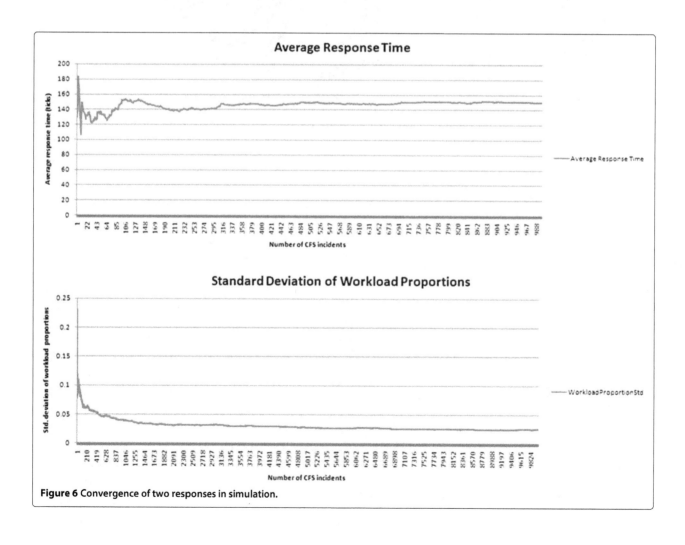

Figure 6 Convergence of two responses in simulation.

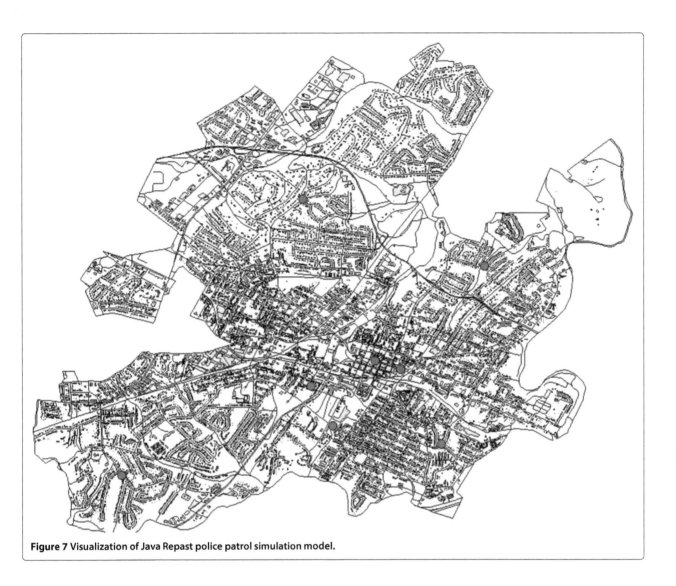

Figure 7 Visualization of Java Repast police patrol simulation model.

The current districting plan was also evaluated by the simulation system. The simulation results show both performance measurements can be improved. The average response time of current districting plan was 180.50 ticks (simulation time unit), which was reduced to 167.70 (Plan No.179). The standard deviation of workload proportion among 8 districts was reduced from 0.0340 to 0.0142 (Plan No.229).

Due to the NP-completeness of the graph-partition problem, there are too many possibilities of districting plans. We cannot use exact method to evaluate each of them. The evaluated districting plans in this case study are only a small proportion of the whole solution set and the solutions provided are preliminary. The global optimality cannot be guaranteed. We only find some significant districting parameters and intermediate measurements that may lead to better plans. More rigorous experimental design and statistical analysis can be conducted to further study the relationship between these

factors and responses. With more powerful computational resources, more districting plans can be further generated and evaluated. It is possible to make improvements on both response variables.

Pareto frontier for bi-criteria decision making

Because we have a multiple objective problem (i.e., we want to minimize the average response time and minimize the variation in workload) we cannot choose a districting plan with a single objective. Further no single plan was best in both average response time and workload variation. To provide a multiple objective solution we used Pareto analysis. This analysis shows the positioning of each of the alternative districting plans with respect to each other on the two dimensional plot of both metrics. Using this plot we can trace the Pareto frontier which is the set of non-dominated districting plans. These plans are not dominated because no other plan is better than them in at least one of the performance metrics.

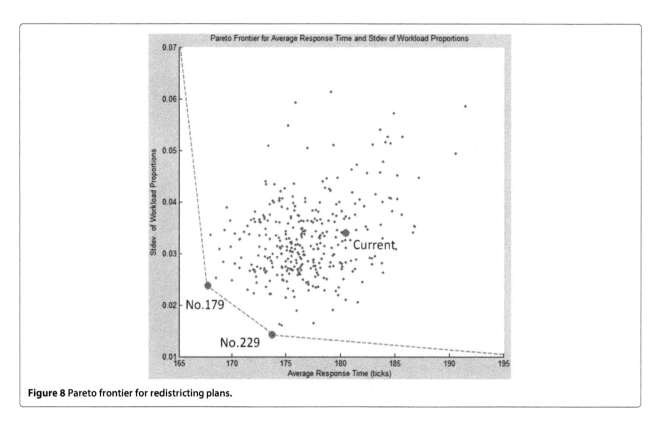

Figure 8 Pareto frontier for redistricting plans.

Figure 8 shows the Pareto frontier of average response time and workload standard deviation for the Charlottesville case study. This figure shows that 2 out of 300 districting plans are on the Pareto frontier. They are No.179 (best districting plan for response time), No.229 (best districting plan for workload variation). Under any weighting of response time and workload variation, one of the two districting plans dominates the others. So, they are the best 2 districting plans. The police department can

choose one of them based on their needs and some practical considerations. The actual physical compositions of districting plan No.179 and No.229 are shown in Figure 9.

Replacing grid boundaries

As noted in Section "Generation of alternative districting plans", the police patrol boundaries should consider some administrative boundaries, natural boundaries and important roads. Clearly, the boundaries based on the grid

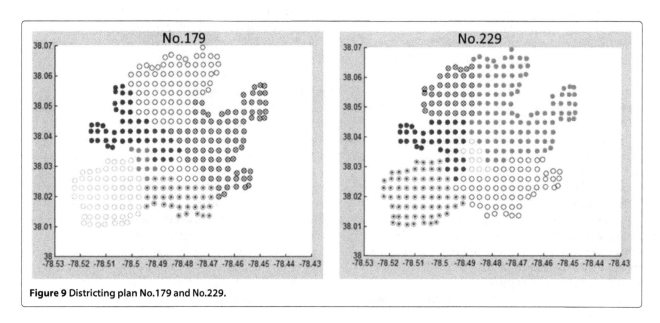

Figure 9 Districting plan No.179 and No.229.

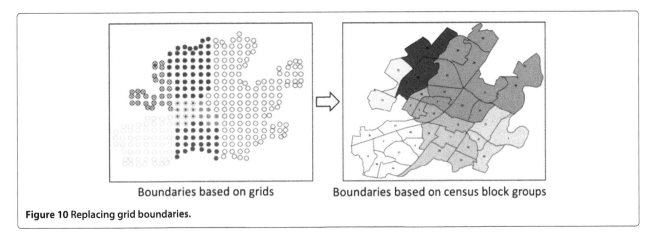

Boundaries based on grids   Boundaries based on census block groups

Figure 10 Replacing grid boundaries.

network violate these boundaries. However, some existing geographical units such as police beats and census
block groups consider these boundaries. So, replacing the
grid boundaries needs to consulting with police departments. If patrol boundaries must be drawn based on police
beats or census blocks, conversion can be made between
grid network and these units. Example can be seen in
Figure 10. If not necessary, the grid boundaries can be
replaced by the nearest roads. In this way, the performance of the districting plan may be close the optimal
solution based on grid network.

Conclusions and future work
In this paper, we reviewed the characteristics of the police
patrol district design problem from the perspective of past
and current work. We also showed the complexity of the
problem from both computational and evaluation perspectives. In Section "Approach to police patrol districting" we described our approach to this problem. First, an
algorithm for automatically generating police patrol districting plans was developed by growing them incrementally using small atomic geographic units as the building
blocks. The second step is to screen these plans to obtain
a smaller number of promising plans that can undergo
more detailed and rigorous evaluation. Our last step is
the perform evaluation using an agent-based simulation
that provides high fidelity measures of performance. The
case study presented in this paper shows the use of our
police patrol districting approach for the Charlottesville
Police Department. Compared with the current patrol district boundaries, the solution generated from our patrol
districting approach shows improvement on both average
response time and variation of the workload through the
detailed simulation study.

While our simulation provides high fidelity it does not
affectively capture changes over the course of an entire
year. The changes include significant changes in weather
and traffic patterns. To make our simulation in its current
form work for an entire year would require run lengths

of several months. Hence we must develop improvements, either through sub-sampling, meta-modeling or
other data reduction strategies. We also need to improve
the screening method to ensure that we do not inadver-
tently remove an alternative that may prove superior in
our more intensive simulation based evaluation.

Additional file

Additional file 1: Simulation dynamic view. This file is video record of
Java Repast's visualization, which shows the dynamic view of the police
patrol simulation system.

Competing interests
Both authors declare that they have no competing interests.

Authors' contributions
YZ implemented the simulation system, developed the districting algorithm in
this paper, tested them, and drafted the manuscript. DB provided theoretical
guidance in the whole procedure and revised the manuscript. Both authors
read and approved the final manuscript.

References
1. M Rosenshine, Contributions to a theory of patrol scheduling. Oper. Res.
    Q (1970-1977). **21**, 99–106 (1970)
2. PE Taylor, SJ Huxley, A break from tradition for the San Francisco Police:
    patrol officer scheduling using an optimization-based decision support
    system. Interfaces. **19**, 4–24 (1989)
3. CD Hale, *Police Patrol, Operations and Management*. (Prentice Hall, Upper
    Saddle River, 1980)
4. SJ D'Amico, SJ Wang, R Batta, CM Rump, A simulated annealing approach
    to police district design. Comput. Oper. Res. **29**(6), 667–684 (2002)
5. PG Hancock, NC Simpson, Fifty years of operational research and
    emergency response. J. Oper. Res. Soc. **60**(51), 126–139 (2009)
6. GW Cordner, KE Scarborough, *Police Administration*. (Anderson,
    Cincinnati, 2010)
7. RC Larson, Measuring the Response Patterns of New York City Police
    Patrol Cars (1971). New York City Rand Institute R-673-NYC/HUD
8. PS Mitchell, Optimal selection of police patrol beats. J. Crim. Law.
    63(4), 577–584 (1972)
9. KM Curtin, K Hayslett-McCall, F Qiu, Determining optimal police patrol
    areas with maximal covering and backup covering location models.
    Netw. Spat. Econ. **10**, 125–145 (2010)

10. AAAly, DWLitwhiler, Police briefing stations: a location problem. AIIE Trans. (0569-5554). **11**, 12–22 (1979)

11. M Altman, The computational complexity of automated redistricting: Is automation the answer? Rutgers Comput. Technol. Law J. **23**, 81–142 (1997)

12. DS Johnson, The NP-completeness column: an ongoing guide. J. Algorithms. **3**(2), 182–195 (1982)

13. D Joshi, LK Soh, A Samal, in *Data Min, 2009. ICDM '09.Ninth IEEE. Int Conf.* Redistricting Using Heuristic-Based Polygonal Clustering, (2009), pp. 830–835

14. BA Knoppers, HF Miller, in *International Symposium on Criminal Justice Information and Statistics Systems Proceedings.* Computer simulation of police dispatching and patrol functions, (1972)

15. Official website of Java Repast. http://repast.sourceforge.net/

16. N Malleson, Agent-Based Modelling of Burglary, *PhD thesis.* (School of Geography, University of Leeds, 2010)

4

Predicting sentencing outcomes with centrality measures

Carlo Morselli[1*], Victor Hugo Masias[2,3], Fernando Crespo[4] and Sigifredo Laengle[3]

Abstract

Despite their importance for stakeholders in the criminal justice system, few methods have been developed for determining which criminal behavior variables will produce accurate sentence predictions. Some approaches found in the literature resort to techniques based on indirect variables, but not on the social network behavior with exception of the work of Baker and Faulkner [ASR 58: 837–860, 1993]. Using information on the *Caviar Network* narcotics trafficking group as a real-world case, we attempt to explain *sentencing outcomes* employing the social network indicators. Specifically, we report the ability of centrality measures to predict a) the verdict (innocent or guilty) and b) the sentence length in years. We show that while the set of indicators described by Baker and Faulkner yields good predictions, introduction of the additional centrality measures generates better predictions. Some ideas for orienting future research on further improvements to sentencing outcome prediction are discussed.

Keywords: Criminology, Sentencing outcomes, Social networks

Introduction

This study examines the prediction of criminal trial *sentencing outcomes* on the basis of social network measures. Though it has received relatively little attention in criminology, sentencing predictions are extremely important to various stakeholders in the criminal justice system [1,2]. In general terms, law enforcement entities are responsible for three central tasks: a) monitoring, b) making arrests, and c) charging one or more persons [2]. In their pursuit of these activities, however, they normally do not have the necessary data and methods at their disposal to identify which individual and group characteristics influence the fate of those they lay charges against. Furthermore, attempts at prediction are complicated by the fact that judicial processes are not free of bias due to discrimination or errors stemming from the lack of standard sentencing guidelines [3-7].

While studies aimed at specifying the factors influencing criminal conduct may be found in past research [8], few focus on explaining sentencing outcome based on the networking features of offenders. Research has concentrated rather on explaining outcomes using sociodemographic and socioeconomic variables. For example, sentences have

been shown to fluctuate in accordance with political environment indicators [9], an individual's race and age [10,11], and an individual's criminal history and the presence of a police confession [12].

Our concern is to access *sentencing outcomes* as a function of behavior and positioning in criminal networks in order to determine whether the judicial processes that define sentences capture and take this behavior into account. From a social network perspective, networks of nodes represent individuals (or actors) and the direct and indirect relationships between them [13]. As Sarnecki has noted: "One of the most important tasks of network analysis is to attempt to explain, at least in part, the behavior of the elements in a network by studying specific properties of the relations between these elements" [14] p. 5. This method is already established as a powerful tool in many fields such as marketing, political science, organizational behavior, epidemiology, sociology, and software development [15-17]. Other theoretical and empirical initiatives have extended its use to the analysis of the social behavior of criminal groups and organizations [2,18-20] and terrorists operations [21,22].

A key aspect of the social network approach was pointed to by McGloin and Kirk: "[n]etwork analysis requires different data than most criminologists typically employ. It may be clear by now that the unit of analysis in network

* Correspondence: carlo.morselli@umontreal.ca
[1]School of Criminology, Université de Montréal, C.P. 6128, succursale Centre-ville, Montreal, QC H3C-3 J7, Canada
Full list of author information is available at the end of the article

studies is not the node or individual, but the tie between entities (i.e., links among the nodes)" [23], p. 212. More specifically, this approach allows us to identify a) the central individuals in a criminal network, b) its subgroups, c) interactions between the subgroups, d) the network's structure, e) the impact of removing an individual from the network, and f) the network's information flows [20,23]. It also affords a broad array of measures and technologies from various generations that facilitate the study of organized criminal behavior [24]. In short, network analysis provides both a theoretical basis and practical methods criminologists can employ to study the variables that explain criminal behavior and the interpersonal relationships underlying it.

Most existing studies of criminal networks focus on characterizing the roles of individual members, especially those whose roles are central [1,20,23,25] or who serve as brokers [18,26-31]. Yet despite the growing popularity among criminologists of these social network applications, their practical usefulness is still limited [32]. The state of the art suggests there is little information regarding which social network variables can predict who will or will not be arrested or convicted and how long a sentence will be. One of the few works that explores the explanatory ability of certain social network and sentencing outcome measures is Baker and Faulkner [1]. The authors use various centrality indicators defined in Freeman [33] to explore the capacity of social network metrics to explain verdicts and prison sentence length. Thus, they explore whether a predictive model of sentencing outcome can be constructed from measures of degree centrality, betweenness centrality, and closeness centrality together with graph density and centralization metrics. Their results show that degree centrality explains the likelihood of a guilty or innocent verdict but is less successful in predicting sentence length [1]. What is certain, however, is that these efforts have played a pioneering role in the search for explanatory relationships between sentencing outcome and social network indicators.

Our aim in this study is to pursue Baker and Faulkner's initial findings by assessing variations in criminal justice outcomes in one specific case study. Our analysis expands the repertoire of network measures by integrating a variety of centrality measures that were not assessed by Baker and Faulkner or other researchers since. These variables and the main data source for this case study will be presented in the subsequent section. This data and method description is followed by a series of analyses that demonstrate how positioning in a criminal network is key to understanding how an individual will be reacted to by criminal justice agents.

Centrality measures and criminal behavior

Centrality is a key concept in social network analysis [13,34] and in academic literature there are different indexes of centrality [33,35,36] which have the common purpose of "quantify an intuitive feeling that in most networks some vertices or edges are more central than others" [37], p. 16. Centrality can be assessed by three types of measures: local, distance, and feedback [38]. Baker and Faulkner [1] already demonstrated criminal justice risks and trade-offs generated by degree centrality, betweenness centrality, and closeness centrality. The additional indicators proposed for this study include out-degree centrality, eigenvector centrality [35], authority centrality and hub centrality [39]. Each of these measures offers a different way of measuring the centrality of an individual in a network.

Degree centrality and its derivative, in-degree and out-degree centrality, are local measures [13]. Degree centrality is a straightforward count of the number of direct contacts that are linked to a node. Out-degree centrality measures the number of direct contacts to whom the node communicates toward (out-flow communication). In-degree centrality measures the number of these direct contacts that communicate toward a node (in-flow communication).

Betweenness centrality and closeness centrality are distance measures [40]. Betweenness centrality measures the extent to which a node mediates relationships between other nodes by its position along the geodesics within the network. A geodesic is the shortest path (or number of degrees) connecting a dyad (a pair of nodes). The greater a node is located along the geodesics in the network, the greater its betweenness centrality. This measure essentially represents the ability of some nodes to control the flow of connectivity (or communication, in this case) within a network. Controlling the flow within the network in this indirect manner is the broker's edge. Closeness centrality is also based on geodesic paths, but unlike betweenness centrality which accounts for mediation within these paths, closeness measures the extent to which a node is in proximity to others. This measure is essentially a calculation of the mean geodesic distance between a node and all other reachable nodes in the network.

Feedback measures in this analysis were accounted for by eigenvector centrality [35], authority centrality and hub centrality [39]. Eigenvector is a derivative of degree centrality in that it measures the extent to which a node is connected to well-connected nodes. Authority centrality and hub centrality are measures that were designed for directed networks. The two are analyzed together and may be described as a mix of in-degree/out-degree centrality and eigenvector centrality. Authority centrality is similar to in-degree centrality in that it measures incoming relationships, while hub centrality is similar to out-degree centrality because it measures outgoing relationships. The difference between the two sets of measures lies in the connectivity of actors that are connected to a node. A node with high authority centrality is one that receives a high volume of communications from nodes with high hub centrality. A node with high hub centrality is one that receives a high volume of communications from nodes with high authority centrality. Kleinberg [39] emphasizes the *mutually reinforcing relationship* between authorities and hubs in that a good hub points to many good authorities, while a good authority points to by many good hubs.

These variables will be used to examine and interpret the patterns surrounding variations in criminal justice outcomes in the *Caviar Network*. Each set of analysis integrating these variables carry their own rationale. Out-degree centrality measures explain the propagation of messages in a telephone communication network [41,42]. This is important for the present case study since our data are drawn from intercepted communications between criminal network participants. Our hypothesis follows that participants who are more active in this intercepted communication network are more visible (and thus vulnerable) and this will translate into more severe *sentencing outcomes*.

Betweenness centrality was presented as a more strategic networking pattern [19] in that it represents those participants who are active and pivotal in a network, but less directly involved. Indeed, the broker advantage has been recognized consistent across past research on illegal drug-trafficking [43-46], human smuggling [47-49], stolen-vehicle exportation [50] and general criminal enterprise settings [51-53]. Our hypothesis in the present case study follows that, once a participant is arrested, the brokerage edge is considerably hindered and the key positioning of high-betweenness centrality participants emerges as a heavy burden, thus leading to higher *sentencing outcomes*.

Baker and Faulkner [1] proposed that closeness centrality is positively related to an unfavorable judicial outcome. However, it should be noted that closeness centrality can also indicate that nodes are distant from a node that has high closeness centrality. In this sense, low closeness centrality helps to identify who was or were the last persons in the flow of communication in a drug trafficking network. We can deduce that an individual with a relatively low closeness centrality may be most vulnerable in the judicial process due to his high visibility and high-risk tasks. Therefore, we expect that the closeness centrality indicator is negatively associated with the likelihood of an unfavorable judicial outcome.

Eigenvector centrality [35,54] represents a participant's connections to well-connected participants. Nodes with the same degree centrality are not necessarily equally central as this will depend on how their contacts are connected. Eigenvector centrality adds this important nuance and captures the problems often associated to proximity to the most visible. In this sense, participants with higher eigenvector centrality should receive more sever sentencing

because of their proximity to well-connected individuals in the network who, as hypothesized above, are themselves more likely to receive harsher punishment.

To further nuance the implications of being well connected in a criminal network and being connected to others who are well connected, the authority and hub centrality measures will be introduced to the analysis to assess the reciprocal features that are offered by these variables. Kleinberg argues that these indicators offer "a richer notion of importance, or prominence, [that] contains an intrinsic element of circularity: it arises from the fragile intuition that a node is important if it receives links from other important nodes" [55], p. 611. Our hypothesis therefore posits that a sentencing outcome should penalize more heavily those individuals whose values for these measures reveal a relatively high authority or hub level within the network.

Method
Case study
This study is based on the *Caviar Network*, a hashish and cocaine importation and trafficking network that operated out of Montreal, Canada, during the 1990's [2,19,56,57]. The *Caviar Network* was an international network engaged in hashish and cocaine importation that was the targeted during a 2-year investigation (1994–1996) by the Royal Canadian Mounted Police and the Montreal Police. The strategy adopted by the two forces was unique in that large drug shipments were seize on several occasions[a], but no arrests were made until the final phase of the investigation. This enabled investigators to gain detailed knowledge of the criminal behavior and organization of the network participants during the various phases of the investigative process.

Data source
The source for the network data is the evidence derived from electronic surveillance transcripts that were presented in court during the trials of some of the participants. The more than 1, 000 pages of transcripts released to the public reveal the communication network that existed between network participants. These transcripts were used to create a social network matrix of the drug trafficking operation's communication system during the investigation. The network is valued and directed and is made up of 110 participants. At the end of the investigation, 25 participants were arrested, 22 were charged, and 14 were found guilty. So as not to reveal the identity of the monitored individuals, an identification number was assigned to each (e.g., node $N_1, \ldots, N_{110}$)[b]. Below is a graph of the *Caviar Network*[c].

Figure 1 shows a sociogram of the *Caviar Network*, where each node represents an individual member while arrows describe the communications flow. The nodes in

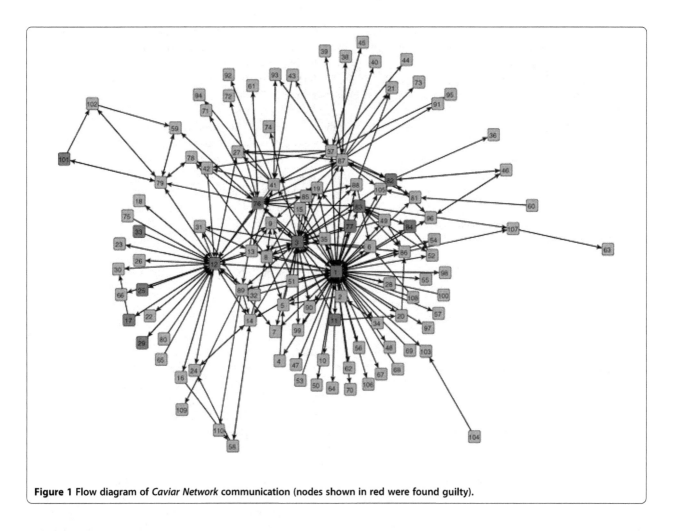

Figure 1 Flow diagram of *Caviar Network* communication (nodes shown in red were found guilty).

red are the individuals who were found guilty by the courts. As can be seen in the sociogram, there are some nodes that have a clear centrality in the network (N_1, N_2 and N_3), but we can also realize that by using only this kind of visual information it is difficult to figure out how the position of each node in the network has a relationship with a coordinated criminal behavior. In fact, some of the participants had heterogeneous and highly specialized roles. For example, individual N_1 initiated the importation network and was the main coordinator of hashish importations. N_{12} was a Colombian associate who was the main coordinator for cocaine importations. N_3 was the described as a N_1's *lieutenant*, but more detailed analysis demonstrated that he was a key liaison between N_1 and N_3 [2]. Individual N_{87} was the owner of a legitimate importation enterprise and was one of many participants who did not participate directly in the trafficking activities, but served as key facilitators by supplying legitimate fronts, financial resources, and logistic resources during the importation activities[d] (for this specific analysis, see [56]).

Let us note that the sociogram does not contain data on verbal or written communication, ie., the explicit content of communication between the network's members). Rather, the sociogram shows us the communicative behavior of each individual based on two primitive data types: a) data about who called who and b) data about the number of times where communication occurred between each pair of individuals. Thus, because the social network measure is built from these two simple data types, it is both practical and challenging to analyze whether the centrality measures have the ability to predict the outcomes of a judicial process.

Statistical data analysis

In this study, two variables are used to indicate the criminal justice outcomes. The first variable is dichotomous and indicates an innocent (coded 0) or guilty (coded 1) verdict ($M = .13$, $SD = .33$). The second variable is continuous and indicate the sentence in years which ranged from 0 to 15 years ($M = .86$ years, $SD = 2.59$). The number of cases, minimum and maximum values, means, standard deviations and inter- correlations between outcome measures (variables 1–2) and predictor variables (variables 3–9) are presented in Table 1.

Table 1 Minima, Maxima, Means, Standard Deviations and Intercorrelations for Outcome Measures and Centrality Measures ($N = 110$)

Variable	Min.	Max.	M	SD	2	3	4	5	6	7	8	9
Outcome Measures												
1 Verdict	.00	1.00	.13	.33	.87**	.28**	.46**	.44**	.43**	.49**	.41**	.31**
2 Year Sentence	.00	15.00	.86	2.59	–	.26**	.63**	.68**	.59**	.58**	.39**	.45**
Predictor Variable												
3 Closeness Centrality	.00	.00	.00	.00		–	.23*	.20*	.21*	.24*	.21*	.13
4 Degree Centrality	.11	218.00	6.87	23.07			–	.94**	.99**	.90**	.42**	.93**
5 Betweenness Centrality	.00	4, 663.00	118.09	524.68				–	.93**	.73**	.23*	.88**
6 Out-Degree Centrality	.00	109.00	2.76	11.03					–	.86**	.30**	.96**
7 Eigenvector Centrality	.00	1.00	.04	.13						–	.71**	.80**
8 Authority Centrality	.00	1.00	.04	.11							–	.14
9 Hub Centrality	.00	1.00	.04	.11								–

*$p < .01$ level (2 – tailed).
**$p < .05$ level (2 – tailed).

The strategy behind our analysis was to establish which subset of centrality measures had greater predictive ability for *sentencing outcomes* in the *Caviar Network* case. More specifically, we set out to determine how the predictive abilities of the measures used in the existing literature (variables 3–5) compared with those discussed in our literature survey above (variables 6–9). There were three steps in the strategy:

1. The first step was to verify whether the degree centrality, betweenness centrality and closeness centrality measures (that is, the measures proposed as sentencing outcome predictors by [1]) were able to predict the outcome of the *Caviar Network* trial. This was done by conducting an initial logistic regression to predict the verdict of guilt or innocence and an initial multiple linear regression to predict the sentence in years. Both regression models were carried out using the stepwise selection method. The candidate variables in the two regression models were closeness centrality (variable 3), degree centrality (variable 4), and betweenness centrality (variable 5). The analysis yielded a) a first model for predicting the verdict (see Table 2), and b) a first model for predicting the sentence length in years (see Table 3).

2. The second step was to select the variables with the best explanatory ability for sentencing outcomes of all the centrality measures studied. This was done using a second logistic regression analysis for predicting the verdict and a second multiple linear regression to predict sentence length. Once again, stepwise selection was employed. The candidate variables in this second step were all the centrality measures (variables 3–9 in Table 1).

The analysis yielded a) a second model for predicting the verdict (see Table 4), and b) a second model for predicting sentence length (see Table 5).

3. The third step consisted in making the various comparisons of the model results. The final models for predicting the verdict were compared by observing their respective correct classification percentages. The final models for predicting the sentence (see second Sub-section of Results) were then compared on the basis of the coefficient of determination (R^2) and the error variance (S^2) of the multiple linear regressions.

Results

The results will be reported as follows. First, we report the summary of logistic regression for predicting the verdict (first Subsection). Second, we report the summary of multiple regressions for predicting the sentence in years (second Subsection).

Logistic regression analysis for centrality measures predicting verdict

A first logistic regression analysis was conducted to discriminate the verdict, using the Wald statistic to select the significant variables in terms of their prediction ability.

Table 2 Final Regression Model 1 Predicting Verdict

Predictor	B	SE	OR	95%CI	Wald Statistics	p
Closeness Centrality	−4,910-60	926.76	.00	[.00,.00]	28.08	<.001
Degree Centrality	.13	.04	1.14	[1.05,1.24]	10.52	.001

Note. *CI* = confidence interval for odds ratio *(OR)*.

Table 3 Final Regression Model 1 Predicting Length of Imposed Sentences

Predictor	B	SE B	β	t	p
Betweenness Centrality	<.01	.00	.63	8.95	< .001
Closeness Centrality	1,118.80	362.14	.22	3.09	.003

Note. R^2 = .51, (N = 110, p < .05).

The independent variables for this step are betweenness, closeness and degree centrality. The final model used closeness and degree centrality variables to predict the verdict variable (see Table 2).

A test of the full model against a constant only model was statistically significant, indicating that the predictors as a set reliably distinguished between guilty and innocent (X^2 23.121, p < .003 with df = 8). Nagelkerke's R^2 of .585 indicated a moderately relationship between prediction and grouping. Prediction success overall was 90.9% (35.7% for guilty and 99% for innocent).

As can be seen in Table 2, the Wald criterion demonstrated that closeness centrality, p < .001, and degree centrality, p < .01, made a significant contribution to prediction. In the final model the classification was improved by eliminating the regression constant, and the betweenness centrality variable, p = .655, was also dropped due to its high residual probability. The odds ratio for closeness centrality is almost 0 (OR < .0001), indicating that the higher is this measure, the less likely is a guilty verdict. For degree centrality the odds ratio is 1.14, meaning that the higher is this indicator, the more likely is a guilty verdict.

The independent variables in the second regression logistic analysis were the betweenness, closeness and degree centrality indicators, as was the case in the first regression, with the addition of the authority centrality, eigenvector centrality, hub centrality, and out-degree centrality measures. For this logistic regression the Wald statistic was applied in iterative steps to select the significant variables that discriminate the verdict, eliminating the non-significant variables (p ≥ .05). The final model used the out-degree centrality and a constant to predict the verdict variable (see Table 4).

A test of the full model against a constant only model was statistically significant, indicating that the predictors as a set reliably distinguished between guilty and innocent (X^2 = 7.228, p < .300 with df = 6). Nagelkerke's R^2 of .375 implies that the model explained 37.5% of the relationship

Table 4 Final Regression Model 2 Predicting Verdict

Predictor	B	SE	OR	95%CI	Wald Statistics	p
Out-Degree Centrality	.29	.08	1.34	[1.14,1.57]	12.73	<.001
Constant	-2.85	.44	.06		42.94	<.001

Note. CI = confidence interval for odds ratio (OR).

Table 5 Final Regression model 2 Predicting length of Imposed Sentences

Predictor	B	SE B	β	t	p
Authority Centrality	−10,640.00	4.81	-.46	−2.21	.029
Closeness Centrality	< .01	.001	1.10	8.73	< .001
Eigenvector Centrality	21.79	6.18	1.11	3.52	.001
Hub Centrality	−35.82	7.02	−1.27	−5.11	< .001

Note. R^2 = .64, (N = 110, p < .05).

between prediction and grouping. Prediction success overall was 91.8% (42.9% for guilty[e] and 99% for innocent).

As can be seen in Table 4, the Wald criterion demonstrated that only out-degree centrality made a significant contribution to prediction, p < .001. In the final model the classification was improved by eliminating the authority centrality variable, p = .451, betweenness centrality, p = .329, degree centrality, p = .454, eigenvector centrality, p = .854, hub centrality, p = .329, were also dropped due to their high residual probability. Thus, for out-degree centrality the odds ratio is 1.34, meaning that the higher is this indicator, the more likely is a guilty verdict.

Then, by comparing the percentage correct classification in the first and second logistic regression model, we can report that the second one provides a better prediction of the verdict.

Multiple regression analysis for centrality measures predicting the imposed sentence

An alpha level of .05 was used. The means, standard deviations and intercorrelations between the variables was presented in Table 1[f].

A first linear regression was then run to predict the imposed sentence based on the three independent variables: betweenness centrality, closeness centrality and degree centrality. As can be seen in Table 3, the analysis of the data using a linear regression technique revealed that the combined predictors explained 51.5% of the variance in sentence in years, R^2 = .515, adjusted R^2 = .521, F (3.107) = 37.95, p < .0001. Betweenness centrality, β = .003, p < .001, and closeness centrality, β = 1, 118.800, p < .01, were significant predictors of the length of the sentence; degree centrality, β = −.003, p = .905, is not a statistically significant predictor of sentence length. Thus, the regression coefficients indicate that betweenness and closeness centrality increase the length of the sentence.

A second linear regression was run to predict the imposed sentence length. This included the same two sets of centrality measures as independent variables: betweenness, closeness and to degree centrality plus authority centrality, eigenvector centrality, hub centrality, and out-degree centrality. As can be seen in Table 5, the analysis of the data using a linear regression equation revealed that the combined predictors explained 64.4%

of the variance in the length of the sentence, $R^2 = .644$, adjusted $R^2 = .631$, $F (4, 106) = 49.93$, $p < .0001$. Authority centrality, $\beta = -10,640$, $p < .05$, betweenness centrality, $\beta = .006$, $p < .001$, eigenvector centrality, $\beta = 21.749$, $p < .01$, hub centrality, $\beta = -35.822$, $p < .001$, were significant predictors of the length of the sentence; closeness centrality, $\beta = 294.998$, $p = .431$, degree centrality, $\beta = -.059$, $p = .596$; out-degree centrality, $\beta = .201$, $p = .268$, were not statistically significant predictors of the imposed sentence length. Thus, the regression coefficients indicate that betweenness and eigenvector centrality increase the length of the sentence while authority centrality and hub centrality reduce it.

Upon comparing the R^2 of the first linear regression model (Table 3) with that of the second linear regression model (Table 5), we can then report that the second model provides a better prediction of the sentence in years. In addition, because the error variance in the first regression model, $S^2 = 1.90$, is larger than that of the second regression model, $S^2 = 1.62$, the second model generates errors that are less dispersed. This implies that using the additional set of proposed indicators generates a better prediction.

Discussion and conclusion

This study has shown that social network centrality indicators have good predictive abilities that can strengthen the efforts of criminologists to explain criminal trial *sentencing outcomes* using data on the communication behavior of a criminal network. In what follows we offer a number of observations on our findings.

The first point to note is that using a single network analysis centrality measure leads to good verdict predictions (see Table 4). The results were in fact better than the ones generated by the binary regression model reported in [1], although it must be kept in mind that the cases analyzed were different. Our model posits that the out-degree variable explains the finding of innocence or guilt in that it shows that nodes making calls to other nodes are more likely to be classified as guilty, while those found innocent are those who communicate with relatively fewer individuals. It is also true, however, that the model is better at classifying the innocent than the guilty. This result may be due to the fact that the values of the social network indicators are close to 0, which creates numerical stability problems (on numerical stability in matrices, (see [58,59]). Furthermore, the number of individuals convicted is low compared to the total number observed (14 out of 110, or 12.7%) and a value in the classification is missing, suggesting a separation problem [60]. We therefore conclude that the model predicts guilt or innocence well with a single social network indicator but classifies those found innocent better than those found guilty.

Second, the use of four social network centrality measures generates good predictions of the length of imposed sentences (see Table 5). Certain variables were found to increase or decrease the length of the sentence. Thus, individuals who mediate communication more (betweenness centrality) and those who communicate more with individuals having high centrality levels (eigenvector centrality) receive longer sentences. By contrast, high values for authority or hub centrality decrease sentence length while low values increase it. Individual N_1, for example, had the highest hub centrality value whereas individual N_3 displayed the highest authority centrality value, and both were given relatively short sentences.

This last finding might seem to contradict our working hypothesis that higher values for hub and authority centrality should increase sentence length. But it must be kept in mind that in order to be a good hub or authority an individual's node must point to good hubs or good authorities. We suspect that the judicial process imposed light sentences to some nodes that had high hub or authority centralities because the investigative process did not recognize the Caviar Network's complex communication structure. The complexity of the algorithm for computing the hub and authority variables makes it virtually impossible to interpret these variables visually in a graph or sociogram. It appears that the complexity of the network's behavior and authority distribution structures *protected* certain members while making others *vulnerable*. In this sense we conclude that our approach explains sentence length based on social network variables.

Although the model generates good predictions, it is noteworthy that the negative weights indicate reductions in sentence length as hub and authority centrality increase, just the opposite of what we would have expected. We believe this occurred because some individuals with high values for these indicators were not punished. This is not to say that the investigation was poorly handled, but nor do we feel obliged to conclude these measures are not good sentence length predictors. A more likely explanation is that the investigators and judges on the case did not have the information generated for this study available to them given the impossibility of obtaining it or observing it directly and were thus not in a position to ensure sentence length was related to network communication behavior. The information they would have needed was derived from a complex algorithmic computation and a sociogram of 110 individuals that is difficult to represent visually. Indeed, at the time of the investigation into the *Caviar Network* the hub and authority computation algorithm [39] had not yet been formulated. Identifying the authorities in a criminal network is therefore highly important, for without this data the sentences handed down will not be proportional to the actual communication behavior of the Network's member individuals.

To conclude, the social network indicators used in previous studies already generated good sentencing outcome predictions, the inclusion of additional network centrality measures improves their accuracy. In light of this, three principal considerations should guide future research in this area.

1. The addition of sociodemographic and socioeconomic variables used in the conventional literature to those posited in this study should be explored to determine whether they would improve sentence prediction. In our view, the criminal history variable has already demonstrated its predictive ability regarding sentencing outcome [3,7,12,61]. In the *Caviar Network* case, for example, the node given the longest sentence was individual N_{12}, who was condemned to 15 years in prison because of previous convictions.

2. Whereas [1] only included local and distance measures as predictor variables, our results show that local variables function best for predicting the verdict while distance and network feedback variables do a better job of explaining sentence length. Further investigation of *sentencing outcomes* should include various types of social network measures.

3. There is still no methodology for identifying criminals over time. In the present study we aggregated the 11 matrices describing the behavior of the *Caviar Network* over a two-year period. The next step would be to carry out a dynamic classification analysis such as the one proposed by [62] to create behavior profiles or patterns for different groups in terms of their social network indicators.

This study has attempted to respond to a number of questions and define new tasks for explaining *sentencing outcomes*. The ultimate goal is to provide criminologists with valuable feedback for decisions regarding future research and the allocation of resources and effort to issues of public interest. The application of the social network approach requires further study of criminal networks, particularly as regards ethical and legal questions that arise in real-world cases [63]. We agree fully with the observation of McGloin and Kirk that "the use of formal social network analysis is still quite limited in the fields of criminology and criminal justice" [23], p. 222. Greater application of this approach together with the development of new social network measures could provide valuable information on the centrality of individuals in these networks and their network behavior.

Endnotes

[a] Morselli [2] reports that these seizures led to a loss of approximately US$32 million for participants in the network.

[b] Data was organized and analyzed with the Organizational Risk Analyzer (see [64]), a program made available by the CASOS project at Carnegie Mellon University.

[c] This sociogram was produced using visone software [65]. For more information on graph-layout algorithms and their application in networks social analysis, see the work of [38,66-69].

[d] Individuals N_{82} to N_{110} represented such facilitators in the network.

[e] A guilty verdict was correctly predicted for individual N_{11} that the first logistic regression model were unable to classify.

[f] The correlation matrix of all variables presented in Table 1 suggests that there is no problem of multicollinearity. As can be note, there is no one variable highly correlated with all others variables.

Competing interests
The authors declare that they have no competing interests.

Authors' contributions
CM carried out the data collection and studied the research domain, CM and VM designed the research, VM, FC and SL conducted the empirical tests, and VM and SL wrote the paper. All authors read and approved the final manuscript.

Acknowledgement
We thank all anonymous reviewers for their thorough evaluation and constructive recommendations for improving this manuscript.

Author details
[1]School of Criminology, Université de Montréal, C.P. 6128, succursale Centre-ville, Montreal, QC H3C-3 J7, Canada. [2]Faculty of Economics and Business, Universidad Diego Portales, Manuel Rodríguez Sur 253, 8370057, Santiago de, Chile. [3]Department of Management Control, University of Chile, Diagonal Paraguay 257, 8330015, Santiago de, Chile. [4]Universidad de Valparaíso, Brigadier de La Cruz 1050, 8900183, Santiago de, Chile.

References
1. WE Baker, RR Faulkner, The Social Organization Of Conspiracy: Illegal Networks in the Heavy Electrical Equipment Industry. Am. Sociol. Rev. **58**(6), 837–860 (1993)
2. C Morselli, *Inside Criminal Networks* (Springer Verlag, New York, 2009)
3. SD Bushway, AM Piehl, Judging Judicial Discretion: Legal Factors and Racial Discrimination in Sentencing. Law Soc Rev **35**(4), 733–764 (2001)
4. J Dixon, The Organizational Context of Criminal Sentencing. Am. J. Sociol. **100**(5), 1157–1198 (1995)
5. MP Harrington, C Spohn, Defining Sentence Type: Further Evidence Against Use of the Total Incarceration Variable. J Res Crime Delinquency **44**, 36–63 (2007)
6. S Nicholson-Crotty, KJ Meier, Crime and Punishment: The Politics of Federal Criminal Justice Sanctions. Pol Res Q **56**(2), 119–126 (2003)
7. D Steffensmeier, S Demuth, Ethnicity and Sentencing Outcomes in U.S. Federal Courts: Who Is Punished More Harshly? Am. Sociol. Rev. **65**(5), 705–729 (2000)
8. L Ellis, KM Beaver, JP Wright, *Handbook of Crime Correlates* (Academic, San Diego, CA, 2009)
9. R Helms, Modeling the Politics of Punishment: A Conceptual and Empirical Analysis of'Law in Action' in Criminal Sentencing. J Crim Justice **37**, 10–20 (2009)
10. C Spohn, D Holleran, The Imprisonment Penalty Paid by Young, Unemployed Black and Hispanic Male Offenders. Criminol **38**, 281–306 (2000)

11. RJ Thomson, MT Zingraff, Detecting Sentencing Disparity: Some Problems and Evidence. Am. J. Sociol. **86**(4), 869–880 (1981)

12. SD Bushway, AM Piehl, The Inextricable Link Between Age and Criminal History in Sentencing. Crime & Delinquency **53**, 156–183 (2007)

13. S Wasserman, K Faust, *Social Network Analysis: Methods and Applications* (Cambridge University Press, Cambridge, 1994)

14. J Sarnecki, *Delinquent Networks: Youth Co-Offending in Stockholm* (Cambridge University Press, Cambridge, 2001)

15. A Abraham, AE Hassanien, V Snášel, *Computational Social Network Analysis: Trends, Tools and Research Advances* (Springer, London, 2010)

16. P Carrington, JC Scott, *The SAGE Handbook of Social Networks* (Sage Publications, London, 2011)

17. JC Scott, *Social Network Analysis* (Sage Publications, New Park, CA, 1991)

18. P Klerks, The Network Paradigm Applied to Criminal Organizations: Theoretical Nitpicking or a Relevant Doctrine for Investigators? Recent Developments in the Netherlands. Connections **24**(3), 53–65 (2001)

19. C Morselli, Assessing Vulnerable and Strategic Positions in a Criminal Network. J Contemp Crim Justice **26**(4), 382–392 (2010)

20. MK Sparrow, The Application of Network Analysis to Criminal Intelligence: An Assessment of the Prospects. Soc Netw **13**(3), 251–274 (1991)

21. KM Carley, J Reminga, S Borgatti, Destabilizing Dynamic Networks Under Conditions of Uncertainty, in *International Conference on Integration of Knowledge Intensive Multi-Agent Systems* (IEEE KIMAS, Boston MA, 2003), pp. 121–126

22. VE Krebs, Mapping Networks of Terrorist Cells. Connections **24**(3), 43–52 (2002)

23. D McAndrew, The Structural Analysis of Criminal Networks, in *The Social Psychology of Crime: Groups, Teams, and Networks*, ed. by D Canter, L Alison (Ashgate, Aldershot, 1999), pp. 52–92

24. JJ Xu, H Chen, CrimeNet Explorer: A Framework for Criminal Network Knowledge Discovery. ACM Trans. Inf. Syst. **23**(2), 201–226 (2005)

25. KM Carley, JS Lee, D Krackhardt, Destabilizing Networks. Connections **24**(3), 31–34 (2001)

26. RS Burt, *Applied Network Analysis: A Methodological Introduction* (Sage Publications, Beverly Hills, 1983)

27. RS Burt, *Brokerage and Closure: An Introduction to Social Capital* (Oxford University Press, Oxford, 2005)

28. N Coles, It's Not What You Know, It's Who You Know That Counts: Analyzing Serious Crime Groups as Social Networks. Br. J. Criminol. **4**(41), 580–594 (2001)

29. RL Cross, A Parker, *The Hidden Power of Social Networks: Understanding How Work Really Gets Done in Organizations* (Harvard Business School Press, Boston, 2004)

30. PV Marsden, Brokerage Behavior in Restricted Exchange Networks. Soc. Struct. Netw. Anal. **7**(4), 341–410 (1982)

31. P Williams, The Nature of Drug-Trafficking Networks. Curr. History **97**(618), 154–159 (1998)

32. JM McGloin, DS Kirk, Social Network Analysis, in *Handbook of Quantitative Criminology*, ed. by AR Piquero, D Weisburd (Springer, New York, 2010), pp. 209–224

33. LC Freeman, Centrality in Social Networks Conceptual Clarification. Soc. Netw. **1**(3), 215–239 (1979)

34. G Sabidussi, The Centrality Index of a Graph. Psychometrika **31**(4), 581–603 (1966)

35. P Bonacich, Power and Centrality: A Family of Measures. Am. J. Sociol. **92**, 11170–1182 (1987)

36. SP Borgatti, Centrality and Network Flow. Social Networks **27**, 55–71 (2005)

37. D Koschutzki, KA Lehmann, L Peeters, S Richter, D Tenfelde-Podehl, O Zlotowski, Centrality Indices, in *Network Analysis*, ed. by U Brandes, T Erlebach (Springer, New York, 2005), pp. 16–61

38. U Brandes, T Erlebach, *Network Analysis: Methodological Foundations* (Springer Verlag, New York, 2005)

39. JM Kleinberg, Authoritative Sources in a Hyperlinked Environment. J. Assoc. Comput. Machinery **46**(5), 604–632 (1999)

40. LC Freeman, A Set of Measures of Centrality Based on Betweenness. Sociometry **4**(1), 35–41 (1977) [http://www.jstor.org/stable/3033543]

41. MU Khan, SA Khan, Social Networks Identification and Analysis Using Call Detail Records, in *Proceedings of the 2nd International Conference on Interaction Sciences: Information Technology, Culture and Human* (Association for Computing Machinery, New York, 2009), pp. 192–196

42. C Kiss, A Scholz, M Bichler, Evaluating Centrality Measures in Large Call Graphs, in *Proceedings of the 8th IEEE International Conference on E-Commerce Technology* (IEEE, San Francisco CA, 2006), pp. 47–55

43. FJ Desroches, *The Crime that Pays: Drug Trafficking and Organized Crime in Canada* (Canadian Scholars' Press, Toronto, ON, 2005)

44. M Natarajan, Understanding the Structure of a Large Heroin Distribution Network: A Quantitative Analysis of Qualitative Data. J. Quant. Criminol. **22**(2), 171–192 (2006)

45. G Pearson, D Hobbs, *Middle Market Drug Distribution (Home Office Research Study No. 227)* (Home Office, London, 2001)

46. D Zaitch, *Trafficking Cocaine: Colombian Drug Entrepreneurs in the Netherlands* (Springer, The Hague, 2002)

47. E Kleemans, HG Van de Bunt, The Social Organisation of Human Trafficking, in *Global Organized Crime: Trends and Developments*, ed. by D Siegel, HG van de Bunt, D Zaitch (Kluwer Academic Publishers, Dordrecht, 2003), pp. 97–104

48. S Zhang, *Chinese Human Smuggling Organizations: Families, Social Networks, and Cultural Imperatives* (Stanford University Press, Stanford, CA, 2008)

49. S Zhang, KL Chin, Enter the Dragon: Inside Chinese Human Smuggling Operations. Criminology **40**(4), 737–767 (2002)

50. G Bruinsma, W Bernasco, Criminal Groups and Transnational Illegal Markets. Crime, Law Soc. Change **41**, 79–94 (2004)

51. JO Finckenauer, EJ Waring, *Russian Mafia in America: Immigration, Culture, and Crime* (Northeastern University Press, Boston, 1998)

52. MH Haller, Illegal Enterprise: A Theoretical and Historical Interpretation. Criminology **28**, 207–236 (1990)

53. C Morselli, *Contacts, Opportunities, and Criminal Enterprise* (University of Toronto Press, Toronto, ON, 2005)

54. P Bonacich, Factoring and Weighting Approaches to Status Scores and Clique Identification. J. Math. Sociol. **2**, 113–120 (1972)

55. JM Kleinberg, Hubs, Authorities, and Communities. ACM Comput. Surveys (CSUR) **31**(4), 1–5 (1999)

56. C Morselli, C Giguère, Legitimate Strengths in Criminal Networks. Crime, Law and Social Change **45**(3), 185–200 (2006)

57. C Morselli, K Petit, Law-Enforcement Disruption of a Drug Importation Network. Global Crime **8**(2), 109–130 (2007)

58. PG Ciarlet, *Introduction to Numerical Linear Algebra and Optimisation* (Cambridge University Press, Cambridge, 1989)

59. GH Golub, CF Van Loan, *Matrix Computations* (Johns Hopkins University Press, Baltimore, 1996)

60. C Zorn, A Solution to Separation in Binary Response Models. Polit. Anal. **13**(2), 157–170 (2005)

61. D Steffensmeier, J Ulmer, J Kramer, The Interaction of Race, Gender, and Age in Criminal Sentencing: The Punishment Cost of Being Young, Black, and Male. Criminology **36**(4), 763–798 (1998)

62. F Crespo, R Weber, A Methodology for Dynamic Data Mining Based on Fuzzy Clustering. Fuzzy Set Syst. **150**(2), 267–284 (2005)

63. C Kadushin, Who Benefits from Network Analysis: Ethics of Social Network Research. Social Networks **27**(2), 139–153 (2005)

64. Q Yin, Q Chen, *A Social Network Analysis Platform for Organizational Risk Analysis – ORA*. In *Second International Conference on Intelligent System Design and Engineering Application* (IEEE, Sanya, 2012), pp. 760–763

65. U Brandes, D Wagner, Visone: Analysis and Visualization of Social Networks, in *Graph Drawing Software*, ed. by M Jünger, P Mutzel (Springer Verlag, New York, 2004), pp. 321–340

66. U Brandes, P Kenis, J Raab, Explanation Through Network Visualization. Methodology: European J. Res. Methods Behav. Soc. Sci. **2**, 16–23 (2006)

67. W Huang, SH Hong, P Eades, Effects of Sociogram Drawing Conventions and Edge Crossings in Social Network Visualization. J. Graph Algorithms Appl. **11**(2), 397–429 (2007)

68. M Huisman, MA Van Duijn, Software for Social Network Analysis, in *Models and Methods in Social Network Analysis*, ed. by P Carrington, J Scott, S Wasserman (Cambridge University Press, New York, 2005), pp. 270–316

69. D Wagner, Analysis and Visualization of Social Networks, in *Proceedings of the 2nd International Conference on Experimental and Efficient Algorithms (WEA'03)* (Springer Verlag, New York, 2003), pp. 261–266

5

An "Estimate & Score Algorithm" for simultaneous parameter estimation and reconstruction of incomplete data on social networks

Rachel A Hegemann*, Erik A Lewis and Andrea L Bertozzi

Abstract

Dynamic activity involving social networks often has distinctive temporal patterns that can be exploited in situations involving incomplete information. Gang rivalry networks, in particular, display a high degree of temporal clustering of activity associated with retaliatory behavior. A recent study of a Los Angeles gang network shows that known gang activity between rivals can be modeled as a self-exciting point process on an edge of the rivalry network. In real-life situations, data is incomplete and law-enforcement agencies may not know which gang is involved. However, even when gang activity is highly stochastic, localized excitations in parts of the known dataset can help identify gangs responsible for unsolved crimes. Previous work successfully incorporated the observed clustering in time of the data to identify gangs responsible for unsolved crimes. However, the authors assumed that the parameters of the model are known, when in reality they have to be estimated from the data itself. We propose an iterative method that simultaneously estimates the parameters in the underlying point process and assigns weights to the unknown events with a directly calculable score function. The results of the estimation, weights, error propagation, convergence and runtime are presented.

Keywords: Inferring incomplete data, Social networks, Gang rivalries, Hawkes process, Self-exciting point processes

Introduction

In this work we focus our attention on data sets of events involving rival gangs on a social network. Each event in the data set corresponds to a crime that occurs at a specified time and involves a pair of rival gangs. A subset of these events are unsolved crimes in which one or both of the rival gangs is not known. The method developed in this paper could be broadly applied to any social network involving activities in time between pairs of nodes on the network. However the interest in the problem came about by examining data from the Hollenbeck Division of the Los Angeles Police Department, home to 29 street gangs with a well-known rivalry network [1-3].

Unlike other methods used to address incomplete data relating to social networks [4,5], the question at hand is

not if a rivalry exists, but rather to which rivalry a violent event belongs. This structure of between gang rivalries can be viewed as a social network [6] often embedded in space [1,2]. Violent events involving gangs tend to be dyadic, and so we can formulate these events as a realization of a stochastic process occurring on the edges of the rivalry network. For each edge in the network there exists a different stochastic process. In our analysis however, we use identical parameters to generate synthetic data. The method does not assume that the underlying parameters generating each process are identical.

The first step to inferring the affiliation of the violent events is to understand the underlying stochastic process. This requires us to capture the behavior of criminal activity through computational means, much like in [7-9]. Recently methods have been proposed in the literature to mathematically model gang violence. The authors in [10] employ an agent-based model to investigate the geographic influences in the formation of the gang rivalry

*Correspondence: Rachel.A.Hegemann@gmail.com
Department of Mathematics, University of California Los Angeles, 520 Portola Plaza, Los Angeles CA, USA

structure observed in Hollenbeck. These authors consider the long-term structure of the rivalry network embedded in space. In terms of the rivalry violence, a shorter timescale must be considered.

Violence among gangs exhibits retaliatory behavior [11]. In other words, given an event has happened between two gangs, the likelihood that another event will happen shortly after is increased. A problem such as this is modeled naturally by a self-exciting point process. It is interesting to note that these models were first used to analyze earthquakes [12-15]. Since then, they have been used to model financial contagion in credit markets [16,17], viral videos on the web [18], terrorist activity in Indonesia [19], and the spread of infectious disease [20]. In this analysis we limit the scope of our model to include time only, thus providing a baseline model.

The authors in [21] and [22] have successfully modeled the pairwise gang violence as a Hawkes process [23]. All of the events are associated with exactly one rivalry, or edge of a social network. The violence on each edge, k, is assumed to have the conditional intensity

$$\lambda_k(t|H_{\tau,k}) = \mu_k + \alpha_k \sum_{t>t_j} \omega_k e^{-\omega_k(t-t_j)}. \tag{1}$$

In this Hawkes process, the intensity $\lambda_k(t|H_{\tau,k})$ depends on the history of the process $H_{\tau,k} = \{t_1, t_2, \cdots t_{M_k}\}$, where M_k is the number of events for process, k. In this framework, the window of time, $[0, T]$, observed for each process in the network is the same. However, the number of events in each process, M_k, is stochastic, and therefore varies from process to process. In practice the final time, T, is determined by the end of the data collection period. Further, the edges of the window introduce boundary effects that are adjusted for in the parameter approximation, see Equations 10 and 11.

The background rate of the process is defined by the constant μ_k. In the context of gang rivalries, background events can be thought of as random occurrences between rival gangs that trigger retaliatory events. The expected number of offspring for any event is determined by the constant α_k, and the decay of the intensity back to the background rate is ω_k. Offspring events, in this context, could be interpreted as retaliatory events. Larger values for μ_k and α_k produce more background and offspring events respectively. Larger values of ω_k do not influence the total number of events, but rather the amount of clustering in time.

The authors of [24] produce a mathematical framework to solve the incomplete data problem observed in gang violence data sets. In their work they use an optimization strategy that computes the weights to infer the rivalry affiliation of the incomplete data. In this formulation the authors prove that their optimization has a unique solution under mild constraints. This is substantial contribution in inferring the affiliation of the unknown violent events. However, the authors of [24] assume that the process parameters are known, an assumption that is often not feasible in practice. Further, finding the weights requires solving a computationally expensive optimization problem.

We propose an iterative method that (A) estimates the process parameters assuming the data is generated by the process defined by Equation 1 and (B) infers the process affiliation of simulated data via a direct method of computation. We iterate between (A) and (B) until the estimates for the unknown events converge. We call this the Estimate & Score Algorithm (ESA). The details of the ESA are described in Section "The Estimation & Score Algorithm (ESA)". The ESA is tested on simulated data in Section "Results", with analysis of the estimation of the parameters in the presence of incomplete data (see Subsection "Estimation analysis") and comparison of the proposed score functions with that of the Stomakhin-Short-Bertozzi (SSB) method in [24] (see Subsection "Updating Weights analysis"). In Subsection "Runtime Analysis" there is an analysis of the runtime between the Stomakhin-Short-Bertozzi and the Forward Backward score functions used to update the weights (see Subsection "Runtime Analysis"). Subsection "Convergence Results" contains an analysis of the convergence of the Estimation & Score Algorithm. This method solves the more realistic problem of estimating the process and the weights. Further, the computation for the weight updates is more direct and therefore avoids performing the costly optimization scheme used in [24]. This is a novel piece of work with many exciting extensions. A final discussion of the results and future work is presented in Section "Discussion and Future Work". As in [24] we do not use field data in this paper, rather we generated point process data using similar parameters as observed in the field data for Hollenbeck [22]. By using simulated data to test the algorithms we have actual ground truth evaluate the performance of the method.

Problem Formulation

The data is assumed to lie on a known social network containing K processes, where each of the K processes is a pairwise rivalry between two gangs. From this set of events, there are a total of N events where the time is known, but the processes affiliation is not known. These events are referred to as *unknown events*. Each of the N unknown events are placed into each of the K processes. Since the process affiliation is not known for all of the events in the network, each event is given an associated weight, $S_{i,k}$. Here $S_{i,k}$ is the ith element of the kth process. If the event is known $S_{i,k} = 1$. If $S_{i,k}$ is unknown then it is

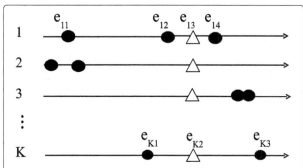

Figure 1 Simplified representation of the rivalry network with known (circle) and unknown (triangle) events. The known events are depicted with circles and the one unknown event is depicted with a triangle. Note that since we do not know the affiliated process of this event, we place it in all processes. Associated with this event is a weights $S_{i,k} \in [0,1]$ such that $\sum_{k=1}^{K} S_{i,k} = 1$.

assigned a number between 0 and 1 by our algorithm. We enforce the constraint that $\sum_{k=1}^{K} S_{i,k} = 1$.

A simplified representation of our problem formulation can be found in Figure 1. The known events are represented by circles and the unknown event is

represented by a triangle. Here we can see that since we do not know the affiliation of the triangle event, it is placed in all of the other processes. We emphasize that this represents our lack of information about which rivalry it belongs to.

As indicated in Figure 1, for each process in the network events $e_{i,k}$ are indexed by increasing time, $t_1 \leq t_2 \leq t_3 \cdots \leq t_{M_k}$. Ordering the events in such a way has the consequence that the first unknown element in time, for example, may have different indexes for different processes. In Figure 1 the triangle index in first process is the third event, $e_{1,3}$. However the triangle in the Kth process is the second event, $e_{K,2}$. One can easily keep track of the local index of a unknown event for each process.

The Estimation & Score Algorithm (ESA)

The proposed Estimation & Score Algorithm can be broken into three basic stages: initialization, parameter estimation, and updating the weights. This method is succinctly described in Figure 2.

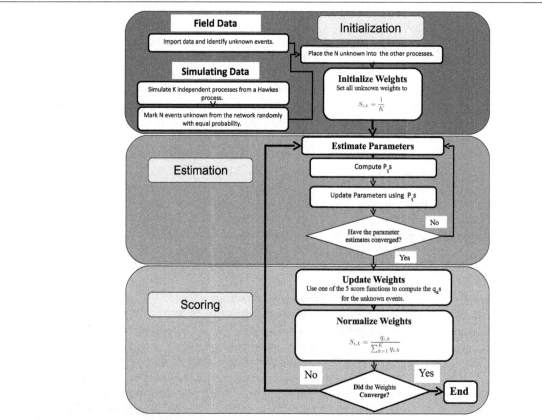

Figure 2 Flow chart of the Estimation & Score Algorithm. There are two ways to implement this method. The first, (left of initialization), is the algorithm used when given an incomplete data set. The second, (right of initialization), is the algorithm used in this paper to simulate the data and test the components of the ESA. The two main phases of the algorithm are the Estimation phase (see Section "Estimation analysis") and the Update Weights phase (see Section "Updating weights").

Initialization

For this paper, there were two ways of initializing the Estimate & Score Algorithm. The first is used to infer rivalry affiliation given field data. After importing the data, the unknown events are identified and placed into each of the of the K processes. The weights, $S_{i,k}$, must also be initialized. If the event is known, then $S_{i,k}=1$. If the event is unknown then $S_{i,k} = \frac{1}{K}$.

An alternate initialization utilizes simulated data in order to test the components of the Estimate & Score Algorithm. In this case, data is generated from K independent Hawkes processes with given μ_k, α_k, and ω_k. From these data, choose N events at random from the network to mark as unknown. Place these N unknown events into each of the other processes. Initialize the weights such that for known events $S_{i,k} = 1$ and for unknown events $S_{i,k} = 1/K$. This initialization process is used in this paper to test the method and produce the results in Section "Results".

Parameter Estimation

In the presence of no unknown events, there are both parametric [12] and nonparametric [25-28] ways to model the underlying stochastic process on each edge of the social network. For this work, we chose a parametric form for the triggering density to validate the model but the results could easily be extended to the nonparametric case. We note that, as is usual with nonparametric estimates, speed would be compromised for the sake of flexibility.

For this paper, the data is assumed to be a realization of Equation 1, where the parameters are estimated using a method similar to the Expectation Maximization (EM) algorithm [29]. An EM-like approach is taken because of the branching structure present in a Hawkes process. In such a process each event can be associated with a background or response event. However, given a realization from this process it is not immediately obvious whether an event is a background or response event. We can view this information as a hidden variable that we must estimate. In this way, every event in each of the K processes is assigned a probability $P_{i,j}^k$. The probability that event i is a background event is denoted $P_{i,i}^k$, and probability that event i caused event j is denoted $P_{i,j}^k$. This assumes that $t_i < t_j$. From this EM estimation, the approximation for each of the variables is altered to include the weights for the unknown events. In fact, in the case where all the events are known, the estimation formulas are the same. This section derives the EM estimates when in the presence of incomplete data.

The classical log-likelihood function $\hat{\ell}_k(H_{\tau,k}|\mu_k,\alpha_k,\omega_k)$ for a general point process with a fixed window $[0,T]$ is

$$\hat{\ell}_k(H_{\tau,k}|\mu_k,\alpha_k,\omega_k) = \sum_{i=1}^{M_k} \lambda_k(t_i|H_{\tau,k}) - \int_0^T \lambda_k(t|H_{\tau,k})dt. \quad (2)$$

Incorporating the branching structure into the log-likelihood function, the event association is added as a random variable, $\chi_{i,j}$ such that

$$\chi_{i,j} = \begin{cases} 1 & \text{if event } i \text{ caused event } j \text{ and } i \neq j \\ 1 & \text{if event } i \text{ is a background event and } i = j \\ 0 & \text{else} \end{cases} . \quad (3)$$

This branching allows us to separate those events associated with the background μ_k and the response $g(t) = \alpha_k \omega_k e^{-\omega_k t}$. This leads to the altered log-likelihood function

$$\ell_k(H_{\tau,k}|\mu_k,\alpha_k,\omega_k) = \sum_{i=1}^{M_k} \chi_{i,i} \log(\mu_k) - \int_0^T \mu_k dt \quad (4)$$

$$+ \sum_{i=1}^{M_k} \left\{ \sum_{j=i+1}^{M_k} \chi_{i,j} \log\left(\alpha_k \omega_k e^{-\omega_k(t_j-t_i)}\right) \right.$$

$$\left. - \int_0^{T-t_i} \alpha_k \omega_k e^{-\omega_k(s)} ds \right\}.$$

Taking the expectation of $\ell_k(H_{\tau,k}|\mu_k,\alpha_k,\omega_k)$ with respect to $\chi_{i,j}$ results in

$$E_\chi[\ell_k(H_{\tau,k}|\mu_k,\alpha_k,\omega_k)] = \sum_{i=1}^{M_k} P_{i,i}^k \log(\mu_k) - \int_0^T \mu_k dt \quad (5)$$

$$+ \sum_{i=1}^{M_k} \left\{ \sum_{j=i+1}^{M_k} P_{i,j}^k \log\left(\alpha_k \omega_k e^{-\omega_k(t_j-t_i)}\right) \right.$$

$$\left. - \int_0^{T-t_i} \alpha_k \omega_k e^{-\omega_k(s)} ds \right\}.$$

In the EM algorithm, the quantity $E_\chi[\ell_k(H_{\tau,k}|\mu_k,\alpha_k,\omega_k)]$ is maximized with respect to each of the variables $\mu_k, \alpha_k, \omega_k$ given the data $H_{\tau,k}$. This leads to the EM estimates

$$\mu_k = \frac{\sum_{i=1}^{M_k} P_{i,i}^k}{T}, \quad \alpha_k = \frac{\sum_{i<j}^{M_k} P_{i,j}^k}{M_k - \sum_{i=1}^{M_k} e^{-\omega_k(T-t_i)}} \quad (6)$$

$$\omega_k = \frac{\sum_{i<j}^{M_k} P_{i,j}^k}{\sum_{i<j}(t_j - t_i)P_{i,j}^k + \alpha_k \sum_{i=1}^{M_k}(T-t_i)e^{-\omega_k(T-t_i)}}. \quad (7)$$

Where $P_{i,j}^k$ is defined by

$$P_{i,j}^k = \frac{\alpha_k \omega_k e^{-\omega_k(t_j-t_i)}}{\lambda_k(t_i|H_{\tau,k})}, \quad P_{i,i}^k = \frac{\mu_k}{\lambda_k(t_i|H_{\tau,k})}, \quad (8)$$

for $t_i < t_j$. The EM algorithm then becomes a matter of iterating between estimating the probabilities and the parameters. It has been proven that this algorithm will converge under mild assumptions [29]. Further, Equation 6 adjusts for boundary effects.

In the presence of events with unknown process affiliation in the network, we assign weights to the contribution of each event to the log-likelihood function. Specifically, each of the unknown events in process k have a weight $S_{i,k}$, such that $\sum_k S_{i,k} = 1$. For the known events $S_{i,k} = 1$. These weights are incorporated for each process via

$$
L_k(H_{\tau,k}|\mu_k,\alpha_k,\omega_k)
$$

$$
= \sum_{i=1}^{M_k} P_{i,i}^k S_{i,k} \log(\mu_k) - \int_0^T \mu_k dt
$$

$$
+ \sum_{i=1}^{M_k-1} \sum_{j=i+1}^{M_k} S_{i,k} S_{j,k} P_{i,j}^k \log\left(\alpha_k \omega_k e^{-\omega_k(t_j-t_i)}\right)
$$

$$
- \sum_{i=1}^{M_k} S_{i,k} \int_0^{T-t_i} \alpha_k \omega_k e^{-\omega_k(s)} ds. \tag{9}
$$

Note that $L_k(H_{\tau,k}|\mu_k,\alpha_k,\omega_k)$ is no longer an EM log likelihood in the presence of unknown data. Maximizing $L_k(H_{\tau,k}|\mu_k,\alpha_k,\omega_k)$ with respect to each of the parameters the estimates become

$$
\mu_k = \frac{\sum_{i=1}^{M_k} P_{i,i}^k S_{i,k}}{T},
$$

$$
\alpha_k = \frac{\sum_{i<j}^{M_k} P_{i,j}^k S_{i,k} S_{j,k}}{\sum_{i=1}^{M_k} S_{i,k} - \sum_{i=1}^{M_k} S_{i,k} e^{-\omega_k(T-t_i)}} \tag{10}
$$

$$
\omega_k = \frac{\sum_{i<j}^{M_k} P_{i,j}^k S_{i,k} S_{j,k}}{\sum_{i<j}(t_j-t_i) P_{i,j}^k S_{i,k} S_{j,k} + \alpha_k \sum_{i=1}^{M_k} S_{i,k}(T-t_i) e^{-\omega_k(T-t_i)}}. \tag{11}
$$

When all of the events are known, i.e. $S_{i,k} = 1$ when unknown event i, k belongs to process k and is zero otherwise, these estimates become identical to the EM parameter estimates.

Updating weights

At the start of the Estimation & Score algorithm all of the weights for the unknown events are $S_{i,k} = 1/K$. Once the parameters are estimated using the altered EM algorithm described in Equation 11, the weights, $S_{i,k}$, are updated, see Figure 2. Here we present four different score functions and the Stomakhin-Short-Bertozzi method [24], used to define, $q_{i,k}$, the intermediate process affiliation. Each of these score functions synthesize information from different portions of the data set. Given an event early in the data set, a score function that uses future events would be ideal. On the other hand, for later events a score function using previous events is desired. Similar considerations should be made if there are portion of the data with more incomplete data. After all of these intermediate weights, $q_{i,k}$, have been calculated, they are re-normalized

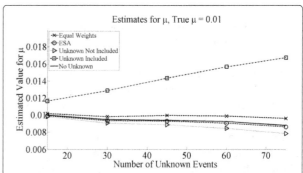

Figure 3 Plot of the parameter estimates for μ_k as the number of unknown events increase. Plots of the estimates for μ_k for the Unknown Not Included (dash-triangle), Unknown Included (dash-square), Equal Weights (dash-x), ESA (dash-circle), and No Unknown (solid). In each of the three figures, the estimates are plotted vs the number of unknown events. Each network has five processes with the true parameters $\mu_k = 0.01$, $\omega_k = 0.1$, and $\alpha_k = 0.5$. Each data point presented is the average of the results from 100 simulated networks.

as a probability via $S_{i,k} = \frac{q_{i,k}}{\sum_k q_{i,k}}$. For simplicity we consider a response function of the form, $g_k(t) = \alpha_k \omega_k e^{-\omega_k(t)}$.

Ratio Score Function

The *Ratio* score function considers the ratio of the background rate μ_k and the sum of all the future events, $\sum_{i<j} g_k(t_j-t_i)$. Mathematically the score is determined by

$$
q_{i,k}^{Ratio} = \frac{\sum_{i<j} g_k(t_j - t_i)}{\mu_k(t_i)}. \tag{12}
$$

Lambda Score Function

The *Lambda* score function uses only previous information by taking the ratio of the intensities evaluated at the unknown event time t_i.

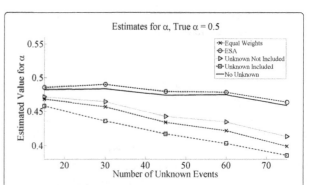

Figure 4 Plot of the parameter estimates for α_k as the number of unknown events increase. Plots of the estimates for α_k for the Unknown Not Included (dash-triangle), Unknown Included (dash-square), Equal Weights (dash-x), ESA (dash-circle), and No Unknown (solid). In each of the three figures, the estimates are plotted vs the number of unknown events. Each network has five processes with the true parameters $\mu_k = 0.01$, $\omega_k = 0.1$, and $\alpha_k = 0.5$. Each data point presented is the average of the results from 100 simulated networks.

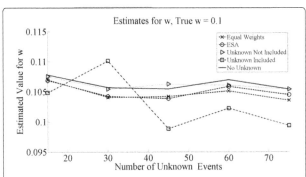

Figure 5 Plot of the parameter estimates for ω_k as the number of unknown events increase. Plots of the estimates for ω_k for the Unknown Not Included (dash-triangle), Unknown Included (dash-square), Equal Weights (dash-x), ESA (dash-circle), and No Unknown (solid). In each of the three figures, the estimates are plotted vs the number of unknown events. Each network has five processes with the true parameters $\mu_k = 0.01$, $\omega_k = 0.1$, and $\alpha_k = 0.5$. Each data point presented is the average of the results from 100 simulated networks.

$$q_{i,k}^{Lambda} = \frac{\lambda_k(t_i|H_{\tau,k})}{\sum_{m=1}^{K} \lambda_m(t_i|H_{\tau,k})} \quad (13)$$

Stomakhin-Short-Bertozzi (SSB) method
The method defined in [24] is summarized by

$$\max\left\{\sum_k \sum_{ij} \delta_{i,j}\mu_k q_{i,k}^{SSB} + \frac{1}{2}(1-\delta_{ij})\alpha_k\omega_k e^{-\omega_k|t_i^k - t_j^k|} q_{i,k}^{SSB} q_{j,k}^{SSB}\right\}, \quad (14)$$

subject to

$$\sum_{k=1}^{K} \left(q_{i,k}^{SSB}\right)^2 = 1. \quad (15)$$

This method is motivated by the Hawkes process defined in Equation 1.

Probability Score Function
The *Probability* score function uses the approximation of the branching structure of the underlying process. The idea behind this method is events that are background events with no corresponding response events should not belong in the process. An event that is a background with many response events or an event that is a response to another event should be part of that process.

$$q_{i,k}^{Prob} = \frac{\sum_{t_j > t_i} P_{i,j}^k}{P_{i,i}^k} \quad (16)$$

$$P_{i,i}^k = \frac{\mu_k(t_i)}{\lambda_k(t_i|H_{\tau,k})} \quad P_{i,j}^k = \frac{g_k(t_j - t_i)}{\lambda_k(t_j|H_{\tau,k})} \quad (17)$$

Forward Backward Score Function
This method is the ratio of the summation of the response for the events in the future and the past, $\sum_{i \neq j} g_k(|t_i - t_j|)$ over the background rate μ_k.

$$q_{i,k}^{FB} = \frac{\sum_{i \neq j} g_k(|t_i - t_j|)}{\mu_k} \quad (18)$$

Results
The Estimation & Score Algorithm is tested for accuracy on simulated data from the Hawkes process defined in Equation 1. An analysis of the parameter estimation method outlined in Subsection "Parameter Estimation" is conducted in Subsection "Estimation analysis". A comparison of the score functions when assuming the true parameters is found in Subsection "Updating Weights analysis". Subsection "Runtime Analysis" provides a comparison of the runtime between the Forward Backward score function and the Stomakhin-Short-Bertozzi method. A example of convergence of the Estimate & Score Algorithm is provided in Subsection "Convergence Results".

Table 1 Average and standard deviations for μ_k on 100 networks, true value is $\mu_k = 0.01$

	# unknown	15	30	45	60	75
Equal	(Ave)	0.0102	0.0098	0.0100	0.0099	0.0096
Weights	(StDev)	±0.0014	±0.0014	±0.0017	±0.0015	±0.0015
ESA	(Ave)	0.0099	0.0093	0.0093	0.0091	0.0086
	(StDev)	±0.0014	±0.0014	±0.0017	±0.0014	±0.0014
Unknown	(Ave)	0.0098	0.0091	0.0089	0.0085	0.0079
Not Included	(StDev)	±0.0014	±0.0014	±0.0017	±0.0015	±0.0015
Unknown	(Ave)	0.0117	0.0129	0.0143	0.0157	0.0167
Included	(StDev)	±0.0014	±0.0017	±0.0019	±0.0016	±0.0019
No Unknown	(Ave)	0.0100	0.0095	0.0094	0.0093	0.0088
	(StDev)	±0.0014	±0.0014	±0.0017	±0.0015	±0.0015

Table 2 Average and standard deviations for α_k on 100 networks, true value is $\alpha_k = 0.5$

	# unknown	15	30	45	60	75
Equal	(Ave)	0.4678	0.4573	0.4340	0.4220	0.3989
Weights	(StDev)	±0.0636	±0.0759	±0.0686	±0.0726	±0.0699
ESA	(Ave)	0.4853	0.4903	0.4795	0.4786	0.4642
	(StDev)	±0.0640	±0.0767	±0.0712	±0.0741	±0.0719
Unknown	(Ave)	0.4712	0.4646	0.4429	0.4348	0.4132
Not Included	(StDev)	±0.0638	±0.0779	±0.0700	±0.0737	±0.0702
Unknown	(Ave)	0.4580	0.4364	0.4172	0.4032	0.3855
Included	(StDev)	±0.0668	±0.0822	±0.0705	±0.0799	±0.0818
No Unknown	(Ave)	0.4820	0.4838	0.4741	0.4750	0.4595
	(StDev)	±0.0647	±0.0759	±0.0726	±0.0748	±0.0689

Estimation analysis

There are many ways we could allow the unknown events to influence our estimates of the underlying parameters for each process. There are two extremes. On the one hand, we could exclude all of the unknown events from the parameter estimation. This would be equivalent to setting the $S_{i,k} = 0$ for all unknown events. On the other hand, we could include all of the unknown events in the estimation of the parameters for each process. This would be equivalent to letting $S_{i,k} = 1$ for all i and k. Another possible estimation method is some combination of these two. We propose this as a way of allowing the unaffiliated events to play some role in the estimation process. The naive choice is allowing each event to play the same role in each process. This amounts to setting $S_{i,k} = 1/K$ for the unknown events. We compare these three choices to the estimations obtained by the Estimate & Score Algorithm (ESA) using the Forward Backward score function. Finally, we want to compare all four of these possible estimation techniques to the best we could possibly do. In this case, that would mean we knew all the affiliations for the events (i.e. there are no unknown events).

Figures 3, 4, 5 displays the results for the μ_k, α_k, and ω_k estimates for the five cases: $S_{i,k} = 0$ for unknown events (dash-triangle), $S_{i,k} = 1$ for unknown events (dash-square), $S_{i,k} = 1/K$ for unknown events (dash-x), the results using ESA (dash-circle), and the estimates you get when you know all the affiliations for the unknown events (solid). These results with standard deviations are displayed in Tables 1, 2, 3. In each of the three figures, the estimates are plotted vs the number of unknown events. Each network has five processes with the true parameters $\mu_k = 0.01$, $\omega_k = 0.1$, and $\alpha_k = 0.5$. Different networks are created with 15, 30, 45, 60, and 75 unknown events. We estimate the parameters using each of the five methods explained above. This procedure is repeated 100 times with different random seed values and then the average estimate is calculated.

Notice in the estimates for μ_k in Figure 3 and Table 1, the ESA performs the best compared to the true value and has only a slight reduction in accuracy as the number of unknown events increases. On average the other three estimates seem to degrade more rapidly as the number of unknown events increases. When $S_{i,k} = 1$, the estimates

Table 3 Average and standard deviations for ω_k on 100 networks, True Estimate is $\omega_k = 0.1$

	# unknown	15	30	45	60	75
Equal	(Ave)	0.1070	0.1041	0.1042	0.1051	0.10364
Weights	(StDev)	±0.0264	±0.0274	±0.0262	±0.0248	±0.0255
ESA	(Ave)	0.1069	0.1042	0.1039	0.1059	0.1045
	(StDev)	±0.0263	±0.0273	±0.0264	±0.0255	±0.0240
Unknown	(Ave)	0.1075	0.1054	0.1063	0.1060	0.1054
Not Included	(StDev)	±0.0264	±0.0286	±0.0269	±0.0246	±0.0269
Unknown	(Ave)	0.1048	0.1101	0.0988	0.1022	0.0993
Included	(StDev)	±0.0275	±0.1035	±0.0273	±0.0301	±0.0285
No Unknown	(Ave)	0.1078	0.1057	0.1055	0.1070	0.1054
	(StDev)	±0.0265	±0.0277	±0.0256	±0.0241	±0.0230

for μ_k are far above the true value and growing as the number of unknown events increases. This follows from the fact that letting $S_{i,k} = 1$ means we are effectively adding events to the network. Take the case when $K = 2$. Assume that each process has 1000 events, and there are 100 unknown events from each process. When we estimate the parameters for the first process, we will use the 900 events we know plus the 200 unknown events from the network. We will get the identical number of events in our estimation for process two. This creates 200 new events and thus biases the estimates for μ_k. This motivated the idea of equal weighting for each unknown event, and that choice is validated by the estimates for μ_k. A similar argument shows why $S_{i,k} = 0$ (i.e. ignoring all the unknown events) has the lowest estimate for μ_k at each level of incomplete data.

In the estimates for the branching ratio α_k, the ESA on average yields the best estimates and maintains its accuracy in the presence of unknown events. It is interesting to note that equal weighting performs worse here than if we let $S_{i,k} = 0$ for all unknown events. Using the ESA overcomes this drawback. Again, setting $S_{i,k} = 1$ for all unknown events performs the worst. This could stem from the fact that most of the unknown events are being labeled background and thus this estimation technique underestimates the branching ratio because fewer events are considered offspring. Notice that the estimate for ESA (dash-circle) tracks the best possible estimate (solid) well while the other three start to trail off as more and more information is labeled as unknown.

Finally, in Figure 5 and Table 1, it is shown that the ESA estimate (dash-circle) for ω_k tracks the behavior of the best estimate (solid) closer than the other methods. Including all of the unknown events (dash-square) provides the poorest estimate for ω_k. For the other three estimation techniques we see that they are all comparable.

Updating Weights analysis

To understand the strengths and weaknesses of each of the five score functions, defined in Subsection "Updating weights", the score functions were evaluated for 100 incomplete events using the true values for μ_k, α_k, and ω_k when taking the Top 1, Top 2, and Top 3 best inferences. For comparison to [24], the true parameters were taken to be $\mu_k = 0.01$, $\omega_k = 0.1$, and $\alpha_k = 0.5$. Due to the stochastic nature of the processes, for each level of process number 100 random networks were tested. The average results of this analysis are found in Figure 6. The number correctly identified by the each of the score functions is on the vertical axis. The horizontal axis displays the number of processes in the network.

From Figure 6 it is clear that the Stomakhin-Short-Bertozzi score function in solid dark blue, and the

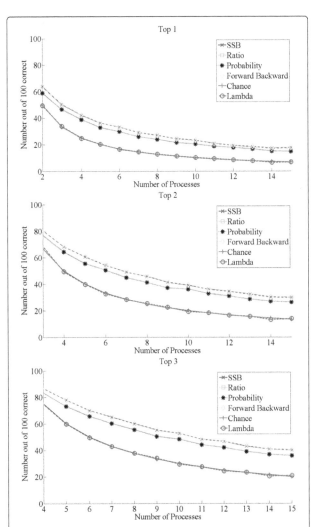

Figure 6 **Display of the number of correctly identified unknown events out of 100.** Display of the number of correctly identified unknown events when the Top 1, Top 2, and Top 3 inferences are taken into consideration. For all score functions, the parameters are $\mu_k = 0.01$, $\omega_k = 0.1$, and $\alpha_k = 0.5$, and assumed to be known. The Stomakhin-Short-Bertozzi score function (solid dark blue x) and the Forward Backward score (cyan dashed diamond), the Probability (black dashed asterisk) and Ratio (solid green square) score functions, and the Lambda (magenta dashed circle) score function and chance (solid dark green plus) produce comparable results with these parameters.

Forward Backward score function (cyan dashed diamond) perform nearly identically when looking at the Top 1, Top 2, and Top 3 inferences. These functions look both forward and backward in time from the incomplete event, and are therefore able to identify clusters of events in time. The Probability (black dashed asterisk) and Ratio (solid green square) score functions don't do nearly as well the Stomakhin-Short-Bertozzi and Forward Backward score functions, but better than the Lambda (magenta dashed circle) score function. The Lambda score function appears to perform close to chance (dark green solid plus) for the Top 1, Top 2, and Top 3 inferred process affiliation. Due to the success of the Forward Backward score function and the Stomakhin-Short-Bertozzi method, only these are used for further analysis.

The analysis comparing the score functions assumed that the true parameters were known. However, when applying this method in practice there will be error in the estimated parameters. This estimation error will propagate through to the score functions. To understand how deviations of the estimated parameters influence the score functions pairwise combinations of the parameters were increased and decreased by 90% from the target values $\mu_k = 0.01$, $\omega_k = 0.1$, and $\alpha_k = 0.5$ in 10% increments. In particular the Forward Backward and SSB score functions are computed for pairwise combinations of μ in the range of $[\,0.001, 0.019\,]$, ω in the range of $[\,0.01, 0.19\,]$, and α in the range of $[\,0.05, 0.95\,]$. Further, in these pairwise combinations, the third parameter is kept at the target value. Notice that a 90% change is larger than the errors observed in the parameter estimates in Subsection "Estimation analysis".

To examine the propagation of errors of the parameters to the score functions one event from a network with 10 processes is chosen to be unknown. The score function $S_{1,true}$ with the target parameters, $\mu_k = 0.01$, $\omega_k = 0.1$, and $\alpha_k = 0.5$ for the true process is calculated. Then, on the same network, the parameters are offset by

$$\widehat{\text{parameter}} = \text{parameter} \pm \%\text{change} \cdot \text{parameter}. \quad (19)$$

The offset score function $\hat{S}_{1,true}$ is calculated from these offset parameters. The difference between $S_{1,true} - \hat{S}_{1,true}$ is taken for each pairwise combination of parameters. Again, due to the stochastic nature of the processes, each analysis was done for 100 runs and the average difference in score functions is recorded. The results of this analysis are displayed in Figure 7 with those of the Forward Backward score function (left), and those for the Stomakhin-Short-Bertozzi score function (right). In general the Stomakhin-Short-Bertozzi score function is more sensitive to the changes than the Forward Backward score functions for the μ_k and α_k parameters. Changes in the

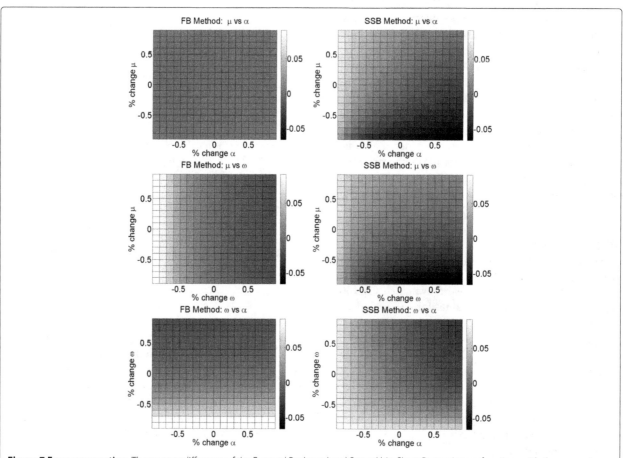

Figure 7 Error propagation. The average difference of the Forward Backward and Stomakhin-Short-Bertozzi score functions with the parameters varied by ±90% of the target values, $\mu_k = 0.01$, $\omega_k = 0.1$, and $\alpha_k = 0.5$.

Forward Backward score functions are minimal for most changes of parameters except for small values of ω_k. As ω_k decreases then the approximated Forward Backward score function decreases, causing a positive difference. As seen in Subsection "Estimation analysis", Figure 5, when estimating ω_k, there is a tendency to over, not under estimate the parameter, and so this does not appear to occur within these parameters. The changes in the Stomakhin-Short-Bertozzi score function depend on all of the pairwise changes of the parameters. As μ_k increases the computed Stomakhin-Short-Bertozzi decreases. On the other hand, as ω_k or α_k increase the score function increases. This analysis shows that though the Stomakhin-Short-Bertozzi method and the Forward Backward score functions preform similarly when the parameters are known exactly, under the influence of estimation error the Stomakhin-Short-Bertozzi score function varies more than the Forward Backward score function.

Runtime Analysis

Though the Forward Backward score function and the SSB method produce comparable results in terms of accuracy, there is a sizable difference in the time it takes to update the weights using these methods.

The Forward Backward score function is designed to be direct, meaning calculates the weights using available information without need for iteration. The Stomakhin-Short-Bertozzi method, however, determines the weight by solving a optimization problem. A closed form solution for the maximized weights is not known to these authors, so the weights are found by numerically approximating the weights that maximize Equation 14. In the implementation of the Stomakhin-Short-Bertozzi we employ a gradient ascent method which requires 4-11 iterations to reach convergence with a tolerance of 0.001. The direct methods, Forward Backward, Probability, Ratio, and Lambda score functions, are on the same order of operations as one iteration of the gradient ascent used to solve Equation 14. Specifically, one iteration of the gradient ascent method and calculating the direct score functions are $O(N \cdot K \cdot M)$ where N is the number of unknown events, K is the number of processes and M is the expected number of events in process k. The expected number of events in process k can be further analyzed via,

$$M = E[M_k] = \mu_k \cdot T \cdot \frac{1}{1 - \alpha_k} + \frac{K - 1}{K} N. \qquad (20)$$

The run time of both the Forward Backward function and the Stomakhin-Short-Bertozzi method are empirically examined in Figure 8. Both score functions were calculated with 20 networks for each level of number unknown events and number of processes with the known parameter values of $\mu_k = 0.01$, $\omega_k = 0.1$, and $\alpha_k = 0.5$. All of the run times are calculated in milliseconds. It can

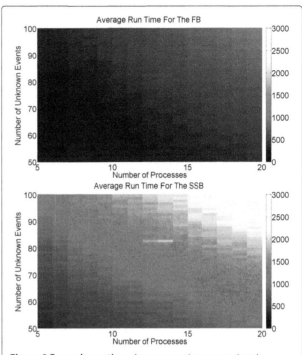

Figure 8 Example run time. Average run time comparison in milliseconds between the Forward Backward function and the Stomakhin-Short-Bertozzi method.

be seen that the average run time needed to compute the Forward Backward function at every level of N and K is substantially less than that of the Stomakhin-Short-Bertozzi method. Also, it is clear from this figure that the time needed to calculate both of these methods increases as N and K increase.

Convergence Results

The Estimation & Score Algorithm converges quickly when either the Forward Backward score function or Stomakhin-Short-Bertozzi method are used. Figure 9 displays the parameter estimates for a typical run of the Estimation & Score Algorithm for both the Forward Backward (left) and Stomakhin-Short-Bertozzi (right). Both score functions produce qualitatively similar results, and it appears that the rate of convergence is comparable for both cases. The estimated weights for one unknown data event for this typical run versus the iteration for each process are plotted in Figure 10. The weights plotted are obtained from the Forward Backward score function (left) and the Stomakhin-Short-Bertozzi method (right). It is interesting to note that both methods of weighting choose the same process affiliation as the most likely. Further tests were conducted with a variable initial weighting. These runs showed similar behavior as initializing the Estimate & Score Algorithm with $S_{i,k} = 1/K$, implying that the Estimate & Score Algorithm is robust to small perturbations of the initial weighting.

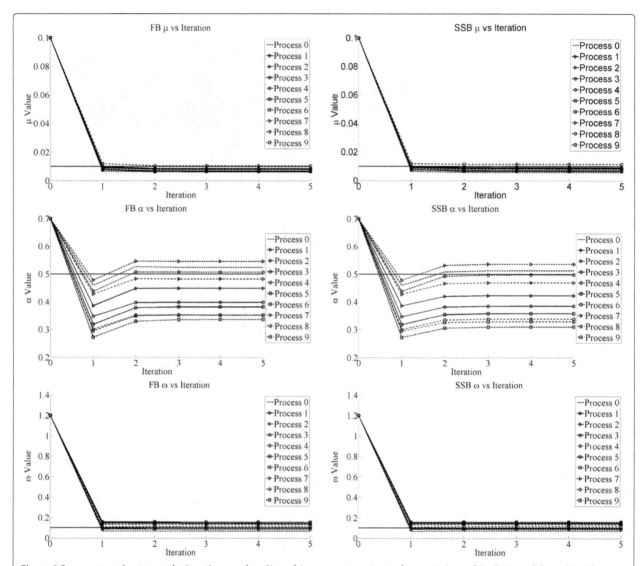

Figure 9 Parameter estimates vs. the iteration number. Plots of the parameter estimates for a typical run of the Estimate & Score Algorithm using the Forward Backward (left) and Stomakhin-Short-Bertozzi (right) methods. Both methods compute nearly identical estimates of the parameters for each of the ten processes. The choice for plotting event 99 was random.

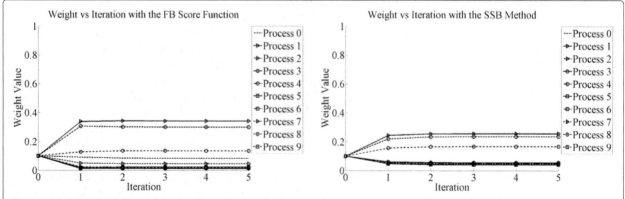

Figure 10 Estimated weights vs. iteration. Plots of the weights for one unknown event computed by a typical run of the Estimate & Score Algorithm using the Forward Backward (left) and Stomakhin-Short-Bertozzi method (right). The choice for plotting event 99 was random.

Discussion and Future Work

In this paper we propose an effective method for simultaneously estimating the parameters and assigning process affiliation in case of incomplete field data from self-exciting point processes on a network. This problem comes from the demand for law enforcement agencies to identify gang affiliation in the case of unsolved crimes in an area of highly complex gang rivalry activity. We present a new framework we name the Estimate & Score Algorithm for possible application to field data. By testing the method on simulated datasets we can understand its performance features and liabilities. The method is an iterative procedure in which process parameters are estimated alternately with the calculation of network affiliation probabilities. We identify several useful 'score functions' for calculating the network affiliations. We also compare the use of unknown events in the parameter estimation. One upshot of our analysis is that the inclusion of unknown events may increase the accuracy of the parameter estimation. Several score functions are considered and the Forward Backward score function shows the most promise with comparable results to that of the Stomakhin-Short-Bertozzi method of [24] in the parameter regime tested. The score function calculation is a direct method that does not rely on solving a variational problem, and thus is more computationally efficient than [24].

For future work, space often plays a role in understanding criminal activity [8,30-33]. Further, criminal behavior has non-random structure and can often be framed in terms of routine activity theory [34,35]. In the case of gang violence, there is a strong spatial component [1,10,36]. One can extend the Estimate & Score Algorithm to include space. There is a precedence in the earthquake literature of adding space to self-exciting point processes [13,15], however, in the case of gang violence, the spatial response may be different. Instead of retaliatory events clustering around prior events, it appears that the data is clustered around regions in space. A spatial model similar to that of [37] could be employed, where the triggering density in space is related to their respective gang set-space, or center of activity [38]. Statistically when modeling spatial point processes one needs to tease out the difference between hot spots due to risk heterogeneity versus event dependence. The data given will be one realization of the underlying process, however using techniques such as prototyping [39], one could potentially reformulate the data into multiple realization of the same process and distinguish between these two phenomena.

There are other factors in the data that can be fused into the model, though more analysis would be required. For example, in earthquake modeling the magnitude of the earthquake is often included. To include such a factor to the intensity $\lambda_k(t|H_{\tau,k})$ one would need to determine a numerical metric to define the impact of each event

type. This is not a straightforward task and would require further investigation. Extending this model in this way could allow for the inclusion of events involving tagging, or other low level gang crimes, which could be a precursor to more extreme violent interactions between gangs. Including this data is outside of the scope of the current model but has a strong potential to enrich the overall data set allowing for better analysis.

It is important to note that there are other methods to approximate the underlying form of the self exciting process. For example the authors in [28] consider the general form of the intensity function $\lambda_k(t|H_{\tau,k})$ to be

$$\lambda(t|H_\tau) = \mu(t) + \alpha \sum_{t>t_j} g(t-t_j). \tag{21}$$

Using a non-parametric method, they are able to approximated the background function $\mu(t)$ and the response function $g(t)$ for a broader class of functions. In this paper, the data was assumed to come from a Hawkes process with constant background rate and an exponential response to previous events. There are cases where the background rate is not constant [40]. Further it is conceivable that the response function could be of a form other than an exponential decay. In this circumstances, the model for $\lambda(t|H_\tau)$ in Equation 1 would not be appropriate.

Finally, this method has a great potential in the field of policing. Once such a model has been calibrated correctly, the Estimation & Score Algorithm using the quicker Forward Backward score function can be used to infer the gang association in real time, while the investigation is on going. Given an accurate model of the underlying process, such a method could identify rivalries that have heightened activity.

Abbreviations
EM: Expectation Maximization; SSB: Stomakhin-Short-Bertozzi; ESA: Estimation & Score Algorithm; Avg: Average; StDev: Standard deviation.

Competing interests
The authors declare that they have no competing interests.

Author's contributions
RH led in the construction of the Estimation & Score algorithm, coding, analysis of the results and writing of the manuscript. EL contributed to the construction of the Estimation & Score algorithm, coding, analysis of the results, and writing of the manuscript. AB contributed to the analysis of the results, editing of the manuscript, and conception and design of the Estimation & Score algorithm. All authors read and approved the final manuscript.

Acknowledgements
This work was supported by NSF grant DMS-0968309, ONR grant N000141010221, ARO grants W911NF1010472 and W911NF1110332, and AFOSR MURI grant FA9550-10-1-0569. Further, we would like to thank Martin Short, Jeff Brantingham, and George Mohler for their helpful comments and conversations.

References

1. SM Radilm, C Flint, GE Tita, Spatializing Social Networks: Using Social Network Analysis to Investigate Geographies of Gang Rivalry, Territoriality, and Violence in Los Angeles. Annals of the Association of American Geographers. **100**(2), 307–326 (2010). http://www.tandfonline.com/doi/abs/10.1080/00045600903550428

2. G Tita, S Radil, Spatializing the social networks of gangs to explore patterns of violence. Journal of Quantitative Criminology. **27**, 1–25 (2011)

3. G Tita, JK Riley, G Ridgeway, AF Abrahamse, P Greenwood, *Reducing Gun Violence: Results from an Intervention in East Los Angeles*. (RAND Press, Santa Monica, CA, 2004)

4. P Hoff, Multiplicative latent factor models for description and prediction of social networks. Computational & Mathematical Organization Theory. **15**, 261–272 (2009). http://dx.doi.org/10.1007/s10588-008-9040-4. [10.1007/s10588-008-9040-4].

5. JH Koskinen, GL Robins, PE Pattison, Analysing exponential random graph (p-star) models with missing data using Bayesian data augmentation. Statistical Methodology. **7**(3), 366–384 (2010). http://www.sciencedirect.com/science/article/pii/S1572312709000628. [ice:title¿SPECIAL ISSUE ON STATISTICAL METHODS FOR THE SOCIAL SCIENCES Honoring the 10th Anniversary of the Center for Statistics and the Social Sciences at the University of Washingtonj/ce:title¿].

6. MB Short, GO Mohler, P Brantingham, GE Tita, Gang rivalry dynamics via coupled point process networks (2011)

7. P Brantingham, U Glässer, P Jackson, M Vajihollahi, in *Mathematical Methods in Counterterrorism*, ed. by N Memon, J David Farley, DL Hicks, and Rosenorn T. Modeling Criminal Activity in Urban Landscapes (Springer Vienna , 2009), pp. 9–31. http://dx.doi.org/10.1007/978-3-211-09442-6_2. [10.1007/978-3-211-09442-6_2]

8. P Brantingham, U Glasser, B Kinney, K Singh, M Vajihollahi, in *Systems, Man and Cybernetics, 2005 IEEE International Conference on Volume 4*, vol. 4. A computational model for simulating spatial aspects of crime in urban environments (IEEE, 2005), pp. 3667–3674

9. P Brantingham, P Brantingham, Computer simulation as a tool for environmental criminologistsm. Security Journal. **17**, 21–30 (2004)

10. RA Hegemann, LM Smith, AB Barbaro, AL Bertozzi, SE Reid, GE Tita, Geographical influences of an emerging network of gang rivalries. Physica A: Statistical Mechanics and its Applications. **390**(21-22), 3894–3914 (2011). http://www.sciencedirect.com/science/article/pii/S037843711100447X

11. S Decker, Collective and normative features of gang violence*. Justice Quarterly. **13**(2), 243–264 (1996). http://www.ingentaconnect.com/content/routledg/rjqy/1996/00000013/00000002/art00005

12. A Veen, FP Schoenberg, Estimation of Space–Time Branching Process Models in Seismology Using an EM Type Algorithm. Journal of the American Statistical Association. **103**(482), 614–624 (2008). http://pubs.amstat.org/doi/abs/10.1198/016214508000000148

13. Y Ogata, Space-Time Point-Process Models for Earthquake Occurrences. Annals of the Institute of Statistical Mathematics. **50**, 379–402 (1998). http://dx.doi.org/10.1023/A:1003403601725. [10.1023/A:1003403601725]

14. Y Ogata, Statistical models for earthquake occurrences and residual analysis for point processes. J. Amer. Statist. Assoc. **83**(401), 9–27 (1988)

15. J Zhuang, Y Ogata, D Vere-Jones, Stochastic declustering of space-time earthquake occurrences. Journal of the American Statistical Association. **97**(458), 369–380 (2002)

16. E Errais, K Giesecke, LR Goldberg, Affine Point Processes and Portfolio Credit Risk. SIAM Journal on Financial Mathematics. **1**, 642–665 (2010). http://link.aip.org/link/?SJF/1/642/1

17. Y Aït-Sahalia, J Cacho-Diaz, R Laeven, *Modeling financial contagion using mutually exciting jump processes, Tech. rep.* (National Bureau of Economic Research, 2010)

18. R Crane, D Sornette, Robust dynamic classes revealed by measuring the response function of a social system. Proceedings of the National Academy of Sciences. **105**(41), 15649–15653 (2008). http://www.pnas.org/content/105/41/15649.abstract

19. M Porter, G White, Self-exciting hurdle models for terrorist activity. The Annals of Applied Statistics. **6**, 106–124 (2011)

20. S Meyer, J Elias, M Höhle, A Space–Time Conditional Intensity Model for Invasive Meningococcal Disease Occurrence. Biometrics. **68**, 607–616 (2011)

21. GO Mohler, MB Short, PJ Brantingham, FP Schoenberg, GE Tita, Self-Exciting Point Process Modeling of Crime. Journal of the American Statistical Association. **106**(493), 100–108 (2011). http://pubs.amstat.org/doi/abs/10.1198/jasa.2011.ap09546

22. M Egesdal, C Fathauer, K Louie, J Neuman, Statistical and Stochastic Modeling of Gang Rivalries in Los Angeles. SIAM Undergraduate Research Online. **3**, 72–94 (2010)

23. AG Hawkes, Spectra of some self-exciting and mutually exciting point processes. Biometrika. **58**, 83–90 (1971). http://biomet.oxfordjournals.org/content/58/1/83.abstract

24. A Stomakhin, MB Short, AL Bertozzi, Reconstruction of missing data in social networks based on temporal patterns of interactions. Inverse Problems. **27**(11), 115013 (2011). http://stacks.iop.org/0266-5611/27/i=11/a=115013

25. D Marsan, O Lengline, Extending earthquakes' reach through cascading. Science. **319**(5866), 1076 (2008)

26. D Marsan, O Lengliné, A new estimation of the decay of aftershock density with distance to the mainshock. Journal of Geophysical Research. **115**(B9), B09302 (2010)

27. D Sornette, S Utkin, Limits of declustering methods for disentangling exogenous from endogenous events in time series with foreshocks, main shocks, and aftershocks. Physical Review E. **79**(6), 61110 (2009)

28. E Lewis, G Mohler, A Nonparametric EM Algorithm for Multiscale Hawkes Processes. Preprint (2011)

29. AP Dempster, NM Laird, DB Rubin, Maximum likelihood from incomplete data via the EM algorithm. J. Roy. Statist. Soc. Ser. B. **39**, 1–38 (1977). [With discussion]

30. PJ Brantingham, PL Brantingham, *Environmental Criminology*. (Sage Publications, Inc, Beverly Hills, CA, 1981)

31. DT Herbert, *Geography of Urban Crime*. (Longman Inc, London, 1982)

32. JE Eck, S Chainey, JGCM Leitner, RE Wilson, Mapping Crime: Understanding Hot Spots, National Institute of Justice, 1–71 (2005). http://www.ojp.usdoj.gov/nij

33. PL Brantingham, PJ Brantingham, Criminality of place. European Journal on Criminal Policy and Research. **3**, 5–26 (1995). http://dx.doi.org/10.1007/BF02242925. [10.1007/BF02242925]

34. PJ Brantingham, PL Brantingham, Environment, routine situation: Toward a pattern theory of crime. Advances in Criminological Theory. **5**, 259–294 (1993)

35. LE Cohen, M Felson, Social Change and Crime Rate Trends: A Routine Activity Approach. American Sociological Review. **44**(4), 588–608 (1979). http://www.jstor.org/stable/2094589

36. R Block, Gang Activity and Overall Levels of Crime: A New Mapping Tool for Defining Areas of Gang Activity Using Police Records. Journal of Quantitative Criminology. **16**, 369–383 (2000). http://dx.doi.org/10.1023/A:1007579007011. [10.1023/A:1007579007011]

37. M O'Leary, Modeling Criminal Distance Decay. Cityscape: A Journal of Policy Development and Research. **13**(3), 161–198 (2011)

38. G Tita, J Cohen, J Engberg, An Ecological Study of the Location of Gang "Set Space". Soc. Probl. **52**(2), 272–299 (2005)

39. K Nichols, F Schoenberg, J Keeley, A Bray, D Diez, The application of prototype point processes for the summary and description of California wildfires. Journal of Time Series Analysis. **32**(4), 420–429 (2011)

40. E Lewis, G Mohler, PJ Brantingham, A Bertozzi, Self-exciting point process of Insurgency in Iraq. Security Journal. **25**, 0955–1662 (2011)

Social and organizational influences on psychological hardiness: How leaders can increase stress resilience

Paul T Bartone

Abstract

Today's security forces must operate in environments of increasing complexity, uncertainty and change, a fact that has led to increased stress levels along with the challenge to adapt. For many people, such stressful conditions can lead to a range of health problems and performance decrements. But others remain healthy, showing resilience under stress. What accounts for such resilience? This paper focuses on psychological hardiness, a set of mental qualities that has been found to distinguish resilient from non-resilient people. Those high in psychological hardiness show greater commitment – the abiding sense that life is meaningful and worth living; control – the belief that one chooses and can influence his/her own future; and challenge – a perspective on change in life as something that is interesting and exciting. This paper begins with a brief discussion of the major stress sources in modern military and security operations, and the broad range of factors that can influence resilience in organizations. Next the concept of psychological hardiness is described, including theoretical background, representative research findings, and biological underpinnings. Finally, some strategies are suggested for how psychological hardiness can be built up in organizations, primarily through leader actions and policies. By focusing more attention on increasing psychological hardiness, security organizations can realize enhanced health and performance in the workforce, while also preventing many stress-related problems.

Keywords: Hardiness, Resilience, Leaders, Social influence, Security operations

Introduction

Modern life is inherently stressful, and is getting moreso as the pace of technological change continues to increase. And while much attention has been devoted to studying those who break down under stress, the majority of people appear to respond with remarkable resilience even to severe or traumatic stress [1]. What accounts for such resilience? If the factors or pathways that lead to human resiliency under stress were better understood, perhaps some of these resiliency factors could be developed or amplified in those who are initially low in resilience, and more vulnerable to stress.

This paper focuses attention on psychological hardiness, one of several potential "pathways to resilience" posited by Bonanno [1]. Following a brief discussion of the key psychological stress factors in modern military

and security operations, I describe the cognitive style of psychological hardiness, considering the theoretical basis as well as representative research findings. With this as background, I consider some of the ways that hardiness response patterns can be increased in persons and organizations. Based on both theoretical and empirical grounds, I argue that leaders in organizations can foster increases in the kinds of cognitions and behaviors that typify the high-hardy person's response to stressful circumstances.

Psychological stress factors in military and security operations

Military and security operations entail stressors of various kinds for the personnel involved. Combat-related stressors and the threat of violent attacks are the most obvious ones, and have received the most attention (e.g., [2]). But security operations carry additional challenges and stressors, beyond the threat of harm to life and limb.

Correspondence: bartonep@ndu.edu
Center for Technology & National Security Policy, National Defense University, Ft. McNair, Washington, DC 20319-5062, USA

In the military for example, units are deploying more often and for longer periods of time, as operational demands increase while force size and budgets shrink. Increased operational requirements also lead to more frequent training exercises, planning sessions, and equipment inspections, all of which adds to the workload stress [3]. Also, more frequent deployments require more family separations, a well-recognized stressor for military personnel [4].

Given this, one avenue for reducing the stress associated with military operations is to lessen the frequency and duration of deployments. Unfortunately, such an approach is not always possible given political and strategic realities and limited resources. The military is not alone in this regard; the same is often true in other occupations and contexts. For example, following the 9/11 terrorist strike on the World Trade Center, fire, police, and other emergency and security personnel maintained continuous operations around the clock, in order to maintain security, locate survivors, and restore essential services to the affected areas. Similar situations are seen when natural disasters strike. For example, thousands of police, National Guard and disaster response workers were involved in rescuing victims, establishing security and restoring basic services in New Orleans following Hurricane Katrina in August of 2005. In such crisis situations, continuous operations and extreme efforts are necessary to save lives, and relaxing the pace of work may be considered unacceptable or even unethical.

When reducing stressful operations or activities is not a policy option, what can be done to minimize or counter the stressors associated with such operations? In order to answer this question in the case of military and security personnel, we should begin with a good understanding of the nature of the stressors encountered in operations. Extensive field research with United States military units deployed to Croatia, Bosnia, Kuwait and Saudi Arabia from 1993 through 1996, including interviews, observations and survey data, identified five primary psychological stress dimensions in modern military operations: (1)Isolation; (2)Ambiguity; (3)Powerlessness; (4)Boredom; and (5)Danger [5,6]. Today, with the greatly increased frequency and pace of deployments for U.S. forces and the long work periods involved [3], an additional significant stress factor should be added to the list: workload or "operations tempo." These dimensions are summarized in Table 1.

1. Isolation: Military personnel typically deploy to remote areas, far away from home, separated from their families, and frequently without good methods for communicating. Troops are in a strange land and culture, away from familiar surroundings. Also, fellow workers are also often strangers, since the

Table 1 Primary stressor dimensions in modern military operations

Stressor	Characteristics
1. Isolation	-Remote location
	-Foreign culture & language
	-Distant from family/friends
	-Unreliable communication tools
	-Newly configured units, don't know your co-workers
2. Ambiguity	-Unclear mission – changing mission
	-Unclear Rules-of-Engagement (ROE)
	-Unclear command/leadership structure
	-Role confusion (what's my job?)
	-Unclear norms, standards of behavior (what's acceptable here & what is not?)
3. Powerlessness	-Movement restrictions
	-Rules of Engagement (ROE) constraints on response options
	-Policies prevent intervening, providing help
	-Forced separation from local culture, people, events, places
	-Unresponsive supply chain – trouble getting needed supplies & repair parts
	-Differing standards of pay, movement, behavior etc. for different units in area
	-Indeterminate deployment length – don't know when we're going home
	-Don't know/can't influence what is happening with family back home
4. Boredom (alienation)	-Long periods of repetitive work activities without variety
	-Lack of work that can be construed as meaningful, important
	-Overall mission/purpose not understood as worthwhile or important
	-Few options for play, entertainment
5. Danger (threat)	-Real risk of serious injury or death, from:
	-enemy fire, bullets, mortars, mines, explosive devices etc.
	-accidents, including "friendly fire"
	-disease, infection, toxins in the environment
	-chemical, biological, or nuclear materials used as weapons
6. Workload	-High frequency, duration, and pace of deployments
	-Long work hours/days during the deployments
	-Long work hours/days in periods before and after deployments

deployed unit is typically a task force specially constituted for a particular mission. This creates a sense of psychological isolation.

2. Ambiguity: In modern military operations, the mission and rules-of-engagement are often unclear, or there may be multiple missions that are in conflict, or the mission changes over time. The role and purpose of the military person may be similarly unclear. Confusion and mystery in the command structure often adds to the uncertainty (who is in charge of what?). Lack of understanding of host nation language and cultural practices, and how these may impact on deployed forces, also increases the uncertainty (which norms and practices are acceptable in the host culture, and which are not?). These ambiguities can also pertain with respect to other military contingents as well as contractors in a multinational coalition force. All of this generates a highly ambiguous social environment.

3. Powerlessness: Security and operational concerns (e.g., "force protection") often lead to movement restrictions, as for example when troops are restricted from leaving their base camp. Troops may also be banned from any interaction with the local populace, and prevented from participating in familiar activities such as running/jogging for exercise, or displaying the flag. There are frequently also multiple constraints on dress and activities. They have few choices in their daily existence. Movement and communication restrictions also impede troops from learning about local culture and language, and resources that might be available locally. All of this adds to a sense of powerlessness, that one has little control over the surrounding environment. Troops may also see military personnel from other services or countries operating with different rules and privileges in the same environment, but have no explanation for these different standards. And soldiers may observe local people in need of help – wounded, ill, hungry, – but be unable to proffer assistance due to movement and contact rules and rules of engagement.[a]

4. Boredom: Modern military missions frequently involve long periods of "staying in place," often without much real work to do. As the weeks and months crawl by, troops start to get bored. To some degree, this boredom can be countered by providing more entertainment and sports activities. But the real problem of boredom is traceable to the lack of meaningful work or constructive activities to engage in. Daily tasks often take on a repetitive dullness, with a sense that nothing very important is being accomplished.

5. Danger: This dimension encompasses the real physical dangers and threats that are often present in the deployed environment, threats that can result in injury or death. Things like bullets, mines, bombs, or other hazards in the deployed setting are included here, as well as the risk of accidents, disease, and exposure to toxic substances. In current U.S. and coalition operations in Iraq and Afghanistan, this includes many hidden dangers such as suicide bombers, snipers, and "improvised explosive devices" or IEDs. This source of stress can be direct, representing threats to oneself, or indirect, representing threats to one's comrades. Exposure to severely injured or dead people, and the psychological stress this can entail, also adds to the sense of danger for troops.

6. Workload: This factor represents the increasing frequency, length, and rapid pace of deployments that many military units are encountering. Also, most deployments are characterized by a "24 hour, 7-days a week" work schedule in which soldiers are always on duty, with no time-off. Work-related sleep deprivation is often a related feature. Training and preparation activities in the period leading up to a deployment also usually entail a heavy workload and extremely long days. The same is generally true for military units returning home from a deployment, who must work overtime to assure that all vehicles and equipment are properly cleaned, maintained and accounted for.

Multiple factors can influence resilience

While the main focus of this paper is on psychological qualities that contribute to resilience, it's also important to put this discussion in a larger context. Many factors at multiple levels can contribute to resilience, exerting some influence over how individuals behave and respond to work-related stress. Taking the military organization as an example, Figure 1 lists some of these factors at the individual, organizational policy, and organizational structure levels.

Individual level factors are relevant first of all in the selection process. These would include for example social background, personality (including psychopathology), previous experience and education, maturity, intelligence, physical fitness, and family circumstances. Training and education programs can also influence individuals in various ways, for example in building knowledge, skills and fitness. Organizational policies also can exert an important influence on resilience, in terms of how the organization and its members respond to challenging or stressful events. Here it is useful to distinguish between "macro-level" policies, such as agency rules, regulations and directives, mission statements,

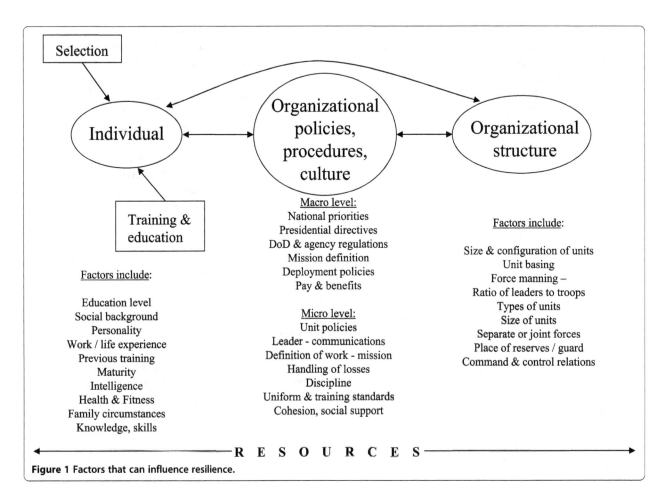

Figure 1 Factors that can influence resilience.

deployment and rotation policies, Rules-of-Engagement and the like, and "micro-level" policies, such as small unit policies, leader directives and communications, training schedules and policies, and so forth. At the same time it's important to recognize that some (but not all) micro-level policies and procedures are influenced rather directly by larger, macro-level policies and standards.

Organizational structural factors also have an influence on how the military organization responds to challenges. The size, type, and configuration of units may be more or less appropriate for the demands of the environment at a particular time. Other structural considerations include where units are based and how they are staffed or manned, the ratio of leaders to troops, and the integration of National Guard and Reserve forces, as well as joint and coalition forces. The integration issue here applies both in the context of specific missions, as well as regarding extended alliances (e.g., NATO coalition forces in Afghanistan). The arrows in Figure 1 serve as a reminder that these different major factors interact and influence each other as well. For example, organizational policies clearly influence (and in some cases determine) structures, while existing structures,

force levels and types have an influence on policies that are developed and implemented regarding their utilization. Structures and policies have an influence on individuals in a myriad of ways, as for example when force structures and rotation policies determine when and for how long an individual will be deployed. The line labeled "Resources" at the bottom of Figure 1 is meant to indicate that all of these factors—individual, organizational policies, and organizational structures—are influence importantly by resource considerations. Budgets are limited, and what is done in any area always depends on available time and money.

What tools, strategies, or coping mechanisms can be applied in order to increase resilience or resistance to these stressors, both at the individual and organizational levels? We focus below on the psychological style known as mental hardiness, and discuss how leaders can leverage this construct to increase individual and group resiliency under stress.

Psychological hardiness

The "hardiness" theoretical model first presented by Kobasa [7] provides insight for understanding highly resilient stress response patterns in individuals and groups.

Conceptually, hardiness was originally seen as a personality trait or style that distinguishes people who remain healthy under stress from those who develop symptoms and health problems [7,8]. Hardy persons have a strong sense of life and work commitment, a greater feeling of control, and are more open to change and challenges in life. They tend to interpret stressful and painful experiences as a normal aspect of existence, part of life that is overall interesting and worthwhile [9].

Rather than a personality trait, psychological hardiness is better considered a "worldview" in Adler's [10] sense, a more general framework that people apply to interpret their entire life experience. It is a generalized style of functioning that includes cognitive, emotional and behavioral features, and characterizes people who stay healthy under stress in contrast to those who develop stress-related problems. The hardy style person is also courageous in the face of new experiences as well as disappointments, and tends to be highly competent. The high-hardy person, while not impervious to the ill-effects of stress, is strongly resilient in responding to highly stressful conditions.

The concept of hardiness is theoretically grounded in the work of existential philosophers and psychologists such as Heidegger [11], Frankl [12], and Binswanger [13]. It involves the creation of meaning in life, even life that is sometimes painful or absurd, and having the courage to live life fully despite its inherent pain and futility. It is a broad, generalized perspective that affects how one views the self, others, work, and even the physical world (in existential terms, *Umwelt*, the "around" or physical world; *Mitwelt*, the "with" or social world, and *Eigenwelt*, the world of the self or me). As early as 1967, using somewhat different terms, Maddi outlined the hardy personality type and contrasted it with the non-hardy "existential neurotic" [14]. He used the term "ideal identity" to describe the person who lives a vigorous and proactive life, with an abiding sense of meaning and purpose, and a belief in his own ability to influence things.

Since Kobasa's original report on hardiness and health in executives [7], an extensive body of research has accumulated showing that hardiness protects against the ill effects of stress on health and performance. Studies with diverse occupational groups have found that hardiness operates as a significant moderator or buffer of stress (e.g. [15-18]). Hardiness has also been identified as a moderator of combat exposure stress in Gulf War soldiers [19-21]. Psychological hardiness has emerged as a stress buffer in other military and security groups as well, including U.S. Army casualty assistance workers [22], peacekeeping soldiers [23,24], Israeli soldiers in combat training [25], Israeli officer candidates [26], and Norwegian Navy cadets [27]. Studies have found that troops who develop PTSD symptoms following exposure to combat stressors are significantly lower in hardiness, compared to those who don't get PTSD [20]. Using data from Bartone's [20] study of U.S. soldiers in the Gulf War, Figure 2 shows the typical, and rather robust interaction effect of hardiness and stress. Under low-stress conditions, those high in hardiness are fairly similar to those low in hardiness in terms of health, in this case PTSD symptoms. However, under high-stress conditions, the resiliency effects of hardiness are most apparent. Here, those high in hardiness report significantly fewer PTSD symptoms than those low in hardiness (PTSD symptoms measured by the Impact of Events Scale; [28]).

Hardiness as a protective factor against stress-related disease: The psychobiology of hardiness

Psychosocial stress is a significant risk factor in the development of many health problems, including coronary disease [29-31]. Cardiovascular disease is the leading cause of death in the world, accounting for an estimated 17.5 million deaths in 2005 or about 30% of the total [32]. Most of these deaths are from heart attacks and strokes. Many factors increase the risk of cardiovascular disease, including obesity, diet, physical inactivity, health habits, and cholesterol levels (LDL) in the blood, as well as stress (Expert Panel on Detection, Evaluation, and Treatment of High Blood Cholesterol in Adults; [33]). Furthermore, stress is associated with a number of "precursor" physiological and endocrinological changes including increased glucose and lowered insulin levels, high blood pressure, and elevated serum lipids, changes that can lead to serious disease states [34-37].

While these risk factors are well-recognized, the effect sizes are often small, suggesting that their influence is not uniform across individuals. Part of this variation may be explained by individual differences in traits and dispositions that can increase vulnerability (or resistance) to traditional risk factors. Probably the most well-studied of these is the "Type A" behavior style, which is

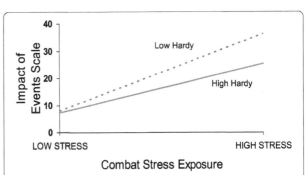

Figure 2 Stress X Hardiness interaction effect in Gulf War soldiers (N = 824), with Combat Stress Exposure predicting PTSD symptoms for low and high hardy groups.

marked by impatience, competitiveness, time urgency, and hostility [38]. Many studies have linked Type A style to increased risk for Coronary Heart Disease (CHD) (e.g., [39,40]). However, this effect likewise is not universal, and many people who are high in the Type A pattern show no such ill effects. This suggests that other, currently unrecognized variables may be at work to influence how stressors and other risk factors impact on a person's cardiovascular status.

A relevant study by Howard, Cunningham & Rechnitzer [41] examined both hardiness and Type A behavior pattern as potential moderators of the impact of occupational stress on several cardiovascular indicators. They found significant interaction effects between hardiness and Type A behavior, with low-hardy/high Type A persons also highest in systolic and diastolic blood pressure, triglycerides, and total cholesterol. This pattern of results suggests that persons high in hardiness are less reactive on a physiological/endocrinological level to stress, as compared to their low hardiness counterparts, who display more extreme reactions. A subsequent study by Contrada [15] also looked at hardiness and Type A style as potential moderators of cardiovascular responses to stress. Using an experimental approach to increase stress, Contrada found that systolic and diastolic blood pressures were elevated in the Type A group, and that hardiness was associated with lower diastolic blood pressure (DBP) reactivity. The lowest DBP reactivity of all was seen in the high-hardy, low Type A (Type B) subjects. Contrada took the additional step of examining the hardiness facets of Commitment, Control and Challenge, determining that the Challenge facet accounted for the lower DBP reactivity in the high hardy subjects. These two studies together suggest that hardiness is an important variable for understanding differential physiological reactivity to stress.

Additional studies have found that hardiness is related to a number of HPA hypothalamus-pituitary-adrenal axis stress response hormones [42], as well as to immune system functioning [43]. In the Zorrilla et al. [42] study, high self-esteem, hardiness and affective stability were found to be correlated with higher basal pituitary-adrenal hormone levels, notably plasma cortisol and b-endorphin. The authors suggested that high hardy persons may be less stress-reactive, and that although basal levels of HPA hormones may be somewhat elevated, hardiness is associated with less volatility in reaction to stressors. Some indirect support for this notion is taken from well established differences in stress responsiveness that track circadian patterns of glucocorticoid levels; stress responsiveness is lowest at the circadian peak of glucocorticoid levels, and highest at the circadian nadir. Similarly, high hardy persons, with consistently higher levels of basal cortisol (a potent glucocorticoid) are also less reactive to stressful conditions.

In their study of hardiness and immune functioning, Dolbier et al. [43] identified very high and low hardy persons based on DRS scores, collected blood samples, and then performed functional immune assays *in vitro*. They found that samples from the high hardy group showed significantly stronger functional immune response, in terms of T and B lymphocyte proliferation in response to several pathogens including Candida albicans ($p < .008$) (antigen), Mycobacterium tuberculosis – PPD ($p < .001$) (antigen), Concanavalin A (Con A) ($p < .002$) (a T-lymphocyte mitogen), and Staphylococcus enterotoxin (Staph A) ($p < .005$) (T-lymphocyte mitogen).

Another recent study found that hardiness was related to high-density lipoprotein, the type of cholesterol that appears to be protective against coronary heart disease and atherosclerosis [44]. While these findings do not demonstrate causal directionality, it may be that the mental processes employed by people high in hardiness are influencing distal bodily functions including cholesterol metabolism. This could happen through central neural pathways involving the balance between executive, rational functioning localized in the pre-frontal cortex region, and emotional responding involving limbic system structures such as the amygdala. "Executive functioning" includes threat appraisal, consideration of response options, and the decision to respond in certain ways based upon context, past experience, and long-term goals and expectations [45,46]. These executive - prefrontal cortex brain areas have abundant bidirectional communication pathways to a variety of limbic structures including the amygdala and hypothalamus. When confronted by novel situations and challenges, appraisals made by high hardy persons tend to be positive, with an expectation of successful coping and good outcomes. These positive appraisals would tend to maintain the inhibitory control exercised by prefrontal cortical executive function over more primitive subcortical structures and related automatic response patterns, such as the amygdala-regulated fear response. In contrast, more pessimistic (non-hardy) threat appraisals would lead to more rapid relinquishing of executive control, and reversion to more basic fear-based responses, and the extended activation states associated with sympathetic nervous system dominance. This lack of autonomic balance is known to be linked to multiple disease states, including cardiovascular disease [47]. And while specific processes remain poorly understood, recent neuroscience research has confirmed that cholesterol levels are controlled in part by central brain and neurochemical processes [48].

Measuring psychological hardiness

Early approaches to measuring hardiness were problematic in a number of ways. Hardiness was originally assessed by Kobasa [7] with an amalgam of 18 different scales and over 100 items to assess the dimensions of Commitment, Control and Challenge. For example, this measure and several others derived from it contained only negatively worded items, and so was really measuring non-hardiness. This increased the potential for measurement confounding with negative factors like neuroticism and depression [49]. In addition, many studies failed to find the three core hardiness factors of commitment, control and challenge. These measurement problems led to the creation of a new, improved hardiness scale developed by Bartone for use in a study of stress and health in Chicago bus drivers [50]. This hardiness scale was further refined into a 45-item measure (the Dispositional Resilience Scale-DRS) reported in 1989 [22]. Additional psychometric work led to shorter 30-item and 15-item versions [51]. The DRS has been used extensively in U.S. military and non-military samples, with excellent results (eg., [22,24]). In his review of hardiness theory and research, Funk [52] recommended the DRS as the best available hardiness measure. Also using the DRS, Sinclair & Tetrick [53] confirmed a factor structure of three facets, commitment control and challenge, nested under a more general hardiness construct. The short DRS-15 scale was translated into Norwegian in 1998, and has since been used in multiple studies in Norway [27,54]. The DRS-15 scale has been further improved in cross-cultural studies with Norwegian and American samples [55,56].[b]

Psychological hardiness as a framework for understanding positive leader influence

How does hardiness increase resiliency to stress? While the underlying mechanisms are still not fully understood, a critical aspect of the hardiness resiliency mechanism likely involves the interpretation, or the meaning that people attach to events around them and their own place in the experiential world. As discussed earlier, this involves the executive mental functions of memory, recognition, appraisal and judgment. High hardy people typically interpret experience as (1)overall interesting and worthwhile, (2)something they can exert control over, and (3)challenging, presenting opportunities to learn and grow. In organized work groups such as the military and many security organizations, this "meaning-making" process is something that can be influenced by leader actions and policies. Military units by their nature are group-oriented and highly interdependent. Common tasks and missions are group ones, and the hierarchical authority structure frequently puts leaders in a position to exercise substantial control and influence over subordinates. By the policies and priorities they establish, the directives they give, the advice and counsel they offer, the stories they tell, and perhaps most importantly the examples they set, leaders may alter the manner in which their subordinates interpret and make sense of experiences. Some empirical support for this notion comes from a study by Britt, Adler and Bartone [24], who found (using structural equation modeling) that hardiness increases the perception of meaningful work, which in turn increases the perception of positive benefits associated with a stressful military deployment to Bosnia.

Many writers have commented on how social processes can influence the creation of meaning by individuals. For example, Janis [57] used the term "groupthink" to describe how people in groups can come to premature closure on issues, with multiple individuals conforming to whatever is the dominant viewpoint in the group. Berger and Luckmann [58] argue that "reality" or perceptions of individuals reflect "social constructions," an incorporation into the individual mind of social definitions of the world. Karl Weick [59] discusses the process by which organizational policies and programs can influence how individuals within the organization "make sense of" or interpret their experiences, particularly at work. Even Gordon Allport [60], distinguished American personality psychologist, viewed individual meaning as often largely the result of social influence processes. Peers, leaders, and entire work units or organizational cultures can influence how experiences get interpreted. In particular, leaders who are high in hardiness themselves can exert substantial influence on those around them to process stressful experiences in ways characteristic of high hardy persons.

Thus, the operative power of psychological hardiness to lessen the ill-effects of stressful experiences is related to the particular interpretations of such experiences that are typically made by the hardy person. If a stressful or painful experience can be cognitively framed and made-sense-of within a broader perspective which holds that all of existence is essentially interesting, worthwhile, a matter of personal choice, and providing chances to learn and grow, then the stressful experience can have beneficial psychological effects instead of harmful ones. In a small group context, leaders are in a unique position to shape how stressful experiences are understood by members of the group. The leader who, through example and discussion, communicates a positive construction or re-construction of shared stressful experiences, may exert an influence on the entire group in the direction of his/her interpretation of experience.

Leaders who are high in hardiness likely have a greater impact in their groups under high-stress conditions, when by their example, as well as by the explanations they give to the group, they encourage others to interpret stressful events as interesting challenges which can be met, and in any case provide opportunities to learn. This process itself, as well as the positive result (a shared understanding of the stressful event as something worth-while and beneficial) could be expected to also generate an increased sense of shared values, mutual respect, and cohesion. Further support for this interpretation comes from a study showing that hardiness and leadership interact to affect small group cohesion levels following a rigorous military training exercise [27]. This interaction effect signifies that the positive influence of leaders on the growth of unit cohesion is greater when hardiness levels in the unit are high. This suggests that effective leaders encourage positive interpretations of stressful events and increase group solidarity, especially in a context of higher psychological hardiness levels.

Although more research is needed on this issue, there is now sufficient evidence to support the view that leaders can increase high-hardiness response patterns within their organizations, and to provide a preliminary sketch of how the high-hardy leader behaves in order to influence hardiness and stress resilience in the organization. The prototypical hardy leader: (1) Leads by example, providing subordinates with a role model of the hardy approach to life, work, and reactions to stressful experiences. Through actions and words, he/she demonstrates the strong sense of commitment, control, and challenge, and a way of responding to stressful circumstances that demonstrates stress can be valuable, and that stressful events always at least provide the opportunity to learn and grow; (2) facilitates "hardy" group sense making of experience, in how tasks, missions are planned, discussed, and executed, and also as to how mistakes, failures, and casualties are spoken about and interpreted. While most of this sense making influence occurs through normal day-to-day interactions and communications, occasionally it can happen in the context of more formal "After-Action Reviews," or debriefings that can focus attention on events as learning opportunities and create shared positive constructions of events and responses around events;[c] (3) seeks out (creates if necessary) meaningful/challenging group tasks, and then capitalizes on group accomplishments by providing recognition, awards, and opportunities to reflect on and magnify positive results (e.g., photographs, news accounts, and other tangible mementos).

In work groups such as the military and security organizations, where individuals are regularly exposed to a range of stressors and hazards, leaders are in a unique position to shape how stressful experiences are made sense of, interpreted and understood by members of the group. The leader who by example, discussion, and established policies communicates a positive construction or reconstruction of shared stressful experiences, exerts a positive influence on the entire group in the direction of his/her interpretation of experience – toward more resilient and hardy sense-making. And

while leadership is of core importance, multiple other factors also may influence how individuals make sense of experiences. For example, policies and regulations throughout the organization can have the effect not only of increasing or decreasing stress levels, but may also directly and indirectly influence hardiness commitment, control and challenge tendencies in employees. A better knowledge of these various factors will permit more effective approaches to building stress resilience not just in security organizations, but anywhere people are exposed to highly stressful circumstances.

Endnotes

[a] Other studies have also identified powerlessness as a damaging influence for soldiers on peacekeeping operations For example, Weisaeth & Sund [61] found that in Norwegian soldiers serving in Lebanon under the UNIFIL United Nations peacekeeping mission, the feeling of being powerless to act or intervene when witnessing some atrocity was a main contributor to post-traumatic stress symptoms.

[b] The DRS-15 is available at www.kbmetrics.com.

[c] An NIMH report on best practices for early psychological interventions following mass violence events [62] noted great confusion regarding the term "debriefing." The authors recommend that the term "debriefing" be reserved for operational after-action reviews, and not be applied to psychological treatment interventions such as Critical Incident Stress Debriefing [63]. For groups such as the military, after-action group debriefings, properly timed and conducted and focused on events rather than emotions and reactions, can have great therapeutic value for many participants by helping them to place potentially traumatizing events in a broader context of positive meaning [64].

Competing interests
The author declares no competing interests.

Authors' contributions
The primary author is respnsible for the research and all aspects of the manuscript.

References
1. GA Bonanno, Loss, trauma and human resilience: Have we underestimated the human capacity to thrive after extremely aversive events? Am Psychol **59**, 20–28 (2004)
2. CW Hoge, CA Castro, SC Messer, D McGurk, DI Cotting, RL Koffman, Combat duty in Iraq and Afghanistan, mental health problems, and barriers to care. N Engl J Med **351**, 13–22 (2004)
3. C Castro, A Adler, OPTEMPO: Effects on soldier and unit readiness. Parameters **29**, 86–95 (1999)
4. DB Bell, J Bartone, PT Bartone, WR Schumm, PA Gade, *USAREUR family support during Operation Joint Endeavor: Summary report (ARI Special Report 34)* (U. S. Army Research Institute for the Behavioral and Social Sciences, Alexandria, VA, 1997), p. ADA339016

5. PT Bartone, *Psychosocial stressors in future military operations* (Paper presented at the Cantigny Conference Series on Future of Armed Conflict, Wheaton, Illinois, 2001)

6. PT Bartone, AB Adler, MA Vaitkus, Dimensions of psychological stress in peacekeeping operations. Military Medicine **163**, 587–593 (1998)

7. SC Kobasa, Stressful life events, personality, and health: An inquiry into hardiness. J Personal Soc Psychol **37**, 1–11 (1979)

8. SR Maddi, SC Kobasa, *The hardy executive* (Dow Jones-Irwin, Homewood, IL, 1984)

9. SC Kobasa, SR Maddi, Existential personality theory, in *Existential Personality Theories*, ed. by R Corsini (Peacock, Itasca, IL, 1977), pp. 243–276

10. A Adler, The Individual Psychology of Alfred Adler, in, ed. by HL Ansbacher, RR Ansbacher (Harper Torchbooks, New York, 1956)

11. M Heidegger, *Being and time* (Harper Collins Publishers, New York, 1986)

12. V Frankl, *The doctor and the soul* (Knopf, New York, 1960)

13. L Binswanger, *Being in the world: Selected papers of Ludwig Binswanger* (Basic Books, New York, 1963)

14. SR Maddi, The existential neurosis. J Abnorm Psychol **72**, 311–325 (1967)

15. RJ Contrada, Type A behavior, personality hardiness, and cardiovascular responses to stress. J Personal Soc Psychol **57**, 895–903 (1989)

16. SC Kobasa, SR Maddi, S Kahn, Hardiness and health: A prospective study. J Personal Soc Psychol **42**, 168–177 (1982)

17. DL Roth, DJ Wiebe, RB Fillingim, KA Shay, Life events, fitness, hardiness, and health: A simultaneous analysis of proposed stress-resistance effects. J Personal Soc Psychol **57**, 136–142 (1989)

18. DJ Wiebe, Hardiness and stress moderation: A test of proposed mechanisms. J Personal Soc Psychol **60**, 89–99 (1991)

19. PT Bartone, Hardiness as a resiliency factor for United States forces in the Gulf War, in *Posttraumatic stress intervention: Challenges, issues, and perspectives*, ed. by JM Violanti, D Paton, C Dunning (C. Thomas, Springfield, Illinois, 2000), pp. 115–133

20. PT Bartone, Hardiness protects against war-related stress in Army reserve forces. Consulting Psychology Journal **51**, 72–82 (1999)

21. PT Bartone, *Psychosocial predictors of soldier adjustment to combat stress* (Paper presented at the Third European Conference on Traumatic Stress, Bergen, Norway, 1993)

22. PT Bartone, RJ Ursano, KW Wright, LH Ingraham, The impact of a military air disaster on the health of assistance workers: A prospective study. J Nerv Ment Dis **177**, 317–328 (1989)

23. PT Bartone, *Stress and hardiness in U.S. peacekeeping soldiers* (Paper presented at the annual convention of the American Psychological Association, Toronto, Ontario, 1996)

24. TW Britt, AB Adler, PT Bartone, Deriving benefits from stressful events: The role of engagement in meaningful work and hardiness. J Occup Heal Psychol **6**, 53–63 (2001)

25. V Florian, M Mikulincer, O Taubman, Does hardiness contribute to mental health during a stressful real life situation? The role of appraisal and coping. J Personal Soc Psychol **68**, 687–695 (1995)

26. M Westman, The relationship between stress and performance: The moderating effect of hardiness. Hum Perform **3**, 141–155 (1990)

27. PT Bartone, BH Johnsen, J Eid, JC Laberg, W Brun, Factors influencing small unit cohesion in Norwegian Navy officer cadets. Mil Psychol **14**, 1–22 (2002)

28. M Horowitz, N Wilner, W Alvarez, Impact of Events Scale: A measure of subjective stress. Psychosomatic Medicine **41**, 209–218 (1979)

29. M Kivimäki, P Leino-Arjas, R Luukkonen, H Riihimäki, J Vahtera, J Kirjonen, Work stress and risk of cardiovascular mortality: Prospective cohort study of industrial employees. British Medical Journal **325**, 857–860 (2002)

30. DS Krantz, DS Sheps, RM Carney, BH Natelson, Effects of Mental Stress in Patients with Coronary Artery Disease: Evidence and Clinical Implications. JAMA **283**, 1800–1802 (2000)

31. TW Smith, JM Ruiz, Psychosocial influences on the development and course of coronary heart disease: Current status and implications for research and practice. J Consult Clin Psychol **70**, 548–568 (2002)

32. World Health Organization, cardiovascular diseases data for 2005. http://www.who.int/cardiovascular_diseases/en/ (accessed 28 August, 2008)

33. WP Castelli, RJ Garrison, PW Wilson, RD Abbott, S Kalousdian, BW Kannel, Incidence of coronary heart disease and lipoprotein cholesterol levels: The Framingham Study. JAMA **256**, 2835–2838 (1986)

34. NS Bhacca, Five hourly measurements of serum cholesterol levels: A new methodology to assess and evaluate stress, good health and disease. Medical Hypotheses **54**, 962–968 (2000)

35. RB Singh, H Mori, Risk factors for coronary heart disease: Synthesis of a new hypothesis through adaptation. Medical Hypotheses **39**, 334–341 (1992)

36. A Steptoe, L Brydon, Associations between acute lipid stress responss and fasting lipid levels 3 years later. Heal Psychol **24**, 601–607 (2005)

37. WR Ware, High cholesterol and coronary heart disease in younger men: The potential role of stress induced exaggerated blood pressure response. Medical Hypotheses **70**, 543–547 (2007)

38. M Friedman, R Rosenman, *Type A Behavior and Your Heart* (Knopf, New York, 1974)

39. T Cooper, T Detre, SM Weiss, JD Bristow, R Carleton, HP Dustan, RS Eliot, M Feinleib, MJ Jesse, FJ Klocke, GE Schwartz, JL Shields, RA Stallones, Coronary-prone behavior and coronary heart disease: a critical review. Circulation **63**, 1199–1215 (1981)

40. BK Houston, CR Snyder, *Type A behavior pattern: Research, theory, and practice* (Wiley, New York, 1988)

41. JH Howard, DA Cunningham, PA Rechnitzer, Personality (hardiness) as a moderator of job stress and coronary risk in Type A individuals: A longitudinal study. J of Behavioral Medicine **9**, 229–244 (1986)

42. EP Zorrilla, RJ DeRubeis, E Redei, High self-esteem, hardiness and affective stability are associated with higher basal pituitary –adrenal hormone levels. Psychoneuroendocrinology **20**, 591–601 (1995)

43. CL Dolbier, RR Cocke, JA Leiferman, MA Steinhardt, SJ Schapiro, PN Nehete, JE Perlman, J Sastry, Differences in immune responses of high vs. low hardy healthy individuals. J of Behavioral Medicine **24**, 219–229 (2001)

44. PT Bartone, A Spinosa, J Robb, *Psychological hardiness is related to baseline high-density lipoprotein (HDL) cholesterol levels* (Presented at the Association for Psychological Science annual convention, San Francisco, CA, 2009)

45. E Koechlin, G Basso, P Pietrini, S Panzer, J Grafman, The role of the anterior prefrontal cortex in human cognition. Nature **399**, 148–151 (1999)

46. Y Suchy, Executive functioning: Overview, assessment, and research issues for non-neuropsychologists. Annals of Behavioral Medicine **37**, 106–116 (2009)

47. JF Thayer, RD Lane, The role of vagal function in the risk for cardiovascular disease and mortality. Biol Psychol **74**, 224–242 (2007)

48. D Perez-Tilve, SM Hofmann, J Basford, R Nogueiras, PT Pfluger, JT Patterson, E Grant, HE Wilson-Perez, NA Granholm, M Arnold et al., Melanocortin signaling in the CNS directly regulates circulating cholesterol. Nat Neurosci **13**, 877–882 (2010)

49. SC Funk, BK Houston, A critique analysis of the hardiness scale's validity and utility. J Personal Soc Psychol **53**, 572–578 (1987)

50. PT Bartone, Predictors of stress-related illness in city bus drivers. Journal of Occupational Medicine **31**, 657–663 (1989)

51. PT Bartone, *A short hardiness scale* (Paper presented at the Annual Convention of the American Psychological Society, New York, 1995)

52. SC Funk, Hardiness: A review of theory and research. Heal Psychol **11**, 335–345 (1992)

53. RR Sinclair, LE Tetrick, Implications of item wording for hardiness structure, relation with neuroticism, and stress buffering. J Res Personal **34**, 1–25 (2000)

54. BH Johnsen, J Eid, PT Bartone, Psykologisk "hardførhet": Kortversjonen av The Short Hardiness Scale. Tidsskrift for Norsk Psykologforening **41**, 476–477 (2004)

55. PT Bartone, BH Johnsen, J Eid, H Molde, SW Hystad, JC Laberg, *DIF- Differential Item Functioning analysis of Norwegian and American hardiness measures* (Presented at the Association for Psychological Science annual convention, Washington, DC, 2007)

56. SW Hystad, J Eid, BH Johnsen, JC Laberg, PT Bartone, Psychometric properties of the revised Norwegian dispositional resilience (hardiness) scale. Scand J Psychol **51**, 237–245 (2010)

57. I Janis, *Groupthink*, 2dth edn. (Houghton Mifflin, Boston, 1982)

58. PL Berger, T Luckmann, *The social construction of reality* (Doubleday, Garden City, NY, 1966)

59. KE Weick, *Sensemaking in organizations* (Sage, Thousand Oaks, CA, 1995)

60. GW Allport, The historical background of social psychology, in *Handbook of Social Psychology*, ed. by G Lindzey, E. Aronson, vol. 1, 3rd edn. (Random House, New York, 1985), pp. 1–46

61. L Weisaeth, A Sund, Psychiatric problems in UNIFIL and the UN-Soldier's stress syndrome. International Review of Army, Air Force and Navy Medical Service **55**, 109–116 (1982)

62. National Institute of Mental health, *Mental health and mass violence: Evidence-based early psychological intervention for victims/survivors of mass violence. A workshop to reach consensus on best practices. NIH Publication No. 02–5138* (U.S. Government Printing Office, Washington, DC, 2002). also at www.nimh.nih.gov/research/massviolence.pdf

63. JT Mitchell, GS Everly, Critical incident stress management and critical incident stress debriefing: Evolutions, effects, and outcomes, in *Psychological debriefing: Theory, practice and evidence*, ed. by B Raphael, JP Wilson (Cambridge University Press, Cambridge, England, 2000), pp. 71–90

64. PT Bartone, Einsatzorientierte Nachbesprechung (Debriefing): Was jeder militärische Führer wissen sollte (Event-oriented debriefing following military operations: What every leader should know), in *Streßbewältigung und Psychotraumatologie im UN- und humanitären Hilfseinsatz (Coping with stress and psychological trauma in UN and peacekeeping operations)*, ed. by T Sporner (Beta Verlag, Bonn, 1997), pp. 126–133

7

A psychological perspective on virtual communities supporting terrorist & extremist ideologies as a tool for recruitment

Lorraine Bowman-Grieve

Abstract

This paper considers the role of virtual communities as a tool for recruitment used by terrorist and extremist movements. Considering involvement as a psychological process and thinking about recruitment from a psychological perspective, the facilitation of online elements important to this process are highlighted in this paper. In addition a short case study taken from the use of the Internet by the Radical Right movement provides examples of how the Internet can be used to promote involvement and encourage recruitment into terrorist and extremist movements.

Keywords: Psychology, Terrorism, Extremism, Virtual communities, Recruitment

Background
Understanding terrorism: a group phenomenon
Terrorism is, first and foremost, a group phenomenon [1], the dynamics of which have traditionally been difficult to assess due to the predominantly clandestine nature of these organisations. However, the Internet and its use by terrorist movements, individual members, and potential supporters and recruits afford new avenues for accessing information about terrorist groups and their activities.

Crenshaw (1990) [2] argues that because terrorist behaviour cannot be labelled as pathological or irrational due to the lack of empirical evidence to support such notions, it must therefore be considered a choice which is made following a process of logical reasoning. As such terrorist activity can be described as rational and comprehensible in light of the circumstances and contexts in which it occurs. Individual psychological processes toward involvement can be described as rational and logical because of the primarily psychological benefits associated with involvement in terrorism for example, a sense of belonging, status, or power; perceptions of excitement or empowerment. Individual reasons why people become involved are many and varied, with no single catalyst event that explains involvement [3],

however research indicates that involvement is a gradual process that occurs over time. This gradual process of becoming involved is mediated by 'group' factors, the social aspects of which provide justifications and support for increasing involvement over time.

Despite the clandestine nature of terrorist movements and their predominant incompatibility with first-hand research our understanding of involvement and recruitment processes has increased in recent years. For example, it has been noted in numerous studies that inter-personal bonds play an important role in this recruitment process. Della Porta (1992) [4] for example, from empirical research with Italian militants, suggests that an important stage in the socialisation process, which leads to involvement in a terrorist or underground movement, is the construction of peer groups during adolescence. Similarly, in a more recent study Post, Sprinzak and Denny (2003) [5], based on semi-structured interviews with incarcerated Middle Eastern terrorists, found that peer influence was cited as a dominant reason for joining a terrorist group. Furthermore recent studies relating to Islamic fundamentalist recruitment indicate that kinship and social bonds also play a key role in this process. Sageman (2004) [6] for example, in an analysis of 400 terrorist biographies, found that sixty-eight percent had pre-existing friendship bonds to others involved in the Jihad or joined the Jihad as a collective decision, while a further twenty percent joined

Correspondence: lbowmangrieve@lincoln.ac.uk
School of Psychology, University of Lincoln, Lincoln, UK

through kinship bonds, meaning that the individual had a close relative in the Jihad.

Passy (2000) [7] states that social networks play an important role in influencing the behaviour of the individual and their readiness to take part in collective action because of their inherent functions, such as socialising, recruitment and decision shaping; success or failure in the recruitment process ultimately is dependent on the relationship formed by the recruiter with the potential recruit. According to Starks and Sims Bainbridge (1980) [8] the recruiter must 'bond' with the potential recruit for the process to be successful. The Internet and virtual communities in particular may aid in facilitating this process. For example, Back (2002) [9] draws attention to the use of websites and virtual communities to recruit new members, by providing contact information and details on how to join and contribute to support activities. Encouraging Internet users to become involved in online support activities serve to draw supporters further into the movement. Members can also use virtual communities to make contact with other supporters within their localities, forming both on and offline communities, networks and bonds through the Internet. Arguably the most potent combination will be involvement online and identification with the terrorist group, in addition to exposure to recruiters and opportunities to engage in support behaviours in the physical world.

Case description
The internet, virtual communities, recruitment & processes of involvement
While the effectiveness of the bomb remains essential to the terrorist movement in terms of the psychological element of terrorism and to draw attention to the movement and their goals, the Internet provides a safe, easy and cheap means of communicating, disseminating propaganda, gathering intelligence, promoting support, demonising the enemy and raising funds. Terrorist use of the Internet and the communicative value the use of this technology brings, are wide ranging and far-reaching. In essence the Internet provides a new solution to the old problem of communication; where once terrorist movements were reliant on 'traditional' forms of media to bring their 'cause' to the public, the Internet now facilitates a broad spectrum of communication possibilities, from websites to virtual communities.

The term 'virtual community' can be used here as an anchor, an already formulated notion of shared online space and communicative interaction between users [10], from which it is possible to examine the content and nature of online communities in support of terrorist movements and extremist ideologies. Virtual communities of this nature have important functions for the individual and the group, providing a 'safe haven' for supporters of

extremist ideologies, a forum of validation and support and the means to become knowledgeable and increasingly involved within the movement over time. Analysis and interpretation of online interactions within virtual communities [11] indicate that community interaction may play a role in the earlier phases of the recruitment process particularly those relating to initial support and involvement.

The discourses created and sustained within virtual communities can be used to disseminate information, to communicate ideologies, to promote and propagandise, to encourage involvement and throughout all of these to potentially facilitate the recruitment of individuals to specific groups. The sustenance of discourses that seek to dehumanise the enemy and justify the ideology of the movement contributes to a community of validation that exists for members and potential members of the movement. It can be argued that virtual community members exist in some kind of a pre- or semi-radicalized state; they are groups of members, potential members, recruiters and recruits.

Discussion & evaluation
Recruitment online: some examples from the radical right
As early as 2001 Ray and March II [12] investigated the use of Internet by white extremists for recruitment purposes. These authors found that white extremist movements were indeed using the services and facilities provided by the Internet to recruit new members and encourage investment and further online involvement in the activities of the organisation. The ease of access to material provided by the Internet has increased the likelihood of both adults and young people searching online to find something to believe in or to reaffirm their already existing beliefs, as such the Internet can be used as a gateway into the particular culture, ideals and beliefs of a movement in question [13]. The following quote from a member of the radical right virtual community of Stormfront illustrates the important role the Internet can play in recruitment and involvement processes - *"It was the Internet that got me interested: checking out sites like the Hammerskins and Combat 18/Screwdriver.net in particular. Then after a few emails etc., I got contacts and then was able to meet up with like minded people in the flesh...it all just grew from there. Never underestimate the power of the Internet when it comes to recruiting new folk to our movement."*

The availability of White Power music and white supremacist computer games online (made available through websites and virtual communities), are used to target youths specifically in an attempt to interest them in the movement with the aim of recruitment. Similarly 'white' dating services can function effectively in the promotion and sustenance of right wing networking [14].

White power music

The significance of White Power music to the recruitment process involving young people is worthy of mention particularly in light of the many websites that exist to promote such music. The White Power music scene remains one of the fundamental links promoting a wide radical right (in particular neo-Nazi/skinhead) network, with music and lyrics used not only to promote violence against minorities but also to reflect the socio-economic issues and grievances of importance to the movement, such as immigration policies, the 'Jewish conspiracy' and belief in the inevitability of a race war [15]. According to Cotter (1999) [15], the lyrics of such music reinforce the White Power rhetoric and acts as an important recruitment tool; representing primarily the youth sub-culture of the movement.

In the following example a user of the radical right virtual community 'Stormfront' refers to the role of White Power music and the Internet in his involvement process - *"I was on the Internet one night looking for a song on some file sharing program. I came across one called "White Power" by a band called Skrewdriver. I hated negroes, spics, gays, etc. and decided to download it. The second Ian Stuart shouted out "White Power 1,2,3,4" i was HOOKED."* In this case the music downloaded from the Internet lead to this individual 'surfing the net' further to find the website of a White Power record label and subsequently the purchasing of David Duke's book 'My Awakening' which is in turn cited by many individuals as playing an important role in becoming involved in support of the radical right.

Computer games

The increasing popularity and sophistication of computer games is being utilised by extremist elements online to draw in potential new recruits, targeting primarily the youth demographic [12]. The increasing sophistication of these games and their potential as a propaganda and recruitment tool should not be ignored. For example according to the Anti-Defamation League (2002) [16] Resistance Records (owned by The National Alliance and considered the main distributors of White Power rock), have widened their product base to include racist and anti-Semitic games such as 'Ethnic Cleansing'. This particular game is based on other more mainstream games such as Doom and Quake. It is a city-based game and the player can choose his attire, with KKK robes or Skinhead garb as the options. The player moves through the game murdering 'predatory sub-humans' and their Jewish 'masters' in order to save the white world. Throughout the game National Alliance signs and posters can be seen in the background while White Power rock bands provide the background music. In the final stages of the game the player is confronted by the 'end

boss' (Ariel Sharon) who shouts statements such as "We have destroyed your culture", when the Sharon character is killed he says "Filthy white dog, you have destroyed thousands of years of planning" (reflecting the conspiracy theory of the Jews being the Master planners plotting the downfall of the white race) [16]. Ethnic Cleansing is just one of the games promoted and sold by the National Alliance and affiliate Resistance Records. Another game White Law is also for sale from the site and is reminiscent of The Turner Diaries[a] (which had been rumoured to be planned for release as a computer game in 2002). The associated blurb for 'White Law' claims, "More weapons, more levels, much more challenging than Ethnic Cleansing". (These games can be purchased for just US$10 each). While the link between right wing inspired online gaming & computer gaming in general remains tentative at best it continues to serve an important propaganda dissemination function for Right Wing extremist movements in general [11].

Online dating service – 'Whites Only'

In relation to the facilitation of interpersonal bonds online, some Radical Right communities (and websites) have set up dating services. Such services target white men and women who desire contact on a personal level, and can have an impact on lifestyle choices for members of the movement making it easier for them to meet a partner with similar political/ideological views. For example, a number of websites are dedicated purely to 'White Pride' dating services, such as euro datelink (www.eurodatelink.com/). The Stormfront discussion forum also provides a forum section dedicated to white singles seeking dates, this section of the board is divided into two subsections, one dedicated to 'talk', the other dedicated to 'dating advice'. These facilities are popular among single users and appear to be well used. They provide information and links to other white dating services, for example this information posted by one of the moderators:

"Dating web sites are very popular on the Internet. There are many dating sites for many different ethnic groups -- Jewish, Black, Indian, Native American, Arab, and Asian. However, if you look for White singles, there isn't much. We needed a dedicated dating site for normal White people of European descent who would like to meet people with a similar background. Therefore we decided to launch Eurodatelink.net. Eurodatelink is for people of European descent wherever they may live, rich or poor, Christian, pagan, or atheist who share one common desire: to meet other White people for dating, romance, or friendship. http://www.eurodatelink.net/ is a real dating site for White heterosexual people looking to meet singles or who just want to make new friends."

The use of the Internet, particularly websites and discussion forum services, to promote in-group networking and 'dating' services for whites only, are noteworthy not simply because they represent a means for individuals to meet other like minded individuals but also because they can arguably be seen as facilitating increased involvement. For example, in encouraging others to date within their own race group members promote the ideology of the group as important in relation to life decisions outside of the virtual realm. Similarly, such services provide a way for people to become involved in this movement and to become acquainted with others within the movement on a more personal level. The fostering of personal relationships with others involved within extremist movements has been identified as a contributing factor toward increasing involvement over time. The potential for relationships formed online to contribute to the involvement process of individuals has not been empirically studied and perhaps warrants further investigation, particularly given the large number of Internet and community members who apparently avail of this service.

Conclusions

The radical right represents a factionalised movement with dispersed networked organisational structure which primarily adheres to the notion of 'leaderless resistance'. While the radical right have not actively orchestrated a large-scale terrorist campaign to achieve their aims they continue to retain an interested body of supporters and promoters, as exemplified by their online presence, in particular sophisticated virtual communities of support with large number of registered members.

Essentially virtual support communities facilitate social interaction and the formation of social bonds, which in turn can lead to changes in attitudes and behaviour over time. These changes in attitude might include adopting the most prevalent ideology expressed within the community. Similarly changes in behaviour might include involvement in a range of both on and off line activities in support of the ideology/organisation. Just as individuals who may be open to supporting an organisation do not necessarily become further involved, so is the case for virtual community members. Although virtual community members may freely express their opinions online, not all of them will take the next step and become new members or recruits (of either the online or offline organisations), similarly not all individuals become increasingly involved.

However given that virtual communities promote discussion, interaction and the formation of interpersonal bonds and relationships, which often occur when individuals use the communities regularly, they are potential recruiting grounds and should be recognised as such. This is particularly the case in light of research that

suggests this may be an important factor in the recruitment process [12]. Limited numbers of people decide to become members of terrorist organisations however the Internet has the potential to facilitate at least some level of recruitment. Arguably this will be most apparent where there is a strong online presence that encourages and promotes involvement in support related activities such as donating funds, distributing fliers, supporting Prisoners of War and/or engaging in online support activities (with the potential to later engage in offline support activities). With this in mind it is important to continue investigating how and why terrorist movements and their supporters use the Internet and to consider that these uses are open to innovation and change reflecting the dynamic nature of modern technology.

Endnotes
[a]The Turner Diaries (1978), written by William Pierce (former leader of the National Alliance) under the pseudonym Andrew Macdonald, provide a blueprint for the organisation and strategic development of a clandestine terrorist group.

Competing interests
The authors declare that they have no competing interests.

Acknowledgements
Journal instruction requires an Acknowledgements section however none was provided. In this regard, please provide the missing section. Many thanks to Alison Torn and EISIC reviewers who commented on earlier drafts of this paper.

References
1. N Friedland, Becoming a terrorist: Social and individual antecedents, in *Terrorism: Roots, impact, responses*, ed. by L Howard (Praeger, New York, 1992), pp. 81–94
2. M Crenshaw, The logic of terrorism: Terrorist behaviour as a product of strategic choice, in *Origins of terrorism: Psychologies, ideologies, theologies, states of mind*, ed. by W Reich (Cambridge University Press, Cambridge, 1990), pp. 7–24
3. J Horgan, *The Psychology of Terrorism* (Routledge, Oxon, 2005)
4. Dd Porta, Political socialization in left-wing underground organizations: Biographies of Italian and German militants, in *Social movements and violence: Participation in underground organizations*, ed. by Dd Porta (JAI Press, Greenwich, CT, 1992), pp. 259–290
5. J Post, E Sprinzak, L Denny, The terrorists in their own words: Interviews with 35 incarcerated Middle Eastern Terrorists. Terrorism & Political Violence 15(1), 171–184 (2003)
6. M Sageman, *Understanding terrorist networks* (University of Pennsylvania Press, Philadelphia, 2004)
7. F Passy, Socialization, recruitment, and the structure/agency gap. A specification of the impact of networks on participation in social movements, 2000. Retrieved June 20th, 2011 from http://www.nd.edu/~dmyers/lomond/passy.pdf
8. R Starks, W Sims Bainbridge, Networks of faith: Interpersonal bonds and recruitment to cults and sects. The American Journal of Sociology 85(6), 1376–1395 (1980)
9. L Back, Aryans reading Adorno: Cyber-culture and twenty-first century Racism. Ethnic & Racial Studies 25(4), 628–651 (2002)
10. S Jones, *Cybersociety: Computer Mediated Communication and Community* (Sage Publications, Thousand Oaks, 1995)

11. L Bowman-Grieve, Exploring Stormfront: The Virtual Community of the Radical Right. Studies in Conflict & Terrorism **32**(11), 989–1007 (2009)
12. B Ray, & GE Marsh II, Recruitment by extremist groups on the Internet. (Electronic version) *First Monday, 6 (2)*, 2001. Retrieved June 20th, 2011 from http://firstmonday.org/htbin/cgiwrap/bin/ojs/index.php/fm/article/view/834/743
13. L Bowman-Grieve, Irish Republicanism and the Internet: Support for new wave dissidents. Perspectives on Terrorism **4**(2), 22–34 (2010)
14. R Ezekiel, *The racist mind* (Viking, New York, 1995)
15. JM Cotter, Sounds of Hate: White Power rock and roll and the Neo-Nazi Skinhead subculture. Terrorism and Political Violence **11**(2), 111–140 (1999)
16. Anti-Defamation League. Racist Groups Using Computer Gaming to Promote Violence against Blacks, Latinos and Jews, 2002. Retrieved June 20th, 2011 from http://www.adl.org/videogames/default.asp

8

Algorithmic criminology

Richard Berk

Abstract

Computational criminology has been seen primarily as computer-intensive simulations of criminal wrongdoing. But there is a growing menu of computer-intensive applications in criminology that one might call "computational," which employ different methods and have different goals. This paper provides an introduction to computer-intensive, tree-based, machine learning as the method of choice, with the goal of *forecasting* criminal behavior. The approach is "black box," for which no apologies are made. There are now in the criminology literature several such applications that have been favorably evaluated with proper hold-out samples. Peeks into the black box indicate that conventional, causal modeling in criminology is missing significant features of crime etiology.

Keywords: Machine learning, Forecasting, Criminal behavior, Classification, Random forests, Stochastic gradient boosting, Bayesian additive regression trees

Introduction

Computational Criminology is a hybrid of computer science, applied mathematics, and criminology. Procedures from computer science and applied mathematics are used to animate theories about crime and law enforcement [1-3]. The primary goal is to learn how underlying mechanisms work; computational criminology is primarily about explanation. Data play a secondary role either to help tune the simulations or, at least ideally, to evaluate how well the simulations perform [4].

There are other computer-intensive application in criminology that one might also call "computational." Procedures from statistics, computer science, and applied mathematics can be used to develop powerful visualization tools that are as engaging as they are effective [5,6]. These tools have been recently used in a criminology application [7], and with the growing popularity of electronic postings, will eventually become important components of circulated papers and books.

There are also a wide variety of computer-intensive methods used in law enforcement to assemble datasets, provide forensic information, or more broadly to inform administrative activities such as COMPSTAT [8]. Although these methods can be very useful for criminal justice practice, their role in academic criminology has yet to be clearly articulated.

Correspondence: berkr@wharton.upenn.edu
Department of Statistics, Department of Criminology, University of Pennsylvania, Philadelphia, USA

In this paper, yet another form of computational criminology is discussed. Very much in the tradition of exploratory data analysis developed by John Tukey, Frederick Mosteller and others three decade ago [9], powerful computational tools are being developed to inductively characterize important but elusive structures in a dataset. The computational muscle has grown so rapidly over the past decade that the new applications have the look and feel of dramatic, qualitative advances. Machine learning is probably the poster-child for these approaches [10-13].

There are many new journals specializing in machine learning (e.g., *Journal of Machine Learning*) and many older journals that are now routinely sprinkled with machine learning papers (e.g., *Journal of the American Statistical Association*). So far, however, applications in criminology are hard to find. Part of the reason is time; it takes a while for new technology to diffuse. Part of the reason is software; the popular statistical packages can be at least five years behind recent developments. Yet another part of the reason is the need for a dramatic attitude adjustment among criminologists. Empirical research in criminology is thoroughly dominated by a culture of causal modeling in which the intent is to explain in detail the mechanisms by which nature generated the values of a response variable as a particular function of designated predictors and stochastic disturbances.[a] Machine learning comes from a different culture characterized by an "algorithmic" perspective.

"The approach is that nature produces data in a black box whose insides are complex, mysterious, and, at least, partly unknowable. What is observed is a set of $\mathbf{x}$'s that go in and a subsequent set of $\mathbf{y}$'s that come out. The problem is to find an algorithm $f(\mathbf{x})$ such that for future $\mathbf{x}$ in a test set, $f(\mathbf{x})$ will be a good predictor of $\mathbf{y}$." [14]

As I discuss at some length elsewhere [15], the most common applications of machine learning in criminology have been to inform decisions about whom to place on probation, the granting of parole, and parole supervision practices. These are basically classification problems that build directly on parole risk assessments dating back to the 1920s. There are related applications informing police decisions in domestic violence incidents, the placement of inmates in different security levels, and the supervision of juveniles already in custody. These can all be seen successful *forecasting* exercises, at least in practical terms. Current decisions are informed by projections of subsequent risk. Such criminal justice applications guide the discussion of machine learning undertaken here. We will focus on *tree-based*, machine learning procedures as an instructive special case. Four broad points will be made.

First, machine learning is computational not just because it is computer-intensive, but because it relies algorithmic procedures rather than causal models.[b] Second, the key activity is data exploration in ways that can be surprisingly thorough. Patterns in the data commonly overlooked by conventional methods can be effectively exploited. Third, the forecasting procedures can be hand-tailored so that the consequences of different kinds of forecasting errors can be properly anticipated. In particular, false positives can be given more or less weight than false negatives. Finally, the forecasting skill can be impressive, at least relative to past efforts.

Conceptual foundations

It all starts with what some call "meta-issues." These represent the conceptual foundation on which any statistical procedure rests. Without a solid conceptual foundation, all that follows will be *ad hoc*. Moreover, the conceptual foundation provides whatever links there may be between the empirical analyses undertaken and subject-matter theory or policy applications.

Conventional regression models

Conventional causal models are based on a quantitative theory of how the data were generated. Although there can be important difference in detail, the canonical account takes the form of a linear regression model such as

$$y_i = \mathbf{X}_i \boldsymbol{\beta} + \varepsilon_i, \tag{1}$$

where for each case i, the response y_i is a linear function of fixed predictors $\mathbf{X}_i$ (usually including a column if 1's for the intercept), with regression coefficients $\boldsymbol{\beta}$, and a disturbance term $\varepsilon_i \sim NIID(0, \sigma^2)$. For a given case, nature (1) sets the value of each predictor, (2) combines them in a linear fashion using the regression coefficients as weights, (3) adds the value of the intercept, and (4) adds a random disturbance from a normal distribution with a mean of zero and a given variance. The result is the value of y_i. Nature can repeat these operations a limitless number of times for a given case with the random disturbances drawn independently of one another. The same formulation applies to all cases.

When the response is categorical or a count, there are some differences in how nature generates the data. For example, if the response variable $\mathbf{Y}$ is binary,

$$p_i = \frac{1}{1 + e^{-(\mathbf{X}_i \boldsymbol{\beta})}}, \tag{2}$$

where p_i is the probability of some event defined by $\mathbf{Y}$. Suppose that $\mathbf{Y}$ is coded "1" if a particular event occurs and "0" otherwise. (e.g., A parolee is arrested or not.) Nature combines the predictors as before, but now applies a logistic transformation to arrive at a value for p_i. (e.g., The cumulative normal is also sometimes used.) That probability leads to the equivalent of a coin flip with the probability that the coin comes up "1" equal to p_i. The side on which that "coin" lands determines for case i if the response is a "1" or a "0." As before, the process can be repeated independently a limitless number of times for each case.

The links to linear regression become more clear when Equation 2 is rewritten as

$$\ln \left(\frac{p_i}{1 - p_i} \right) = \mathbf{X}_i \boldsymbol{\beta}, \tag{3}$$

where p_i is, again, the probability of the some binary response whose "logit" depends linearly on the predictors.[c]

For either Equation 1, 2 or 3, a causal account can be overlaid by claiming that nature can manipulate the value of any given predictor independently of all other predictors. Conventional statistical inference can also be introduced because the sources of random variation are clearly specified and statistically tractable.

Forecasting would seem to naturally follow. With an estimate $\mathbf{X}_i \hat{\boldsymbol{\beta}}$ in hand, new values for $\mathbf{X}$ can be inserted to arrive at values for $\hat{\mathbf{Y}}$ that may be used as forecasts. Conventional tests and confidence intervals can then be applied. There are, however, potential conceptual complications. If $\mathbf{X}$ is fixed, how does one explain the appearance of new predictor values $\mathbf{X}^*$ whose outcomes one wants to forecast? For better or worse, such matters are typically ignored in practice.

Powerful critiques of conventional regression have appeared since the 1970s. They are easily summarized: the causal models popular in criminology, and in the social sciences more generally, are laced with far too many untestable assumptions of convenience. The modeling has gotten far out ahead of existing subject-matter knowledge.[d]

Interested readers should consult the writings of economists such as Leamer, LaLonde, Manski, Imbens and Angrist, and statisticians such as Rubin, Holland, Breiman, and Freedman. I have written on this too [16].

The machine learning model

Machine Learning can rest on a rather different model that demands far less of nature and of subject matter knowledge. For given case, nature generates data as a random realization from a joint probability distribution for some collection of variables. The variables may be quantitative or categorical. A limitless number of realizations can be independently produced from that joint distribution. The same applies to every case. That's it.

From nature's perspective, there are no predictors or response variables. It follows that there is no such thing as omitted variables or disturbances. Often, however, researchers will use subject-matter considerations to designate one variable as a response Y and other variables as predictors X. It is then sometimes handy to denote the joint probability distribution as $\Pr(Y, X)$. One must be clear that the distinction between Y and X has absolutely nothing to do with how the data were generated. It has everything to do the what interests the researcher.

For a quantitative response variable in $\Pr(Y, X)$, researchers often want to characterize how the means of the response variable, denoted here by μ, may be related to X. That is, researchers are interested in the conditional distribution $\mu|X$. They may even write down a regression-like expression

$$y_i = f(X_i) + \xi_i, \tag{4}$$

where $f(X_i)$ is the unknown relationship in nature's joint probability distribution for which

$$\mu_i = f(X_i). \tag{5}$$

It follows that the mean of ξ_i in the joint distribution equals zero.[e] Some notational and conceptual license is being taken here. The predictors are random variables and formally should be represented as such. But in this instance, the extra complexity is probably not worth the trouble.

Equations 4 and 5 constitute a theory of how the response is related to the predictors in $\Pr(Y, X)$. But any relationships between the response and the predictors are "merely" associations. There is no causal overlay.

Equation 4 is not a causal model. Nor is it a representation of how the data were generated — we already have a model for that.

Generalizations to categorical response variables and their conditional distributions can be relatively straightforward. We denote a given outcome class by G_k, with classes $k = 1 \ldots K$ (e.g., for $K = 3$, released on bail, released on recognizance, not released). For nature's joint probability distribution, there can be for any case i interest in the conditional probability of any outcome class: $p_{ki} = f(X_i)$. There also can be interest in the conditional outcome class itself: $g_{ki} = f(X_i)$.[f]

One can get from the conditional probability to the conditional class using the Bayes classifier. The class with the largest probability is the class assigned to a case. For example, if for a given individual under supervision the probability of failing on parole is .35, and the probability of succeeding on parole is .65, the assigned class for that individual is success. It is also possible with some estimation procedures to proceed directly to the outcome class. There is no need to estimate intervening probabilities.

When the response variable is quantitative, forecasting can be undertaken with the conditional means for the response. If $f(X)$ is known, predictor values are simply inserted. Then $\mu = f(X^*)$, where as before, X^* represents the predictor values for the cases whose response values are to be forecasted. The same basic rationale applies when outcome is categorical, either through the predicted probability or directly. That is, $\mathbf{p}_k = f(X^*)$ and $\mathbf{G}_k = f(X^*)$.

The $f(X)$ is usually unknown. An estimate, $\hat{f}(X)$, then replaces $f(X)$ when forecasts are made. The forecasts become estimates too. (e.g., μ becomes $\hat{\mu}$.) In a machine learning context, there can be difficult complications for which satisfying solutions may not exist. Estimation is considered in more depth shortly.

Just like the conventional regression model, the joint probability distribution model can be wrong too. In particular, the assumption of independent realizations can be problematic for spatial or temporal data, although in principle, adjustments for such difficulties sometimes can be made. A natural question, therefore, is why have any model at all? Why not just treat the data as a population and describe its important features?

Under many circumstances treating the data as all there is can be a fine approach. But if an important goal of the analysis is to apply the findings beyond the data on hand, the destination for those inferences needs to be clearly defined, and a mathematical road map to the destination provided. A proper model promises both. If there is no model, it is very difficult to generalize any findings in a credible manner.[g]

A credible model is critical for forecasting applications. Training data used to build a forecasting procedure and subsequent forecasting data for which projections into the future are desired, should be realizations of the same data generation process. If they are not, formal justification for any forecasts breaks down and at an intuitive level, the enterprise seems misguided. Why would one employ a realization from one data generation process to make forecasts about another data generation process?[h]

In summary, the joint probability distribution model is simple by conventional regression modeling standards. But it provides nevertheless an instructive way for thinking about the data on hand. It is also less restrictive and far more appropriate for an inductive approach to data analysis.

Estimation

Even if one fully accepts the joint probably distribution model, its use in practice depends on estimating some of its key parameters. There are then at least three major complications.

1. In most cases, $f(\mathbf{X})$ is unknown. In conventional linear regression, one assumes that $f(\mathbf{X})$ is linear. The only unknowns are the values of the regression coefficients and the variance of the disturbances. With the joint probability distribution model, any assumed functional form is typically a matter descriptive convenience [17]. It is not informed by the model. Moreover, the functional form is often arrived at in an inductive manner. As result, the functional form as well as its parameters usually needs to be estimated.
2. Any analogy to covariance adjustments is also far more demanding. To adjust the fitted values for associations among predictors, one must know the functional forms. But one cannot know those functional forms unless the adjustments are properly in place.
3. $\mathbf{X}$ is now a random variable. One key consequence is that estimates of $f(\mathbf{X})$ can depend *systematically* on which values of the predictors happen to be in the realized data. There is the likely prospect of bias. Because $f(\mathbf{X})$ is allowed to be nonlinear, which parts of the function one can "see" depends upon which values of the predictors are realized in the data. For example, a key turning point may be systematically missed in some realizations. When $f(\mathbf{X})$ is linear, it will materialize as linear no matter what predictor values are realized.

This is where the computational issues first surface. There are useful responses all three problems if one has the right algorithms, enough computer memory, and one or more fast CPUs. Large samples are also important.

Data partitions as a key idea

We will focus on categorical outcomes because they are far more common than quantitative outcomes in the criminal justice applications emphasized here. Examples of categorical outcomes include whether or not an individual on probation or parole is arrested for a homicide [18], whether there is a repeat incident of domestic violence in a household [19], and different rule infractions for which a prison inmate may have been reported [20].

Consider a 3-dimensional scatter plot of sorts. The response is three color-coded kinds of parole outcomes: an arrest for a violent crime (red), an arrest for a crime that is not violent (yellow), and no arrest at all (green). There are two predictors in this cartoon example: age in years and the number of prior arrests.

The rectangle is a two-dimension predictor space. In that space, there are concentrations of outcomes by color. For example, there is a concentration of red circles toward the left hand side of the rectangle, and a concentration of green circles toward the lower right. The clustering of certain colors means that there is structure in the data, and because the predictor space is defined by age and priors, the structure can be given substantive meaning. Younger individuals and individuals with a greater number of priors, for instance, are more likely to be arrested for violent crimes.

To make use of the structure in the data, a researcher must locate that structure in the predictor space. One way to locate the structure is to partition the predictor space in a manner that tends to isolate important patterns. There will be, for example, regions in which violent offenders are disproportionately found, or regions where nonviolent offenders are disproportionately found.

Suppose the space is partitioned as in Figure 1, where the partitions are defined by the horizontal and vertical lines cutting through the predictor space. Now what? The partitions can be used to assign classes to observations. Applying the Bayes classifier, the partition at the upper right, for example, would be assigned the class of no crime — the vote is 2 to 1. The partition at the upper left would be assigned the class of violent crime — the vote is 4 to 1. The large middle partition would be assigned the class of nonviolent crime — the vote is 7 to 2 to 1. Classes would be assigned to each partition by the same reasoning. The class with the largest estimated probability wins.

The assigned classes can be used for forecasting. Cases with unknown outcomes but predictor values for age and priors can be located in the predictor space. Then, the class of the partition in which the case falls can serve as a forecast. For example, a case falling in the large middle partition would be forecasted to fail through an arrest for a nonviolent crime.

The two predictors function much like longitude and latitude. They locate a case in the predictor space. The

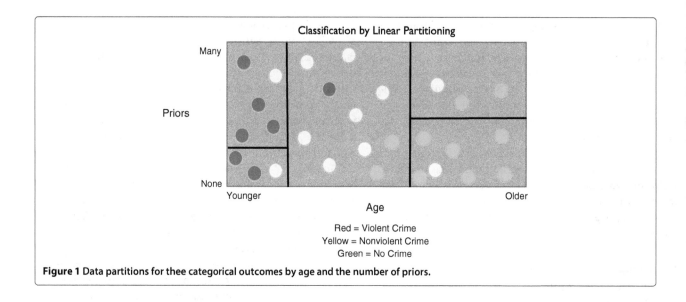

Figure 1 Data partitions for thee categorical outcomes by age and the number of priors.

partition in which a case falls determines its assigned class. That class can be the forecasted class. But there need be nothing about longitude and latitude beyond their role as map coordinates. One does not need to know that one is a measure of age, and one is a measure of the number of priors. We will see soon, somewhat counter-intuitively, that separating predictors from what they are supposed to measure can improve forecasting accuracy enormously. If the primary goal is to search for structure, how well one searches drives everything else. This is a key feature of the algorithmic approach.

Nevertheless, in some circumstances, the partitions can be used to described how the predictors and the response are related in subject-matter terms. In this cartoon illustration, younger individuals are much more likely to commit a violent crime, individuals with more priors are much more likely to commit a violent crime, and there looks to be a strong statistical interaction effect between the two. By taking into account the meaning of the predictors that locate the partition lines (e.g., priors more than 2 and age less than 25) the meaning of any associations sometimes can be made more clear. We can learn something about $f(\mathbf{X})$.

How are the partitions determined? The intent is to carve up the space so that overall the partitions are as homogeneous as possible with respect to the outcome. The lower right partition, for instance, has six individuals who were not arrested and one individual arrested for a nonviolent crime. Intuitively, that partition is quite homogeneous. In contrast, the large middle partition has two individuals who were not arrested, seven individuals who were arrested for a crime that was not violent, and one individual arrested for a violent crime. Intuitively, that partition is less homogenous. One might further intuit that any partition with equal numbers of individuals for

each outcome class is the least homogenous it can be, and that any partition with all cases in a single outcome class is the most homogeneous it can be.

These ideas can be made more rigorous by noting that with greater homogeneity partition by partition, there are fewer classification errors overall. For example, the lower left partition has an assigned class of violent crime. There is, therefore, one classification error in that partition. The large middle category has an assigned class of nonviolent crime, and there are three classification errors in that partition. One can imagine trying to partition the predictor space so that the total number of classification errors is as small as possible. Although for technical reasons this is rarely the criterion used in practice, it provides a good sense of the intent. More details are provided shortly.

At this point, we need computational muscle to get the job done. One option is to try all possible partitions of the data (except the trivial one in which partitions can contain a single observation). However, this approach is impractical, especially as the number of predictors grows, even with very powerful computers.

A far more practical and surprisingly effective approach is to employ a "greedy algorithm." For example, beginning with no partitions, a single partition is constructed that minimizes the sum of the classification errors in the two partitions that result. All possible splits for each predictor are evaluated and the best split for single predictor is chosen. The same approach is applied separately to each of the two new partitions. There are now four, and the same approach is applied once again separately to each. This recursive partitioning continues until the number of classification errors cannot be further reduced. The algorithm is called "greedy" because it takes the best result at each step and never looks back; early splits are never revisited.

Actual practice is somewhat more sophisticated. Beginning with the first subsetting of the data, it is common to evaluate a function of the proportion of cases in each outcome class (e.g., .10 for violent crime, .35 for nonviolent crime, and .55 for no crime). Two popular functions of the proportions are

$$\text{Gini Index:} \quad \sum_{k \neq k'} \hat{p}_{mk}\hat{p}_{mk'} \tag{6}$$

and

$$\text{Cross Entropy or Deviance:} \quad -\sum_{k=1}^{K} \hat{p}_{mk} \log \hat{p}_{mk}. \tag{7}$$

The notation denotes different estimates of proportions $\hat{p}_{mk}$ over different outcome categories indexed by k, and different partitions of the data indexed by m. The Gini Index and the Cross-Entropy take advantage of the arithmetic fact that when the proportions over classes are more alike, their product is larger (e.g., $[.5 \times .5] > [.6 \times .4]$). Intuitively, when the proportions are more alike, there is less homogeneity. For technical reasons we cannot consider here, the Gini Index is probably the preferred measure.

Some readers have may have already figured out that this form of recursive partitioning is the approach used for classification trees [21]. Indeed, the classification tree shown in Figure 2 is consistent with the partitioning shown in Figure 1.[i]

The final partitions are color-coded for the class assigned by vote, and the number of cases in each final partition are color coded for their actual outcome class. In classification tree parlance, the full dataset at the top before any partitioning is called the "root node," and the final partitions at the bottom are called "terminal nodes."

There are a number of ways this relatively simple approach can be extended. For example, the partition boundaries do not have to be linear. There are also procedures called "pruning" that can be used to remove lower nodes having too few cases or that do not sufficiently improve the Gini Index.

Classification trees are rarely used these days as stand-alone procedures. They are well known to be very unstable over realizations of the data, especially if one wants to use the tree structure for explanatory purposes. In addition, implicit in the binary partitions are step functions — a classification tree can be written as a form of regression in which the right hand side is a linear combination of step functions. However, it will be unusual if step functions provide a good approximation of $f(\mathbf{X})$. Smoother functions are likely to be more appropriate. Nevertheless, machine learning procedures often make use of classification trees as a component of much more effective and computer-intensive algorithms. Refinements that might be used for classification trees themselves are not needed; classification trees are means to an estimation end, not the estimation end itself.

Random forests

Machine learning methods that build on classification trees have proved very effective in criminal justice classification and forecasting applications. Of those, random forecasts has been by far the most popular. We consider now random forests, but will provide a brief discussion of

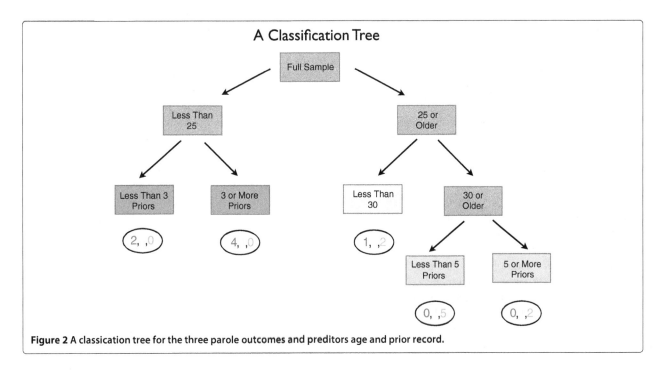

Figure 2 A classication tree for the three parole outcomes and preditors age and prior record.

two other tree-based methods later. They are both worthy competitors to random forests.

A good place to start is with the basic random forests algorithm that combines the results from a large ensemble of classification trees [22].

1. From a training dataset with N observations, a random sample of size N is drawn with replacement. A classification tree will be grown for the chosen observations. Observations that are not selected are stored as the "out-of-bag" (OOB) data. They serve as test data for that tree and will on average be about a third the size of the original training data.
2. A small sample of predictors is drawn at random (e.g., 3 predictors).
3. After selecting the best split from among the random subset of predictors, the first partition is determined. There are then two subsets of the data that together maximize the improvement in the Gini index.
4. Steps 2 and 3 are repeated for all later partitions until the model's fit does not improve or the observations are spread too thinly over terminal nodes.
5. The Bayes classifier is applied to each terminal node to assign a class.
6. The OOB data are "dropped" down the tree. Each observation is assigned the class associated with the terminal node in which it lands. The result is the predicted class for each observation in the OOB data for that tree.
7. Steps 1 through 6 are repeated a large number of times to produce a large number of classification trees. There are usually several hundred trees or more.
8. For each observation, the final classification is by vote over all trees when that observation is OOB. The class with the most votes is chosen. That class can be used for forecasting when the predictor values are known but the outcome class is not.

Because random forests is an ensemble of classification trees, many of the benefits from recursive partitioning remain. In particular, nonlinear functions and high order interaction effects can found inductively. There is no need to specify them in advance.

But, random forests brings its own benefits as well. The sampling of training data for each tree facilitates finding structures that would ordinarily be overlooked. Signals that might be weak in one sample might be strong in another. Each random sample provides a look at the predictor space from different vantage point.

Sampling predictors at each split results in a wide variety of classification trees. Predictors that might dominate in one tree are excluded at random from others. As a result, predictors that might otherwise be masked can surface.

Sampling predictors also means that the number of predictors in the training data can be *greater* than the number of observations. This is forbidden in conventional regression models. Researchers do not have to be selective in the predictors used. "Kitchen sink" specifications are fine.

The consequences of different forecasting errors are rarely the same, and it follows that their costs can differ too, often dramatically. Random forests accommodates in several ways different forecasting-error costs. Perhaps the best way is to use stratified sampling each time the training data are sampled. Oversampling the less frequent outcomes changes the prior distribution of the response and gives such cases more weight. In effect, one is altering the loss function. Asymmetric loss functions can be built into the algorithm right from the start. An illustration is provided below.

Random forests does not overfit [22] even if thousands are trees are grown. The OOB data serve as a test sample to keep the procedure honest. For other popular machine learning procedures, overfitting can be a problem. One important consequence is that random forests can provide consistent estimates of generalization error in nature's joint probability distribution for the particular response and predictors employed.[j]

Confusion tables

The random forests algorithm can provide several different kinds of output. Most important is the "confusion table." Using the OOB data, actual outcome classes are cross-tabulated against forecasted outcome classes. There is a lot of information in such tables. In this paper, we only hit the highlights.

Illustrative data come from a homicide prevention project for individuals on probation or parole [23]. A "failure" was defined as (1) being arrested for homicide, (2) being arrest for an attempted homicide, (3) being a homicide victim, or (4) being a victim of a non-fatal shooting. Because for this population, perpetrators and victims often had the same profiles, no empirical distinction was made between the two. If a homicide was prevented, it did not matter if the intervention was with a prospective perpetrator or prospective victim.

However, prospective perpetrators or victims had first to be identified. This was done by applying random forests with the usual kinds predictor variables routinely available (e.g., age, prior record, age at first arrest, history of drug use, and so on). The number of classification trees was set at 500.[k]

Table 1 shows a confusion table from that project. The results are broadly representative of recent forecasting performance using random forests [15]. Of those who failed, about 77% were correctly identified by the random forests algorithm. Of those who did not fail, 91% were correctly identified by the algorithm. Because the table is

Table 1 Confusion table for forecasts of perpetrators and victims

	Forecasted Not Fail	Forecasted Fail	Accuracy
Not Fail	9972	987	.91
Fail	45	153	.77

True negatives are identified with 91% accuracy. True positives are identified with 77% accuracy. (Fail = perpetrator or victim. No Fail = not a perpetrator or victim).

constructed from OOB data, these figures capture true forecasting accuracy.

But was this good enough for stakeholders? The failure base rate was about 2%. Failure was, thankfully, a rare event. Yet, random forests was able to search through a high dimensional predictor space containing over 10,000 observations and correctly forecast failures about 3 times out of 4 among those who then failed. Stakeholders correctly thought this was impressive.

How well the procedure would perform *in practice* is better revealed by the proportion of times when a forecast is made, the forecast is correct. This, in turn, depends on stakeholders' costs of false positives (i.e., individuals incorrectly forecasted to be perpetrators or victims) relative to the costs of false negatives (i.e., individuals incorrectly forecasted to neither be perpetrators nor victims). Because the relative costs associated with failing to correctly identify prospective perpetrators or victims were taken to be very high, a substantial number of false positives were to be tolerated. The cost ratio of false negatives to false positives was set at 20 to 1 *a priori* and built into the algorithm. This meant that relatively weak evidence of failure would be sufficient to forecast a failure. The price was necessarily an increase in the number of individuals incorrectly forecasted to be failures.

The results reflect this policy choice; there are in the confusion table about 6.5 false positives for every true positive (i.e., 987/153). As a result, when a failure is the forecasted, is it correct only about 15% of the time. When a success is the forecasted, it is correct 99.6% of the time. This also results from the tolerance for false positives. When a success is forecasted, the evidence is very strong. Stakeholders were satisfied with these figures, and the procedures were adopted.

Variable importance for forecasting

Although forecasting is the main goal, information on the predictive importance of each predictor also can be of interest. Figure 3 is an example from another application [15]. The policy question was whether to release an individual on parole. Each inmate's projected threat to public safety had to be a consideration in the release decision.

The response variable defined three outcome categories measured over 2 years on parole: being arrested for a

violent crime ("Level 2"), being arrested for a crime but not a violent one ("Level 1"), and not being arrested at all ("Level 0"). The goal was to assign one such outcome class to each inmate when a parole was being considered. The set of predictors included nothing unusual except that several were derived from behavior while in prison: "Charge Record Count," "Recent Report Count," and "Recent Category 1 Count" refer to misconduct in prison. Category1 incidents were considered serious.

Figure 3 shows the predictive importance for each predictor. The baseline is the proportion of times the true outcome is correctly identified (as shown in the rows of a confusion table). Importance is measured by the drop in accuracy when each predictor in turn is precluded from contributing. This is accomplished by randomly shuffling one predictor at a time when forecasts are being made. The set of trees constituting the random forest is not changed. All that changes is the information each predictor brings when a forecast is made.[1]

Because there are three outcome classes, there are three such figures. Figure 3 shows the results when an arrest for a violent crime is forecasted. Forecasting importance for each predictor is shown. For example, when the number of prison misconduct charges is shuffled, accuracy declines approximately 4 percentage points (e.g., from 60% accurate to 56% accurate).

This may seem small for the most important predictor, but because of associations between predictors, there is substantial forecasting power that cannot be cleanly attributed to single predictors. Recall that the use of classification trees in random forests means that a large number of interaction terms can be introduced. These are product variables that can be highly correlated with their constituent predictors. In short, the goal of maximizing forecasting accuracy can compromise subject-matter explanation.

Still, many of the usual predictors surface with perhaps a few surprises. For example, age and gender matter just as one would expect. But behavior in prison is at least as important. Parole risk instruments have in the past largely neglected such measures perhaps because they may be "only" indicators, not "real" causes. Yet for forecasting purposes, behavior in prison looks to be more important by itself than prior record. And the widely used LSIR adds nothing to forecasting accuracy beyond what the other predictors bring.

Partial response plots

The partial response plots that one can get from random forecasts and other machine learning procedures can also be descriptively helpful. The plots shows how a given predictor is related to the response with all other predictors held constant. An outline of the algorithm is as follows.

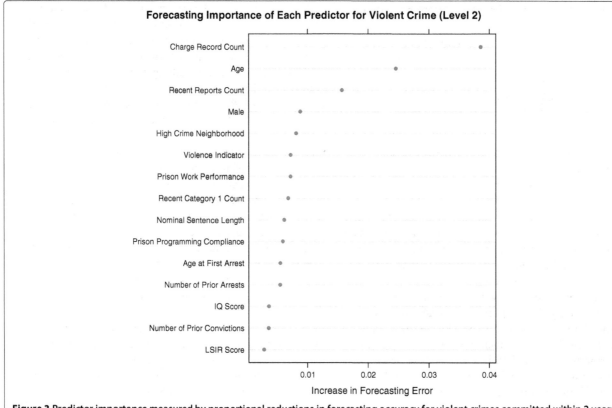

Figure 3 Predictor importance measured by proportional reductions in forecasting accuracy for violent crimes committed within 2 years of release on parole.

1. A predictor and a response class are chosen. Suppose the predictor is IQ, and the response class is an arrest for a violent crime.
2. For each case, the value of IQ is set to one of the IQ values in the dataset. All other predictors are fixed at their existing values.
3. The fitted values of are computed for each case, and their mean calculated.
4. Steps 2 and 3 are repeated for all other IQ values.
5. The means are plotted against IQ.
6. Steps 2 through 5 are repeated for all other response variable classes.
7. Steps 1 through 6 are repeated for all other predictors.

Figure 4 shows how IQ is related to commission of a violent crime while on parole, all other predictors held constant. The vertical axis is in centered logits. Logits are used just as in logistic regression. The centering is employed so that when the outcome has more than two classes, no single class need be designated as the baseline.[m] A larger value indicates a greater probability of failure.

IQ as measured in prison has a nonlinear relationship with the log odds are being arrested for a violent crime. There is a strong, negative relationship for IQ scores from about 50 to 100. For higher IQ scores, there no apparent association. Some might have expected a negative association in general, but there seems to be no research anticipating a nonlinear relationship of the kind shown in Figure 4.

Other tree-based algorithms

For a variety of reasons, random forests is a particularly effective machine learning procedure for criminal justice forecasting [15]. But there are at least two other tree-based methods than can also perform well: stochastic gradient boosting [24,25] and Bayesian additive regression trees [26]. Both are computer intensive and algorithmic in conception.

Stochastic gradient boosting

The core idea in stochastic gradient boosting is that one applies a "weak learner" over and over to the data. After each pass, the data are reweighted so that observations that are more difficult to accurately classify are given more weight. The fitted values from each pass through the data are used to update earlier fitted values so that the weak learner is "boosted" to become a strong learner. Here is an outline of the algorithm.

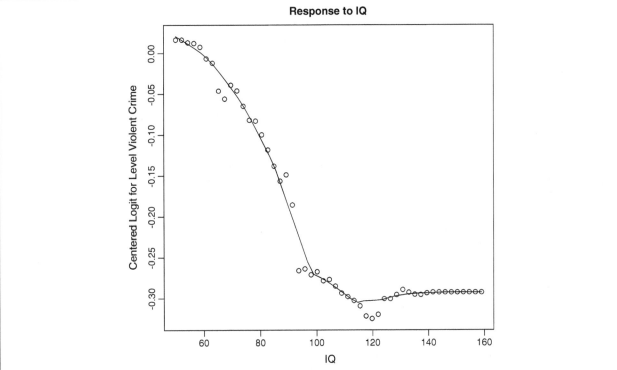

Figure 4 **How inmate IQ is related to whether a violent crime is committed while on parole.** The relationship is negative for below average IQ scores and flat thereafter.

Imagine a training dataset in which the response is binary. Suppose "fail" is coded as "1" and "succeed" is coded as "0."

1. The algorithm is initialized with fitted values for the response. The overall proportion of cases that fail is a popular choice.
2. A simple random sample of the training data is drawn with a sample size about half the sample size of the training data.[n]
3. The negative gradient, also called "pseudo residuals," is computed. Just like with conventional residuals, each fitted value is subtracted from its corresponding observed value of 1 or 0. The residual will be *quantitive* not categorical: $(1 - p)$ or $-p$, where p is the overall proportion coded as "1."
4. Using the randomly-selected observations, a *regression* tree is fit to the pseudo residuals.[o]
5. The conditional mean in each terminal node serves as an estimate of the probability of failure.
6. The fitted values are updated by adding to the existing fitted values the new fitted values weighted to get the best fit.
7. Steps 2 through 6 are repeated until the fitted values no longer improve a meaningful amount. The number of passes can in practice be quite large (e.g., 10,000), but unlike random forests, stochastic

gradient boosting can overfit [25]. Some care is needed because there is formally no convergence.
8. The fitted probability estimates can be used as is, or with the Bayes classifier transformed into assigned classes.

Stochastic gradient boosting handles wide range of response variable types in the spirit of the generalized linear model and more. Its forecasting performance is comparable to the forecasting performance of random forests. A major current liability is the requirement of symmetric loss functions for categorical response variables.

Bayesian additive regression trees

Bayesian additive regression trees [26] is a procedure that capitalizes on an ensemble of classification (or regression) trees is a clever manner. Random forests generates an ensemble of trees by treating the tree parameters as fixed but the data as random — data and predictors are sampled. Stochastic gradient boosting proceeds in an analogous fashion. Bayesian additive trees turns this upside-down. Consistent with Bayesian methods more generally, the data are treated as fixed once they are realized, and tree parameters are treated as random — the parameters are sampled. Uncertainty comes from the parameters, not from the data. Another difference is that one needs a model well beyond the joint probability distribution model. That model is essentially a form of linear regression. The outcome is regressed in a special way on a linear additive function of the fitted values from each tree combined with an additive disturbance term [27].

The parameter sampling takes four forms:

1. Whether or not to consider any partition of a node is determined by chance in a fashion that discourages larger trees;
2. if there is to be a split, the particular partitioning is determined by chance;
3. the proportion for each terminal node is selected at random from a distribution of proportions; and
4. the overall probability for each class is selected at random from a distribution of proportions.

The result can be a large ensemble classification trees (e.g., 300) that one might call a Bayesian forest.[p]

The forest is intended to be a representative sample of classification trees constrained so that trees more consistent with prior information are more heavily represented.

The growing of Bayesian trees is embedded in the algorithm by which the fitted values from the trees are additively combined. The algorithm, a form of "back-fitting" [28], starts out with each tree in its simplest possible form. The algorithm cycles though each tree in turn making it more complicated as needed to improve the fit while holding all other trees fixed at their current structure. Each tree may be revisited and revised many times. The process continues until there is no meaningful improvement in the fitted values. One can think of the result as a form of nonparametric regression in which a linear combination of fitted values is constructed, one set from each tree. In that sense, it is in the spirit of boosting.[q]

If one takes the model and the Bayesian apparatus seriously, the approach is not longer algorithmic. If one treats the model as a procedure, an algorithmic perspective is maintained. The perspective one takes can make a difference in practice. For example, if the model parameters are treated as tuning parameters, they are of little substantive interest and can be directly manipulated to improve performance. They are a means to an end, not an end in themselves.

Forecasting performance for Bayesian trees seems to be comparable to forecasting performance for random forests and stochastic gradient boosting. However, a significant weakness is that currently, categorical outcomes are limited to two classes. There is work in progress to handle the multinomial case. Another weakness is an inability to incorporate asymmetric loss, but here too there may soon be solutions.

Statistical inference for tree-based machine learning

Even when the training data are treated as a random realization from nature's joint probability distribution, conventional statistical tests and confidence intervals are problematic for random forests and stochastic gradient boosting. Bayesian additive regression trees raises different issues to be briefly addressed shortly.

Consider statistical inference for forecasts, which figure so centrally in our discussion. In conventional practice, forecasting confidence intervals can be very useful. There is a model representing how outcome probabilities and/or classes are generated. That model specifies the correct functional form and disturbance distribution, and typically treats the predictors as fixed. A 95% confidence interval will cover each true probability 95% of the time over random realizations of the response variable. There can be similar reasoning for the outcome classes themselves.

The conventional formulation does not apply under the joint probability distribution model. There can be a "true" probability for every outcome class that one would like to estimate. There can be a "true" class, also a potential estimation target. But, there are no credible claims that estimates of either have their usual convenient properties. In particular, they not assumed to be an unbiased or even consistent estimates.

For reasons given at the beginning of Section Estimation, $\hat{f}(\mathbf{X})$ is taken to be some approximation of $f(\mathbf{X})$ that can contain both systematic and random error. Biased estimated are essentially guaranteed. When there is bias, confidence intervals do not have their stated coverage and test statistics computed under the null hypothesis do not have their stated probabilities.

In a forecasting setting, there is nevertheless the prospect of appropriate 95% "error bands." One takes the machine learning results as fixed, as they would be in a forecasting exercise, and considers bands around the fitted values that would contain 95% of the forecasts. Work is under way on how to construct such bands, and there is no doubt useful information in the residuals or a bootstrap using those residuals [29]. There are also useful, though less complete, approaches that can be applied to random forests in particular. The votes over trees provide some purchase on uncertainty associated with a forecasted class [15].

Bayesian additive regression trees can generate a predictive distribution of the fitted probabilities for either outcome class. These probabilities are treated like much like another set of parameters whose values are unknown but can be characterized by a particular distribution. Bayesian forecasting intervals then can be constructed [30]. One can determine, for instance, the range in which the middle 95% of the forecasted probabilities fall. And by placing a threshold through these probabilities at an appropriate location (e.g., .50), probabilities can be transformed into classes. However, one must not forget that the uncertainty being represented comes from uncertainty in the parameters that influence how the trees are grown. These depend on priors that can seem to some as fictions of convenience. In addition, some may not favor the Bayesian approach to begin with. In either case, an algorithmic interpretation can still be appropriate and then forecasts and forecast uncertainty can be addressed in much the same fashion as for other kinds of tree-based machine learning.

Conclusions

Random forests, stochastic gradient boosting, and Bayesian additive trees are very different in conception and implementation. Yet in practice, they all can forecast well and typically much better than conventional regression models. Is there something important these tree-based method share beyond the use of large number of classification trees?

The use of tree ensembles can be viewed more abstractly as a way to effectively search a large predictor space for structure. With a large number of trees, the predictor space is sliced up in many different ways. Some sets of partitions will have stronger associations with the response variable than others and in the end, will have more weight in the forecasts that result. From this point of view, the subject-matter meaning of the predictors is a secondary concern. The predictors serve as little more than very high-dimensional coordinates for the predictor space.

Ensembles of classification trees are effective search engines for that space because of the following features that tree-based methods can share.

1. Using nature's joint probability distribution, compared to a regression causal model, as an account of how the data were generated removes a range of complications that are irrelevant for forecasting and otherwise put unnecessary constraints on the predictor-space search.

2. The use of step functions as each tree is grown can produce a very large number of new predictors. A single predictor such as age, might ultimately be represented by many indicator variables for different break points and many indicators for interaction effects. A search using, for example, 20 identified predictors such as gender and prior record, may be implemented with several hundred indicator variables. As a result, information in the initial 20 predictors can be more effectively exploited.

3. The use of indicator variables means that the search can arrive inductively at highly nonlinear relationships and very high order interactions, neither of which have to be specified in advance. Moreover, because any of the original predictors or sets of predictor can define splits differently over different trees, nonlinear relationships that are not step functions can be smoothed out as needed when the trees are aggregated to more accurately represent any associations.

4. When some form of random sampling is part of the algorithm — whether sampling of the data or sampling of the parameters — the content of the predictor space or the predictor space itself will vary [31]. Structure that might be masked for one tree might not be masked for another.

5. Aggregating fitted values over trees can add stability to forecasts. In effect, noise tends to cancel out.

6. Each of these assets are most evident in forecasting procedures built from large data sets. The high-dimensional predictor space needs lots of observations to be properly explored, especially because much of the search is for associations that one by one can be small. Their importance for forecasting materializes when the many small associations are allowed to contribute as a group. Consequently, training data sample sizes in the hundreds creates no formal problems, but the power of machine learning may not be fully exploited. Ideally, samples sizes should be at least in the 10s of thousands. Sample sizes of 100,000 or more are still better. It is sometimes surprising how much more accurate forecasts can be when the forecasting procedure is developed with massive datasets.

In summary, when subject-matter theory is well-developed and the training data set contains the key predictors, conventional regression methods can forecast well. When existing theory is weak or available data are incomplete, conventional regression will likely perform poorly, but tree-based forecasting methods can shine.[r]

There is growing evidence of another benefit from tree-based forecasting methods. Overall forecasting accuracy is usually substantially more than the sum of the accuracies that can be attributed to particular predictors. Tree-based methods are finding structure beyond what the usual predictors can explain.

Part of the reason is the black-box manner in a very large number of new predictors are generated as a component of the search process. A new linear basis can be defined for each predictor and various sets of predictors. Another part of the reason is that tree-based methods capitalize on regions in which associations with the response are weak. One by one, such regions do matter much, and conventional regression approaches bent on explanation might properly choose to ignore them. But when a large number of such regions is taken seriously, forecasting accuracy can dramatically improve. There is important predictive information in the collection of regions, not in each region by itself.

An important implication is that there is structure for a wide variety of criminal justice outcomes that current social science does not see. In conventional regression, these factors are swept into the disturbance term that, in turn, is assumed to be noise. Some will argue that this is a necessary simplification for causal modeling and explanation, but it is at least wasteful for forecasting and means that researchers are neglecting large chunks of the criminal justice phenomena. There are things to be learned from the "dark structure" that tree-based, machine learning shows to be real, but whose nature is unknown.

Endnotes

[a]A recent critique of this approach and a discussion of more promising, model-based alternatives can be found in [17].

[b]Usual criminology practice begins with a statistical model of some criminal justice process assumed to have generated the data. The statistical model has parameters whose values need to be estimated. Estimates are produced by conventional numerical methods. At the other extreme are algorithmic approaches found in machine learning and emphasized in this paper. But, there can be hybrids. One may have a statistical model that motivates a computer-intensive search of a dataset, but there need be no direct connection between the parameters of the model and the algorithm used in that search. Porter and Brown [32] use this approach to detect simulated terrorist "hot spots" and actual concentrations of breaking and entering in Richmond, Virginia.

[c]Normal regression, Poisson regression, and logistic regression are all special cases of the generalized linear model. There are other special cases and close cousins such as multinomial logistic regression. And there are relatively straightforward extensions to multiple equation models, including hierarchical models. But in broad brush strokes, the models are motivated in a similar fashion.

[d]A very instructive illustration is research claiming to show that the death penalty deters crime. A recent National Research Council report on that research [33] is devastating.

[e]Recall that in a sample, the sum of the deviation scores around a mean or proportion (coded 1/0) is zero.

[f]The notation $f(\mathbf{X})$ is meant to represent *some* function of the predictors that will vary depending on the context.

[g]Sometimes, the training data used to build the model and the forecasting data for which projections are sought are probability samples from the same finite population. There is still a model of how the data were generated, but now that model can be demonstrably correct. The data were generated by a particular (known) form of probability sampling.

[h]One might argue that the two are sufficiently alike. But then one is saying that the two data generations processes are similar enough to be treated as the same.

[i]In the interest of space, we do not consider the order in which the partitions shown in Figure 1 were constructed. One particular order would lead precisely to the classification tree in Figure 2.

[j]Roughly speaking, Breiman's generalization error is the probability that a case will be classified incorrectly in limitless number of independent realizations of the data. Breiman provides an accessible formal treatment [22] in his classic paper on random forests. One must be clear that this is not generalization error for the "right" response and predictors. There is no such thing. The generalization error is for the particular response and predictors analyzed.

[k]Although the number of trees is a tuning parameter, the precise number of trees does not usually matter as long as there are at least several hundred. Because random forests does not overfit, having more trees than necessary is not a serious problem. 500 trees typically is an appropriate number.

[l]In more conventional language, the "model" is fixed. It is not reconstructed as each predictor in turn is excluded from the forecasting exercise. This is very different from dropping each predictor in turn and regrowing the forest each time. Then, both the forest and the effective set of predictors would change. The two would be confounded. The goal here is to characterize the importance of each predictor for a *given* random forest.

[m]For any fitted value, the vertical axis units can be expressed as

$$f_k(m) = \log p_k(m) - \frac{1}{K}\sum_{l=1}^{K}\log p_l(m).$$

The function is the difference in log units between the proportion for outcome class k computed at the value m of a given predictor and the average proportion at that value over the K classes for that predictor.

[n]This serves much the same purpose as the sampling with replacement used in random forests. A smaller sample is adequate because when sampling without replacement, no case is selected more than once; there are no "duplicates."

[o]The procedure is much the same as for classification trees, but the fitting criterion is the error sum of squares or a closely related measure of fit.

[p]As before, the number of trees is a tuning parameter, but several hundred seems to be a good number.

[q]The procedure is very computationally intensive because each time fitted values are required in the backfitting process, a posterior distribution must be approximated. This

leads to the repeated use of an MCMC algorithm that by itself is computer intensive.

ᵣAnother very good machine learning candidate is support vector machines. There is no ensemble of trees. Other means are employed to explore the predictor space effectively. Hastie and his colleagues [12] provide an excellent overview.

Competing interests

The authors declare that he have no competing interests.

References

1. E Groff, L Mazerolle (eds.), Special issue: simulated experiments in criminology and criminology justice. J. Exp. Criminol. **4**(3)
2. L Liu, J Eck (eds.), *Artificial crime analysis: using computer simulations and geographical information systems*. (IGI Global, Hershey, 2008)
3. PL Brantingham, in *Intelligence and Security Informatics Conference (EISIC)*. Computational Criminology European, (2011)
4. RA Berk, How you can tell if the simulations in computational criminology are any good. J. Exp. Criminol. **3**, 289–308 (2008)
5. D Cook, DF Swayne, *Interactive and dynamic graphics for data analysis*. (Springer, New York, 2007)
6. H Wickham, *ggplot: elegant graphics for data analysis*. (Springer, New York, 2009)
7. RA Berk, J MacDonald, The dynamics of crime regimes. Criminology. **47**(3), 971–1008 (2009)
8. DE Brown, S Hagan, Data association methods with applications to law enforcement. Decis Support Syst. **34**, 369–378 (2002)
9. DC Hoaglin, F Mosteller, J Tukey (eds.), *Exploring data tables, trends, and shapes*. (John Wiley, New York, 1985)
10. RA Berk, *Statistical learning from a regression perspective*. (Springer, New York, 2008)
11. C Bishop, *Pattern recognition and machine learning*. (Springer, New York, 2006)
12. T Hastie, R Tibshirani, J Friedman, *The elements of statistical learning*, Second Edition. (Springer, New York, 2009)
13. Marsland S, *Machine learning: an algorithmic perspective*. (CRC Press, Boca Raton, Florida, 2009)
14. L Breiman, Statistical modeling: two cultures. (with discussion) Stat. Sci. **16**, 199–231 (2001)
15. RA Berk, *Criminal justice forecasts of risk: a machine learning approach*. (Springer, New York, 2012)
16. RA Berk, *Regression analysis: a constructive critique*. (Sage publications, Newbury Park, 2003)
17. RA Berk, L Brown, E George, E Pitkin, M Traskin, K Zhang, L Zhao, in *Handbook of causal analysis for social research*, ed. by S Morgan. What you can learn from wrong causal models (Springer, New York, 2012)
18. RA Berk, L Sherman, G Barnes, E Kurtz, L Ahlman, Forecasting murder within a population of probationers and parolees: a high stakes application of statistical learning. J. R. Stat. Soc. Ser. A. **172**(part I), 191–211 (2009)
19. RA Berk, SB Sorenson, Y He, Developing a practical forecasting screener for domestic violence incidents. Eval. Rev. **29**(4), 358–382 (2005)
20. RA Berk, B Kriegler, J-H Baek, Forecasting dangerous inmate misconduct: an application of ensemble statistical procedures. J. Quant. Criminol. **22**(2), 135–145 (2006)
21. L Breiman, JH Friedman, RA Olshen, CJ Stone, *Classification and regression trees*. (Wadsworth Press, Independence, 1984)
22. L Breiman, Random forests. Mach. Learn. **45**, 5–32 (2001)
23. RA Berk, The role of race in forecasts of violent crime. Race Soc. Probl. **1**, 231–242 (2009)
24. JH Friedman, Stochastic gradient boosting. Comput. Stat. Data Anal. **38**, 367–378 (2002)
25. D Mease, AJ Wyner, A Buja, Boosted classification trees class probability/quantile estimation. J. Mach. Lear. Res. **8**, 409–439 (2007)
26. HA Chipman, EI George, RE McCulloch, BART: bayesian additive regression trees. Ann. Appl. Stat. **4**(1), 266–298 (2010)
27. HA Chipman, EI George, RE McCulloch, Bayesian Ensemble Learning. Adv. Neural Inf Process. Syst. **19**, 265–272 (2007)
28. TJ Hastie, RJ Tibshirani, *Generalized additive models*. (Chapman & Hall, New York, 1990)
29. BJ Efron, RJ Tibshirani, *An introduction to the bootstrap*. (Chapman & Hall, New York, 1993)
30. J Gweke, C Whiteman, in *Handbook of Forecasting, Volume 1*, Bayesian Forecasting. ed. by G Elliot, CWJ Granger, and A Timmermann (Elsevier, New York, 2006)
31. TK Ho, The random subspace method for constructing decision trees. IEEE Trans. Pattern Recognizition Mach. Intell. **20**(8), 832–844 (1998)
32. MD Porter, DE Brown, Detecting local regions of change in high-dimensional criminal or terrorist point processes. Comput. Stat. Data. Anal. **51**, 2753–2768 (2007)
33. DS Nagin, JV Pepper, *Deterrence and the death penalty*, Committee on Law and Justice; Division on Behavioral and Social Sciences and Education; National Research Council, (2012)

9

Biologically-inspired analysis in the real world: computing, informatics, and ecologies of use

Laura A McNamara[*]

Abstract

Biological metaphors abound in computational modeling and simulation, inspiring creative and novel approaches to conceptualizing, representing, simulating and analyzing a wide range of phenomena. Proponents of this research suggest that biologically-inspired informatics have practical national security importance, because they represent a new way to analyze sociopolitical dynamics and trends, from terrorist recruitment to cyber warfare. However, translating innovative basic research into useful, usable, adoptable, and trustworthy tools that benefit the daily work of national security experts is challenging. Drawing on several years' worth of ethnographic fieldwork among national security experts, this paper suggests that information ecology, activity theory, and participatory modeling provide theoretical frameworks and practical suggestions to support design and development of useful, usable, and adoptable modeling and simulation approaches for complex national security challenges.

Background

Making analytic software useful, usable, and adoptable in the context of the United States' national security community is a difficult challenge. Not only is the "national security community" a massive, complicated, and heterogeneous set of institutions, but its members are responsible for providing timely and trustworthy assessments of significant trends. Analysts are taught to think critically about the data and information they are examining, as well as the cognitive biases they bring to its interpretation. Critical thinking and skepticism often extend to innovative and exotic technologies, such as new informatics tools, particularly those developed outside the analytic workplace. As Philip Huxtable, a researcher at the United States Joint Forces Command, has observed, national security analysts are not likely to adopt a technology if they do not "...trust the tool or method's validity and usefulness for their tasks" [1].

Biologically-inspired algorithms and frameworks are certainly innovative and exotic. Although biological metaphors have long influenced computer science (for example, in the form of neural nets), innovations in biology have more recently inspired creative, interdisciplinary approaches to conceptualizing, representing, simulating

and analyzing social, economic and cultural trends. In relation to the national security community, proponents of biologically-inspired informatics believe these approaches might shed light on trends and threats that are not well-addressed by traditional social science theory and methods. However, before biologically-inspired informatics can be usefully applied in national security settings, proponents must pay attention to the challenge of translating innovative science into working tools. This is a complicated process [2]; innovation and novelty alone will not guarantee that biologically-inspired informatics will find a productive niche in national security analysis and decision-making.

In keeping with the biologically-inspired theme of this special issue, this essay draws on Nardi and O'Day's metaphor of information ecologies as a holistic framework for understanding the relationships among tools, people, and information in potential contexts of use [3]. Approaching contexts of use from an ecological perspective can help developers appreciate the design challenges associated with introducing new technologies into existing organizational cultures. Two complementary methodological frameworks, activity theory and participatory modeling, provide practical guidance for translating ecological perspectives into usable and useful design knowledge, while building productive working relationships with the people responsible for making sense of complex national security challenges. Hopefully, this essay will

Correspondence: lamcnam@sandia.gov
Sandia National Laboratories, PO Box 5800, MS 0519, Albuquerque, NM 87185-0519, USA

inspire proponents of biologically-inspired informatics to seek new ways of engaging national security analysts and decision-makers as informed and committed stakeholders in informatics research and development.

New problems, new methods

The 9/11 attacks highlighted significant problems with information collection, sharing, and analysis in the United States' national security community. Since 9/11, the United States has taken many steps to improve the analysis and communication of intelligence assessments. Significant investments in analytic practices have led to new paradigms for evaluating intelligence information and communicating assessments to decision-makers; i.e., the Analysis of Competing Hypotheses (ACH) and Words of Estimative Probabilities (WEP) [4,5]. As part of this reform, government agencies have sought out computer software and hardware that will improve the processes and products of intelligence analysis: not just new search engines and databases, but information visualization and visual analytics platforms, computer-supported collaborative environments, even classified versions of social media such as Twitter and Facebook [6]. These days, both military and civilian agencies are awash in new software, from 'grass-roots' analyst-driven initiatives such as the collaborative platforms of Intelli-pedia and A-Space [7] to vendor-provided visual analytics software, such as Analysts' Notebook and Palantir [8,9].

Informatics research and development is also playing a role in the evolution of analytic practice and technology. Of particular importance is the recent emergence of the interdisciplinary field of computational social science, which is a trading zone [10] that brings framings from other disciplines, such as biological metaphors, to bear on the analysis of social, political, and cultural trends. The new methods and theories have emerged from these intersections have researchers extolling the potential for interdisciplinary computational science to "...[extend] our cognitive range [and provide] a new means of knowing the world, which is fundamentally different from that of experimental control" [11].

As computational social science has grown, researchers have sought funding and application areas in the national security community [12,13]. Computational modeling and simulation have long track record of informing government decision-making, and decision-makers are hungry for better forecasting capabilities, even rudimentary ones, to support resource allocation decisions and timely policy, operational, and tactical responses in an uncertain and rapidly changing world [14-18]. As a result, a number of national security thought leaders have suggested that new computational science techniques, including a wide range of modeling,

simulation, and informatics approaches, might give decision-makers a jump on complex, seemingly intractable sociopolitical trends. Perhaps the best-known funding vehicle for this intersection is the Human Social, Cultural, and Behavior (HSCB) program, under the Director of Defense Research and Engineering (DDR&E) in the Office of the Secretary of Defense (OSD). Since its inception, HSCB has itself funded over fifty research projects in government, industry and academia [16,17]. Overall, the DoD's publicly available research portfolio indicates at least thirty different interdisciplinary sociocultural research and development projects [17], many of which involve computational modeling, simulation, and informatics [17-21].

Such research investments have led to tremendous innovation in algorithms, data, and technology. Yet the long-term viability of any application depends less on its scientific novelty than whether it is presented in a way that people can use it.[a] Unfortunately, very little attention been paid to the problem of translating the innovations of biologically-inspired informatics into useful, usable, and adoptable tool for the analysts who ostensibly comprise the intended user communities [20,22,23].

Usability, utility, and adoptability

Usability, utility, and adoptability each describe distinct but interrelated qualities associated with the potential impact of a new technology; i.e., the degree to which humans can employ an artifact to achieve a desired goal, end, or effect on the world around them. Usability refers to such qualities as learnability, efficiency, and whether important operations are easily performed and remembered. Utility or usefulness describes the degree to which people can use the technology to perform tasks that matter to them, and a rich literature provides guidance and techniques for assessing these qualities [22-27]. Lastly, adoptability addresses the goodness-of-fit between a tool or technology and the sociocultural characteristics of an intended user community [28].

The relationships among usability, utility, and adoptability are complicated: although they can be mutually reinforcing, none is sufficient (nor perhaps even necessary) to achieve the other two. This is because all are context- and user-dependent. For example, a software application that has a highly learnable and efficient interface may not provide capabilities that align well with a user community's core tasks. Similarly, high utility can overcome mediocre usability, as when technically proficient users are comfortable employing unfinished software. A prototype optimization toolkit that incorporates a new solver may be useful enough that engineers are willing to overlook a nonexistent interface or annoying bugs, at least temporarily. Lastly, both usability and utility tend to emphasize the relationship between a human user and a particular technology; neither quite addresses whether or not tools can be adopted into existing work environments. Adoptability brings additional consideration to higher-order social and organizational factors that may enable and constrain tool adoption, such as norms for technology acquisition and organizational modes of communication [28].

A vignette may help explain how usability, utility, and adoptability play out in the development and deployment of new software tools. Several years ago, the author became acquainted with a computer science research group embedded in a large government agency. Seeking to have a positive impact on analytic approaches in the agency, a few of the computer scientists decided to redesign a search engine that analysts commonly used with the agency's largest database. The researchers selected the project after hearing analysts complain about the non-intuitive nature of the current search engine. They elicited suggestions from experienced personnel to ensure that the new search engine would provide smoother navigation experience than the existing one. When the prototype was ready, the team invited analysts to test it and provide feedback. The testers praised the simplicity and learnability of the interface and the efficiency with which they could review records in the database.

Surprisingly, however, the new search engine was not widely adopted; in fact, only a handful of analysts expressed interest in getting the interface installed on their desktop machines. In discussing this mystery with the research and development team and with some of the agency's analysts, it became apparent that the older, clunkier search engine had considerable inertia in the work environment. For one thing, it was well-integrated into the suite of commercial tools that most analysts were already using. Not only would switching to the new search engine require additional steps to export and import data, but searching the database was only one of many tasks analysts did in a day, and time spent retrieving information was relatively low compared to other work tasks. In addition, because of cyber security concerns, the agency's software acquisition policies required extensive review of new code, even when developed internally. Lastly, as one analyst explained, she had "grown up" using the older search engine and felt comfortable with it. She believed her peers felt similarly; after all, it did not appear that using the existing search engine was hurting her group's overall performance. Such factors made it difficult for the research group's innovation to gain the momentum necessary for successful adoption.

The search engine project described in the preceding vignette would probably have benefitted from more structured and careful elicitation, documentation, and

management of basic technology and user requirements. The field of software engineering provides extensive guidance in this regard, including user-oriented design approaches that emphasize the importance of user priorities, tasks, and workflows in the development of new tools (e.g., [25,29]). Yet the intersection of "national security" and "biologically-inspired security informatics" introduces challenges to usability, utility, and adoptability that may not be adequately addressed by standard software engineering paradigms, even those that emphasize active user participation in the design, development, and testing of new technologies. Computer scientist Jean Scholtz has written that developing applications that take advantage of innovative computational science, such as the biologically-inspired research described in this issue, challenge mainstream software development paradigms [30]. These challenges are due to the organizational complexity and cognitive demands of national security analysis; cultural differences between researchers and national security analysts; and the interdisciplinary character of computational modeling and simulation itself. Each is briefly reviewed below.

First, the national security community is diverse, with workplaces that include trailers on forward operating bases in Afghanistan or (until recently) Iraq; buzzing cubicle farms in federal office buildings in Maryland or Virginia, and secure facilities located in bland industrial parks or university campuses around the country. Even analysts working on similar problems within the same agency may have very different customer sets, geographical focus areas, timelines, tools and technologies, and data sources. To make matters more complicated, multiple analytic groups in different agencies can be working on similar issues with quite different methodologies. Simply identifying the appropriate user community for a new software tool, analytic method or technique is a non-trivial problem, even for people within the national security community.

Related to this is the fact that informatics research and development tends to occur in industrial and/or academic domains that are organizationally, physically, and culturally distinct from the bureaucratic domains of the national security community. It is helpful to think of each domain as a distinct epistemic culture. These are cross-institutional communities whose members are engaged in shared activities, discussions, objectives, techniques, technologies, and practices, all of which have emerged over time as people pursue collectively-valued forms of knowledge [31].

The epistemic culture of computational social science tends to be grounded in academic, private nonprofit, and/or industrial research settings. It is intensely interdisciplinary, and emphasizes computational modeling and simulation as an empirical approach to the study of social phenomena for which data can be difficult to acquire. In contrast, national security analysis and decision-making is located squarely in the realm of government and deals with real-world, high-consequence outcomes on a daily basis. National security analysts, civilian and military, are responsible for identifying, assessing, and ensuring that the United States can interdict potential tactical and strategic threats. Analysts identify important issues and respond to difficult questions, piecing together information sources that may be incomplete, uncertain, ambiguous, evolving, even conflicting or deceptive. Analytic assessments are routinely promulgated throughout the intelligence community, shared across multiple government agencies, and may find their way into policy discussions at very high levels of government, where they may be cited to support significantly risky courses of action. As most analysts can attest, errors in judgment or communication can disastrous for national security, which is one of the most politically charged and least forgiving areas of American public life. Rarely, if ever, do computer science researchers face the possibility of being held responsible for decision outcomes that may be literally existential.

Given explosive growth in information, analytical techniques, and computing power over the past two decades, it is not surprising that both the research and the policy- and decision-making communities are seeking practical benefit from computationally-driven analytical techniques. At the same time, the potential stakeholders may find biologically-inspired informatics opaque, particularly when projects leverage cross-disciplinary methods and frameworks in conceptually innovative and risky ways. Because of this gulf, "...it is frequently the case that policy-makers dismiss academic research as too theoretical, unrelated to the actual problems they are wrestling with, or in other ways irrelevant to their concerns" [32].

Last, the interdisciplinary novelty of biologically-inspired computational social modeling and simulation is itself problematic, because the rapid evolution and heterogeneity of these projects can make it difficult for non-practitioners to judge the quality of a model and/or its simulation outputs [33,34]. Anyone who has tried to rid their kitchen of sugar ants can appreciate the communicative talents and collective resilience of the ant colony. However, the assumptions and constraints associated with ant colony-inspired mathematical models of social networks or power markets are probably not intuitive to all-source intelligence analysts who lack familiarity with the mathematical formalisms of ant colony-inspired algorithms [35,36]. The ability to develop a good sense of how one's tools interact with data and information is a major factor that influences adoptability: national security work products can have significant existential consequences, and trust in one's work processes is perhaps the most important metric that attends technology design activities in this space.

Wanted: a new development model

Philip Huxtable and others who are familiar with efforts to bring modeling and simulation into national security analysis have emphasized the importance of breaking down organizational barriers between researchers and government analysts, so that analysts can develop "an understanding of [the tool's] strengths and weaknesses and thus develop confidence in using it for tasks on which significant decisions (and their professional reputations) will be based" [1,23,33,34]. Yet within the national security community, most modeling, simulation, and other informatics projects follow an "over the fence" development model: researchers develop and demonstrate working systems in a research setting; the resulting systems are then thrown "over the fence" to the users who are presumably waiting to receive them. Even when informatics projects have explicitly identified an impact area or use context, much of the research tends to occur at a distance from the analytic workplace. Even national security R&D programs that are organizationally proximate to analytic workplaces are not necessarily integrated with the analytic and/or decision-making processes they seek to affect. This is not a new problem: As Huxtable laments, "Everyone in the community knows [the over the fence] approach doesn't work, yet the vast majority of analytic capability projects are executed this way, and most are unlikely to transition in any way that makes use of their apparent potential" [1].

For the national security community to realize return on its informatics investments, proponents of such methodologies must pay far greater attention to the characteristics of end-user communities. In this regard, social science theory and method can provide valuable frameworks and techniques for identifying key aspects of the organizational, political, and social contexts of national security and relating these to tool development. In the following pages, I suggest that information ecology can help proponents of biosecurity innovations appreciate the complex challenges associated with technology adoption in the national security community. Activity theory provides a complementary set of techniques and methods for eliciting the key aspects of work environments that bear on the usability, utility, and adoptability of new tools. Developing richer relationships with user communities inside the national security environment opens the door to effective collaboration, such as participatory modeling, a development approach specifically aimed at cultivating informed and committed stakeholders for modeling and simulation technologies.

Moving beyond "the user:" information ecologies

Over the past fifty years, the fields of human factors and human-computer interaction have established a set of well-recognized principles for designing technologies that fit the physiological and cognitive requirements of human users. However, the rapid evolution of personal computing, the Internet, and the explosion of collaborative technologies and social media has expanded technology design paradigms, so that it is no longer enough to consider the Everyman User in design. Instead, design thinking now emphasizes humans as actors engaged in the act of sense making: the assembly of meaningful narratives that explain what is happening, so that actors can respond appropriately. Technology must be designed to enable and empower people to engage, assess and act upon the social, political, and cultural contexts in which they are embedded.

One provocative example of this contextual, more humanistic trend in design thinking is Bonnie Nardi and Vicki O'Day's discussion of information ecologies [3]. Nardi and O'Day's biological metaphor makes this framework particularly appropriate for this special issue of Security Informatics. More importantly, however, the metaphorical casting of an office workplace as a living ecology helps break down taken-for-granted assumptions about what makes a technology "better" than its predecessors.

The ecologies that interest Nardi and O'Day are human settings where people collectively pursue the creation, maintenance, exchange, and retrieval of information. Libraries, school classrooms, the cubicle farms of an intelligence agency: these are not just workplaces, but living systems that engage human actors in meaningful activity. Importantly, unlike biological ecologies, information ecologies are socially purposive: inhabitants engage in goal-directed behavior toward the accomplishment of a broader, socially-sanctioned outcome - for example, the monitoring and interdiction of sub-state criminal networks that are involved in human trafficking. Because information ecologies are living and dynamic sets of "...people, practices, values and technologies in a particular local environment," write Nardi and O'Day, design work must begin with an understanding of the "...human activities that are served by technology" ([3]; emphasis added). They describe how different elements of an ecology - tools, specific methods, even humans who occupy specific roles - become established as niches that provide specific functions in support of human activity. As Nardi and O'Day explain, the most important niches are occupied by keystone species whose removal fundamentally change the nature of the ecosystem, even threaten its survival.

Consider the search engine vignette in relation to Nardi and O'Day's ecologies. The story illustrates the difficulty of changing a single element in a system without accounting for the full range of activities in which that element is embedded. Perhaps the search engine occupied a critical niche: i.e., human users had over time connected it with other elements of the system to support myriad functions, such as communication among analysts and information traceability. Even though the developers had visibly improved the search engine's primary function - retrieving information from a database - the existing system was deeply embedded in other processes and functions. Technologies that span multiple users, such search engines or email services, often play a keystone role in information ecologies. As Nardi and O'Day point out, removal of a keystone species can jeopardize the very survival of an ecology; for example, many forms of analytic work might grind to a halt if the search engine disappeared. Not surprisingly, people tend to react strongly (and often negatively) to abrupt changes in keystone species, because so many of their activities depend on the functions such species afford.

Yet innovation in system elements, even in keystone species, is important if an information ecology is to adapt and grow. Just as natural ecologies survive by adapting to the pressures of an evolving environment, so are information ecologies engaged in ongoing and dynamic process of evolution, as people perceive and respond to emerging trends and pressures. The fact of evolution should be inspiring to new technology developers, because it means that opportunities for innovation are always present in an information ecology. Indeed, information ecologies thrive on diversity in people, tools, roles, tasks, activities, technologies, and resources, because diversity lends resilience when external pressures or the failure of some internal element put stress on the ecology's systems [3].

Imaginatively recasting national security software users as species in a complex information ecology should give proponents of biologically-inspired informatics technologies pause and optimism. It is naïve, and probably counterproductive, to assume that "better" informatics technologies will be embraced by national security decision-makers purely because these technologies embody some type of scientific, mathematical, or computational superiority. However, because the national security workplace is a living ecology, there are always opportunities for cultivating and establishing viable niches for new sense making activities, with their accompanying technologies and expertise. The challenge is decomposing the ecology in question to identify the most viable niches for an envisioned innovation.

Ecologies and activities

Nardi and O'Day's metaphorical mapping between biological ecologies and office workplaces helps us re-think our assumptions about human-tool relationships. However, its practical applications may not be immediately apparent. At this point, it is appropriate to introduce a related framework for studying human-technology interaction known as activity theory. Information ecology and activity theory are complementary, which is not coincidental; Bonnie Nardi is one of the United States' foremost proponents of activity theory-based approaches to technology design and development [37]. Like information ecology, activity theory emphasizes the embeddedness of individual human activity in broader systems of social relationships. However, activity theory's framework has very clear methodological implications for eliciting contextual factors related to the design and development of usable, useful, and adoptable software.

Activity theory is derived from the work of Soviet developmental psychology, which emphasized the importance of cultural and contextual factors in shaping human cognitive development and consciousness. In the 1980s, Scandinavian, British, and later American researchers adopted the principles of activity theory as an alternative approach to the individualist paradigms that dominated Western research on human communication, reasoning, work and learning [37-39]. Today, activity theory is widely seen as an important "post-cognitivist" and "post-technologist" approach to human-computer interaction and system engineering because it provides accessible and highly practical guidance for mapping what people are doing, what they are using and creating as they do it, and how social,

organizational, and cultural factors make their activity meaningful [25,37,39].

Figure 1 illustrates activity theory's main conceptual relationships. As the name suggests, activity theory begins with the activity, or purposeful, goal-directed human action, as the unit of analysis. Activities comprise human actors who put various resources or instruments to use toward achievement of an object. At this very basic level, activity theory resembles established theories of human-computer interaction, such as Card and Moran's GOMS [39,40]. However, activity theory goes beyond the immediacy of micro-interactions between individuals and technologies to examine the relationship between individuals and social collectives.

Of particular importance in this regard is the concept of outcome, which indicates the broader set of values and purpose that lend meaning to human action. Outcomes explain why an individual's work matters to a larger set of human actors and individuals. In activity theory, that larger set is captured in concept of a community, which refers to objectively defined social location in which an actor is embedded (e.g., an intelligence analyst in a three-letter agency), as well as the actor's subjective sense of membership and responsibility vis-à-vis other actors (e.g., a young analyst is part of a group of novices being mentored by a particular expert). Roles and rules provide structure and regularity to communities. They comprise a mix of formal and informal elements that not only give individuals a sense of social location vis-à-vis other members; but which also support the achievement of organizational purpose by formalizing

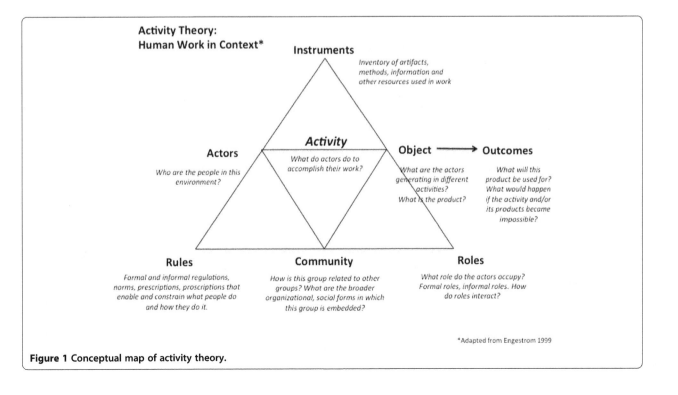

Figure 1 Conceptual map of activity theory.

the distribution of responsibilities, resources, power, and labor across a community.

Over the past decade, activity theory has become an increasingly popular framework because the approach generates rich descriptive data that helps designers identify relationships that bear on the introduction of new technologies. Although a full description of activity theory's methods is beyond the scope of this article, some of the questions that that emerge from activity theoretic approach are depicted in Figure 1. These questions can be used to identify and categorize key elements in a work environment. For example, a hypothetical activity might consist of an intelligence analyst (the actor, occupying a particular role) who uses a search engine (a computer software/hardware instrument) to identify high-quality satellite imagery covering a particular geographical region during a given time period (identifying imagery is object of the search activity; imagery is also an instrument). Once the imagery is retrieved, the analyst will conduct a systematic search of the imagery (the imagery, the displays, the software, and even the analyst's search methods are instruments) to identify indicators of illicit activity (the object of the search). The analyst will assemble a report (the object of the search and analysis activities), which she will mark with appropriate distribution restrictions (marking requirements are rules) so that she can distribute the report to law enforcement (which she identifies as part of the national security community) to support an investigation into maritime criminal activity (the outcome).

Activity theoretic studies are typically iterative, because digging into one area of the framework is likely to raise questions or reveal information about other areas. For example, as people identify instruments and resources, they will probably describe how they use particular resources in performing various tasks, which leads to identifying activities, their objects, and the intended outcomes. Indeed, when trying to build familiarity with a new user community, it is often easiest to begin at the apex of the triangle and conduct an inventory of the instruments that people use in their work. This is because physical resources are relatively easy to identify and can include computers, software, books, maps, communication devices, and displays; as well as key places - offices, conference rooms, cubicles.

Activity theory is not the only way to approach studies of work, but it does provide an efficient way to bootstrap one's knowledge of a work context. It also helps designers identify specific work activities that deserve more intensive study, as through cognitive task analysis [41,42]. Most importantly, however, activity theory helps technology developers build relationships with the people whose work they seek to impact: as Kuutti points out, activity theory "...aims at reconstructing contexts in practice so that people are not just objects or subordinate parts, but regain their role as creators" [43]. In

this sense, activity theory is complementary with another paradigm that may be useful to proponents of biologically-informed informatics: namely, participatory modeling.

Cultivating a niche: participatory modeling

Participatory modeling is a methodology that leverages the principles of user-oriented design to ensure that computational applications, including modeling, simulation, and informatics technologies, are comprehensible to stakeholders in a decision space. Participatory approaches use the development of analytic technologies, such as models, to integrate multiple goals and perspectives across stakeholder communities. Participatory approaches developed in the context of natural resource decision-making, where stakeholders often have diverse and conflicting goals for management of shared resources. Successful management of shared resources requires that stakeholders comprehend and trust the decision-making process, including data, information, and analysis. The participatory modeling philosophy is expressed in a number of methodological frameworks that vary according to the mechanisms and degree of stakeholder participation: Barreteau has noted, participatory modeling and simulation paradigms are quite diverse in the details of their implementation [44,45]. However, all seek to build comprehensibility and trust by incorporating stakeholders as active participants in the modeling process: negotiating a shared conceptual framework, identifying data and information, examining and mitigating sources of bias, establishing appropriate contexts of use, and setting goals for verification and validation of the model's software and products.

This emphasis on trust, transparency, and the creation of comprehensible analytic processes and tools maps well to the challenges that informatics proponents face when engaging the national security community. As previously discussed, analysts are often reluctant to adopt computational technologies that they do not understand; it makes sense that incorporating end-users in development process is might generate the contextual knowledge required to make sense of a modeling approach. If nothing else, coupling participatory modeling approaches with the activity theoretic approach described above can help technology developers appreciate the goals, constraints, outcomes, and impacts associated with national security analysis and decision-making. However, participatory modeling is also consonant with the political philosophy of activity theory, which explicitly calls for users to have an ownership role in the design and development of technologies that will impact their work and lives. In addition, activity theoretic investigations of national security workplaces engage users in the derivation of design principles careful study of a use environment. The resulting relationships can be leveraged toward participatory development of next-generation informatics technologies. In doing so, developers can mitigate lack-of-knowledge issues that might otherwise prevent end-users from, for example, appreciating the benefits and limitations and associated with using bee colony metaphors to understand political memes.

Review and conclusion

This paper has provided a cursory overview of three related theoretical frameworks - information ecologies, activity theory, and participatory modeling - for approaching design challenges associated with informatics for national security decision-making. Mainstream software engineering is a starting point for rethinking how we introduce new analytic approaches into the national security workplace. For example, professional associations have identified standards associated with basic usability, while the software engineering literature provides a variety of methods for eliciting user requirements. However, while an elegant user interface and well-written documentation can enhance a tool's usability, utility, and adoptability, the cognitive and epistemological complexity of interdisciplinary informatics requires additional investment in building relationships between researchers and intended user communities.

Humanistic, holistic frameworks like information ecology, activity theory, and participatory modeling emphasize that qualities like usability, utility, and adoptability are more than "interface deep." Successful transition of new informatics technologies will require the entire community - funders, users, researchers - to evolve models of success beyond software- and model-oriented measures, such as algorithmic elegance or the quality of software implementation. Instead, when people adopt an innovation, they are making a conscious (if subtle) decision to change how they engage with some area of their lives, work, and perhaps even their relationships with a community of peers. Not only can new tools change how individuals solve problems, but the adoption of new technologies can stimulate far-reaching changes in community identity and culture, challenging established norms for "who we are" and "how we do things here" [46].

In this regard, proponents of analytic innovations, including biologically-inspired informatics, must ask themselves if methodological improvements in national security analysis will be driven by technological innovation. From the perspective of ecology and activity theory, this assumption is tremendously naïve because it neglects the agency of human analysts as users who decide how they will perform their work. These theories suggest that novel computational science approaches can only be successful if everyone - funders, researchers, and analysts - actively seek ways to bridge the organizational, cultural, and epistemological divides that separate "researchers" from "analysts."

In this regard, proponents of national security informatics should look for ways to incorporate analysts and researchers together into the development of new technologies. For example, a specialist analysis cell might be asked to design its own call for proposals in conjunction with a funding agency. The deal would require a commitment from the analyst cell and a research team to work side-by-side for a period of time. Not only would the researchers begin to understand the analysts' activities, resources, goals, outcomes, and constituents; but the analysts would have the opportunity to become familiar with researchers' techniques and theories, so that approaches like the biologically-inspired ones described in this issue become less exotic and more comfortable. Frameworks such as activity theory can help guide these relationships; questions derived from its elements can help technology designers and analysts jointly identify critical elements and relationships in a workplace. This structured relationship building can establish foundational trust relationships, adding momentum to the participatory development of a new informatics technology.

If modeling and simulation technologies are to bring the revolutionary analytical changes that they promise, modelers and analysts alike must be encouraged to recast themselves as co-owners of new technologies. In particular, researchers who want their technologies to have real-world impacts must become familiar with, even become participating members of, the very security ecologies they seek to influence. Just as biologically-inspired informatics are an interdisciplinary creation, so too must their application bring disparate communities into collaborative relationships. Paying attention to context is critical to establish a viable niche for informatics, modeling, and simulation as methodological species that add diversity and strength to the constantly evolving ecology of national security.

Endnotes

[a]A reviewer of an earlier draft pointed out that usability, utility, and adoptability are not the only problems associated with using new computational science approaches in national security. In fact, they might not even be the most important ones: Empirical evaluation using high-quality datasets is rarely performed; and standards for verification, validation, and accreditation technologies are largely undefined. While the paucity of validation quality data and robust verification, validation, and accreditation approaches are indeed problematic, that topic is beyond the scope of this paper.

Competing interests
The author declare that he have no competing interests.

Acknowledgements
The author wishes to thank Jennifer Perry of the Defense Threat Reduction Agency's Advanced Systems and Concepts Office for her insight and support of work related to this paper. In addition, Timothy Trucano, Rich Colbaugh, Kristen Glass, and numerous intelligence analysts in several federal

workplaces have contributed to the author's thinking on the topics discussed in this paper. Any errors or omissions are solely the responsibility of the author.

Sandia National Laboratories is a multi-program laboratory managed and operated by Sandia Corporation, a wholly owned subsidiary of Lockheed Martin Corporation, for the U.S. Department of Energy's National Nuclear Security Administration under contract DE-AC04-94AL85000.

References

1. P. Huxtable, Leveraging Computational Social Science for National Security, in *Challenges in Computational Social Modeling and Simulation for National Security Decision Making*, ed. by L. McNamara, T. Trucano, C. Gieseler (Defense Threat Reduction Agency, Advanced Systems and Concepts Office, Ft. Belvoir, VA, 2011), pp. 157–168

2. L.M. Murphy, P.L. Edwards, *"Bridging the Valley of Death: Transitioning from Public Sector to Private Sector Funding,"* National Renewable Energy Laboratory (NREL) (Golden, Colorado, 2003)

3. B. Nardi, V.L. O'Day, *Information Ecologies: Using Technology with Heart* (MIT Press, Boston, 1996)

4. National Intelligence Council, *Iran: Nuclear Intentions and Capabilities* (Office of the Director of National Intelligence, Washington, DC, 2007)

5. National Commission on Terrorist Attacks Against the United States, *The 9/11 Commission Report* (United States Government Printing Office, Washington, DC, 2004)

6. L. Resnyansky, The internet and the changing nature of intelligence. IEEE Technol. Soc. Mag. **28**, 41–48 (2009). Spring 2009

7. D.C. Andrus, *The Wiki and the Blog: Toward A Complex Adaptive Intelligence Community* (Central Intelligence Agency, Washington, DC, 2005). June 15

8. *Palantir Technologies*. Available: http://www.palantirtech.com/

9. *Analyst's Notebook*. Available: http://www.coplink.com/us/products–services/analysis-product-line/analysts-notebook

10. P. Galison, *Image and Logic: A Material Culture of Microphysics* (University of Chicago, Chicago, 1997)

11. D. Byrne, Simulation - a way forward. Sociol. Res. Online **2** (1997). http://www.socresonline.org.uk/socresonline/2/2/4.html

12. C. Cioffi-Revilla, S. O'Brien, *"Computational Analysis in US Foreign and Defense Policy,"* presented at the First International Conference on Computational Cultural Dynamics (College Park, MD, 2007)

13. Committee on Behavioral and Social Science Research to Improve Intelligence Analysis for National Security, *Intelligence Analysis for Tomorrow: Advances from the Behavioral and Social Sciences* (National Research Council, National Academy of Sciences, Washington, DC, 2011)

14. S. Magnuson, Military swimming in sensors and drowning in data. Nat. Def. (2010). http://www.nationaldefensemagazine.org/archive/2010/January/Pages/Military%E2%80%98SwimminglnSensorsandDrowninginData%E2%80%99.aspx, 2010

15. R.L. Popp, D. Allen, C. Cioffi-Revilla, Utilizing Information and Social Science Technology to Understand and Counter the Twenty-First Century Strategic Threat, in *Emergent Information Technologies and Enabling Policies for Counter-Terrorism*, ed. by R.L. Popp, J. Yen (IEEE/John Wiley and Sons, Hoboken, NJ, 2006)

16. Human Social Behavior Culture Modeling Program, HSCB Phase One and Two Summary, in *Human Social Culture Behavior Modeling Program Newsletter Winter 2010*, ed. by D. Schmorrow, vol. 3rd edn. (Strategic Analysis, Inc./Deputy Undersecretary of Defense for Science and Technology, Arlington, VA, 2010)

17. Human Social Behavior Culture Modeling Program, DoD-Wide Programs, in *Human Social Behavior Culture Modeling Program Newsletter, Spring 2010*, ed. by D. Schmorrow (Strategic Analysis, Inc./Deputy Undersecretary of Defense for Science and Technology, Arlington, VA, 2010), p. 8

18. H. Liu, J.J. Salerno, M. Young, *Social Computing, Behavioral Modeling and Prediction* (Springer, New York, 2008)

19. S.K. Chai, J.J. Salerno, P. Mabry, *Lecture Notes in Computer Science: Advances in Social Computing*, vol. 2010: 6007th edn. (Springer, New York, 2010)

20. R. Goolsby, Ethics and defense agency funding: some considerations. Soc. Netw. **27**, 95–106 (2005)

21. R. Goolsby, Combating terrorist networks: an evolutionary approach. Comput. Math. Org. Theory **12**, 7–20 (2006)

22. J. Scholtz, E. Morse, T. Hewett, *"In Depth Observational Studies of Professional Intelligence Analysts 2005,"* presented at the International Conference on Intelligence Analysis (MacLean, VA, 2006)

23. J. Scholtz, E. Morse, M.P. Steves, Evaluation metrics and methodologies for user-centered evaluation of intelligent systems. Interact. Comput. **18**, 1186–1214 (2006)

24. J. Nielsen, Guerrilla HCI: Using Discount Usability Engineering to Penetrate the Intimidation Barrier, in *Cost-Justifying Usability*, ed. by R.G. Bias, D.J. Mayhew (Academic, Boston, MA, 1994), pp. 245–272. available at http://www.useit.com/jakob/publications.html

25. J. Nielsen, Usability Engineering, in *The Computer Science and Engineering Handbook*, ed. by A.B. Tucker (Chapman and Hall/CRC Press, Boca Raton, FL, 2004), pp. 1139–1160

26. C.W. Turner, J.R. Lewis, J. Nielsen, Determining usability test sample size. Int. Encycl. Ergon. Hum. Factors **3**, 3084–3088 (2006)

27. B. Nardi, Activity Theory and Human-Computer Interaction, in *Context and Consciousness: Activity Theory and Human-Computer Interaction*, ed. by B. Nardi (MIT Press, Cambridge, MA, 1996)

28. E. Rogers, *Diffusion of Innovations*, 5th edn. (Free Press, New York, 2003)

29. K. Vredenburg, J.Y. Mao, P.W. Smith, T. Carey, *"A Survey of User-Centered Design Practice,"* presented at the CHI '02: Proceedings of the SIGCHI Conference on Human Factors in Computing Systems: Changing our World (Changing Ourselves, Minneapolis, MN, 2002)

30. J. Scholtz, A User-Centered Approach to Social Modeling and Simulation for Decision Making, in *Challenges in Computational Social Modeling and Simulation for National Security Decision Making*, ed. by L. McNamara, T. Trucano, C. Gieseler (Defense Threat Reduction Agency, Advanced Systems and Concepts Office, Ft. Belvoir, VA, 2011), pp. 227–240

31. K. Knorr-Cetina, *Epstemic Cultures: How the Sciences Make Knowledge* (Harvard University Press, Cambridge, MA, 1999)

32. N. Gilbert, Modellers claim wars are predictable. Nature **462**, 836 (2009)

33. L. Resnyansky, Social modeling as an interdisciplinary research practice. IEEE Intell. Syst. **23**, 20–27 (2008). July/August 2008

34. J.G. Turnley, Assessing the Goodness of Computational Social Models, in *Challenges in Computational Social Modeling and Simulation for National Security Decision Making*, ed. by L. McNamara, T. Trucano, C. Gieseler (Defense Threat Reduction Agency, Advanced Systems and Concepts Office, Ft. Belvoir, VA, 2011), pp. 241–254

35. M. Al-Fayoumi, S. Banerjee, P.K. Mananti, Analysis of social network using clever ant colony metaphor. World Acad. Sci. Eng. Technol. **53**, 970–974 (2009)

36. S. Li, L. Gao, G. Xu, *"The Best Bidding Price Based on Ant Colony Algorithms in Electric Power Markets,"* presented at the Sustainable Power Generation and Supply (Nanjing, China, 2009)

37. B. Nardi, Studying Context: A Comparison of Activity Theory, Situated Action Models, and Distributed Cognition, in *Context and Consciousness: Activity Theory and Human-Computer Interaction*, ed. by B.A. Nardi (MIT Press, Cambridge, MA, 1995), pp. 70–102

38. Y. Engeström, *Developmental Studies of Work as a Testbench of Activity Theory: The Case of Primary Care Medical Practice* (Cambridge University Press, New York, 1996)

39. Y. Engeström, Activity Theory and Individual and Social Transformation, in *Perspectives on Activity Theory*, ed. by Y. Engeström, R. Miettinen, R.L. Punamäki (Cambridge University Press, New York, 1999), pp. 19–38

40. S.K. Card, T.P. Moran, A. Newell, *The Psychology of Human-Computer Interaction* (Lawrence Erbaum Associates, Hillsdale, NJ, 1983)

41. B. Crandall, G. Klein, R.R. Hoffman, *Working Minds: A Practitioner's Guide to Cognitive Task Analysis* (MIT Press, Cambridge, MA, 2006)

42. R.R. Hoffman, L.G. Militello, *Perspectives on Cognitive Task Analysis: Historical Origins and Modern Community of Practice* (Psychology Press (Taylor and Francis), New York, 2009)

43. K. Kuutti, Activity Theory, Transformation of Work, and Information Systems Design, in *Perspectives on Activity Theory*, ed. by Y. Engeström, R. Miettinen, R.L. Punamäki (Cambridge University Press, New York, 1999), pp. 360–376

44. O. Barreteau, Our companion modelling approach. J. Artif. Soc. Soc. Simul. **6**, 1 (2003)

45. W. Dare, O. Barreteau, A role playing game in irrigated system negotiation: between playing and reality. J. Artif. Soc. Soc. Simul. **6** (2003). http://jasss. soc.surrey.ac.uk/6/3/6.html

46. P.E. Becker, *Congregations in Conflict: Cultural Models of Local Religious Life* (Cambridge, New York, 1999)

10

Evaluating text visualization for authorship analysis

Victor Benjamin[1*], Wingyan Chung[2], Ahmed Abbasi[3], Joshua Chuang[4], Catherine A Larson[1] and Hsinchun Chen[1]

Abstract

Methods and tools to conduct authorship analysis of web contents is of growing interest to researchers and practitioners in various security-focused disciplines, including cybersecurity, counter-terrorism, and other fields in which authorship of text may at times be uncertain or obfuscated. Here we demonstrate an automated approach for authorship analysis of web contents. Analysis is conducted through the use of machine learning methodologies, an expansive stylometric feature set, and a series of visualizations intended to help facilitate authorship analysis at the author, message, and feature levels. To operationalize this, we utilize a testbed containing 506,554 forum messages in English and Arabic, source from 14,901 authors that participated in an online web forum. A prototype portal system providing authorship comparisons and visualizations was then designed and constructed in order to support feasibility analysis and real world value of the automated authorship analysis approach. A preliminary user evaluation was performed to assess the efficacy of visualizations, with evaluation results demonstrating task performance accuracy and efficiency was improved through use of the portal.

Keywords: Terrorism; Text visualization; Online forum; Authorship analysis; Cybercrime

Introduction

Authorship analysis is useful in any application context where authorship attribution is uncertain, unknown, or otherwise obfuscated. Such occurrences often arise in disciplines such as history and criminology. Traditionally, authorship analysis has been performed through manual analysis. However, manual analysis has become increasingly difficult with growing usage of electronic text (e.g. e-mail, websites) and social media (e.g. forums, blogs). Problems with manual analysis arise when processing large volumes of text content or adapting traditional stylometric analysis (e.g. handwriting style) to electronic text. As a result, researchers have become interested in developing techniques to conduct automated authorship analysis on electronic text across various languages. By borrowing perspectives and techniques from computational linguistics, many traditional features used to evaluate authorship have been operationalized for use with electronic texts.

In particular, there is great interest in developing authorship visualization tools to support greater user accountability in online communities and social media. The anonymity provided by the Internet makes it an attractive platform for those wishing to conduct various forms of crime, including drug trafficking, piracy, cybercrime, and terrorism [1–3]. Additionally, there are several trust issues with online deception between individuals and organizations that could be mitigated with better authentication services; visualization tools could help deter abuse of the anonymity the Internet provides.

However, there are several basic hurdles researchers and practitioners must overcome to perform automated authorship analysis. First, a corpus or data must be contained for analysis to be performed. If attempting to conduct analysis on social media data, data must be collected through the usage of an API or by using an automated crawler. Second, stylometric features must be extracted from the text to conduct analysis. Features must be systematically chosen, often times by borrowing from previous research and also through rigorous feature selection. Techniques borrowed from linguistics are often utilized during feature extraction. Next, there is a need for a systematic mechanism to analyze and compare the writing styles of different authors. Different computational techniques rooted in machine learning

* Correspondence: vabenji@email.arizona.edu
[1]MIS Department, University of Arizona, Tucson, AZ, USA
Full list of author information is available at the end of the article

can be utilized. Finally, results must also be transformed into informative visualizations.

Due to the growing need for automated authorship analysis and visualization tools, the Arizona Authorship Analysis Portal (AzAA) was conceived as a platform on which analyses could be developed and assessed. The portal integrates machine learning methods, a robust stylometric feature set, and a series of visualizations designed to facilitate analysis at the feature, author, and message levels. It allows identification of "extreme" jihadi authors, and also supports analysis and comparison of author writing styles. Additionally, for the purpose of providing a testbed for analyses to be run against, the system contains two datasets from an Arabic and English forum identified to contain extremist content.

In this paper, we present the AzAA portal and discuss its relevance and effectiveness in the space of automated authorship analysis. To do this, we first describe the task of authorship analysis and cover previous related works. We then move on to more deeply discuss previous works that contributed directly to the AzAA portal's development. Next we provide an overview of the AzAA system and describe the many components necessary for the system to work. We demonstrate various case studies on how the system is of use, and present results of a preliminary user evaluation of the portal's text visualization function. We conclude with an outline of our next steps and future development.

Related work

To implement a system such as the AzAA portal, a review of important, recent works in relevant disciplines is necessary. First, an understanding of authorship analysis and its purpose must be established to provide trajectory in the design and implementation of the AzAA portal. Next, perspectives and methodology from previous research in text analysis provide direction for developing and operationalizing features for authorship analysis of electronic text. Visualizations can provide richer understanding during authorship analysis, and thus we briefly discuss previous practices in text visualization domain. Lastly, to build a corpus for the AzAA portal, computational approaches based on previous works are utilized to collect, transform, and store data from Arabic and English forums.

Authorship analysis

Authorship analysis is useful when authorship attribution is uncertain, unknown, or otherwise obfuscated. The goal of any such analysis is usually one of three purposes: authorship identification, authorship characterization, and authorship similarity detection. Authorship identification compares a particular author's known writings to a particular unattributed or mis-attributed document in order to determine the level of possibility that he or she is the author. Traditionally, authorship analysis has been applied to domains such as history, the humanities, criminology, etc. Based on stylometric analysis, or the statistical analysis of writing style, authorship analysis has grown increasingly important to those wishing to examine the virtual space. As more individuals access the Internet and participate in social media, the volume of misconduct and abuse of cyber infrastructure becomes more frequent.

Previous researchers have experimented with authorship analysis techniques in some virtual contexts such as e-mail and web forums [4–7]. For example, Li et al. [6] explored and tested key features important to identifying authorship of online texts; Argamon et al. [8] developed methodology to construct various "profiles" of an author's characteristics (such as age, gender, personality) and analyzed which features were most effective for profiling each characteristic type. Similarly, Abbasi and Chen [9] focused on stylistic features for an authorship similarity detection experiment; they conducted a study where authors' identities were not known ahead of time, but writing samples of each author could be compared for similarity/dissimilarity to one another.

However, web content often poses difficulties for authorship analysis as compared to traditional forms of writing. The most often cited challenge of authorship experiments with web content is the shorter length of online messages, which tend to average no more than a couple of hundred words [7]. Additionally, online messages tend to vary greatly in length, adding yet another challenge to balanced analysis. The ability to automatically perform authorship analysis on web contents, despite challenges identified in research, is of great asset to both researchers and practitioners. A review of recent improvements to authorship analysis on web contents reveals that improvements have been largely grounded in the development and use of writing style markers (features) of electronic text, and also in machine learning classification techniques adopted for authorship identification and similarity comparisons.

Stylometric & text analysis

The two most important analytical techniques for authorship analysis of web contents are stylometric analysis and text analysis based on machine learning approaches; both are grounded in statistics. Stylometric analysis refers to utilizing domain-specific features (i.e. characteristics) in statistical analyses to compare and distinguish one text document from another. Statistical techniques have the benefit of providing greater explanatory potential which can be useful for evaluating trends and variances over larger amounts of text; in particular, various multivariate statistical approaches have been tested and shown to provide a high level of accuracy [10,11]. Similarly, recent years have seen the usage of statistical machine learning-based text analysis techniques grow in authorship analysis studies [4,5,7,12]. Such techniques provide scalability and performance helpful when conducting analyses on web forum messages.

Stylometric features, or writing style features, are characteristics that help in comparing and distinguishing between two documents or bodies of text. Depending on the domain that authorship analysis is applied to, features are categorized in different ways. In the context of web content, text style features, HTML features, and content-specific features are often used [9,13,14]. Text style features generally include structural features, syntactic features, and lexical features. Structural features generally include features that describe the overall organization of a document or text. When referring to web content, structural features include the usage of HTML-encoded text, which includes the ability to format text with word bolding, italics, font coloring, font size, etc. [15]. Syntactic features refer to the sentence-level of a document, including patterns used for formulating sentences. This category often includes features such as punctuation usage, function and stop word usage, etc. Syntactic features have been found to be quite useful in many different studies analyzing web content [3,4]. Lastly, lexical features are associated with word-level characteristics such as word frequency, vocabulary richness, frequency, word length distribution, etc. [13]. Lexical features are particularly important as they help establish content-specific differences among authors when conducting authorship analysis. Keywords relevant to different topics can be mapped to different authors when conducting analysis utilizing lexical features.

Computational analyses of text have grown in popularity with the increase of computational power available to researchers and practitioners. Techniques such as support vector machines, neural networks, genetic algorithms, and decision trees are all useful for text analysis tasks across [4,12,14,16]. The wider acceptance of such techniques has enabled authorship analysis to adapt to electronic text and web contents. Machine learning provides great scalability in terms of the number of features used for analysis, as well as the number of documents analyzed. These benefits over other methods greatly improves the authorship analysis task when applied to web contents, as online messages are often abundant in volume, involve classification of many authors, and provide large feature sets to utilize for analysis.

Two particular types of text analyses that are of interest to authorship analysis are sentiment analysis and affect analysis, both of which can be used to identify attitudes, emotions, moods, and polarity of a document and its author. Additionally, both analyses borrow much from natural language processing, linguistics, and machine learning techniques [1,17,18]. The analyses, often implemented by automated machine learning classifiers, are commonly used to scrutinize a text to potentially reveal the author's opinions and affect state concerning multiple items. Such opinions and affect state can serve as additional important features that are helpful for attributing authorship of text when attribution is difficult.

Text visualization

Text visualization is the representation of large amount of text using visual metaphors [19–21]. It is concerned with getting insight into information obtained from one or more textual documents without users having read those documents. Examples of text visualization applications include generating high-quality keyphrases from text collections [22] and visualizing networks of business stakeholders on the web [23]. Despite the importance, scarce work is found in the analysis and visualization using various aspects of authorship styles and features.

In the context of web content, visualizations have traditionally been often used to create information concerning user activity of web forums, blogs, or other social media, allowing users to be more informed of their own activities and also those of fellow participants [24–27]. Most of the information projected in such visuals is entirely derived from participant activity patterns, and thus there is little evaluation of actual author-message content [13]. From the perspective of authorship analysis, activity patterns alone are not enough to accurately assign attribution to text. Thus, there exists a need for visualizations which utilize the data within message content.

Specifically, visualizations that could help researchers and practitioners assign authorship attribution in the virtual space would be of great asset. Visualizations can be used to help compare different writing samples, emphasize differences between authors, etc. The information projected by visualizations would be based entirely on the lexical, syntactic, and structural features identified in the text where attribution is in question.

There have been a few notable works on authorship visualization. Some research has used statistical techniques such as cosine similarity and principal component analysis to visualize writing style patterns [28]. Writing style patterns were rooted in word usage frequencies, and comparisons were drawn between authorship styles by observing the variance between top n-gram usage among different authors. Another study chose to use latent semantic indexing based on n-gram usage for authorship visualization [29]. Essentially, patterns in the relationships between terms and concepts contained in text are identified; this allows for individuals' authorship styles to be represented as an eigenvectors (i.e. principal components), allowing for further comparison and analysis between different authors. Further, the use of n-gram-based visualizations referred to as

Patterngrams can be used to compute document similarity [30]. Later, the visualization technique *Writeprint* was developed as a method to visualize web content [13]. *Writeprints* are useful for improving authorship identification and attribution by identifying individuals based on their writing style, including syntactic, structural, and lexical features. The visualization technique accounted for each category of features, and allowed researchers and practitioners to view authorship styles through different lenses offered by each feature category. The technique was also used to successfully attribute authorship on multilingual text. Overall, n-gram based techniques and those that account for syntactic, structural, and lexical features appear to be the most effective for authorship analysis of web contents.

Data collection & processing

To conduct authorship analysis and visualization of web content, data must first be collected and processed for use in research. Many recent studies utilizing web-based content commonly make use of automated crawlers for data collection [31,32]. Automated crawlers allow for large amounts of text to be collected very rapidly when compared to manual approaches. After web pages containing text are collected, automated parsers and feature extraction programs can be developed to strip relevant text out of web pages and compute feature usage values [3]. Feature usage values are often times stored permanently in a database and/or transformed into vectors for further analysis utilizing statistical techniques.

The AzAA portal

The AzAA portal was initially designed as an extension of the Dark Web Forum Portal (DWFP), a large archive of international terrorist and extremist web forums. The DWFP containing over 15 M messages in several different languages and supports search and analysis over a dataset of archived forum postings [13,32,33]. Currently, searching and browsing functions, multilingual translation, and social network analysis are supported, but the most recent version of the DW portal did not include the ability to perform authorship analysis, which can be important both for cyber-crime investigation and counter-terrorism [34,35]. The AzAA portal was designed and implemented to fill this gap and provide additional tools for researchers and practitioners.

Research testbed and feature Set

The AzAA portal was conceptualized to help support identification of "extreme" authors of postings in forums from the Dark Web Forum Portal. The portal was designed to allow comparisons of writing samples from multiple authors, helping users identify differences and similarity in authorship style. A design framework for the portal can be viewed in Figure 1.

To construct our data set, automated crawlers were employed. We utilized a popular web crawling package called *Offline Explorer*, but any similar crawling software would work. The crawling program was used to automatically collect web pages from identified Dark Web forums, or forums that contain potentially dangerous, extremist contents. Two forums were selected for analysis; forum contents were in English and Arabic, respective to each forum. After collection, text parsing programs were written in Java to extract relevant message data embedded within collected web pages. Extracted messages could be further processed to develop lexical, syntactic, and structural features for authorship analysis. Messages are also used to identify extreme authors through their language usage.

By referring to past research, we were able to identify a total of 4,000 lexical, syntactic, and structural features to extract for authorship analysis. Lexical features included words and terminology that may indicate potentially extremist contents. User messages can be broken into word vectors, which each unique word mapping to a unique feature that may help with authorship identification [9]. Additionally, as many features can be derived from author messages, lexical features compose the majority of the 4,000 features used in our research. Structural features of web content generally consist of usage of HTML; relevant features include image usage, hyperlink usage, font colors, font type, font size, text alignment, text bolding, italics, etc. Extracted syntactic features included punctuation usage, sentence patterns, etc.

In the interest of performing analysis on "extreme" authors, it is useful to measure author sentiments and affect states as a text analytics-based approximation [36,37]. Thus, we perform sentiment and affect analysis using a J48 classifier [37,38]. We extract content-specific features based on feature frequency and classifier information gain. Such features include religious/cultural terms, sentiment cues, and words associated with violence, anger, hate, and racism [36–38]. These techniques provide some means for identifying authors with the highest sentiment and affect intensities for anger, violence, hate, etc. to be identified and selected through filters. In prior benchmarking, the method has yielded affect intensity mean percentage errors of 5% or less on similar Dark Web forums [36]. Thirty of the authors with the highest average intensities for these affect classes (as well as a minimum of 100 postings) were identified by the classifier. This approach undertaken is consistent with prior work on the use of affect/sentiment analysis to identify highly relevant forum members in the Dark Web [36–39].

All authors do not necessarily have a unique pattern, however; some exhibit writing patterns that are erratic

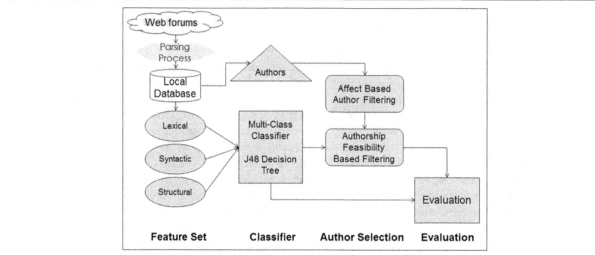

Figure 1 Authorship analysis design framework. Web forum pages are collected, with relevant data extracted and archived in a database. Features are generated from author messages, which are used for both author feasibility testing. Extreme authors are chosen based on affect analysis; identified authors are then tested for their feasibility in this experiment, as not all authors have unique writing styles. Authorship analysis is then performed using a decision tree classifier. Test results are then evaluated.

and/or include considerable reposting, quoting, plagiarism, non-sequiturs, short responses, etc. To evaluate the author selection, feasibility analysis was conducted to determine which authors were detectable. The latest 100 posts for each of the 30 identified authors were used for evaluation purposes. Recent postings were selected to avoid writing style changes that may occur naturally over time. For each author, 50 messages were used for classifier training and the other 50 are for testing. The authorship analysis methods employed were similar to ones utilized in prior studies using supervised machine learning classifiers such as a multi-class decision tree and established stylometric identification feature sets encompassing lexical, syntactic, structural, and content-specific attributes [4–7]. Only authors for which at least 90% of test messages were correctly classified were retained in the AzAA portal. The rational being that if the underlying patterns/insights and descriptive analytics are only meaningful if the associated classification performance is high. Consistent with prior work, using all three feature sets together (text style, HTML, and content-specific features) for authorship identification yielded the best overall performance, with over 90% macro-level accuracy [5,7].

System architecture

The AzAA portal is operationalized with many modern technologies and computing standards. At the core of the AzAA portal is an Apache webserver with Tomcat for JavaServer Pages support. Both of these Java applications are open source software created and maintained by the Apache Foundation. We employ the traditional Model-View-Controller (MVC) perspective for implementing the AzAA portal. In particular, we make use of the Struts2

Framework and Spring framework, two popular enterprise-level open-source frameworks, were adopted for scalability, flexibility, compatibility, and extendibility. With these two frameworks, we can easily apply the MVC perspective, thus allowing the portal to be more easily integrated into other local projects sharing the same frameworks. The front-end design (i.e. "view") and implementation were through JSP and HTML5 elements such as Javascript (JQuery and Bootstrap), HTML and CSS. Feature extraction and analysis (i.e. "model") for each author is calculated and stored in a Microsoft SQL Server database for quick recall at run-time. A NoSQL server for storage is also a viable alternative. The interface allows the user to quickly select various visualizations to view data through, supporting the controller functionality of the MVC perspective.

Use of the AzAA portal

Use of the AzAA portal allows for easy and quick analysis of authorship styles. Specifically, the AzAA portal provides users with multiple perspectives and visualizations for viewing different data, and comparisons between authorship styles can be performed with minimal input required on part of the user. An integrated tool to help support the identification of extreme authors 0Here we showcase and detail portal functionality.

When users log into the system, they are greeted with a welcome screen from which a user may select how to proceed. The welcome screen contains text to introduce the user to the system and to explain different ways to use the system. At this point, the user may choose to view authorship styles at an author-level or message-level perspective (Figure 2). Both perspectives ultimately display the similar data to users, but offer more focus on

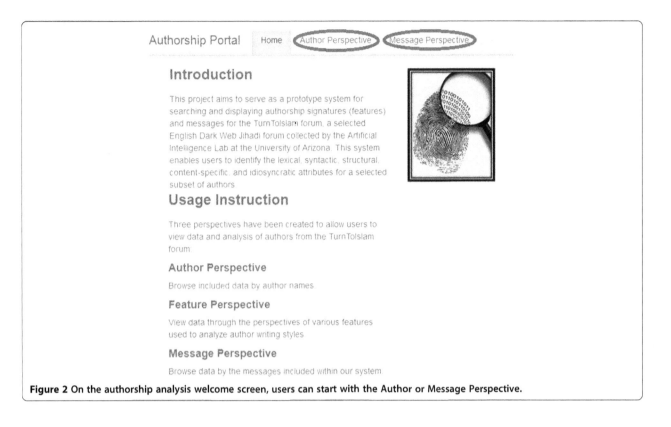

Figure 2 On the authorship analysis welcome screen, users can start with the **Author** or **Message Perspective.**

observing author postings at a cumulative level and at an individual-message level.

In the Author-Based Perspective, users can view the authorship styles of individual forum participants captured within our dataset. The author-based perspective is especially useful for identifying which authors use specific stylometric features the most (Figure 3). On this screen, users are presented with some author information as well as options to proceed. Users are initially presented with columns containing ranked lists of author feature usage for feature categories such as affect words, HTML features, content features, etc. Users can select to keep the columns in a simple summary view, or choose a more detailed heatmap view (Figure 4) for deeper scrutiny. Users also are supplied with dropdown menus to select two authors for which to compare authorship style.

Visualizations provide quick context on author stylometric features. Heatmaps (Figure 4) can show differences in data by coloring data points in various shades to show frequent feature usage. The darker and more intense shades used to color datapoints are representative of greater feature usage or frequency. For example, Figure 4 shows a portion of the heatmap where authors are sorted by their usage of racist terminology. A gradient is formed that visually presents feature usage per author, relative to other authors. The user Muharram23 has the most intensely shaded cell for the racism feature, and thus we can conclude from this visualization that

this author uses racist terminology the most frequently out of all authors in our dataset.

From the author-perspective, users can also select to directly compare the authorship styles of two authors. Users are presented with a table comparing authors through individual feature-level comparisons (Figure 5), while also generating a radar chart to summarize authorship differences and similarities for the user (Figure 6). Comparison of authors on the individual-feature level is particularly useful if the user of the system is interested in evaluating how some particular authors differ on a specific subset of features. If the user of the system has very focused questions, this perspective to view authorship differences may be useful.

Conversely, the radar chart shown in Figure 6 is more suited for providing fast, high-level summaries of authorship style comparisons. In our examples, we compare the author Muharram23 against the author Brother4ever. Differences for various stylometric features can be seen in Figure 5, while Figure 6 highlights differences across the major feature categories. The radar chart supports such comparisons at both the feature category and subcategory level. Here we show a comparison at the subcategory level betweenMuhahrram23 and Brother4-ever. Muharram23 uses a great deal of racist terminology within his messages; conversely, Brother4ever appears to discuss a wider range of topics, particularly religion and culture.

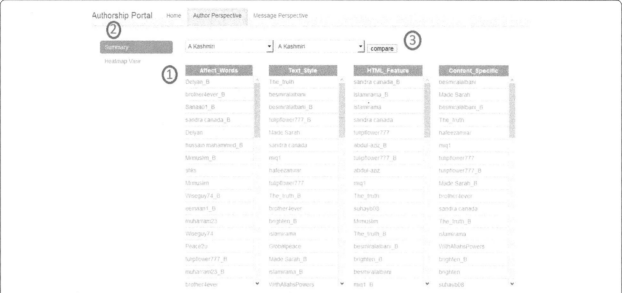

Figure 3 A portion of the Author Perspective screen showing which authors use which stylometric features the most. **(1)** Authors are ranked by feature usage across multiple feature categories. **(2)** Users can select a summary perspective which displays users in a simple ranked list, or a more detailed heatmap view. **(3)** Users can choose to directly compare the authorship styles of two authors.

Users may also browse the raw message contents in their original form or plaintext form, supported by feature highlighting within messages. To do this, users must switch from the author-perspective to the message-perspective, which can be performed as seen in Figure 2. When users select the message-perspective, they land on a screen in which they can select authors from a drop-down menu to view individual messages of. We select the user 'Ahmed ibn Ibrahim' as an example to walk through this section of the system; after choosing the 'Ahmed ibn Ibrahm' via the author drop-down menu, the page is populated with a list the author's messages (Figure 7). From here, one can select to

view a message in plain text or with its original HTML formatting. Additionally, users may also employ a series highlighting tools to easily identify specific features within messages.

Feature highlighting within text can help draw user attention towards more interesting aspects of authorship style. It is particularly useful for aiding in quick identification of lexical features. In Figure 8, one of the author's messages has been selected for viewing, and many feature highlighting options have been toggled on. Specifically, some affect-related features that imply hate, violence, anger, etc. on part of the author are highlighted in the

Author Name	Last Post Date	Anger	Hate	Racism	Religious	Violence
muharram23	08/28/2007	0	0.001	0.0057	0.0546	0.0011
Amir_of_spain_B	10/13/2010	0.0004	0.0011	0.0031	0.011	0.0006
Rashadi	02/23/2009	0.0007	0.0012	0.003	0.0383	0.0003
Akilah_B	03/23/2009	0.0007	0.0001	0.0025	0.029	0.0002
islamrama_B	10/20/2011	0.0002	0.0004	0.0023	0.0059	0.0007
Raihan	07/20/2007	0.0003	0.0005	0.0022	0.0122	0.0011
sandra canada	07/06/2008	0.0001	0.0006	0.0021	0.0348	0.0009
abdul-aziz	11/23/2010	0	0.0001	0.002	0.0169	0.0005
Rashadi_B	01/28/2010	0.0014	0.0007	0.0017	0.0234	0.0012
brighten	11/08/2006	0.0001	0.0004	0.0012	0.0244	0.0007
brother4ever	02/20/2007	0.0003	0.0003	0.0011	0.0452	0.0004
BintMuhammad	10/31/2006	0.0003	0.0004	0.0009	0.0253	0.0004
BintMuhammad_B	11/02/2011	0.0001	0.0002	0.0009	0.0209	0.0001

Figure 4 The "Heatmap view" (here showing usage of racist terms) provides a comprehensive overview of which features are the most distinctive for each author, listed in rows. The darker and more intense shades indicate greater usage.

Feature	Category	Sub-Category	Dominant Author	Mean Usage for muharram23	Mean Usage for brother4ever	Max Mean Usage
force	Affect Words	Violence	muharram23	0	0	0.0004
destroy	Affect Words	Violence	muharram23	0	0	0.0006
battle	Affect Words	Violence	muharram23	0	0	0.0003
defeat	Affect Words	Violence	brother4ever	0	0	0.0001
hit	Affect Words	Violence	muharram23	0.0002	0	0.0002
fight	Affect Words	Violence	brother4ever	0	0.0002	0.0007
torture	Affect Words	Violence	muharram23	0.0002	0.0001	0.0005
war	Affect Words	Violence	muharram23	0.0004	0	0.0016
%	Text Style	Special Characters	muharram23	0.0001	0.0001	0.0004
.	Text Style	Special Characters	muharram23	0.0002	0.0001	0.0015
!	Text Style	Special Characters	brother4ever	0.0001	0.0003	0.0008
?	Text Style	Special Characters	brother4ever	0.0001	0.0003	0.0008
alaykum	Content Specific	Social and Communities	muharram23	0.86	0.04	0.98
BISMILLAH	Affect Words	Religious	brother4ever	0	0.0001	0.001
alaikum	Affect Words	Religious	brother4ever	0	0.0002	0.0156

Figure 5 Feature-level comparisons between two authors, Muharram23 and Brother4ever. This type of comparison is useful to identify differences in individual feature expression between authors.

message with "warm" tones (i.e. red, orange, pink). Features indicating content about topical associations including religion, education, politics, daily life, etc. are highlighted in "cooler" tones (i.e. blues, greens, purples). The interface also provides a simple within-message search, assisting users in locating specific keywords in lengthy messages.

As with any system development, it is helpful to conduct user studies in order to evaluate the effectiveness, usefulness, and usability of a system. To measure the value and effectiveness of the Authorship Portal, we conducted a user study with 31 participants. The overall goal of the experiment was to evaluate the performance of the portal's visualization functionalities, including feature highlighting on the message-level, the stylometric feature radar chart for author-level comparisons, and the stylometric heatmap found within the author-perspective.

A. Experimental Setup

As described previously, the authorship analysis task is useful in any context where authorship attribution is uncertain. Traditional authorship analysis has relied on manual analysis of text and writing style, but manual analysis does not effectively scale to large Internet-based datasets. In the context of identifying extreme authors within virtual communities such as web forums, manual

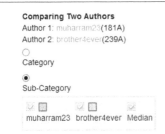
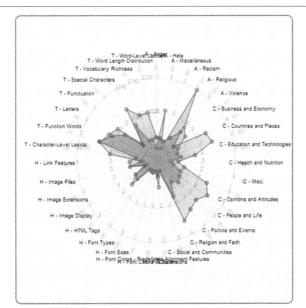

Figure 6 The radar chart visualization of the authorship styles of Muharram23 and Brother4ever. This visualization is particularly useful for quick summaries that highlight the main differences and similarities in authorship style between two authors.

Figure 7 System users can view individual messages of specific authors via the message-perspective feature of the portal. By selecting an author through the drop-down menu, users can view a list of messages written by the author. Users can then select individual messages to read in plaintext or with original HTML formatting, supported by feature-highlighting tools to draw attention to various aspects of authorship style.

analysis techniques are difficult and time-consuming to use. In these cases, automated analyses and integrated tools such as the AAzA portal can help practitioners conduct authorship analyses much more quickly at a greater scale. Further, systems such as the AAzA portal can help support practitioners by allowing for various visualization techniques and pre-programmed analyses that can be quickly executed. However, during and after an integrated tool to support authorship analysis, it is useful to evaluate the effectiveness of the tool in helping complete authorship-related tasks. In our case, the AAzA portal should be evaluated for its effectiveness in helping users identify the writing styles of different extreme authors.

The study participants were undergraduate students at different stages of their academic curriculum. The participants were tasked with using the portal to answer a series of simple questions pertaining to authorship style of specific authors within our dataset. The purpose of such tasks is intended to help evaluate performance of the portal in identifying and comparing "extreme" authors that are present on TurnToIslam online forum.

We adopted a one-factor repeated-measures approach in our experimental design, which has been shown to demonstrate a greater precision than designs that employ only between-subjects factors [40]. Each subject used the Authorship Portal to answer two sections of questions and then provide ratings on a number of

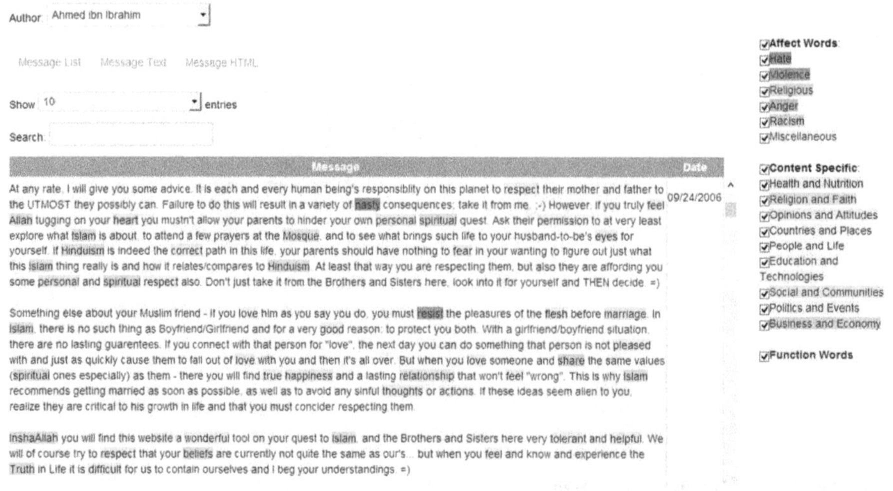

Figure 8 Message-perspective view with original HTML formatting and feature highlighting.

statements and their demographic data in a third section. In one of the first two sections, the participant used the portal's visualization functionality to answer the questions while in the other section the participant did not use the functionality. The subject used the portal to answer two or three questions in the section's three parts. When allowed to use the portal's visualization feature, the participant would be able to use the portal's feature highlighting, authorship comparison spider chart, and stylometric heatmap in the section's three parts respectively. A sample question in Part 1 is "How many times do "Opinions and Attitudes" words appear in the message?" A sample question in Part 2 is "Between BintMuhammad and Raihan, which author has a higher usage of affect words?" A sample question in Part 3 is "Which author has the highest usage of "Politics and Events" content in their authoring of forum messages?" Two different sets of questions were used in the two sections.

The whole experiment took about 60 minutes. In the first 10 minutes, a participant was given a tutorial in which the experimenter guided the use of the portal's functionality. Then the participant worked on the two sections of questions as described above (approximately 20 minutes per section). The order of using or not using the portal's visualization features (i.e., treatment vs. control) was assigned randomly to each participant to remove any bias on the results due to learning effect. The assignment of question sets (i.e., Set 1 or Set 2) was also random. Each question set contained identical items, but the order of items was changed. These two random assignments created four scenarios (T1-C2, T2-C1, C2-T1, and C1-T2 where "T" stands for "treatment," "C" stands for "control," and the two numbers stand for the respective sets of questions). A participant is thus randomly assigned to one of these four scenarios. Upon finishing the two sections of questions, the subject filled out a short questionnaire asking them to rate (on a five-point Likert Scale) their perception on the u6sability of the portal's visualization functionality and to provide demographic data.

The thirty-one participants were undergraduate students (20 males and 11 females) enrolled in a business software application course or a business statistics course offered by a regional university in the United States. The students were primarily college-age (between 18 and 25 years old), with an average age of 22.98 years old.

B. Performance Measures

1) *Accuracy:* The accuracy of the task performance was measured by how close the subject's answer was to the correct answer (for tasks in in Part 1 where a number was expected), as shown in the following formula. The accuracies in all tasks in Part 1 were averaged to obtained an overall accuracy of that part.

$$\text{Accuracy} = 1 - \min\left(\left|\frac{\text{Correct Answer} - \text{Subject's Answer}}{\text{Correct Answer}}\right|, 1\right)$$

For tasks in Parts 2 and 3 where written responses are expected, the accuracy was calculated by averaging the correctness of each task's performance (correct response = 1, incorrect response = 0).

2) *Efficiency:* The efficiency was measured by the time elapsed (in minutes) between the beginning of a task and the completion of the task.

3) *User Rating:* The user rating was measured in a five-point Likert Scale, where 5 means "strongly agree" and 1 means "strongly disagree."

C. Hypothesis Testing

We are interested in testing these hypotheses about the accuracy and efficiency of the Authorship Portal.

H1. The Authorship Portal's feature highlighting function enables users to achieve a significantly higher accuracy in authorship analysis (counting and relating category-specific words) than not using the function.

H2. The Authorship Portal's feature highlighting function enables users to achieve a significantly higher efficiency in authorship analysis (counting and relating category-specific words) than not using the function.

H3. The Authorship Portal's authorship comparison spider chart function enables users to achieve a significantly higher accuracy in authorship analysis (comparing authors' use of category-specific features, sub-category features, and similarity of authors' writing profiles) than not using the function.

H4. The Authorship Portal's authorship comparison spider chart function enables users to achieve a significantly higher efficiency in authorship analysis (comparing authors' use of category-specific features, sub-category features, and similarity of authors' writing profiles) than not using the function.

H5. The Authorship Portal's stylometric heatmap function enables users to achieve a significantly higher accuracy in authorship analysis (identifying authors' usage of category-specific features and sub-category features) than not using the function.

H6. The Authorship Portal's stylometric heatmap function enables users to achieve a significantly higher efficiency in authorship analysis (identifying authors' usage of category-specific features and sub-category features) than not using the function.

D. Experimental Results

The accuracy and efficiency of task performance using the Authorship Portal's visualization functions are generally higher than those without using the visualization functions. Table 1 shows the detailed performance levels and the mean differences in all three parts of each section (using or not using visualization). The figures show that the participants achieved higher efficiency in all three parts of the study, and obtained higher accuracy in all parts (except 1b) when they used the visualization functions of the Authorship Portal.

Statistical tests of the differences between using and not using the visualization functions of the portal indicate significance at most parts of the study (alpha error = 0.05). The columns labeled "p-value$_A$" in Table 1 show that the participants achieved significantly higher accuracy in answering the questions of Parts 2a, 2b, 2c, 3a, and 3b when they used the Authorship Portal's visualization functions. Therefore, hypotheses H3 and H5 were confirmed. We believe that the portal's spider chart and stylometric heatmap provided accurate comparison of the authorship features, thus contributing to the significant results. The columns labeled "p-value$_E$" in Table 1 show that the participants used significantly less time in answering the questions in all parts when they used the Authorship Portal's visualization functions. Therefore, hypotheses H2, H4, and H6 were confirmed. We believe that the portal's spider chart and stylometric heatmap functions helped participants to quickly identify the information they needed to answer the questions, thus contributing to the superior efficiency. On the other hand, hypothesis H1 was not confirmed, even though participants obtained a higher accuracy in Part 1a on average when using the portal's feature highlighting. We believe that it was because participants were able to count the category-specific words accurately in simple messages even without using feature highlighting of the portal. However, more complicated tasks such as comparing author style and identifying feature usage among all authors were shown to be more difficult that they must rely on advanced functions such as the Authorship Portal's visualization in order to achieve significantly higher accuracy.

Subjects rated the Authorship Portal very highly. Table 2 shows their ratings on three statements related to the three visualization functions of the portal. All these ratings are close to the maximum of 5 (strongly agree) along a Likert Scale. In particular, the mean rating of the Authorship Comparison Spider Chart is the highest (4.81) among the three, showing subjects' preference toward a novel visualization of the different writing feature values.

E. Discussion and implication

The highly positive results shown in the experimental findings illustrate the power of the Authorship Portal's visualization functions. Using these functions, subjects were able to achieve higher accuracies (in Parts 2 and 3) and efficiencies (in all parts) than using only ordinary message browsing. These results demonstrate a high usability of the portal in supporting authorship analysis. The portal can possibly save analysts' time and enhance accuracy in understanding online messages related to terrorist activities. Considering the increasing use of forum data and social-media-based analysis in security informatics (e.g., [41]), this study provides new empirical findings to confirm the usability and efficiency of using visualization in authorship analysis. The results should be relevant to

Table 1 Accuracy and efficiency of task performance

Pt.	Task (related function of the portal)	A(V)	A(~V)	Diff$_A$	p-value$_A$	E(V)	E(~V)	Diff$_E$	p-value$_E$
1a	Counting category-specific words (feature highlighting)	0.83	0.77	0.06	0.4367	1.45	4.45	−3.00	0.0020 **
1b	Relating category-specific words (feature highlighting)	0.46	0.47	−0.01	0.9286	1.90	2.74	−0.84	0.0084 **
2a	Comparing authors' use of category-specific features (spider chart)	0.90	0.48	0.42	0.0007 **	1.81	4.61	−2.80	0.0000 **
2b	Comparing authors' use of sub-category-specific features (spider chart)	0.94	0.68	0.26	0.0090 **	1.55	2.81	−1.26	0.0001 **
2c	Comparing similarity of authors' writing profiles (spider chart)	1.00	0.81	0.19	0.0118 **	2.00	3.16	−1.16	0.0061 **
3a	Identifying authors' usage of category-specific features (stylometric heatmap)	0.94	0.32	0.62	0.0000 **	1.52	4.03	−2.51	0.0000 **
3b	Identifying authors' usage of sub-category-specific features (stylometric heatmap)	0.90	0.19	0.71	0.0000 **	1.32	4.42	−3.1	0.0075 **

Note:
A(V) = Mean accuracy of task performance using visualization.
A(~V) = Mean accuracy of task performance without using visualization.
Diff$_A$ = Mean difference of A(V) − A(~V).
E(V) = Mean efficiency of task performance using visualization (in minutes).
E(~V) = Mean efficiency of task performance without using visualization (in minutes).
Diff$_E$ = Mean difference of E(V) − E(~V) (in minutes).
**p < 0.01.

Table 2 Subjects' rating of authorship portal

Statement	Mean rating	S.D.
I find the feature highlighting of the Authorship Portal to be more useful in identifying message features than manually reading the forum messages.	4.68	0.54
I find the authorship comparison spider chart of the Authorship Portal to be more useful in comparing authors' writing than manually reading and comparing the authors' messages.	4.81	0.48
I find the stylometric heatmap of the Authorship Portal to be more useful in feature usage than manually reading the forum messages.	4.74	0.51

terrorism and informatics researchers, visualization users, and security practitioners.

Conclusions and future work

The Arizona Authorship Analysis (AzAA) Portal was developed primarily to support efforts in authorship analysis for terrorism research, cybercrime investigation, and intelligence analysis. Presently, the portal supports identification of "extreme" authors, as well as comparison of authorship styles between authors to reveal writing style similarities and differences. Additionally, sentiment analysis incorporating various lexical features was operationalized via a machine learning classifier for deeper analysis. Results of such analysis were useful for formulating the web-based visualizations that serve as graphical summaries of authorship styles. Other useful functions such as message searching, message browsing, and feature highlighting were also implemented within the system interface, allowing users to explore authors' styles from a variety of perspectives and contexts.

A user evaluation was designed and executed to measure the effectiveness and performance of the AzAA portal in assisting with authorship analysis. Specifically, user evaluation participants were asked to complete a series of tasks involving use of portal text visualizations. Evaluation results demonstrate that the visualizations support greater task efficiency and accuracy for task performance. The AzAA portal demonstrates potential to possibly save analysts' time while also enhancing understanding of online messages related to potential terrorist activities.

Future efforts on the AzAA portal will include the operationalization of a larger testbed for investigation with the system. As large-scale, big data analysis has become an important topic in similar research, it is important to consider how the AzAA portal can be extended to handle larger authorship analysis tasks. Technical components of the authorship analysis algorithm itself may be also be improved; for example, the current decision tree classifier may be replaced with a more scalable SVM classifier in the future [2]. More types of visualizations can also be developed to add value and aid in the process of authorship analysis. Finally, further evaluation of the system's efficacy for authorship analysis tasks is always valuable for finding new directions in which to improve the AzAA portal.

Acknowledgements
This work was supported in part by the National Science Foundation (CBET-0730908) and the Defense Threat Reduction Agency (HDTRA1-09-1-0058) at the University of Arizona. Additionally, this paper is based upon work supported partially by funding from the Center for Business Intelligence and Analytics at Stetson University (http://cbia.stetson.edu/). We thank the study participants and research assistants for their help.

Author details
[1]MIS Department, University of Arizona, Tucson, AZ, USA. [2]Department of Decision and Info. Sciences, Stetson University, DeLand, FL, USA. [3]McIntire School of Commerce, University of Virginia, Charlottesville, VA, USA. [4]HC Analytics, Tucson, AZ, USA.

References
1. KKR Choo, Organized crime groups in cyberspace: a topology. Trends Organ Crime 11(3), 270–295 (2008)
2. D Zimbra, H Chen, H, Scalable Sentiment Classification Across Multiple Dark web Forums, in *Proceedings of the 2012 IEEE International Conference on Intelligence and Security Informatics (ISI 2012)*, 2012, pp. 78–83
3. V Benjamin, H Chen, Securing Cyberspace : Identifying key Actors in Hacker Communities, in *Proceedings of the 2012 IEEE International Conference on Intelligence and Security Informatics (ISI 2012)*, 2012, pp. 24–29
4. O De Vel, A Anderson, M Corney, G Mohay, Mining e-mail content for author identification forensics. SIGMOD Record 30(4), 55–64 (2001)
5. A Abbasi, H Chen, Applying authorship analysis to extremist-group web forum messages. IEEE Intell Syst 20(5), 67–75 (2005)
6. J Li, R Zheng, H Chen, From fingerprint to writeprint. Commun ACM 49(4), 76–82 (2006)
7. R Zheng, Y Qin, Z Huang, H Chen, A framework for authorship analysis of online messages: writing-style features and techniques. J Am Soc Inf Sci Technol 57(3), 378–393 (2006)
8. S Argamon, M Koppel, J Pennebaker, J Schler, Automatically profiling the author of an anonymous text. Commun ACM 52(2), 119–123 (2009)
9. A Abbasi, H Chen, Writeprints: a stylometric approach to identify-level identification and similarity detection in cyberspace. ACM Trans Inf Syst 26, 2 (2008)
10. RH Baayen, H Halteren, FJ Tweedie, Outside the cave of shadows: using syntactic annotation to enhance authorship attribution. Literary Ling Comput 2, 110–120 (1996)
11. JF Burrows, Word patterns and story shapes: the statistical analysis of narrative style. Literary Ling Comput 2, 61–67 (1987)
12. FJ Tweedie, S Singh, DI Holmes, Neural network applications in stylometry: the federalist papers. Comput Hum 30(1), 1–10 (1996)
13. A Abbasi, H Chen, Visualizing Authorship for Identification, in *Proceedings of the 4th IEEE Symposium on Intelligence and Security Informatics*, 2006, pp. 60–71
14. V Benjamin, H Chen, Machine Learning for Attack Vector Identification in Malicious Source Code, in *IEEE Intelligence and Security Informatics*, 2013, pp. 21–23
15. T Urvoy, E Chauveau, P Filoche, T Lavergne, Tracking web spam with HTML style similarities. ACM Trans Web 2(1), 3 (2008)
16. X Liu, H Chen, AZDrugMiner: an information extraction system for mining patient-reported adverse drug events in online patient forums. In *Smart Health* (Springer, Berlin Heidelberg, 2013), pp. 134–150

17. A Abbasi, H Chen, CyberGate: a design framework and system for text analysis of computer mediated communication. MIS Q **32**(4), 811–837 (2008)

18. A Balahur, JM Hermida, A Montoyo, Detecting implicit expressions of emotion in text: a comparative analysis. Decis Support Syst **53**(4), 742–753 (2010)

19. W Chung, H Chen, JF Nunamaker, A visual framework for knowledge discovery on the web: an empirical study on business intelligence exploration. J Manag Inf Syst **21**(4), 57–84 (2005)

20. JA Wise, JJ Thoma, K Pennock, D Lantrip, M Pottier, A Schur, V Crow, Visualizing the non-Visual: Spatial Analysis and Interaction With Information from Text Documents, in *IEEE, Proceedings of Information Visualization*, 1995, pp. 51–58

21. V Benjamin, W Chung, A Abbasi, J Chuang, C Larson, H Chen, Evaluating Text Visualization: An Experiment in Authorship Analysis, in *IEEE International Conference on Intelligence and Security Informatics*, 2013, pp. 16–20

22. J Chuang, CD Manning, J Heer, Without the clutter of unimportant words: descriptive keyphrases for text visualization. ACM Trans Comput Hum Interact **19**(3), 1–29 (2012)

23. W Chung, Visualizing e-business stakeholders on the web: a methodology and experimental results. Int J Electron Bus **6**(1), 25–46 (2008)

24. T Erickson, WA Kellogg, Social translucence: an approach to designing systems that support social processes. ACM Trans Comput Hum Interact **7**(1), 59–83 (2001)

25. W Sack, Conversation map: an interface for very large-scale conversations. J Manag Inf Syst **17**(3), 73–92 (2000)

26. J Donath, K Karahalio, F Viegas, Visualizing Conversation, in *Proceedings of the 32nd Hawaii International Conference on System Sciences*, 1999

27. FB Viegas, M Smith, Newsgroup Crowds and Authorlines: Visualizing the Activity of Individuals in Conversational Cyberspaces, in *Proceedings of the 37th Hawaii International Conference on System Sciences*, 2004

28. B Kjell, WA Woods, O Frieder, Discrimination of authorship using visualization. Inf Process Manag **30**(1), 141–150 (1994)

29. CD Shaw, JM Kukla, I Soboroff, DS Ebert, CK Nicholas, A Zwa, EL Miller, DA Roberts, Interactive volumetric information visualization for document corpus management. Int J Digit Libr **2**, 144–156 (1999)

30. RL Ribler, M Abrams, Using Visualization to Detect Plagiarism in Computer Science Classes, in *Proceedings of the IEEE Symposium on Information Vizualization*, 2000, pp. 173–178

31. TJ Fu, A Abbasi, H Chen, A focused crawler for dark web forums. J Am Soc Inf Sci Technol **61**(6), 1213–1231 (2010)

32. Y Zhang, S Zeng, CN Huang, L Fan, X Yu, Y Dang, CA Larson, D Denning, N Roberts, H Chen, Developing a Dark web Collection and Infrastructure for Computational and Social Sciences, in *Intelligence and Security Informatics*, 2010, pp. 59–64

33. H Chen, *Dark web: Exploring and Data Mining the Dark Side of the web* (Integrated Series in, Information Systems, 2011)

34. R Zheng, J Li, H Chen, H, Z Huang, A framework for authorship identification of online messages: writing-style features and classification techniques. J Am Soc Inf Sci Technol **57**(3), 378–393 (2006)

35. G Frantzeskou, S Gritzalis, SG MacDonnel, Source Code Authorship Analysis for Supporting the Cybercrime Investigation Process, in *Proceedings of the 1st International Conference on E-Business and Telecommunication Networks*, 2004, pp. 85–92

36. A Abbasi, H Chen, Analysis of affect intensities in extremist group forums. In *Terrorism informatics* (Springer, US, 2008), pp. 285–307

37. A Abbasi, H Chen, Affect Intensity Analysis of Dark Web Forums, in *Proceedings of the 5th IEEE International Conference on Intelligence and Security Informatics*, 2007, pp. 282–288

38. A Abbasi, H Chen, Analysis of Affect Intensities in Extremist Group Forums, in *Terrorism Informatics*, 2007, pp. 285–307

39. D Zimbra, H Chen, A cyber-archaeology approach to social movement research: framework and case study. J Comput-Mediat Commun **16**, 48–70 (2010)

40. J Myers, A Well, *Research design and statistical analysis* (Lawrence Erlbaum Associates, 1995)

41. W Chung, D Zeng, IMood: Discovering U.S. Immigration Reform Sentiment, in *Proceedings of the 23rd Workshop on Information Technology and Systems*, 2013

11

Automatic detection of cyber-recruitment by violent extremists

Jacob R Scanlon* and Matthew S Gerber

Abstract

Growing use of the Internet as a major means of communication has led to the formation of cyber-communities, which have become increasingly appealing to terrorist groups due to the unregulated nature of Internet communication. Online communities enable violent extremists to increase recruitment by allowing them to build personal relationships with a worldwide audience capable of accessing uncensored content. This article presents methods for identifying the recruitment activities of violent groups within extremist social media websites. Specifically, these methods apply known techniques within supervised learning and natural language processing to the untested task of automatically identifying forum posts intended to recruit new violent extremist members. We used data from the western jihadist website *Ansar AlJihad Network*, which was compiled by the University of Arizona's Dark Web Project. Multiple judges manually annotated a sample of these data, marking 192 randomly sampled posts as recruiting (YES) or non-recruiting (NO). We observed significant agreement between the judges' labels; Cohen's $\kappa = (0.5, 0.9)$ at $p = 0.01$. We tested the feasibility of using naive Bayes models, logistic regression, classification trees, boosting, and support vector machines (SVM) to classify the forum posts. Evaluation with receiver operating characteristic (ROC) curves shows that our SVM classifier achieves an 89% area under the curve (AUC), a significant improvement over the 63% AUC performance achieved by our simplest naive Bayes model (Tukey's test at $p = 0.05$). To our knowledge, this is the first result reported on this task, and our analysis indicates that automatic detection of online terrorist recruitment is a feasible task. We also identify a number of important areas of future work including classifying non-English posts and measuring how recruitment posts and current events change membership numbers over time.

Keywords: Cyber; Recruitment; Extremist; Terrorism; Darkweb; Machine learning; Natural language processing

Introduction

In the last decade, the modern landscape of extremism has expanded to encompass the Internet and online social media [1,2]. In particular, extremist organizations have increasingly used these technologies to recruit new members. Recent research by Torok shows that cyber tools are most influential at the onset of a future member's extremist activity—the recruitment and radicalization phase [2]. Terrorist groups use the free and open nature of the Internet to form online communities [3] and disseminate literature and training materials without having to rely on traditional media outlets which might censor or change their message [2,4]. Terrorist organizations engage in directed communication and advertisement, recruiting members on social websites like Second Life, Facebook,

and radicalized religious web forums [1,2,5]. The intelligence community would benefit from knowledge of how terrorist organizations conduct online recruitment and whom they may be targeting.

The investigation report on FBI counterterrorism intelligence failures leading up to the Ft. Hood shooting on November 7, 2009 cited a "data explosion" and "workload" as contributing factors to analyst and agent oversights. At "nearly 20,000 Aulaqi-related [electronic documents]," keeping up with workload demands was clearly a challenge for the two reviewers assigned to the case at the time [6]. Considering this large volume of possibly relevant text data requiring review by a limited number of FBI agents, automated classification methods would be useful for pre-screening text documents—reducing the workload of human analysts.

Within this article, a violent extremist (VE) group is an organization that uses violent means, like terrorism,

*Correspondence: jrs6du@virginia.edu
Predictive Technology Laboratory, Department of Systems and Information Engineering, University of Virginia, Charlottesville VA, USA

to disrupt a legitimate authority, whereas insurgents and terrorists are common types of violent extremist groups that act with the specific goal of influencing public opinion or inciting political change. A radical religious group organizing inflammatory yet peaceful protests or a politically motivated person engaging in civil disobedience are *not* considered violent extremists under these definitions. Many modern groups, like the Westboro Baptist Church, have radical religious views, but these beliefs are neither necessary nor sufficient to classify them as violent extremists without the intent to carry out or advocate for *specific acts of violence*. Within this article, VE recruitment is any attempt by a group or individual involved in VE to recruit, radicalize, or persuade another person to aid a violent movement. Cyber-recruitment is therefore recruitment activity that makes use of computers and the Internet.

This article presents data and analytic methods for automatically identifying recruitment activities of violent extremist organizations within online social media. Specifically, these methods identify messages recruiting individuals for participation in violent extremism. For these classification purposes, a VE cyber-recruitment message is any message that attempts to persuade the reader to join a violent extremist organization. These recruitment messages must assist readers in finding violent movements to join, or describe ways to become more active or provide material aid. By developing and evaluating an automatic system for identifying such messages, we demonstrate an important and feasible method for identifying the intention/incitement of violent activity within online communities.

The rest of this article is organized as follows. In the section "Related work", we compare offline violent extremist recruitment with the recent increase in cyber-recruitment efforts. Additionally, we discuss previous counterinsurgency efforts and contemporary research that outlines the challenges associated with analyzing VE activities, like recruitment; we emphasize the specific gaps that our article addresses. The "Data collection and annotation" section describes our data requirements and the specific data sources we used, followed by the pre-processing and annotation steps required for supervised learning of VE recruitment. Following the annotation steps, we present our agreement analysis results of the VE recruitment annotations. In the section "Analytic approach", we propose a probabilistic model employing natural language features for automatically classifying VE recruitment in forum posts. We also describe the classification functions used in our supervised learning experiments, such as naive Bayes, logistic regression, and support vector machines. A description of the results obtained from the experiments along with our interpretation is provided in the "Results and discussion" section. Finally, "Conclusions and future work" section

discusses future directions and potential for our proposed techniques along side privacy concerns related to automated monitoring and analysis of ubiquitous communication.

Related work
Offline recruitment and manual social network analysis
The modern jihadist insurgencies in Iraq and Afghanistan operate among the local civilian population and engage in both legal and illegal activities in order to achieve their strategic and political goals. However, the illegal acts are only effective when carried out by an organized and well-manned group [7]. Recruiting new members is thus a critical activity for both daily operations and the underlying political cause. An average terrorist group has a life expectancy of less than a year, so groups wishing to extend their lifespan must replace members lost through arrests, deaths, and defections [3]. Several studies have tried to understand why some people join violent rebellions [8-12], while others only sympathize or cooperate in a non-violent capacity [13-16]. This article facilitates such understanding by providing methods that identify examples of active recruitment activity within a population of individuals who may passively sympathize with violent groups.

Ralph McGehee observed VE recruitment first hand during his 1967 work to identify communist insurgents in the rural villages along the northern border of Thailand. His efforts enabled the joint CIA-Thai counterinsurgency (COIN) to provide targeted aid to at-risk villages and persons, and in doing so simultaneously thwart communist recruitment efforts and improve regional support for the Thai government. The success of McGehee's program can be attributed to his intelligence teams collecting information on nearly every person in the villages, not just the communist sympathizers he was specifically targeting. This provided a more complete picture of the community and allowed this early social network analysis (SNA) effort to better infer the community's support for the communists and successfully identify active members of the insurgency [17]. Although our research problem specifically targets online communities, strong parallels exist between these virtual worlds and the physical communities addressed by McGehee because both contain violent extremist groups that operate within, hide among, and recruit from a passive majority population.

Cyber-recruitment, social network analysis, and data mining
The primary danger of cyber-recruitment is its ability to quickly expose large online communities to a substantial amount of engaging, multimedia content [2,18,19]. COIN experts are increasingly concerned with the potential of these cyber-communities for illegal purposes. Most

literature has focused on how violent extremist groups use legitimate social networking websites along with online discussion forums for recruitment and other activities. This prior research largely provides evidence and case studies of real online VE activity and suggests ways that virtual worlds may be used by these groups in the future [4,5,19-22]. Recent research has evaluated the use of political tools for shutting down websites or shaming material supporters [23]. Some researchers have suggested the use of web-crawling and analysis techniques to monitor for VE activities including recruitment [2,24,25]; however, we are not aware of any implementations of such techniques on recruitment specifically. This article presents new research that fills this gap, addressing the need to detect cyber-recruitment in online social media forums.

Computer-based social network analysis is a large field of research, one objective of which is to identify the organizational structure of VE networks [1,26-29]. With objectives similar to McGehee's manual SNA work, present research hopes to detect the presence of VE groups and their influence within large-scale networks based on the number of interconnections among VEs and influential community members. There have also been preliminary attempts to profile individual users using text mining techniques [30]. However, this prior research has typically focused on violent extremist activity in general without focusing on a particular activity like recruitment. Although much COIN literature has covered cyber-recruitment, and data/text mining techniques have been used in an early capacity to collect/analyze Internet data, no published research has applied such techniques to specifically examine the cyber-recruitment activities of extremist groups in online environments. The present research complements the research surveyed above by building on recent data collection efforts, focusing on online recruitment specifically, and applying current techniques from natural language processing to automatically identify recruitment activities.

Data collection and annotation

The need for cyber-COIN tools has increased interest in methods that analyze so-called "dark web" content. Dark web content is defined as information from typically private social websites where extremists interact. Many early efforts focused on locating, accessing, extracting, and storing data from dark web forums [1,22,24,31,32]. The present research builds on these key efforts. In the section "Data requirements and sources", we describe requirements that must be met by data sources supporting our objectives along with specific data sources used in our study. In the "Data pre-processing and annotation" section, we describe our manual annotation effort, which analyzed individual posts for recruitment content.

Data requirements and sources

This article leverages prior data collection efforts by using pre-compiled forum post data to model violent extremist recruitment within online social media. The following data requirements are needed to support our research objectives.

Violent extremist activity - The collected data should come from sources that are popular among violent extremist groups and their sympathizers and contain overt recruitment for such groups.

Contemporary time-frame - The collected data should cover a contemporary time-frame (e.g., the last decade) in order to be considered relevant to contemporary anti-extremist efforts.

Language - The collected data must use the English language or be translatable to English using an automatic process like Google's machine-translation service [33].

We identified the Dark Web Portal Project [31,34] as an ideal data source according to the requirements described above. The Dark Web Portal is a repository of social media messages compiled from 28 different online discussion forums. These forums focus on extremist religious (e.g., jihadist) and general Islamic discussions, many of which are sympathetic to radical Islamic groups. Most of the thirteen million collected messages come from Arabic sources, but the Dark Web Project provides translation services and compiles information from at least seven dedicated English-language forums. The most relevant forums come from the Ansar AlJihad Network, which we summarize in Table 1 and describe in more detail below.

The Ansar AlJihad Network is a set of invitation-only jihadist forums in Arabic and English that are known to be popular with western jihadists [35]. The Dark Web Project compiled 299,040 total messages posted on Ansar AlJihad between 2008-2012. Fewer posts are compiled from the English forums, called Ansar1, than from the Arabic portion of the site; however, the English subset was sufficiently large for our study and contained contemporary,

Table 1 Forums used in our study, extracted from the Ansar AlJihad Network via the Dark Web Portal

	AsAnsar	Ansar1
Time-frame	11/2008 - 5/2012	12/2008 - 1/2010
Messages	269,548	29,492
Members	5,034	382
Language	Arabic	English

original-English discussions between jihadists and jihadist sympathizers. We used this subset in all of our experiments. The structured data annotations discussed below are the only data elements not originating from this pre-compiled Ansar AlJihad source.

Data pre-processing and annotation

We collected and pre-processed the Ansar1 data as follows:

1. We read in a sample of raw Ansar1 forum posts and compiled the message text and respective message IDs into an initial corpus. We then automatically removed duplicates (same message ID) and empty documents (no message text) from the corpus.
2. Most posts contain exclusively English text as Asnar1 is the English-language forum for the Ansar AlJihad Network. However, occasional posts include non-English words or phrases; these are commonly Arabic passages from the Koran. In these cases the non-English passages were converted to English using Google Translate [33]. We left slang words written in latin characters intact under the assumption that they were meant to be readable by an English language speaker. For example, "Kuffar" is a derogatory Arabic term for unbeliever.

The Dark Web Portal project does not indicate which messages contain VE recruitment content and which do not. Thus, we manually annotated this information within the data. We provided two independent judges with the following instructions:

1. You have been provided with 192 forum posts sampled from a Jihadist forum.
2. Read each post carefully and determine whether that post has the intent to recruit violent extremists to some group or movement. For the purpose of annotation, violent extremist recruitment is defined as any attempt by a group or individual to recruit, radicalize, or persuade another person into aiding a violent movement aimed at disrupting a legitimate authority.
3. Annotate each post by marking it as either (a) contains violent extremist recruitment, or (b) does not contain violent extremist recruitment.

The forum posts' message text had a wide range of sizes with an average of 246 words among the samples (352-word standard deviation); examples of annotated posts are shown in Table 2. We then used Cohen's κ [36] to validate the labeled data for consistency. Agreement, κ, is the proportion of agreement between the judges after chance agreement has been removed. The value of κ is bounded

Table 2 Example text of Ansar1 forum posts and the respective annotations

Annotation	Sample text**
Recruitment	*A Golden chance to join Jihad in Somalia. Abo Dojana invited those who want to participate in jihad to join the militants in Somalia to form what he called a base of martyrdom-seekers who would from there spread to the entire world. Somalia could actually be an ideal base for physical and weapons training...*
Recruitment	*Representing the militant Islamic group Shebab, Abu Mansour makes a pitch for new overseas recruits after praising one militant fighter killed in an apparent ambush. 'So, if you can encourage more of your children and more of your neighbors and anyone around to send people like him to this jihad (holy war), it would be a great asset for us,' he says.*
Not recruitment	*I have now added him as a friend on Facebook. But something tells me that he isn't going to answer to my request. LOL, you had me rolling on the floor man!!!!! So this attack was done my 'Jaish al Mujihadeen' How it that possible?, did they have problems with bounced-checks from the US?*
Not recruitment	*A court in the German city of Koblenz sentenced a German of Pakistani origin to eight years in prison Monday on a conviction of assisting the international Al-Qaeda terror network. The man gave the group financial aid and tried to recruit new members in German territory, according to the indictment*
Not recruitment	*Did Mansoor join the emerat? I heard he is still fighting for Ichkira Republic*

**Incorrect spellings and grammar of original posts have been left as is throughout the table.

on $[-1,+1]$ with zero indicating that observed agreement equals chance agreement. Therefore a positive κ indicates non-random agreement between judges, and a negative κ indicates conflicting annotation between judges. The following terms are used to calculate κ:

$$\kappa = \frac{p_o - p_c}{1 - p_c}$$

$p_o =$ proportion of observations for which judges agree (see Table 3),

$p_c =$ proportion of observations for which agreement is expected by chance (see Table 3)

Table 3 Agreement matrix of proportions for recruitment categories

		Judge A		
	Category	No	Yes	p_{iB}
Judge B	No	0.82 (0.74)*	0.04	0.86
	Yes	0.03	0.11 (0.02)	0.14
	p_{iA}	0.85	0.15	$\sum p_i = 1.00$

$p_o = 0.82 + 0.11 = 0.93$

$p_c = 0.74 + 0.02 = 0.76$ $\kappa = \frac{0.93 - 0.76}{1 - 0.76} = 0.70$

*Parenthetical values are proportions expected due to chance association.

Table 3 shows the agreement results for our manually annotated Ansar1 data. As shown, the two judges found that approximately 11% of the posts contained VE recruitment. The two judges agreed on the labels for 93% of the posts, with an expected chance agreement of 76%, producing a κ of 70% (see Table 3 for details). Significant non-random agreement was observed with a confidence interval of $(0.5, 0.7)$ at $p = 0.01$; however, interpreting strength of agreement is a common problem with agreement metrics. Some studies have attempted to provide a scale and would describe $\kappa = 0.70$ as "substantial" strength of agreement [37,38], but despite considerable debate among statisticians this issue has never been definitively addressed. Considering both the significance and magnitude of agreement, these results adequately justify using the annotated Ansar1 messages in our analytic approach. To increase the final size of our experimental dataset, one of the judges annotated an additional 100 posts from the Ansar1 collection following the same protocol described above. In total, we observed that 13% of forum posts contained recruitment according to our definition.

Analytic approach

We developed a binary classifier that labels forum posts as either containing or not containing VE recruitment. We used the following probability model:

$$Pr[Recruitment = True \mid d_i] = F[w_1(d_i), ..., w_n(d_i)] \tag{1}$$

In Equation 1, *Recruitment* is a binary classification label, $d_i \in D$ is a forum post, and w_j is a feature function of d_i. In the following section, we discuss the features used and then we present different formulations of the classification function F.

Text classification features

We employed a bag-of-words, or unigram only, feature space by parsing each forum post in the corpus into a term-by-document matrix. This matrix of term frequency (*tf*) features was created using the *RTextTools* and *tm* text mining packages in R [39,40] which also performed basic normalization and feature reduction through the removal of URL web addresses, numbers, punctuation, stopwords, and whitespace. The number of features was further reduced through stemming using the Porter Stemming Algorithm [41]. Under this representation, $w_j(d_i)$ is equal to the raw frequency of a stemmed word form, with n (the number of feature functions) equal to the number of distinct words remaining after document processing.

We then normalized each term frequency (*tf$_j$*) and weighted each by its inverse document frequency (*IDF$_j$*),

producing the logarithmically scaled TF-IDF feature function shown below [42]:

$$w_j(d_i) = \frac{(\log_2(tf_j) + 1) \cdot IDF_j}{\sqrt{\sum_{j'} w_{j'}(d_i)}} \tag{2}$$

where the denominator is a normalization of the feature vector for unit length, and the formula for *IDF* is shown below:

$$IDF_j = \log_2 \left(\frac{|D|}{\sum_{d_i \in D} \mathbb{I}[w_j \in d_i]} \right)$$

$|D|$, corpus cardinality, is the total number of posts in the training corpus, and the denominator represents the number of posts containing at least one occurrence of the *jth* feature (i.e. word). In order to keep the test data unbiased we used *IDF* terms computed only from posts in the training portion of the corpus.

Classification functions

We conducted supervised learning over our annotated posts using a variety of classification functions: naive Bayes, logistic regression, classification trees, boosting, and support vector machines (SVM).

Naive Bayes

Our application of a naive Bayes classifier is described below as an example of how we applied the probability model in Equation 1 to the various classification algorithms mentioned in this section. We calculated the posterior probability of VE recruitment $Pr(Rec_j \mid d_i)$, where $Rec_j \in \{+1, -1\}$, by building upon Bayes' rule and the generic probabilistic model defined above [43]:

$$Pr[Rec_j \mid \mathbf{w}(d_i)] = \frac{Pr[\mathbf{w}(d_i) \mid Rec_j] \, Pr(Rec_j)}{Pr[\mathbf{w}(d_i)]}$$

$$= \frac{Pr[\mathbf{w}(d_i) \mid Rec_j] \, Pr(Rec_j)}{\sum_{r \in Rec} Pr[\mathbf{w}(d_i) \mid Rec_r] \, Pr(Rec_r)}$$

The naive Bayes independence assumption reduces the joint probability to the product of component probabilities $Pr[w_k(d_i) \mid Rec_j]$, giving us the posterior probability estimator $F[w_1(d_i), ..., w_n(d_i)]$ from Equation 1. Since the denominator is a constant with respect to class Rec_j, the posterior function F can be further reduced to the following proportion:

$$Pr[Rec_j \mid w_1(d_i), \ldots, w_n(d_i)] \propto Pr(Rec_j) \prod_{k=1}^{n} Pr[w_k(d_i) \mid Rec_j] \tag{3}$$

Our implementation of naive Bayes was adapted from the R package *e1071* for use with the sparse training data typical in a term-by-document matrix [44]. We fit a naive

Bayes model using the default settings of Laplace (add one) smoothing and priors taken from the training data.

Logistic regression

We used our probability model from Equation 1 with a two-class logistic regression model. Given VE recruitment class labels $Rec = \{+1, -1\}$, we applied the following generalized linear model (GLM) using the logit function [45].

$$Pr\left[Rec_j = \pm 1 \mid \mathbf{w}(d_i)\right] = \frac{1}{1 + \exp\left[-Rec_j\left(\beta_0 + \sum_{k=1}^{n} \beta_k \cdot w_k(d_i)\right)\right]}$$

We estimated parameters $\beta_0, \dots, \beta_k$ from training data by minimizing the L2-regularized log-likelihood:

$$\frac{1}{2}\boldsymbol{\beta}^T\boldsymbol{\beta} + C\sum_{i=1}^{n} \log\left(1 + e^{-Rec_i\,\boldsymbol{\beta}^T d_i}\right) \qquad (4)$$

where $C > 0$ is the regularization cost parameter.

We used the *LiblineaR* package in R to minimize Equation 4 and then to predict the VE recruitment classification of testing data [46]. All GLM results shown in the "Results and discussion" section are for L2-regularized logistic regression models fit with the default settings for this R package and an L2-regularization cost parameter C equal to the ratio of negative to positive class labels.

Classification trees

We applied the probability model in Equation 1 to a classification tree by calculating the posterior probability of the recruitment classes at each node of the tree. The R package *tree* was used to train classifiers grown using recursive partitioning with a deviance criterion to select features at each node [47]. We used the default package parameters to control tree growth, including: minimum within-node deviance $= 0.01(deviance_{root})$, minimum allowable node size $= 10$, and minimum observations to a candidate child node $= 5$.

Logit boosting

We applied an ensemble of the tree classifier to this recruitment classification problem using the LogitBoost algorithm implemented in the R package *caTools* [48]. The boosting results shown in the "Results and discussion" section were produced using the package's default weak learner, decision stumps, and 101 boosting iterations. Logit boosting is an application of the original boosting algorithm, AdaBoost, except with the binomial log-likelihood as the minimized loss function (logistic loss) shown below [49]:

$$\sum_{i=1}^{n} \log\left(1 + e^{-2Rec_i\,F(d_i)}\right) \qquad (5)$$

Support vector machines

Finally, we trained a recruitment classifier using the support vector machine (SVM) algorithm implemented in the R package *e1071* [44]. SVMs do not fit into a probability model like Equation 1; however, the R package provides a method for estimating class probabilities if they are required for things like performance comparisons with receiver operating characteristic (ROC) curves. All SVM results shown below were produced using default package parameters, constraint violation cost $= 100$, and a radial basis function as the kernel.

Results and discussion

To make full use of the annotated data available for training and testing, we randomly segmented the data into ten folds and applied cross-validation. The statistics shown in this section come from the aggregated results of those ten models trained on mutually exclusive training data. We evaluated the classification methods using ROC curves, which show trade-offs between the metrics in the contingency table shown in Table 4. Specifically, ROC curves show the trade-offs between the False Positive Rate (FPR) and True Positive Rate (TPR) at various classification thresholds θ, as generated using Equations 6 and 7. We also employed area under the ROC curve (AUC) to compare each method's performance along the entire curve using a single measure.

$$FPR(\theta) = \frac{FP}{FP + TN} = \frac{FP}{N} \qquad (6)$$

$$TPR(\theta) = \frac{TP}{TP + FN} = \frac{TP}{P} \qquad (7)$$

A comparison of five VE recruitment classifiers using the annotated Ansar1 data can be seen in Figure 1. These are mean ROC curves averaged over the ten fold cross-validation experiment. Results show all the classifiers performing better than a random-guess model (the diagonal), with the SVM classifier performing best at an AUC of 0.89. A comparison of bootstrap results estimating the

Table 4 Confusion matrix used to assess the recruitment model's classification performance

Observed classification	Model classification		
	$Pr(Rec_j\mid d_i) \geq \theta$	$Pr(Rec_j\mid d_i) < \theta$	
Recruitment $=$ True	True positives	False negatives	$P = TP + FN$
	(TP)	(FN)	
Recruitment $=$ False	False positives	True negatives	$N = FP + TN$
	(FP)	(TN)	
	$\hat{P} = TP + FP$	$\hat{N} = FN + TN$	$I = P + N$

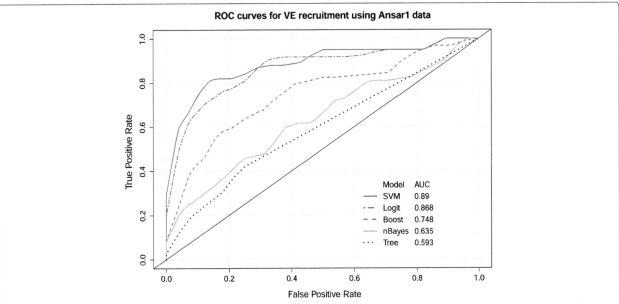

Figure 1 Comparison of VE recruitment classifiers using ROC curves. Curves are averaged over ten cross-validation folds showing classification results for the models.

mean cross-validated AUC can be seen in Figure 2. These bootstrap results were obtained by re-sampling 10,000 times from each testing fold, calculating the AUC on each bootstrapped sample, and then averaging each of those bootstrapped AUCs across the ten cross-validation folds. This resulted in 10,000 mean AUCs for each of the classification models described above. The box-plots

provide a similar graphical performance comparison to Figure 1, but also provide a reference for how widely each method's accuracy varies. All the methods range between 0.2 and 0.3 AUC with SVM having the smallest performance variance and boosting having the widest. A statistical comparison of the five classification methods using the bootstrapped mean AUCs is shown in Table 5.

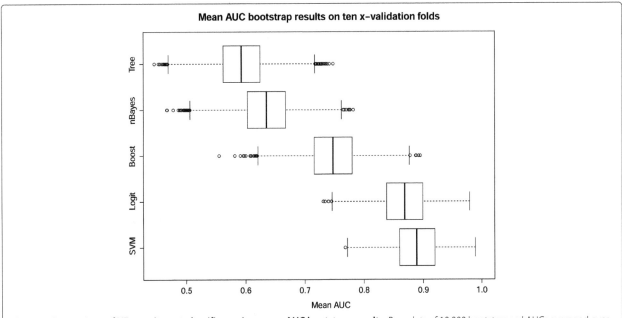

Figure 2 Comparison of VE recruitment classifiers using mean AUC bootstrap results. Box-plots of 10,000 bootstrapped AUCs averaged over ten cross-validation folds.

Table 5 95% confidence intervals for multiple comparisons of bootstrapped mean AUCs using Tukey's range test

Tukey's test comparisons	95% CI Upper	95% CI Lower
SVM – Logit	0.019	0.023
SVM – Boost	0.139	0.143
SVM – nBayes	0.252	0.256
SVM – Tree	0.294	0.297
Logit – Boost	0.119	0.122
Logit – nBayes	0.232	0.235
Logit – Tree	0.273	0.276
Boost – nBayes	0.111	0.115
Boost – Tree	0.153	0.156
nBayes – Tree	0.040	0.043

We used Tukey's range test to determine if the difference in mean AUC between the models is statistically significant [50]. The 95% confidence intervals in Table 5 show a significant difference between each of the classification methods' mean AUC. Therefore, as shown by the ordering of model results in Figure 2 and Table 5, the SVM classifier returned the best performance and classification trees returned the worst mean AUC performance ($p < 0.05$).

The computational complexity of these methods is well documented; however, their runtime performance on this VE recruitment task is not well known. A comparison of time performance benchmarks for two different tasks can be seen in Table 6. The training task results are obtained from trials of each supervised learning algorithm applied to 294 annotated posts per trial. The classification task is the application of each pre-trained classifier to a set of posts resulting in an average classification time per post. Comparing the results in Table 6, we can see that all the methods train in under 30 seconds with SVM, Logistic Regression, and naive Bayes learning two orders of magnitude faster. SVM and logistic regression perform the best on the classification task, but all the methods classify posts in well under a second. Therefore any of these

Table 6 Time performance benchmark results* (a) training time using 294 posts, and (b) mean classification time per post

	Training (s)	Classification (ms/post)
SVM	0.450	0.18
Logit	0.049	0.22
Boost	29.790	0.27
nBayes	0.987	128.57
Tree	11.140	28.18

*Hardware: Intel® Core™ i5 CPU M 480 @ 2.67 GHz; 8 GB RAM.

methods is a feasible VE recruitment classifier if the average time between posts is greater than a tenth of a second; a reasonable assumption for many online forums.

Typically classification research compares results against prior methods as a benchmark for improvements in accuracy; however, we were unable to find any previously published methods for the specific task of identifying violent extremist recruitment using text classification techniques. Thus, our results serve as initial performance benchmarks against which future methods can be compared.

To provide some understanding of how the best performing classification models are being trained to recognize VE recruitment, Table 7 shows a list of the top-weighted features in the logistic regression model. It is clear from the table that posts relating to the escalating conflicts in Nigeria and Somalia were primary topics in the Ansar1 data—an intuitive finding considering the 2009 timeframe of the sampled data. The importance of such terms hints at the Logit model's potential for over-fitting this particular time period. Running the same model on other time periods would likely produce lower performance scores, since different wording is likely. Other important terms like "jihad", "allah", and words stemming from "milit" exemplify the algorithm's ability to recognize typical features of Islamic violent extremism. Perhaps surprisingly, none of the top ten terms are particularly indicative of recruitment. This may be due to the abundant presence of terms like "recruit" and "join". These terms are among the top 30 most frequent, appearing in our corpus 178 and 126 times respectively. High frequency makes these terms more likely to occur in both recruitment and non-recruitment posts and therefore diminishes their discriminating power. Regardless of how they work, performance metrics show that the best models (SVM and Logit) detect VE recruitment with considerable accuracy (mean $AUC > 0.85$).

Conclusions and future work

This work was motivated by increasing online activities of violent extremist organizations along with the lack of automated approaches to analyze such activity.

Table 7 The most discriminating term features as weighted by the cross-validated logistic regression models

Feature	Weight	Feature	Weight
nigeria	0.90	jihad	0.61
hamas	0.72	alandalus	0.61
foreign	0.67	milit (ant,ary,...)	0.60
somalia	0.66	american	0.60
may	-0.65	allah	-0.54

Our research built upon recent data collection and analysis efforts to develop supervised learning and natural language processing methods that automatically identify cyber-recruitment by violent extremists. The results presented in this article support the conclusion that automatic VE recruitment detection is a feasible goal. As the first reported results on this task, our classifiers serve as initial performance benchmarks against which future VE recruitment classifiers can be compared.

In the future, our VE recruitment detection methods could be improved by including support for non-English languages. Whether such future methods use automatic translation or non-English features, support for other languages is an important task considering that violent extremist groups frequently operate in non-English speaking communities. Incorporating non-English text and features could be accomplished through the use of experts to perform the manual annotation. Expert judges might also improve annotation quality if agreement remains strong. Future work could also analyze classifier behavior in depth, and test the effectiveness of more advanced feature selection and modeling techniques. Methods like latent semantic analysis perform singular value decomposition transformations on the feature space and may be employed to further reduce both dimensionality and the effect of non-discriminating terms [51]. Latent Dirichlet allocation may be used to substitute the terms in a high-dimensional feature space with a smaller set of latent topics that represent the major subjects appearing in the corpus [52]. Such latent variable modeling techniques could serve as feature selection and replacement methods while preserving the statistical relationships that are essential for text classification tasks.

By testing the effectiveness of our methods in a proxy for real-world settings we demonstrated that such automated classification tools would clearly fit into the workflow of counterterrorism intelligence teams like the FBI's information review analysts. The current workflow tasks human analysts with manually reviewing and annotating "the ever-increasing [volume of investigative] information" stored in data warehouses like the Electronic Surveillance Data Management System (DWS-EDMS) used by the FBI [6]. An automated classification system using our methods for detecting VE recruitment could serve as a pre-screening step in the current review workflow tasked with reducing the volume of documents requiring human attention. Our automated approach could also complement current lead management systems like eGuardian by automatically detecting potential terrorist recruitment events so they can be efficiently compiled into leads for current investigations or used as evidence to open new terrorism-related investigations.

More generally our automated classification methods could be used as part of a VE recruitment identification

and tracking methodology that would enable the study of recruitment efforts and the membership dynamics of violent organizations. Such a method might be able to measure the effectiveness of extremist and counterinsurgency efforts on new membership by correlating specific recruitment activities and current events with changes in the VE population of a community. As a future research path, this proposed methodology requires (1) an automated system for classifying whether a forum user is a member of a violent extremist group, and (2) time series methods for analyzing recruitment and membership along a timeline.

In light of the still unfolding news regarding the NSA's Boundless Informant and PRISM programs [53], we address some ethical implications of our work. Given that such a comprehensive and intrusive source of text data does exist, there is clearly a potential for abusing a recruitment and membership classification method to target non-combative individuals. Such tracking methods could thwart perfectly legal recruitment efforts of peaceful protesters, or radical yet law-abiding religious sects. These groups might fit the profile of a VE organization in every way except the critical ingredient of violence. Furthermore, recruitment alone rarely necessitates a violent act even though a recruiter may refer to or even encourage such acts. Because of these possible unethical repercussions, we proposed classification methods that target not just extremist groups, but specifically violent groups engaged in acts like terrorism. We hope that tuning the learning algorithms in this way will reduce some risk of misuse.

Abbreviations
AUC: Area under the curve (ROC curve); Boost: Boosting algorithm; COIN: Counterinsurgency; FPR: False positive rate; GLM: Generalized linear model; IDF: Inverse document frequency; Logit: Logistic regression algorithm; nBayes: Naive Bayes algorithm; Rec: Recruitment (of violent extremists); ROC: Receiver operating characteristic; SNA: Social network analysis; SVM: Support vector machines; tf: Term frequency; TPR: True positive rate; VE: Violent extremist.

Competing interests
The authors declare that they have no competing interests.

Authors' contributions
JS developed the recruitment detection methodology, implemented and tested the learning algorithms used in this paper, and drafted the manuscript. MG provided theoretical guidance in the whole procedure and revised the manuscript. Both authors read and approved the final manuscript.

Acknowledgements
This research was financially supported by a grant from the United States Army Research Laboratory (ARL).

References
1. LA Overbey, G McKoy, J Gordon, S McKitrick, Automated sensing and social network analysis in virtual worlds, in *Intelligence and Security Informatics (ISI)* (IEEE Vancouver, BC, Canada, 2010), pp. 179–184
2. R Torok, "Make A Bomb In Your Mums Kitchen": Cyber Recruiting And Socialisation of 'White Moors' and Home Grown Jihadists, in *Australian*

Counter Terrorism Conference (School of Computer and Infomation Science, Edith Cowan University Perth, Western Australia, 2010), pp. 54–61

3. M Rogers, ed. by A Silke, Chapter 4: The Psychology of Cyber-Terrorism, in *Terrorists, Victims and Society: Psychological Perspectives on Terrorism and its Consequences* (John Wiley & Sons Chichester, West Sussex, England, 2003), pp. 77–92

4. S O'Rourke, Virtual radicalisation: Challenges for police, in *8th Australian Information Warfare and Security Conference* (School of Computer and Infomation Science, Edith Cowan University Perth, Western Australia, 2007), pp. 29–35

5. S Mandal, E-P Lim, Second life: Limits of creativity or cyber threat, in *IEEE Conference on Technologies for Homeland Security* (IEEE Waltham, MA, 2008), pp. 498–503

6. WH Webster, DE Winter, L Adrian, J Steel, WM Baker, RJ Bruemmer, KL Wainstein, Final report of the William H.Webster Commission on the Federal Bureau of Investigation, counterterrorism intelligence, and the events at Fort Hood, Texas on November 5, 2009. Technical report, Federal Bureau of Investigation (2012)

7. RR Tomes, Waging war on terror relearning counterinsurgency warfare. Parameters. **34**(1), 16–28 (2004)

8. F Gutiérrez, Recruitment in a civil war: a preliminary discussion of the colombian case, in *Santa Fe Institute, Mimeo*, (2006)

9. M Humphreys, JM Weinstein, Who fights? the determinants of participation in civil war. Am. J. Pol. Sci. **52**(2), 436–455 (2008)

10. MI Lichbach, *The Rebel's Dilemma.* (University of Michigan Press, Ann Arbor, 1998)

11. K Peters, P Richards, 'Why we fight': Voices of youth combatants in Sierra Leone. Africa. **68**(02), 183–210 (1998)

12. JM Weinstein, *Inside Rebellion: The Politics of Insurgent Violence.* (Cambridge University Press, New York, 2007)

13. RD Petersen, *Resistance and Rebellion: Lessons from Eastern Europe.* (Cambridge University Press, New York, 2001)

14. S Popkin, The rational peasant. Theory Soc. **9**(3), 411–471 (1980)

15. JC Scott, *The Moral Economy of the Peasant: Rebellion and Subsistence in Southeast Asia.* (Yale University Press, New Haven & London, 1976)

16. EJ Wood, *Insurgent Collective Action and Civil War in El Salvador.* (Cambridge University Press, New York, 2003)

17. RW McGehee, *Deadly Deceits: My 25 Years in the CIA.* (Sheridan Square Publications, Inc., New York, 1983), pp. 95–116

18. M Conway, Terrorism and the internet: new media–new threat? Parliamentary Aff. **59**(2), 283–298 (2006)

19. R Torok, Developing an explanatory model for the process of online radicalisation and terrorism. Secur. Informatics. **2**(1), 1–10 (2013)

20. L Bowman-Grieve, A psychological perspective on virtual communities supporting terrorist & extremist ideologies as a tool for recruitment. Secur. Informatics. **2**(1), 1–5 (2013)

21. EF Kohlmann, Al-Qaida's MySpace: terrorist recruitment on the internet. CTC Sentinel. **1**(2), 8–9 (2008)

22. LA Overbey, G McKoy, J Gordon, S McKitrick, Jr MH, L Buhler, L Casassa, S Yaryan, Virtual DNA: Investigating cyber-behaviors in virtual worldsL. Technical Report 33-09 E, Space and Naval Warfare System Center Atlantic Charleston, SC (2009)

23. GS McNeal, Cyber embargo: Countering the internet jihad. Case West. Reserv. Univ. J. Int. Law. **39**, 789–826 (2008)

24. H Chen, S Thoms, T Fu, Cyber extremism in web 2.0: An exploratory study of international jihadist groups, in *IEEE International Conference on Intelligence and Security Informatics (ISI)* (IEEE Taipei, 2008), pp. 98–103

25. M Yang, M Kiang, H Chen, Y Li, Artificial immune system for illicit content identification in social media. J. Am. Soc. Inf. Technol. **63**(2), 256–269 (2012)

26. A Basu, Social network analysis of terrorist organizations in India, in *North American Association for Computational Social and Organizational Science (NAACSOS) Conference* (NAACSOS Notre Dame, Indiana, 2005), pp. 26–28

27. KM Carley, Destabilization of covert networks. Comput. Math. Organ. Theory. **12**(1), 51–66 (2006)

28. M Chau, J Xu, Using web mining and social network analysis to study the emergence of cyber communities in blogs, in *Terrorism Informatics* (Springer New York, 2008), pp. 473–494

29. J Diesner, KM Carley, Using network text analysis to detect the organizational structure of covert networks, in *Proceedings of the North*

American Association for Computational Social and Organizational Science (NAACSOS) Conference (NAACSOS Pittsburgh, 2004)

30. Z Chen, B Liu, M Hsu, M Castellanos, R Ghosh, Identifying intention posts in discussion forums, in *Proceedings of NAACL-HLT* (Association for Computational Linguistics Atlanta, Georgia, 2013), pp. 1041–1050

31. H Chen, W Chung, J Qin, E Reid, M Sageman, G Weimann, Uncovering the dark web: A case study of jihad on the web. J. Am. Soc. Inf. Sci. Technol. **59**(8), 1347–1359 (2008)

32. T Fu, A Abbasi, H Chen, A focused crawler for dark web forums. J. Am. Soc. Inf. Sci. Technol. **61**(6), 1213–1231 (2010)

33. Google Inc., Google Translate (2014). http://translate.google.com/

34. H Chen, E Reid, J Sinai, A Silke, B Ganor (eds.), *Terrorism Informatics: Knowledge Management and Data Mining for Homeland Security.* (Springer, New York, 2008)

35. Artificial Intelligence Laboratory, University Of Arizona, Dark Web Forum Portal: Ansar AlJihad Network English Website (2014). http://cri-portal.dyndns.org

36. J Cohen, A coefficient of agreement for nominal scales. Educ. Psychol. Meas. **20**(1), 37–46 (1960)

37. JR Landis, GG Koch, The measurement of observer agreement for categorical data. Biometrics. **33**(1), 159–174 (1977)

38. JL Fleiss, B Levin, MC Paik, The measurement of interrater agreement. Stat. Methods Rates Proportions. **2**, 212–236 (1981)

39. I Feinerer, K Hornik, *Tm: Text Mining Package.* (R Foundation for Statistical Computing, 2014). R package version 0.5-10. http://CRAN.R-project.org/package=tm

40. TP Jurka, L Collingwood, AE Boydstun, E Grossman, W van Atteveldt, RTextTools: Automatic Text Classification Via Supervised Learning (2014). R package version 1.4.2. http://CRAN.R-project.org/package=RTextTools

41. CJ Van Rijsbergen, SE Robertson, MF Porter, *New Models in Probabilistic Information Retrieval.* (British Library Research and Development Dept, 1980)

42. W Cavnar, ed. by DK Harman, Using an n-gram-based document representation with a vector processing retrieval model, in *Overview of the Third Text Retrieval Conference* (Computer Systems Laboratory, National Institute of Standards and Technology Gaithersburg, MD, 1995), pp. 269–277

43. RO Duda, PE Hart, DG Stork, *Pattern Classification*, 2nd edn. (John Wiley & Sons, Inc, New York, 2001), p. 62

44. D Meyer, E Dimitriadou, K Hornik, A Weingessel, F Leisch, E1071: Misc Functions of the Department of Statistics (e1071), TU Wien (2014). R package version 1.6-2. http://CRAN.R-project.org/package=e1071

45. C-J Lin, RC Weng, SS Keerthi, Trust region newton method for logistic regression. J. Mach. Learn. Res. **9**, 627–650 (2008)

46. T Helleputte, LiblineaR: Linear Predictive Models Based On The Liblinear C/C++ Library (2013). R package version 1.80-7. http://CRAN.R-project.org/web/packages/LiblineaR

47. B Ripley, Tree: Classification and Regression Trees (2014). R package version 1.0-35. http://CRAN.R-project.org/package=tree

48. J Tuszynski, caTools: ROC AUC Tools, Moving Window Statistics (2013). R package version 1.16. http://CRAN.R-project.org/package=caTools

49. J Friedman, T Hastie, R Tibshirani, Additive logistic regression: a statistical view of boosting. Ann. Stat. **28**(2), 337–407 (2000)

50. AP Fenech, Tukey's method of multiple comparison in the randomized blocks model. J. Am. Stat. Assoc. **74**(368), 881–884 (1979)

51. S Deerwester, ST Dumais, GW Furnas, TK Landauer, R Harshman, Indexing by latent semantic analysis. J. Am. Soc. Inf. Sci. **41**(6), 391–407 (1990)

52. DM Blei, AY Ng, MI Jordan, Latent dirichlet allocation. J. Mach. Learn. Res. **3**, 993–1022 (2003)

53. G Greenwald, NSA Collecting Phone Records of Millions of Verizon Customers Daily (2013). http://www.guardian.co.uk/world/2013/jun/06/nsa-phone-records-verizon-court-order

12

CrimeFighter Investigator: Integrating synthesis and sense-making for criminal network investigation

Rasmus Rosenqvist Petersen[*] and Uffe Kock Wiil

Abstract

Criminal network investigation involves a number of complex tasks and problems. Overall tasks include collection, processing, and analysis of information, in which analysis is the key to successful use of information since it transforms raw data into intelligence. Analysts have to deal with problems such as information volume and complexity which are typically resolved with more resources. This approach together with sequential thinking introduces compartmentalization, inhibits information sharing, and ultimately results in intelligence failure. We view analysis as an iterative and incremental process of creative synthesis and logic-based sense-making where all stakeholders participate and contribute. This paper presents a novel tool that supports a human-centered, target-centric model for criminal network investigation. The developed tool provides more comprehensive support for analysis tasks than existing tools and measures of performance indicate that the integration of synthesis and sense-making is feasible.

Introduction

Target-centric criminal network investigation involves a number of complex knowledge management tasks such as collection, processing, and analysis of information. The motivation for such work is well described in the training manual of the intelligence analysts of the London Metropolitan Police [1]: *Analysis is the key to successful use of information; it transforms raw data into intelligence. Without the ability to perform effective and useful analysis, the intelligence process is reduced to a simple storage and retrieval system for effectively unrelated data.* Synthesis and sense-making are core analysis tasks; analysts move pieces of information around, stop to look for patterns that can help them relate the information pieces, add new pieces of information and iteration after iteration an information structure appears. Synthesizing emerging and evolving information structures is a creative and cognitive process best performed by humans. Making sense of synthesized information structures (i.e., searching for patterns) is a logic-based process where computers outperform humans as

information volume and complexity increase. Developing useful tool support for target-centric criminal network investigation requires integration of synthesis and sense-making.

We present a novel tool for target-centric criminal network investigation called CrimeFighter Investigator with focus on core investigative processes and tasks. CrimeFighter Investigator is part of the CrimeFighter toolbox for counterterrorism [2]. Besides CrimeFighter Investigator, the toolbox consists of the Explorer tool targeted at open source collection and processing and the Assistant tool targeted at advanced structural analysis and visualization.

The remainder of this paper is organized as follows: In the Section 'Criminal network investigation', we discuss this area of security informatics research and focus on four recurring problems. A generic process model for human-centered, target-centric criminal network investigation is proposed to embrace these problems. A list of investigation tasks is presented to guide the development of tool support. The Section 'CrimeFighter Investigator' describes how a selection of these tasks is supported by CrimeFighter Investigator. The Section 'Evaluation' evaluates CrimeFighter Investigator, and the Section 'Conclusions' summarizes our methods, contributions, and outlines future work.

*Correspondence: rasmusrosenqvistpetersen@gmail.com
The Maersk Mc-Kinney Moeller Institute, University of Southern Denmark, Odense, Denmark

Criminal network investigation

Criminal network investigation involves the collection, processing, and analysis of information related to specified targets. We use three investigation cases to identify criminal network investigation tasks and the challenges associated with these tasks. We propose a generic process model for human-centered, target-centric investigation to embrace the identified challenges. Finally, a list of specific investigative tasks are outlined to guide the development of useful software tool support.

A review and step-by-step reconstruction of three criminal network investigation cases[a] emphasized the following challenges: **Resources** (e.g., [3-5]) are inherently a challenge for criminal network investigations, for example not enough man power to follow up on leads. Contextual pressures such as time constraints, dynamism, and changing goals are typically resolved with more resources. Existing evidence suggests that decision-making and information processing abilities are often not optimal because the informational complexity of the world overwhelms human cognitive abilities and creates bias. **Information volume** challenges (e.g., [3,6-8]) includes information abundance and information scarcity. If information is abundant and the resources required to process the information are limited, potential suspects might not be discovered. On the other hand, if information is scarce, decisions might be based on uncorroborated intelligence later proven to be false. **Information complexity** (e.g., [8-10]) can be introduced by both emerging and evolving information or static collections of information where much of the information is unreliable. Information abundance or scarcity on its own does not necessarily make the network information more complex. The use of aliases, social complexity (e.g., culture and language) and the mix of different information types (e.g., audio, images, signals, video) are all factors that increase the complexity of information. **Information sharing** challenges (e.g., [7,11,12]) are often the consequence of a compartmentalized intelligence process, the culture within intelligence agencies and the trade craft of secret intelligence itself. Several reports have concluded that insufficient information sharing between intelligence agencies is often a root cause of intelligence failure. Examples include the 9/11 commission report and the UK report on whether or not the 7/7 bombings in London could have been prevented.

The main goal of our research is to understand criminal network investigation challenges, processes, and tasks and develop tools to assist the people working with these processes and tasks every day, to help minimize the impact of the challenges.

Investigation model

Based on a specific target-centric model for intelligence analysis [12], we propose a generic process model for human-centered, target-centric criminal network investigation [13,14] in Figure 1.

The customer requests information about a specific target. The investigators search through existing information and request information from the collectors (that may also be investigators). Information related to the target is acquired in disparate pieces over time. The investigators use the acquired information to build a model of the target (synthesis) and extract useful information from the model (sense-making). The extracted information added to new information coming in, results in changes to the model (synthesis). The sense-making - synthesis cycle is continued throughout the investigation as new information is acquired from investigation or extracted from the model. The investigators both work individually and cooperatively as a team. The investigation results are disseminated to the customer at the end of the investigation or at certain intervals (or as requested).

Criminal network investigation is a human-centered process. Investigators (and collectors) rely heavily on their past experience (tacit knowledge) when conducting investigations. Hence, these processes cannot be fully automated. The philosophy of the CrimeFighter Toolbox is that the humans (in this case the investigators) are in charge of the investigative tasks and the software tools are there to support them [2]. The tools should be controlled by the investigators and should support the complex intellectual work (e.g., synthesis and sense-making) to allow the investigators to reach better results faster. CrimeFighter Investigator focuses on providing human-centered, target-centric support for criminal network investigations (acquisition, synthesis, sense-making,

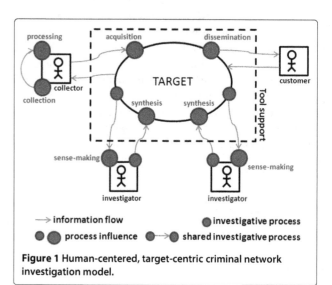

Figure 1 Human-centered, target-centric criminal network investigation model.

and dissemination). Tool support for collection and processing is beyond the scope of this paper: the Crime-Fighter Explorer tool focuses on that. Tool support for advanced structural analysis and visualization of the target model generated is also beyond the scope of this paper: the CrimeFighter Assistant tool focuses on that.

Criminal network investigation tasks

Based on cases and observations of criminal network investigation, contact with experienced end-users from various communities, examination of existing process models and existing tools for criminal network investigation (e.g., [1,10,12,15-24]), and our own ideas for tool support, we maintain a list of investigation tasks for each of the processes: acquisition, synthesis, sense-making, and dissemination. The task lists can be seen as wish lists of requirements for what a tool for criminal network investigation should support; the lists serve as the basis for our tool development efforts. The lists are not exhaustive; we expect to uncover additional requirements for all four processes over time.

Acquisition

Some information may be available at the beginning of an investigation, but new information tends to dribble in over time in disparate pieces of varying size and complexity.

- **Acquisition methods.** Electronic information arrives from various sources and should be easy to insert into the investigation tool using methods such as import, drag-and-drop, and cut-and-paste.
- **Dynamic attributes** are required to support acquisition of various data sets formatted using for example graph markup language (GraphML) or comma separated values (CSV), which are likely to have attributes different from those already in an investigation.
- **Attribute mapping.** To support dynamic attributes it is necessary to map attributes in the acquired information to the investigation data model. For example, mapping attributes to i an information element's visual labels.

Synthesis tasks assist investigators in enhancing their particular criminal network model:

- Creating, editing, and deleting **entities**. Investigators think in terms of people, places, objects, their relationships and groups.
- Creating, editing, and deleting **relationships**. Descriptive associations between entities help discover similarities and ultimately solve criminal network investigations. The impact of link (relation) analysis on the creation of the target model is crucial.

- **Re-structuring.** Information structures typically evolve and new structures emerge during the investigation, through continuous re-structuring of entities and their associations.
- **Grouping.** Investigators often group entities using symbols like color and co-location (weak association), or they use more encapsulating symbols like labeled boxes (strong association).
- **Collapsing and expanding** information is essential since the space available for manipulating information is limited physically, perceptually, and cognitively.
- **Brainstorming** is often used during the early phases of an investigation to get an initial overview of the target and the investigation at hand. Brainstorming is an example of a task that involves both synthesis and sense-making activities. Brainstorming is often supported by tools that allow information elements to be organized in a hierarchical manner.
- **Information types.** Multimedia support is helpful when investigators want to add known locations of individuals to a map or link persons to different segments within an audio file.
- **Emerging attributes.** New attributes are added to entities during synthesis and when importing network information into ongoing investigations.

Sense-making tasks assist investigators in extracting useful information from the synthesized target model:

- **Retracing the steps.** Investigators often retrace the steps of their investigation to see what might have been missed and where to direct resources in the ongoing investigation.
- **Creating hypotheses.** Generating sets of alternative hypotheses is a core task of any investigation that involves making claims and finding supporting and opposing evidence.
- **Adaptive modeling.** Representing the expected structure of networks for pattern and missing link detection is a proactive sense-making task. Adaptive modeling embeds the tacit knowledge of investigators in network models for prediction and analysis.
- **Prediction.** The ability to determine the presence or absence of relationships between and groupings of people, places, and other entity types is invaluable when investigating a case. Prediction at different information levels, i.e., attribute-, entity-, and group-level is often required.
- **Alias detection.** Network structures may contain duplicate or nearly duplicate entities. Alias detection can be used to identify multiple overlapping representations of the same real world object.
- **Exploring perspectives.** To reduce the cognitive biases associated with a particular mind set, exploring

130 Information Security Management

different perspectives (views) of the information is a key criminal network investigation task.

- **Decision-making.** During an investigation, decisions have to be made such as selecting among competing hypotheses, or where to allocate resources on the ground.
- **Social network analysis.** Network centrality measures such as degree, betweenness, closeness, and eigenvector can provide important investigation insights.

Dissemination tasks help investigators to formulate their accumulated knowledge for the customer:

- **Storytelling.** Investigators ultimately need to 'tell stories'. Organizing evidence by events and source documents are important tasks, since the alleged story behind the evidence can then be presented.
- **Report generation** involves graphics, complete reports, parts of investigations, etc. Being able to produce reports fast is important in relation to time-critical environments and frequent briefing summaries, which otherwise take up too much valuable investigation time.

CrimeFighter Investigator

CrimeFighter Investigator is based on a number of overall concepts (see Figure 2). At the center is a shared information space. Spatial hypertext research has inspired the features of the shared information space including the support of investigation history [13]. The view concept provides investigators with different perspectives on

the information in the space and provides alternative interaction options with information (hierarchical view to the left; spatial view at the center; algorithm output view to the right). Finally, a structural parser assists the investigators by relating otherwise unrelated information in different ways, either based on the entities themselves or by applying algorithms to analyze them. In the following, core CrimeFighter Investigator features are presented, but unfortunately space limitations mean that details are limited and not all supported features can be presented (see [13,14,25-27] for more details).

Acquisition support

CrimeFighter Investigator supports the import of network information formatted as comma separated values. Relations are imported as either an adjancy matrix or a list of information element pairs for large criminal networks. When importing criminal network information into investigations, it is necessary to map all network-dependent variables of the existing data model to attributes of the imported entities. Figure 3 shows the entity attributes for a data set containing *Person* information elements. *Person* entities have a label that displays the value of a particular attribute below the graphical abstraction of the entity (in this case, a stick man figure). When importing data, the user is requested to select the attribute to link to the display label by selecting and dragging the attribute from a list of all the entity's attributes to a label reference area. In Figure 3, the attribute *Short Name* is being dragged to the label reference area for person entities.

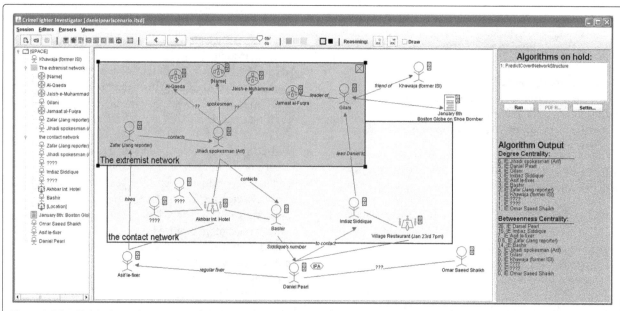

Figure 2 CrimeFighter Investigator screenshot showing an early phase of the Daniel Pearl investigation [9,28].

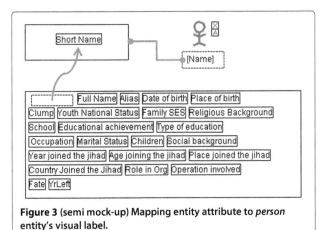

Figure 3 (semi mock-up) **Mapping entity attribute to *person* entity's visual label.**

Synthesis support

Synthesis of entities and their associations is done using well-known interaction metaphors. CrimeFighter Investigator supports three first class entities: **Information elements**, **relations** (between information elements) and **composites** (for grouping information elements and/or relations). Entities are created using a simple mouse drag gesture within the investigation space. Once created, delete and edit functionalities are available from a button menu attached to the entities as shown in Figure 2. Interactive labels provide another way to edit entity attributes linked to entity display labels. The direction and the label of relations are both edited by clicking the relation label. All entities are deleted using a menu button (⊠) positioned relative to the entity. The color of a composite can be set before and after its creation (Figure 2, top).

Our criminal network investigation entities are first class and therefore support continuous **restructuring** of network information. When an information element with multiple relations is deleted, the relation endpoints are considered empty and can be moved freely in the common information space. The investigator can delete the relation endpoints or reconnect them to other entities if desired using a drag and drop gesture. The hierarchical view (Figure 2, left) is used for classification by moving information elements in the hierarchically displayed structure. Different types of composites can be used to group information. The relation composite allows investigators to **group** multiple relations between two entities (such as multiple emails or phone calls between two persons) into a single visible entity (composite). Relation composites group relations by inclusion. Another type of composite supports **collapsing and expanding**. This type of composite groups all information elements by inclusion. Relations that are internal to the composite (have both endpoints inside) are also included, while external

relations (at least one endpoint outside) are referenced. This type of composite supports the concept of a sub-space that allows the investigators to work in detail with a portion of the complete network.

Sense-making support

Retracing the steps of criminal network investigations is facilitated by a history feature. Recording investigation history allows the investigative team to review the path or progress of their investigation or to retrieve information that previously had been deemed irrelevant or deleted, but then found to have greater significance due to new incoming information. The user interface of the investigation history feature is embedded in the tool bar (see Figure 2). Buttons allow navigation of recorded events, and current events are visualized using a slider as well as a label showing both the current event and the total number of events (e.g., 59/59). The history feature records all the interactions that investigators have with entities as events, e.g., "*create* information element", "*resize* composite", "*move* information element", and so on. Each event is given a time stamp and added to the sequential history.

Prediction support includes covert network structure and missing links prediction algorithms [5,29]. Examples of **social network analysis** support are centrality measures such as degree, closeness, and betweenness [30].

An example of two centrality measures running simultaneously can be seen in Figure 2 (right). A structural parser is used to select the algorithms that the investigator wants to run, if they should run sequentially or simultaneously, the order in which they should run, and how to output the results of algorithms. Customized combinations of different algorithms can be created for frequent use. For example, we developed a custom node removal algorithm which can be used by criminal network investigators to ask 'what-if' questions about the secondary effects of removing a key individual from a criminal network [25].

To evaluate the prediction algorithms, we developed three measures of performance and used two different data sets (see 'Evaluation'). One of these data sets is a network of al-Qaeda individuals who were an active part of the organization up to the beginning of 2003. A missing links prediction on a sampled version of 20 individuals from the al-Qaeda network is shown in Figure 4. The investigator can decide whether to append the predictions to the network or simply discard them.

Creating hypotheses is facilitated by the issue-based argumentation view shown in Figure 5. Criminal network investigators use factual evidence or inferential judgments to reason about the issues they come across in their work. Inferential judgments typically require detailed reasoning involving several positions and even more 'pro' and 'con' arguments, while fact-based reasoning typically is done

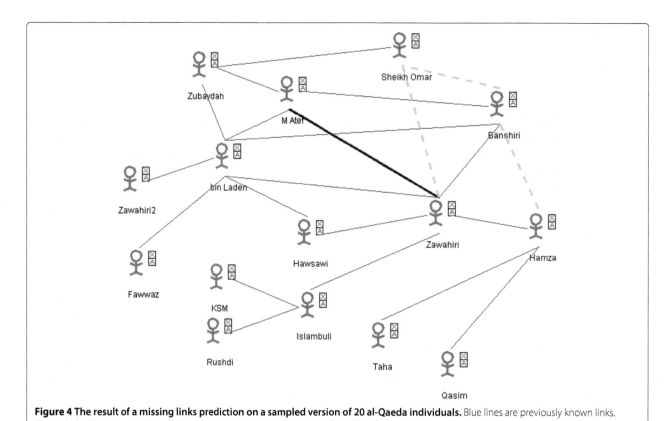

Figure 4 The result of a missing links prediction on a sampled version of 20 al-Qaeda individuals. Blue lines are previously known links. Green dashed lines are predicted links that were ultimately shown to be false. The thick black line is a predicted link that was true.

by creating relations between pieces of evidence (see the person information element 'Daniel Pearl' in Figure 2).

Hypothesis reasoning can be attached to any entity. A small hexagon icon with the text 'IPA' is used to show that reasoning is attached, and clicking the icon opens the issue-based argumentation shown in Figure 5. Reasoning can be used for several purposes: (1) to capture and visualize disagreement in an analysis situation, ensuring that all positions and arguments are heard; (2) to reason convincingly during storytelling (e.g., a senior police officer is creating a briefing based on a recently concluded investigation);

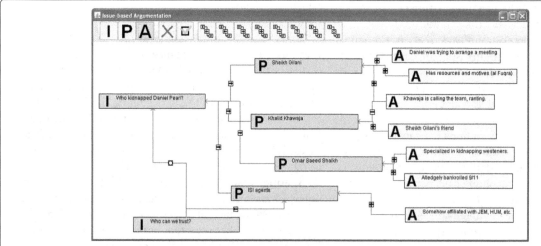

Figure 5 Issue-based argumentation view from the investigation of a kidnapping in Pakistan. The tool bar has buttons for creating issues (I), positions (P), arguments (A), and relations between them.

and (3) to create and explore (competing) hypotheses. According to the IBIS[b] model [31], we have adopted the following predefined relations: is-suggested-by ($\leftarrow$), responds-to ($\rightarrow$), supports ($+$), objects-to ($-$), questions (?), and generalizes or specializes ($\bigcirc$). The relation direction can be both ways in all cases. These predefined relations aid the criminal network investigators in controlling the mapping of their dialogue about issues, positions, and arguments.

Decision-making is currently only supported in the issue-based argumentation view. A "decision" includes a position, the issue it responds to, and associated arguments.

Dissemination support
A history editor is implemented in CrimeFighter Investigator to support **Storytelling**. The granularity of system level history events is often too fine for telling a story. The history editor allows the investigators to group history events that are relevant for the story individually, but when grouped together they explain one important step of the investigation. The investigators can delete events (e.g., if an entity was created by mistake and then deleted), annotate events or groups of events if they feel that the system-generated description is not sufficient, and move events up and down in order to match a time line of real events (e.g., people join a group at a different time from the investigation finding their group membership).

Report generation is available at all stages of a criminal network investigation. All CrimeFighter Investigator features implement a report interface that facilitates the addition or removal of individual report elements. The order in which elements are added to the report is also dynamic. This makes it easier to create reports targeting specific usages. For example, after a prediction is made, reports with or without detailed calculations can be retrieved using the algorithm view (Figure 2, right).

Evaluation
Current criminal network investigation tools aiming to integrate synthesis and sense-making utilize a variety of technologies. Therefore various approaches to evaluation are required. We apply three different evaluation methods. The results of two of these methods are shown in Table 1 and Table 2.

We compared the capabilities of CrimeFighter Investigator with other prominent commercial and research tools for criminal network investigation. In the future, we plan to involve more researchers and end-users in such comparisons. We are currently designing structured usability experiments following [32,33] for evaluation of specific CrimeFighter Investigator features. For now, we present usability feedback gathered from semi-structured interviews with a number of end-users from various criminal network investigation domains. Finally, a sense-making task has been evaluated by developing and testing measures of performance relevant for criminal network investigators.

Capability comparisons
In this section, various tools that support criminal network investigation are compared with CrimeFighter Investigator. The chosen tools include both prominent commercial tools and research prototypes, so that both current and imminent future state-of-the-art is considered. The following three commercial tools have been selected:

- **i2 Analyst's Notebook 8.5** supports a large set of analysis and visualization capabilities support analysts in quickly turning large sets of disparate information into high-quality and actionable intelligence to prevent crime and terrorism [19].
- **Palantir Government 3.0** is a platform for information analysis designed for environments where the fragments of data which an analyst combines to tell the larger story, are spread across a vast set of starting material. Palantir is currently used in various domains such as intelligence, defense, and cyber security [20].
- **Xanalys Link Explorer 6.0** (previously Watson [1]) allows investigators to apply powerful query and analysis techniques to their data, presenting the answers in a range of visualizations such as link charts, time lines, maps, and reports [24].

Also, three research prototype tools have been selected for the comparison:

- **Aruvi** is a prototype implementation of an information visualization framework that supports the analytical reasoning process [22].
- **Sandbox** is a flexible and expressive thinking environment that supports both ad-hoc and formal analytical tasks [23].
- **POLESTAR** (POLicy Explanation using STories and ARguments) is an integrated suite of knowledge management and collaboration tools for intelligence analysts [21].

The evaluation and comparison of the selected tools was made separately for each of the tasks listed in the section 'Criminal network investi- gation'. A thorough examination of each tool has been made by the authors based on the available research literature, books, manuals, and other publicly available information. The results can be seen in Table 1.

Table 1 Overview of tool capability comparison based on support of criminal network investigation processes and tasks

	AN 8.5*	PG 3.0*	XLE 6.0*	Aruvi	Sandbox	POLESTAR	CFI*
Aquisition	3	4	4	2	2	3	2
Acquisition methods	■	■	■	▪	▪	■	▪
Dynamic attributes	▪	■	■	▪	▪	▪	▪
Attribute mapping	▪	▪	■	□	□	■	▪
Synthesis	2	3	2	1	3	2	4
Entities	■	■	■	▪	■	▪	■
Associations	■	■	■	□	▪	▪	□
Re-structuring	▪	▪	▪	□	■	■	■
Grouping	▪	■	□	▪	■	▪	■
Collapsing and expanding	□	■	□	▪	▪	□	■
Brainstorming	▪	▪	▪	□	■	▪	■
Information types	▪	□	▪	□	□	□	□
Emerging attributes	■	▪	▪	□	□	□	□
Sense-making	1	3	1	2	2	2	4
Retracing the steps	□	■	□	▪	□	□	■
Creating hypotheses	▪	▪	□	■	■	■	■
Adaptive modeling	□	□	□	□	□	□	□
Prediction	□	□	□	□	□	□	▪
Alias detection	□	□	□	□	□	□	□
Exploring perspectives	■	■	▪	▪	▪	▪	■
Decision-making	▪	▪	▪	■	▪	▪	▪
Social network analysis	■	■	■	□	□	□	▪
Dissemination	3	4	2	3	2	1	4
Storytelling	□	▪	□	▪	□	▪	■
Report generation	■	■	▪	▪	▪	□	▪

*Tool abbreviations (AN: NB! Analyst's Notebook, PG: Palantir Government, XLE: Xanalys Link Explorer, CFI: CrimeFighter Investigator). Investigative processes (0: no support, 1: fragmentary support, 5: full support). Investigative tasks (■: supported, ▪: partially supported, □: not supported).

Each tool is rated against each task in the list. A judgment has been made whether the tool provides full support, partial support, or no support for the task. This is indicated by different icons in the table. Based on the support for individual tasks, each tool has been given a score for each process based on a judgment of the number of tasks they support. This score is either 0 (no support), 1 (fragmentary support), 2-4 (partial support), or 5 (full support). Fragmentary support means that the core task is in theory supported by the tool through the combination of various features, but it is found to be too time-consuming to be really useful.

CrimeFighter Investigator scores well on three of the four evaluated processes synthesis, sense-making, and dissemination, but scores lower on aquisition. In fact, CrimeFighter Investigator is found to provide more comprehensive support of synthesis and sense-making than any of the other tools, and the same high level of support on dissemination.

Usability feedback

We have received usability feedback from a number of people experienced in investigating criminal networks from various fields such as investigative journalism, counterterrorism, and policing (see Table 3). For the usability feedback interviews (individuals or groups) we followed three steps: First, we gave a general introduction to and demonstration of CrimeFighter Investigator. Second, the criminal network investigators were asked to describe their background and characteristics of their ongoing network investigations. Third, we discussed which CrimeFighter Investigator features would be useful for the criminal network investigators in their work.

Table 2 Overview of end user feedback on the usability and relevance of supporting criminal network investigation processes and tasks within each end user's investigation domain

	Investigative journalism	Counterterrorism	Policing	Research and industry
Aquisition				
Acquisition methods	+	+	+	+
Dynamic attributes	+	+	+	+
Attribute mapping	+	+	+	+
Synthesis				
Entities	+	+	+	+
Associations	+	+	+	+
Re-structuring	+	+	−	+
Grouping	−	−	−	+
Collapsing and expanding	−	+	−	+
Brainstorming	+	−	−	+
Information types	−	+	+	+
Emerging attributes	−	+	+	+
Sense-making				
Retracing the steps	−	+	+	−
Creating hypotheses	+	+	+	−
Adaptive modeling	−	+	−	−
Prediction	+	+	−	+
Alias detection	−	+	−	−
Exploring perspectives	−	+	+	−
Decision-making	−	−	+	−
Social network analysis	+	+	+	−
Dissemination				
Storytelling	+	−	+	−
Report generation	−	−	+	−

To indicate the relevance of supporting the investigative task for end users from a particular investigation domain we use a plus sign (+). A minus sign (−) is used to indicate when support is not a priority for the end users from that domain.

To exemplify our interview approach we provide extracts of an interview held with historian and investigative journalist Alex Strick van Linschoten. The example demonstrates the value of CrimeFighter Investigator usability feedback for both development of future features and evaluation of existing features. At the

Table 3 Investigators interviewed from secret and public criminal network investigation organizations

	Secret	Public	Both
Investigative journalists	0	1	1
Intelligence analysts	1	5	6
Police officers	3	0	3
Research community	0	7	7
TOTAL	**4**	**14**	**24**

time of the interview, Alex is investigating the alleged links between al-Qaeda and the Afghan Taliban, and he has observed several interesting network characteristics (marked using a bold font in the paragraph below).

Alex's data set on the Afghan Taliban spans the **time-period** 1970–2011. As of 2011 the data set had **500–600 individuals,** a network he claims to have more or less memorized. The data set is based on interviews with Taliban members who were asked who they fought with in the '80s, their andiwaal groups (friend groups normally formed by Afghans in their teenage years) and other **relations. Reports** on Afghanistan by the International Security Assistance Force ISAF also contribute to the data set. 70 percent of the **relations** in the network are based on rumors, which is indicated using relation **weights.** When Alex interviews

Taliban members he notes down **attributes** such as 'name', 'date of birth', 'place of birth', 'tribe', 'ethnicity' and 'andiwaal group'. Alex uses Tinderbox [34], a spatial hypertext **tool**, to **record** and **structure** the network information he **collects**.

Alex processes the network information in a number of different ways and has in general many ideas for how a tool such as CrimeFighter Investigator could be applied to organize the information he retrieves. Alex studies the evolution of the network through time (a historical evolution **perspective**). He believes that knowledge about an individual's andiwaal **group** could be used to **predict** who that person might be fighting with in future operations. Alex is **searching** for different **patterns** in the data set like for example changes in age or gender.

Alex has encountered a number of problems for which specialized **tool support** would be an advantage, for instance, a social network analysis tool for support of an actual time line (Tinderbox only supports snapshots of the network). At the time of interview he was **analyzing** the network data to see if there were any important observations that he might have missed. Alex mentions that different **layout** functionality would be useful for this, e.g., laying out nodes according to **betweenness centrality**. Finally, if Alex **exports** information from Tinderbox [34] to **import** it into Analyst's Notebook [19] to create a special visualization, it is not possible to get that visualization back into Tinderbox. The **interchange** of information is not facilitated both ways.

The feedback from potential end users of CrimeFighter Investigator on the usability of the features presented to them, has helped us prioritize those features to focus on the most important ones. In general, the end users found the features supported by CrimeFighter Investigator to be applicable to their work, and in some cases our integration of features was found to be more useful than existing tools (such as i2 Analyst's Notebook, see summary of evaluated tools earlier in this section).

Measures of performance

Our measures of performance (MoPs) focus on the internal structure, characteristics, and nature of criminal network sense-making. We have developed three measures to help us evaluate how CrimeFighter Investigator sense-making performs in terms of 'information volume', 'attribute completeness', and 'attribute accuracy'. In the longer term, these MoPs will help us build a process that criminal network investigators can have confidence in, when going before a decision maker in their organization [35]. We need to make sure that our algorithm-supported sense-making tasks can perform on the criminal networks that investigators are dealing with on a daily basis. More specifically, we want to evaluate if the integration of synthesis and sense-making tasks is feasible.

In this section, we test our support for one sense-making task, prediction, by evaluating the predict missing links algorithm. We use two criminal networks for our evaluation: November 17 and al-Qaeda. The data set of the (believed defunct) Greek terrorist group November 17 (N17) was derived from open source reporting [36]. The N17 group was a small close knit organization of 22 individuals with 63 links out of a potential 231 links. The links of the dataset were obtained from open sources and report some connection between two individuals at some point in the past, but no specific weightings of the links are given [29] (i.e., the link weights are all the same).

The second dataset is the al-Qaeda network at the beginning of 2003. All the network information was gathered from public domain sources: 'documents and transcripts of legal proceedings involving global Salafi mujahedin and their organizations, government documents, press and scholarly articles, and Internet articles' [37]. We have included *acquaintance, friend,* and *post joining jihad* relations, but the algorithm does not differentiate between them. *Nuclear family, relatives, religious leader,* and *ties not in sample* links are excluded from our version of the data set. The topology of all networks are presented in Table 4.

We use sampled versions of the full networks for our evaluations, created by removing either 50 or 25 percent of the links in the network and then seeing what is left. The number of nodes and links alone directly affect algorithm performance in terms of speed. The number of attributes that each node has does not impact the performance of the predict missing links, since tests are run with four attributes every time. We define the complexity of node attributes as the average of valid enumerated values per attribute. Link density is the ratio between the number of links and the number of potential links and indicates for example the connectivity and covertness of the given network.

We logged three variables for each test. Time is the seconds it takes to predict missing links. True positives are predicted links that exist in the non-sampled version of the data set. False positives are predicted links that do not exist in the non-sampled version of the data set. The predict missing links algorithm was customized in the same way for each sampled data set before each test as described in Table 5. The al-Qaeda attributes are selected to match the number of enumerated values for each November 17 attribute.

We evaluate the predict missing links algorithm against all the data sets using the three measures of performance. The results are listed in Table 6.

Table 4 The November 17 and al-Qaeda datasets

	al-Qaeda			November 17	
version →	full	full	id 1–20	full	full
sampling →	100%	25%	50%	100%	50%
Nodes	366	256	15	22	17
Attributes	17	17	17	11	11
Complexity*	9.53	9.53	9.53	2.09	2.09
Links	999	249	18	63	32
Link density	0.015	0.008	0.17	0.27	0.24

*Complexity indicates the average number of enumerated values (text strings) for each entity attribute.

Information volume

This measure of performance is based on the change in processing time and true and false positive ratios when the number of nodes and links increases across the three sampled data sets.

We observe that the sampled al-Qaeda data set increases the time required to process the prediction significantly (as expected). However, in the worst case the logged time is only 63 seconds and this value does not raise any operational concerns for most criminal network investigations. We realize that the network can be much larger, and expect the required time to increase also for the tested data set if attributes with more enumerated values were selected. But it is our experience that for very large networks, criminal network investigators will request predictions within subgroups mostly and not the whole network. And if the network gets very large, then the investigators will be prepared to wait longer for assistance from the algorithm.

Attribute accuracy

The predict missing links algorithm assumes that attribute content (text string) is machine-recognizable, i.e., the content should be one of a list of predefined text strings (e.g., role [LEADERSHIP, OPERATIONAL] or degree centrality [HIGH, MIDDLE, LOW]). We have decreased the attribute accuracy of the sampled data set by scrambling a percentage of the attribute values.

Table 5 Algorithm setup for the November 17 and al-Qaeda data sets

Data set →	November 17	al-Qaeda
L Cutoff	2.5	2.5
Attribute 1	Role	Children
Attribute 2	Faction	Clump
Attribute 3	Resources	Fate
Attribute 4	Degree centrality	Degree centrality

Decreasing the accuracy of attribute content to simulate the data having reduced reliability clearly impacts on the number of predicted links, but the ratio between true and false positives does not change, indicating some robustness of the predict missing links algorithm. The time actually decreases together with the decreasing accuracy of attributes; a decrease in predicted links (due to less attribute content matching up) can more easily be processed by the algorithm. One interesting observation here is that the ratio of true positives dropped significantly for the N17 data set at 70% acurracy to 1 (from 5 at 90% and 9 at 100%). We expect this is caused by N17 having fewer attributes than the al-Qaeda data set, making it more vulnerable to random scrambling of attribute values.

Attribute completeness

End user requirements and usability feedback indicated a need to support dynamic and emerging entity attributes, since limited information is typically available about the individuals in criminal networks. To simulate this, we delete attribute values from the data sets and replace them with empty values.

Like attribute accuracy the total number of predicted links decreases as the number of non-empty attribute values increases but the ratios stay more or less the same. We anticipated this similarity between the accuracy and completeness MoPs as CrimeFighter Investigator does currently not include technology that could improve the attribute accuracy by correcting for example typographical spelling errors.

We chose the predict missing links algorithm to evaluate our developed measures of performance, because we found it promising for investigation of criminal networks of sizes equal to or smaller than the al-Qaeda data set. It is our experience, that criminal network investigators do not synthesize and apply sense-making algorithms to networks significantly bigger than the al-Qaeda data set [37].

Conclusions

The CrimeFighter Investigator approach to target-centric criminal network investigation has been developed based on three types of analysis work:

- **Exploring methods.** We have explored analytical practices, processes, and techniques related to investigative journalism, counterterrorism and policing.
- **Studying related work.** We have found inspiration from existing tools supporting criminal network investigation and from other relevant investigations.
- **Evaluation.** We have compared the capabilities of six existing tools with the CrimeFighter Investigator. We have collected feedback from various criminal network investigation communities regarding which CrimeFighter Investigator features are useful and usable. Finally, we have developed three measures of performance for prediction algorithms.

Together, this analysis work resulted in a list of tasks that guided our development. Many of the tasks envisioned are already now supported. The main contributions to useful integration of criminal network synthesis and sense-making are:

Process model. We have developed a target-centric process model for criminal network investigation, splitting the responsibilities between investigators and tool, empowering humans to make more informed decisions.

Task list. We have outlined and evolved criminal network investigation tasks spanning acquisition, synthesis, sense-making, and dissemination processes, helping us understand how to integrate these tasks.

Tool. We have developed a tool that assists criminal network investigators in target-model synthesis and sense-making, to produce useful intelligence products for their customers.

Evaluation. Our evaluation results from capability comparisons, usability feedback, and measures of performance, indicate that we are on the right path to integrate a broad range of criminal network synthesis and sense-making tasks in one tool. We have observed that existing tools typically focus on either synthesis or sense-making tasks.

Together, this has resulted in a novel tool that combines knowledge from various research domains (including hypertext, knowledge management, software engineering, and criminal network analysis) to address criminal network investigation challenges, processes, and tasks.

As part of our near term future work, we will provide support for the remaining tasks related to synthesis, sense-making, and dissemination. We then plan to thoroughly test the tool in cooperation with experienced investigators. In the longer term, we plan to include

Table 6 Measures of performance for the predict missing links algorithm

	Data set	Version	Sampling	Time (s)	TP*#	TP%	FP*#	FP%
Full data set								
	November 17	(full)	(50%)	0.219	9	42.9	12	57.1
100%	al-Qaeda	(id 1–20)	(50%)	0.078	7	35.0	13	65.0
	al-Qaeda	(full)	(25%)	63.093	288	4.9	5547	95.1
Attribute accuracy								
	November 17	(full)	(50%)	0.235	5	35.7	9	64.3
90%	al-Qaeda	(id 1–20)	(50%)	0.79	6	46.2	7	53.8
	al-Qaeda	(full)	(25%)	37.562	165	5.1	3052	94.9
	November 17	(full)	(50%)	0.124	1	16.7	5	83.3
70%	al-Qaeda	(id 1–20)	(50%)	0.62	5	45.5	6	54.5
	al-Qaeda	(full)	(25%)	24.656	167	5.0	3171	95.0
Attribute completeness								
	November 17	(full)	(50%)	0.282	5	45.5	6	54.5
90%	al-Qaeda	(id 1–20)	(50%)	0.094	7	41.2	10	58.8
	al-Qaeda	(full)	(25%)	41.344	197	4.8	3939	95.2
	November 17	(full)	(50%)	0.531	5	45.5	6	54.5
70%	al-Qaeda	(id 1–20)	(50%)	0.079	5	41.7	7	58.3
	al-Qaeda	(full)	(25%)	24.328	146	4.4	3167	95.6

*TP = true positives, FP = false positives.

support for cooperation beyond the shared information space and provide integration with the CrimeFighter Explorer tool for better acquisition support.

Endnotes

[a] The kidnapping of Daniel Pearl [9,28], the intelligence used for the United States case against Iraq concerning their (alleged) wmd programme [6,11], and the links between Operation Crevice and the 7/7 bombings in United Kingdom [3,4].

[b] Issue Based Information Systems.

Competing interests

Both authors declare that they have no competing interests.

Authors' contributions

RRP carried out the analysis, design, and implementation of support for criminal network investigation processes and tasks in CrimeFighter Investigator. RRP also carried out the analysis that formed the basis of evaluations, designed the experiments for each of the three evaluation methods, and subsequently carried out these experiments. UKW supervised the whole process. In collaboration, UKW and RRP synthesed the capability comparison table and developed the target-centric model for criminal network investigation. Both authors read and approved the final manuscript.

Acknowledgements

This work is based on previous publications by the authors in hypertext and security informatics conference proceedings [13,14,25].

References

1. MK Sparrow, The application of network analysis to criminal intelligence: An assessment of the prospects. Soc. Netw. **13**, 251–274 (1991)
2. UK Wiil, N Memon, J Gniadek, CrimeFighter: A toolbox for counterterrorism. Lect. Notes Commun. Comput Inf. Sci. (Knowl. Discov., Knowl. Eng, Knowl. Manage). **128**, 337–350 (2011)
3. SecurityCommittee Intelligence and, *Could 7/7 have been Prevented? Review of the Intelligence on the London Terrorist Attacks on 7 July 2005*, (UK, 2009)
4. G Woo, in *Mathematical Methods in Counterterrorism*, ed. by N Memon, T Farley, JD Hicks, and DL Rosenorn. Intelligence constraints on terrorist network plots (Springer Wien, 2009), pp. 205–214
5. CJ Rhodes, P Jones, Inferring missing links in partially observed social networks. J. Oper. Res. Soc. **60**(10), 1373–1383 (2009)
6. B Drogin, *Curveball*. (Ebury Press, 2008)
7. National commission on terrorist attacks upon the United States, *The 9/11, Commission Report (Executive Summary)* (USA, 2004). http://www.9-11commission.gov/report/911Report_Exec.pdf
8. MR Kebbell, DA Muller, K Martin, Understanding and managing bias Dealing Uncertainties Policing Serious Crime. (Australian National University, Canberra, 2010), pp. 87–97
9. BH Levy, *Who Killed Daniel Pearl?*. (Melville House Publishing, Brooklyn, 2003)
10. C Atzenbeck, DL Hicks, N Memon, Supporting reasoning and communication for intelligence officers. Int. J. Netw. **8**(1/2), 15–36 (2011). Virtual Organisations
11. T Weiner, *Legacy of Ashes: The History of the CIA*. (Anchor Books, New York, 2008)
12. R Clark, *Intelligence Analysis: A Target-Centric Approach*. (CQ Press, California, 2007)
13. RP Petersen, UK Wiil, in *Proceedings of the 22nd ACM Conference on Hypertext*. Hypertext structures for investigative teams (ACM Press New York, 2011), pp. 123–132
14. RR Petersen, UK Wiil, in *Proceedings of European Intelligence and Security Informatics Conference*. CrimeFighter Investigator: a novel tool for criminal network investigation (IEEE, 2011), pp. 360–365
15. R Adderly, P Musgrove, Police crime recording and investigation systems - A user's view. Int. J. Police Strateg. Manage. **24**, 100–114 (2001)
16. RV Badalamente, FL Greitzer, in *Proceedings of International Conference on Intelligence Analysis*. Top ten needs for intelligence analysis tool development, (2005)
17. EA Bier, SK Card, JW Bodnar, Principles and tools for collaborative entity-based intelligence analysis. IEEE Trans. Vis. Comput. Graph. **16**(2), 178–191 (2010)
18. G Dean, P Gottschalk, *Knowledge Management in Policing and Law Enforcement*. (Oxford University Press, 2007)
19. i2, Analyst's Notebook (2011). http://www.i2group.com/
20. Palantir Government (2011). http://www.palantirtech.com/government
21. NJ Pioch, JO Everett, in *Proceedings of the International Conference on Information and Knowledge Management*. POLESTAR: collaborative knowledge management and sensemaking tools for intelligence analysts (ACM Press New York, 2006), pp. 513–521
22. YB Shrinivasan, JJ Wijk, in *Proceedings of the 26th Conference on Human Factors in Computing Systems*. Supporting the analytical reasoning process in information visualization (ACM Press New York, 2008)
23. W Wright, D Schroh, P Proulx, A Skaburskis, B Cort, in *Proceedings of the Conference on Human Factors in Computing Systems*. The Sandbox for analysis: concepts and methods (ACM Press, 2006), pp. 801–810
24. Xanalys (2011). http://www.xanalys.com/
25. RR Petersen, CJ Rhodes, UK Wiil, in *Proceedings of European Intelligence and Security Informatics Conference*. Node removal in criminal networks (IEEE Computer Society Washington, 2011), pp. 360–365
26. RR Petersen, UK Wiil, in *Handbook of Computational Approaches to Counterterrorism*, ed. by Subrahmanian. V S. CrimeFighter Investigator: criminal network sense-making (Springer New York, 2013), pp. 323–359
27. RR Petersen, in *Criminal Network Investigation: Processes, Tools, and Techniques* (University of Southern Denmark, 2012). Ph.D. dissertation
28. M Pearl, *A Mighty Heart*. (Virago Press, 2004)
29. CJ Rhodes, CMJ Keefe, Social network topology: a Bayesian approach. J. Oper. Res. Soc. **58**(12), 1605–1611 (2007)
30. S Wasserman, K Faust, in *Social Network Analysis: Methods and Applications* (Cambridge University Press Cambridge, 1994)
31. J Conklin, ML Begeman, gIBIS: a hypertext tool for exploratory policy discussion. ACM Trans Inf Syst. **6**(4), 303–331 (1988)
32. A Field, G Hole. How to Design and Report Experiments (Sage Publications Ltd London, 2003)
33. C Atzenbeck. WildDocs - Investigating Construction of Metaphors in Office Work (Aalborg University, 2006). PhD thesis
34. M Bernstein, *The Tinderbox Way*. (Eastgate Systems, Watertown, 2006)
35. JP Stenbit, IL Wells, DS Alberts, *NATO code of best practice for C2 assessment, [Chapter 5: Measures of Merit]*. (CCRP, Washington, 2002)
36. C Irwin, C Roberts, N Mee, in *Defence Science and Technology Laboratory*. Counter Terrorism Overseas, (2002). Dstl/CD053271/1.1 UK
37. M Sageman. Understanding Terrorist Networks (University of Pennsylvania Press (PENN) Philadelphia, Pensylvania, 2004)

13

Emotion classification of social media posts for estimating people's reactions to communicated alert messages during crises

Joel Brynielsson[1,2*], Fredrik Johansson[1], Carl Jonsson[3] and Anders Westling[4]

Abstract

One of the key factors influencing how people react to and behave during a crisis is their digital or non-digital social network, and the information they receive through this network. Publicly available online social media sites make it possible for crisis management organizations to use some of these experiences as input for their decision-making. We describe a methodology for collecting a large number of relevant tweets and annotating them with emotional labels. This methodology has been used for creating a training dataset consisting of manually annotated tweets from the Sandy hurricane. Those tweets have been utilized for building machine learning classifiers able to automatically classify new tweets. Results show that a support vector machine achieves the best results with about 60% accuracy on the multi-classification problem. This classifier has been used as a basis for constructing a decision support tool where emotional trends are visualized. To evaluate the tool, it has been successfully integrated with a pan-European alerting system, and demonstrated as part of a crisis management concept during a public event involving relevant stakeholders.

Keywords: Alert and communication; Social media; Affect analysis; Machine learning; Trend analysis; Information visualization

Introduction

During crises, enormous amounts of user generated content, including tweets, blog posts, and forum messages, are created, as documented in a number of recent publications [1-6]. Undoubtedly, large portions of this user generated content mainly consist of noise with limited or no use to crisis responders, but some of the available information can also be used for detecting that an emergency event has taken place [1], understanding the scope of a crisis, or to find out details about a crisis [4]. That is, parts of the data can be used for increasing the tactical situational awareness [7]. Unfortunately, the flood of information that is broadcast is infeasible for people to effectively extract information from, organize, make sense of, and act upon without appropriate computer support [6]. For this reason, several researchers and practitioners are interested in developing systems for social

media monitoring and analysis to be used in crises. One example is the American Red Cross Digital Operations Center, opened in March 2012 [8]. Another example is the European Union security research project Alert4All, having as its aim to improve the authorities' effectiveness of alert and communication towards the population during crises [9-11]. In order to accomplish this, screening of social media is deemed important for becoming aware of how communicated alert messages are perceived by the citizens [12]. In this paper, we describe our methodology for collecting crisis-related tweets and tagging them manually with the help of a number of annotators. This has been done for tweets sent during the Sandy hurricane, where the annotators have tagged the emotional content as one of the classes *positive* (e.g., happiness), *anger, fear,* or *other* (including non-emotional content as well as emotions not belonging to any of the other classes). The tweets for which we have obtained a good inter-annotator agreement have been utilized in experiments with supervised learning algorithms for creating classifiers being able to classify new tweets as belonging to any of the classes

*Correspondence: joel.brynielsson@foi.se
[1]FOI Swedish Defence Research Agency, Stockholm, Sweden
[2]KTH Royal Institute of Technology, Stockholm, Sweden
Full list of author information is available at the end of the article

of interest. By comparing the results to those achieved when using a rule-based classifier we show that the used machine learning algorithms have been able to generalize from the training data and can be used for classification of new, previously unseen, crisis tweets. Further, the optimum classifier has been integrated with, and constitutes an important part of, the Alert4All proof-of-concept alerting system. In the presence of relevant stakeholders representing politics, industry, end users, and research communities, this system was successfully demonstrated as a cohesive system during a public event. As part of this event, the classification of social media posts was used to visualize emotional trend statistics for the purpose of demonstrating the idea of using social media input for informing crisis management decisions. Overall, the concept was well received, considered novel, and makes it possible for crisis management organizations to use a new type of input for their decision-making.

The rest of this paper is outlined as follows. In the next section we give an overview of related work. A methodology section then follows, where we describe how crisis-related tweets have been collected, selected using automated processing, and tagged manually by a number of annotators in order to create a training set. We also describe how a separate test set has been constructed. After that, we present experimental results achieved for various classifiers and parameter settings. Details regarding the design and implementation of a decision support tool making use of the developed support vector machine classifier is then elaborated on in a separate section. The results and their implications are then discussed in more detail in a separate section before the paper is concluded in the last section.

Related work

The problem of sentiment analysis has attracted much research during the last decade. One reason is probably the growing amounts of opinion-rich text resources made available due to the development of social media, giving researchers and companies access to the opinions of ordinary people [13]. Another important reason for the increased interest in sentiment analysis is the advances that have been made within the fields of natural language processing and machine learning. A survey of various techniques suggested for opinion mining and sentiment analysis is presented in [14]. A seminal work on the use of machine learning for sentiment analysis is the paper by Pang et al. [15], showing that good performance (approximately 80% accuracy for a well-balanced dataset) can be achieved for the problem of classifying movie reviews as either positive or negative.

Although interesting, the classification of movie reviews as positive or negative has limited impact on the security domain. However, the monitoring of social media

to spot emerging trends and to assess public opinion is also of importance to intelligence and security analysts, as demonstrated in [16]. Microblogs such as Twitter pose a particular challenge for sentiment analysis techniques since messages are short (the maximum size of a tweet is 140 characters) and may contain sarcasm and slang. The utilization of machine learning techniques on Twitter data to discriminate between positive and negative tweets is evaluated in [17,18], suggesting that classification accuracies of 60–80% can be obtained. Social media monitoring techniques for collecting large amounts of tweets during crises and classifying them with machine learning algorithms has become a popular topic within the crisis response and management domain. The use of natural language processing and machine learning techniques to extract situation awareness from Twitter messages is suggested in [4] (automatic identification of tweets containing information about infrastructure status), [5] (classification of tweets as positive or negative), and [6] (classification of tweets as contributing to situational awareness or not).

The main difference between our work and the papers mentioned above is that most of the previous work focus on sentiment analysis (classifying crisis tweets as positive or negative), whilst we focus on affect analysis or emotion recognition [19], i.e., classifying crisis tweets as belonging to an emotional state. This problem is even more challenging since it is a multinomial classification problem rather than a binary classification problem. We are not aware of any previous attempts to use machine learning for emotion recognition of crisis-related tweets. The use of affect analysis techniques for the security domain has, however, been proposed previously, such as the affect analysis of extremist web forums and blogs presented in [20,21].

The work presented in this article is the result of a long-term research effort where related studies have been presented along the way. A first visionary paper [10] discusses and presents the concept of using social media monitoring for coming into dialogue with the population. The overall idea is for emergency management organizations to follow what people publish and adjust their information strategies in a way that matches the expectations and needs of the public. A systematic literature review and a parallel interview study were then undertaken [11], where the possibility to use social media analysis for informing crisis communication was deemed promising and important design issues to take into account were highlighted. Based on this insight, we outlined a more detailed design concept for how a screening tool could potentially be used for the purpose of increasing situational awareness during crises [12]. This paper identifies data acquisition and data analysis to be two important parts of such a tool. Then, in parallel to presenting the initial results with regard to tweet classification [22], crisis management stakeholders were involved in a series of user-centered activities in order to understand the user needs and further inform the design of a social media screening tool to be used for crisis management [23]. It became clear that within crisis management it is more important to be able to distinguish between negative emotions such as fear and anger than to be able to differentiate between different positive emotions. Also, a further understanding of crisis management working procedures was obtained, which made it clear that a social media screening tool needs to be focused on trend analysis since, in crisis management, relevant actions are to be undertaken for the purpose of improving some kind of crisis state in order to bring the situation into a better state.

Methodology

Within the research project Alert4All we have discovered the need for automatically finding out whether a tweet (or other kinds of user generated content) is to be classified as containing emotional content [12]. Through a series of user-centered activities involving crisis management stakeholders [23], the classes of interest for command and control have been identified as *positive, anger, fear,* and *other*, where the first class contains positive emotions such as happiness, and the last class contains emotions other than the ones already mentioned, as well as neutral or non-subjective classifications. In the following, we describe the methodology used for collecting crisis-related tweets, selecting a relevant subset of those, and letting human annotators tag them in order to be used for machine learning purposes.

Collecting tweets

The first step in our methodology was to collect a large set of crisis-related tweets. For this purpose we have used the Python package **tweetstream** to retrieve tweets related to the Sandy hurricane, hitting large parts of the Caribbean and the Mid-Atlantic and Northeastern United States during October 2012. The **tweetstream** package fetches tweets from Twitter's streaming API in real-time. It should be noted that the streaming API only gives access to a random sample of the total volume of tweets sent at any given moment, but still this allowed us to collect approximately six million tweets related to Sandy during October 29 to November 1, using the search terms *sandy, hurricane,* and *#sandy*. After automatic removal of non-English tweets, retweets, and duplicated tweets, approximately 2.3 million tweets remained, as exemplified in Table 1. An average tweet in the dataset contained 14.7 words in total and 0.0786 "emotional words" according to the lists of identified keywords as will be described in the next subsection.

Annotation process

After an initial manual review of the remaining collected posts, we quickly discovered that a large proportion of the tweets not unexpectedly belong to the category *other*. Since the objective was to create a classifier being able to discriminate between the different classes, we needed a balanced training dataset, or at least a large number of samples for each class. This caused a problem since random sampling of the collected tweets most likely would result in almost only those belonging to the class *other*.

Table 1 Sample tweets obtained in late 2012 during the Sandy hurricane along with the resulting emotion class output from the developed emotion classifier

Tweet	Predicted class
the anticipation of when the power is going to go out! I NEED TO STUDY WHAT IS HAPPENING STOP SANDY	Anger
God damn it #sandy! There goes my cable...	Anger
Sandy just made landfall on the great State of New Jersey & NYC. Hang tight, you guys.	Anger
Sandy has denied me my jog. I'm crying as much as it's raining right now...	Anger
Shed in backyard was knocked over #sandy	Other
Lovely, there are fallen tree branches in my swimming pool. Eh, It could be worse... #413Sandy #MASandy #Sandy	Positive
So my childhood beach town is basically being destroyed. That's cool.. Stupid Sandy. :/	Anger
So much food in my house because my moms stocking up for Sandy. I'm cool with it.	Anger
Hurricane Sandy might not kill me but this boredom sure will. -__-	Anger
This storm sandy is so scary :0 #scarystuff #mothernature	Fear
Hurricane Sandy is powerful af!!! This wind is NO joke!!!	Other
Power back on. Not sure how much longer that will last. Damn you #sandy - get up off my #raw!	Anger
im like really scared.... stuff like this doesn't happen in Ohio ! #Sandy #Manhattan	Fear
NZ's embassy in Washington is closed as the city hunkers down ahead of #Sandy	Other
11 killed in #Cuba, #Sandy toll reaches 51 in #Haiti	Other

Although this in theory could be solved by sampling a large enough set of tweets to annotate, there is a limit to how many tweets that can be tagged manually in a reasonable time (after all, this is the main motivation for learning such classifiers in the first place). To overcome this problem, we decided to use manual inspection to identify a small set of keywords which were likely to indicate emotional content belonging to any of the emotional classes *positive*, *fear*, or *anger*[a]. The list of identified keywords looks as follows:

- *anger*: anger, angry, bitch, fuck, furious, hate, mad,
- *fear*: afraid, fear, scared,
- *positive*: :), :-), =), :D, :-D, =D, glad, happy, positive, relieved.

Those lists were automatically extended by finding synonyms to the words using WordNet [24]. Some of the resulting words were then removed from the lists as they were considered poor indicators of emotions during a hurricane. An example of a word that was removed is "stormy", which was more likely to describe hurricane Sandy than expressing anger. By using the words in the created lists as search terms, we sampled 1000 tweets which according to our simple rules were likely to correspond to "positive" emotions. The same was done for "anger" and "fear", while a random sampling strategy was used to select the 1000 tweets for "other". In this way we constructed four data files containing 1000 tweets each. The way we selected the tweets may have an impact on the end results since there is a risk that such a biased selection process will lead to classifiers that are only able to learn the rules used to select the tweets in the first place. We were aware of such a potential risk, but could not identify any other way to come up with enough tweets corresponding to the "positive", "anger", and "fear" tags. In order to check the generalizability of the resulting classifiers, we have in the experiments compared the results to a baseline, implemented as a rule-based algorithm based on the keywords used to select the appropriate tweets. The experiments are further described in the next section.

Once the files containing tweets had been constructed, each file was sent by e-mail to three independent annotators, i.e., all annotators were given one file (containing 1000 tweets) each. All annotators were previously familiar with the Alert4All project (either through active work within the project or through acting as advisory board members) and received the instructions which can be found in the appendix. It should be noted that far from all the tweets in a file were tagged as belonging to the corresponding emotion by the annotators. In fact, a majority of the tweets were tagged as *other* also in the "anger", "fear", and "positive" files. In order to get a feeling for the inter-annotator agreement, we have calculated the percentages of tweets for which a majority of the annotators have classified a tweet in the same way (majority agreement) and where all agree (full agreement) as shown in Table 2. As can be seen, the majority agreement is consistently reasonably high. On the other hand, it is seldom that all three annotators agree on the same classification. For a tweet to become part of the resulting training set, we require that there has been a majority agreement regarding how it should be tagged. Now, ignoring which class a tweet was "supposed" to end up in given the used keywords (i.e., the used categories) and instead looking at the emotion classes tweets actually ended up in after the annotation, we received the distribution shown in Table 3. Since we wanted to have a training dataset with equally many samples for each class, we decided to balance the classes, resulting in 461 training samples for each class.

Creating a separate test dataset

While it is popular in the machine learning community to make use of *n*-fold cross validation to allow for training as well as testing on all the available data, we have decided to create a separate test set in this study. The reason for this is the way training data has been generated. If the used strategy to select tweets based on keywords would impact the annotated data and thereby also the learned classifiers too much, this could result in classifiers that perform well using the annotated data, but generalizes poorly to "real" data without the bias. Hence, our test data has been generated by letting a human annotator (not part of the first annotation phase) tag tweets from the originally collected Twitter dataset until sufficiently many tweets had been discovered for each emotion. Since it, as a rule of thumb, is common to use 90% of the available data for training and 10% for testing, we continued the tagging until we got 54 tweets in each class (after balancing the set), corresponding to approximately 10% of the total amount of data used for training and testing.

Experiments

There exists many parameters related to affect analysis that influence the feature set. This section describes the parameters that have been varied during the experiments, and discusses how the parameters affected the achieved experimental results.

Table 2 Inter-annotator agreement for the various categories

Category	Majority agreement	Full agreement
"Positive"	92.7%	47.8%
"Anger"	92.6%	39.2%
"Fear"	95.2%	44.4%
"Other"	99.7%	82.3%

Table 3 Number of annotated tweets per class based on majority agreement

Emotion class	Number of tweets
Positive	622
Anger	461
Fear	470
Other	2249

Classifiers

We have experimented with two standard machine learning algorithms for classification: Naïve Bayes (NB) and Support Vector Machine (SVM) classifiers. Available in Weka [25], the multinomial NB classifier [26] was used for the NB experiments, and the sequential minimal optimization algorithm [27] was used for training a linear kernel SVM. Although many additional features such as part-of-speech could have been used, we have limited the experiments to a simple bag-of-words representation. Initial experimentation showed that feature presence gave better results than feature frequency, wherefore only feature presence has been utilized. Before the training data was used, the tweets were transformed into lower case. Many different parameters have been varied throughout the experiments:

- n-gram size: 1 (unigram)/2 (unigram + bigram),
- stemming: yes/no,
- stop words: yes/no,
- minimum number of occurrences: 2/3/4,
- information gain (in %): 25/50/75/100,
- negation impact (number of words): 0/1/2,
- threshold τ: 0.5/0.6/0.7.

If a unigram representation is used, individual words are utilized as features, whereas if bigrams are used, pairs of words are utilized as features. Stemming refers to the process in which inflected or derived words are reduced to their base form (e.g., fishing → fish). As stop words we have used a list of commonly occurring function words, so if a word in the tweet matches such a stop word it is removed (and is hence not used as a feature). The minimum number of occurrences refers to how many times a term has to occur in the training data in order to be used as a feature. Information gain refers to a method used for feature selection, where the basic idea is to select features that reveal the most information about the classes. When, e.g., setting the information gain parameter to 50, the fifty percent "most informative features" are kept, reducing the size of the resulting model. Negation impact refers to the situation when a negation (such as "not") is detected, and the used algorithm replaces the words following the negation by adding the prefix "NOT_" to them. The specified negation impact determines how many words after

a negation that should be affected by the negation (where 0 means that no negation is used). Finally, the threshold τ has been used for discriminating between emotional content versus other content, as described below.

In the learning phase we used the tweets tagged as *positive*, *anger*, and *fear* as training data, which resulted in classifiers that learned to discriminate between these three classes. For the actual classification of new tweets we then let the machine learning classifiers estimate the probabilities $P(anger|f_1,\ldots,f_n)$, $P(fear|f_1,\ldots,f_n)$, and $P(positive|f_1,\ldots,f_n)$, where $f_1,\ldots,f_n$ refers to the used feature vector extracted from the tweet we want to classify. If the estimated probability for the most probable class is greater than a pre-specified threshold τ, we return the label of the most probable class as the output from the classifier. Otherwise *other* is returned as the output from the classifier. The rationale behind this is that the content of tweets to be classified as *other* cannot be learned in advance (due to the spread of what this class should contain). Instead, we learn what is considered to be representative for the other classes and interpret low posterior probabilities for *anger*, *fear*, and *positive* as *other* being the most likely class.

Experimental results

The best results achieved when evaluating the learned classifiers on the used test set are shown in Figure 1, with the used parameter settings shown in Table 4. The results are also compared to two baseline algorithms: 1) a naïve algorithm that picks a class at random (since all the classes are equally likely in a balanced dataset, this corresponds to a simple majority classifier), and 2) a somewhat more complex rule-based classifier constructed from the heuristics (keywords) used when selecting the tweets to be annotated manually in the training data generation phase. The results suggest that both the NB and SVM classifiers outperform the baseline algorithms, and that the

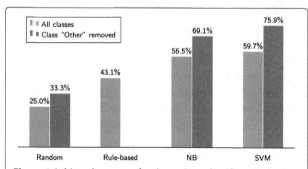

Figure 1 Achieved accuracy for the various classifiers. Blue color shows the results on the full dataset, red color shows the results when the *other* category is removed. The rules used within the rule-based classifier assume that all classes are present, wherefore no results have been obtained on the simplified problem for this classifier.

Table 4 Used parameter settings for the best performing classifiers

Parameter settings	NB	SVM
n-gram size	1 (unigram)	2 (unigram + bigram)
Stemming	Yes	Yes
Stop words	Yes	Yes
Min. no. of occurrences	4	4
Information gain	75%	75%
Negation impact	2	2
Threshold τ	0.6	0.7

SVM (59.7%) performs somewhat better than the NB classifier (56.5%). For a more detailed accuracy assessment, see Tables 5 and 6 where the confusion matrices show how the respective classifiers perform. The use of stemming, stop words, minimum number of occurrences, and information gain according to Table 4 have consistently been providing better results, while the best choices of n-gram size, negation impact, and threshold τ have varied more in the experiments.

For comparison, Table 7 contains the confusion matrix for the baseline classifier, i.e., the rule-based classifier which chooses its class based on possible emotion words found within a tweet. As can be seen in Table 7, the classifications of emotions (i.e., "anger", "fear", or "positive") are often correct, but a large amount of the tweets tend to erroneously fall into the *other* category. Now looking back at the machine learning confusion matrices according to Tables 5 and 6, we see that these classifiers do not exhibit the same behavior as the rule-based classifier with regard to the *other* category, but instead shows more evenly distributed errors. Hence, we can see that the machine learning classifiers have indeed learnt about emotional patterns that cannot be distinguished by simply applying rules based on a predefined list of emotion words.

In addition to evaluating the classifiers' accuracy on the original test set, we have also tested what happens if the task is simplified so that the classifiers only have to distinguish between the emotional classes *positive, fear*, and

Table 6 Confusion matrix for the top-performing NB classifier

Actual class	Predicted class			
	Anger	Fear	Positive	Other
Anger	35	4	5	10
Fear	3	35	9	7
Positive	13	2	19	20
Other	12	6	3	33

anger (i.e., it is assumed that the *other* class is not relevant). This latter task can be of interest in a system where a classifier distinguishing between emotional and non-emotional or subjective and non-subjective content has already been applied. As can be seen in Figure 1, the SVM gets it right in three out of four classifications (75.9%) on this task, while the accuracy of the NB classifier reaches 69.1%. See Tables 8 and 9 for the corresponding confusion matrices.

Design and implementation of a tool for visualizing emotional trends

Based on a series of stakeholder workshops [23], the developed emotion classifier has been used as a basis for the design and implementation of a decision support system entitled the "screening of new media" tool where emotional trends are visualized. To evaluate the tool, it has been integrated with the Alert4All system, which is an implemented prototype of a future pan-European public alert concept. As shown during the final demonstration of the Alert4All system and through the collocated user-centered activities, the social media analysis component of Alert4All provides additional benefit for command and control personnel in terms of providing immediate feedback regarding the development of a crisis in general and regarding the reception of crisis alerts in particular.

Figure 2 shows the developed tool, which has been implemented using HTML5 and JavaScript components. The core component of the tool is the graph which is shown to the upper right in Figure 2 and on its own

Table 5 Confusion matrix for the optimized SVM classifier

Actual class	Predicted class			
	Anger	Fear	Positive	Other
Anger	38	5	6	5
Fear	4	37	3	10
Positive	8	4	29	13
Other	14	12	3	25

The matrix shows how the classifier predictions are distributed, and thereby how well the classifier has learnt to distinguish between the classes.

Table 7 Confusion matrix for the rule-based baseline classifier which chooses class based on the occurrence of certain words

Actual class	Predicted class			
	Anger	Fear	Positive	Other
Anger	21	0	0	33
Fear	0	11	0	43
Positive	1	0	10	43
Other	3	0	0	51

As can be seen, many tweets end up in the *other* category.

Table 8 Confusion matrix for the SVM classifier when the task has been simplified so that the *other* class is not relevant

	Predicted class		
Actual class	Anger	Fear	Positive
Anger	41	5	8
Fear	5	45	4
Positive	13	4	37

in Figure 3. Here, a number of interactive chart components are used in order to visualize how the emotional content in the acquired dataset changes as a function of time. Through interacting with this graph, the user has the possibility to interact with the underlying dataset, and thereby obtain a further understanding of how the feelings expressed on social media vary as time passes.

At the bottom of the tool, the user has the possibility to drill down into the underlying dataset and see the actual posts in the database. From a command and control perspective, it is important to remember that these individual messages cannot and should not be used for inference regarding the whole dataset, but should be used solely for generating new hypotheses that need to be tested further by, e.g., experimenting with the filters in order to obtain sound statistical measures. Also to be noted, the posts are color coded so that it is easy to see which emotion a certain post has been classified as. However, the classification is not always correct, and therefore the user has the possibility to manually reclassify a post and, at a later stage, use the manually classified post as a basis for improving the classifier.

The GUI provides a number of ways to apply filters to the underlying dataset and thereby choose the social media posts to be visualized. The different visualizations are always kept consistent with these filters and with all other settings, i.e., the different parts of the graphical user interface provide different means to visualize one and the same dataset. As can be seen in Figure 2, there exists three main components for applying the filters: a time-line for filtering the time interval to be used, a tag cloud for filtering based on keywords, and the grey box located to the upper left that provides means to filter based on keywords, emotion classes, and data sources.

Table 9 NB classifier confusion matrix for the simplified problem

	Predicted class		
Actual class	Anger	Fear	Positive
Anger	41	5	8
Fear	3	43	8
Positive	19	7	28

An important part of the GUI, and a result of the earlier-mentioned design workshops, is the possibility to shift between the absolute probability distribution according to Figure 2 vis-à-vis the relative probability distribution as depicted in Figure 3. Most often, it will be important to visualize both the relative graph and the absolute graph since it will be easier to visualize the trend using the relative graph whilst the absolute graph is still needed in order to visualize, e.g., trends regarding how the total volume of posts vary.

Discussion

The obtained results show that the machine learning classifiers perform significantly better than chance and the rule-based algorithm that has been used as a baseline. Especially, the comparison to the rule-based algorithm is of interest, since the difference in accuracy indicates that the NB and SVM algorithms have been able to learn something more than just the keywords used to select the tweets to include in the annotation phase. In other words, even though the use of keywords may bias what tweets to include in the training data, this bias is not large enough to stop the machine learning classifiers from learning useful patterns in the data. In this sense the obtained results are successful. The confusion matrices also indicate that even better accuracy could have been achieved using a simple ensemble combining the output from the rule-based and machine learning-based algorithms.

Although the results are promising it can be questioned whether the obtained classification accuracy is good enough to be used in real-world social media analysis systems for crisis management. We believe that the results are good enough to be used on an aggregate level ("the citizens' fear levels are increasing after the last alert message"), but are not necessarily precise enough to be used to correctly assess the emotions in a specific tweet. Nevertheless, this is a first attempt to classify emotions in crisis-related tweets, and by improving the used feature set and combining the machine learning paradigm with more non-domain specific solutions such as the affective lexicon WordNet-Affect [28], better accuracy can most likely be achieved. More training data would probably also improve the accuracy, but the high cost in terms of manpower needed for the creation of even larger training datasets needs to be taken into account. Additionally, the learned classifiers ought to be evaluated on other datasets in order to test the generalizability of the obtained results.

Some of the classification errors were a result of the annotators receiving instructions to classify tweets containing any of the emotions *fear*, *anger*, or *positive* as *other* if the tweets relate to a "historical" state or if the expressed emotion related to someone else than the author of the tweet. Such a distinction can be important if the used classifications should be part of a social

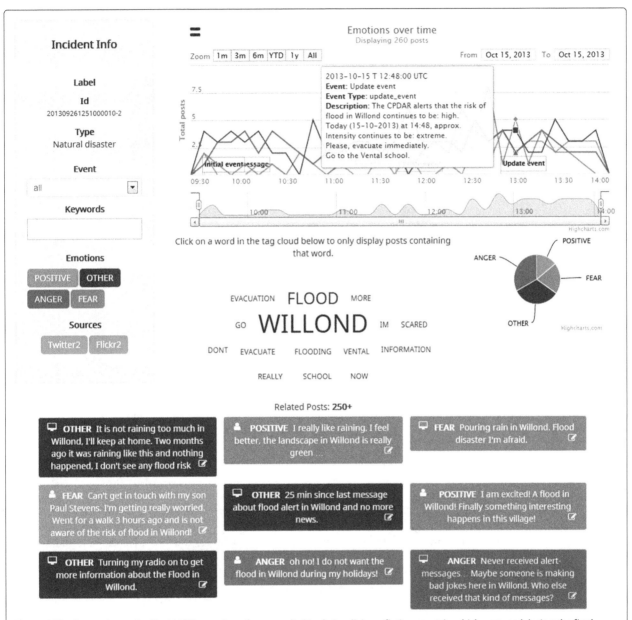

Figure 2 The figure shows the Alert4All "screening of new media" tool visualizing a fictive scenario which was used during the final demonstration in Munich during autumn 2013. As part of the graph, one can see the different messages that have been sent during the development of the crisis. Also, the content of one of these messages is shown due to the mouse pointer being positioned at this location.

media analysis system (since we do not want to take action on emotions that are not present anymore), but no features have been used to explicitly take care of spatio-temporal constraints in the current experiments. If such features were added (e.g., using part-of-speech tags and extraction of terms that contain temporal information), some of the classification errors could probably have been avoided.

Although we in this article have focused on crisis management, there are obviously other potential areas within the intelligence and security domain to which the suggested methodology and algorithms can be applied. As an example, it can be of interest to determine what kind of emotions that are expressed toward particular topics or groups in extremist discussion forums (cf. [20,21]). In the same manner, it can be used to assess the emotions expressed by, e.g., bloggers, in order to try to identify signs of emergent conflicts before they actually take place (cf. [16,29]). Similarly, the tool and algorithms described in this article could also be adapted to be used for evaluating the effects of information campaigns or psychological operations during military missions [30].

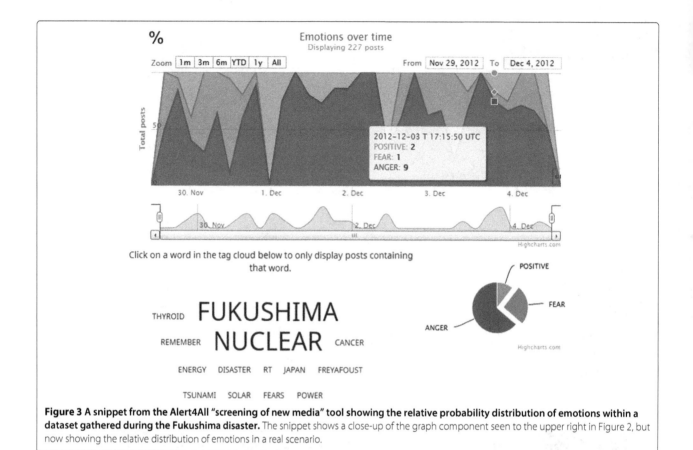

Figure 3 A snippet from the Alert4All "screening of new media" tool showing the relative probability distribution of emotions within a dataset gathered during the Fukushima disaster. The snippet shows a close-up of the graph component seen to the upper right in Figure 2, but now showing the relative distribution of emotions in a real scenario.

Conclusions and future work

We have described a methodology for collecting large amounts of crisis-related tweets and tagging relevant tweets using human annotators. The methodology has been used for annotating large quantities of tweets sent during the Sandy hurricane. The resulting dataset has been utilized when constructing classifiers able to automatically distinguish between the emotional classes *positive*, *fear*, *anger*, and *other*. Evaluation results suggest that a SVM classifier performs better than a NB classifier and a simple rule-based system. The classification task is difficult as suggested by the quite low reported inter-annotator agreement results. Seen in this light and considering that it is a multi-classification problem, the obtained accuracy for the SVM classifier (59.7%) seems promising. The classifications are not good enough to be trusted on the level of individual postings, but on a more aggregate level the citizens' emotions and attitudes toward the crisis can be estimated using the suggested algorithms. Results obtained when ignoring the non-specific category *other* (reaching accuracies over 75% for the SVM) also suggest that combining the learned classifiers with algorithms for subjectivity recognition can be a fruitful way forward.

As future work we see a need for combining machine learning classifiers learned from crisis domain data with more general affective lexicons. In this way we think that better classification performance can be achieved than using the methods individually. Moreover, we suggest extending the used feature set with extracted part-of-speech tags since such information most likely will help determine if it is the author of a tweet who is having a certain emotion, or if it is someone else. Other areas to look into is how to deal with the use of sarcasm and slang in the user generated content.

From a crisis management perspective, it will also be necessary to investigate to what extent the used methodology and the developed classifiers are capable of coping with more generic situations. That is, we hope to have developed classifiers that to at least some significant extent classify based on hurricane and crises behavior in general, rather than solely being able to classifying Sandy-specific data. Investigating this requires that one retrieves and tags new datasets to test the classifiers on. Doing this for several different crisis types and then applying the same classifiers, should make it possible to quantify how capable the developed classifiers are when it comes to classifying tweets from 1) other hurricanes, 2) other types of natural disasters, and 3) crises in general.

Endnote

[a] We use *class* to refer to the class a tweet actually belongs to (given the annotation), and "class" to refer to the class suggested by the used keywords.

Appendix: instructions given to annotators

You have been given 1000 tweets and a category. The tweets were written when hurricane Sandy hit the US in 2012. Hopefully most of the tweets you've been given are associated with your emotion. Your task is to go through these tweets, and for each tweet confirm whether this tweet is associated with the emotion you have been given, and if not, associate it with the correct emotion. To help make sure that the tagging is as consistent as possible between all annotators, you will be given some guidelines to make sure that everyone tags the tweets in a similar way:

- "Fear" is the category containing tweets from people who are scared, afraid or worried.
- "Anger" contains tweets from people that are upset or angry. It's not always obvious whether someone is angry or sad, but if you think they are angry, tag it as "anger". It is acceptable if the person feels sadness as well.
- "Positive" contains tweets from people that are happy or at least feel positive.
- "Other" represents the tweets that don't belong to any of the other three categories. Tweets with none of the three emotions or mixed emotions where one of them isn't dominating belong to this category.
- The emotion should relate to the author of the tweet, not other people mentioned by the author. For example, the tweet "Maggie seems real concerned about Hurricane Sandy..." should not be tagged as "fear", since it's not the author of the tweet that is being concerned. Instead it should be tagged with "other".
- The tag should be based on the author's mood when the tweet was written. For example, the tweet "I was really scared yesterday!" should not be tagged as "fear", since it relates to past events, while we want to know how people were feeling when the tweets were posted. Exceptions can be made to events that happened very recently, for example: "I just fell because sandy scared me", which can be tagged as "fear".
- Obvious sarcasm and irony should be tagged as "Other". If you can't decide whether the author is being sarcastic or not, assume that he is not being sarcastic or ironic.

- A couple of the tweets might not be in English. Non-English tweets belong to "Other" regardless of content.
- A few of the tweets are not related to the hurricane. Treat them in the same way as the rest of the tweets.
- If a tweet contains conflicting emotions, and one of them doesn't clearly dominate the other, it belongs to "Other".
- Some of the tweets will be difficult to tag. Even so, don't leave a text untagged, please choose the alternative you believe is the most correct.

Competing interests
The authors declare that they have no competing interests.

Authors' contributions
All authors drafted, read and approved the final manuscript.

Acknowledgments
We would like to thank Roberta Campo, Luísa Coelho, Patrick Drews, Montserrat Ferrer Julià, Sébastien Grazzini, Paul Hirst, Thomas Ladoire, Håkan Marcusson, Miguel Mendes, María Luisa Moreo, Javier Mulero Chaves, Cristina Párraga Niebla, Joaquín Ramírez, and Leopoldo Santos Santos for their effort during the tagging process.
This work has been supported by the European Union Seventh Framework Programme through the Alert4All research project (contract no 261732), and by the research and development program of the Swedish Armed Forces.

Author details
[1] FOI Swedish Defence Research Agency, Stockholm, Sweden. [2] KTH Royal Institute of Technology, Stockholm, Sweden. [3] Avanti Communications Group plc, London, UK. [4] Ericsson, Stockholm, Sweden.

References
1. A Zielinski, U Bugel, Multilingual analysis of Twitter news in support of mass emergency events, in *Proceedings of the Ninth International Conference on Information Systems for Crisis Response and Management (ISCRAM 2012)* (Vancouver, Canada, 2012)
2. S-Y Perng, M Buscher, R Halvorsrud, L Wood, M Stiso, L Ramirez, A Al-Akkad, Peripheral response: Microblogging during the 22/7/2011 Norway attacks, in *Proceedings of the Ninth International Conference on Information Systems for Crisis Response and Management (ISCRAM 2012)* (Vancouver, Canada, 2012)
3. R Thomson, N Ito, H Suda, F Lin, Y Liu, R Hayasaka, R Isochi, Z Wang, Trusting tweets: The Fukushima disaster and information source credibility on Twitter, in *Proceedings of the Ninth International Conference on Information Systems for Crisis Response and Management (ISCRAM 2012)* (Vancouver, Canada, 2012)
4. J Yin, A Lampert, MA Cameron, B Robinson, R Power, Using social media to enhance emergency situation awareness. IEEE Intell Syst. **27**(6), 52–59 (2012). doi:10.1109/MIS.2012.6
5. A Nagy, J Stamberger, Crowd sentiment detection during disasters and crises, in *Proceedings of the Ninth International Conference on Information Systems for Crisis Response and Management (ISCRAM 2012)* (Vancouver, Canada, 2012)
6. S Verma, S Vieweg, WJ Corvey, L Palen, JH Martin, M Palmer, A Schram, KM Anderson, Natural language processing to the rescue? Extracting "situational awareness" tweets during mass emergency, in *Proceedings of the Fifth International AAAI Conference on Weblogs and Social Media* (Barcelona, Spain, 2011), pp. 385–392
7. MR Endsley, Toward a theory of situation awareness in dynamic systems. Hum Factors. **37**(1), 32–64 (1995)
8. American Red Cross, The American Red Cross and Dell launch first-of-its-kind social media digital operations center for humanitarian relief. Press release 7 March 2012

9. C Párraga Niebla, T Weber, P Skoutaridis, P Hirst, J Ramírez, D Rego, G Gil, W Engelbach, J Brynielsson, H Wigro, S Grazzini, C Dosch, Alert4All: An integrated concept for effective population alerting in crisis situations, in *Proceedings of the Eighth International Conference on Information Systems for Crisis Response and Management (ISCRAM 2011)* (Lisbon, Portugal, 2011)

10. H Artman, J Brynielsson, BJE Johansson, J Trnka, Dialogical emergency management and strategic awareness in emergency communication, in *Proceedings of the Eighth International Conference on Information Systems for Crisis Response and Management (ISCRAM 2011)* (Lisbon, Portugal, 2011)

11. S Nilsson, J Brynielsson, M Granåsen, C Hellgren, S Lindquist, M Lundin, M Narganes Quijano, J Trnka, Making use of new media for pan-European crisis communication, in *Proceedings of the Ninth International Conference on Information Systems for Crisis Response and Management (ISCRAM 2012)* (Vancouver, Canada, 2012)

12. F Johansson, J Brynielsson, M Narganes Quijano, Estimating citizen alertness in crises using social media monitoring and analysis, in *Proceedings of the 2012 European Intelligence and Security Informatics Conference (EISIC 2012)* (Odense, Denmark, 2012), pp. 189–196. doi:10.1109/EISIC.2012.23

13. B Liu, ed. by N Indurkhya, FJ Damerau, Sentiment analysis and subjectivity, in *Handbook of Natural Language Processing, Chapman & Hall/CRC Machine Learning & Pattern Recognition Series.* 2nd edition. Chap. 26 (Taylor & Francis Group, Boca Raton, Florida, 2010), pp. 627–666

14. B Pang, L Lee, Opinion mining and sentiment analysis. Foundations Trends Inf Retrieval. **2**(1–2), 1–135 (2008). doi:10.1561/1500000011

15. B Pang, L Lee, S Vaithyanathan, Thumbs up? Sentiment classification using machine learning techniques, in *Proceedings of the Seventh Conference on Empirical Methods in Natural Language Processing (EMNLP-02)* (Philadelphia, Pennsylvania, 2002), pp. 79–86. doi:10.3115/1118693.1118704

16. K Glass, R Colbaugh, Estimating the sentiment of social media content for security informatics applications. Secur Inform. **1**(3) (2012). doi:10.1186/2190-8532-1-3

17. A Pak, P Paroubek, Twitter as a corpus for sentiment analysis and opinion mining, in *Proceedings of the Seventh International Conference on Language Resources and Evaluation (LREC 2010)* (Valletta, Malta, 2010), pp. 1320–1326

18. L Barbosa, J Feng, Robust sentiment detection on Twitter from biased and noisy data, in *Proceedings of the 23rd International Conference on Computational Linguistics (COLING 2010)* (Beijing, China, 2010), pp. 36–44

19. C Strapparava, R Mihalcea, Learning to identify emotions in text, in *Proceedings of the 2008 ACM Symposium on Applied Computing (SAC'08)* (Fortaleza, Brazil, 2008), pp. 1556–1560. doi:10.1145/1363686.1364052

20. A Abbasi, H Chen, S Thoms, T Fu, Affect analysis of web forums and blogs using correlation ensembles. IEEE Trans Knowl Data Eng. **20**(9), 1168–1180 (2008). doi:10.1109/TKDE.2008.51

21. A Abbasi, H Chen, Affect intensity analysis of dark web forums, in *Proceedings of the Fifth IEEE International Conference on Intelligence and Security Informatics (ISI 2007)* (New Brunswick, New Jersey, 2007), pp. 282–288. doi:10.1109/ISI.2007.379486

22. J Brynielsson, F Johansson, A Westling, Learning to classify emotional content in crisis-related tweets, in *Proceedings of the 11th IEEE International Conference on Intelligence and Security Informatics (ISI 2013)* (Seattle, Washington, 2013), pp. 33–38. doi:10.1109/ISI.2013.6578782

23. J Brynielsson, F Johansson, S Lindquist, Using video prototyping as a means to involving crisis communication personnel in the design process: Innovating crisis management by creating a social media awareness tool, in *Proceedings of the 15th International Conference on Human-Computer Interaction* (Las Vegas, Nevada, 2013), pp. 559–568. doi:10.1007/978-3-642-39226-9_61

24. GA Miller, WordNet: A lexical database for English. Commun ACM. **38**(11), 39–41 (1995). doi:10.1145/219717.219748

25. M Hall, E Frank, G Holmes, B Pfahringer, P Reutemann, IH Witten, The WEKA data mining software: An update. ACM SIGKDD Explorations Newsl. **11**(1), 10–18 (2009). doi:10.1145/1656274.1656278

26. A McCallum, K Nigam, A comparison of event models for naive Bayes text classification, in *AAAI/ICML-98 Workshop on Learning for Text Categorization* (Madison, Wisconsin, 1998), pp. 41–48

27. JC Platt, ed. by B Schölkopf, CJC Burges, and AJ Smola, Fast training of support vector machines using sequential minimal optimization, in *Advances in Kernel Methods: Support Vector Learning.* Chap. 12 (MIT Press, Cambridge, Massachusetts, 1999), pp. 185–208

28. C Strapparava, A Valitutti, WordNet-Affect: an affective extension of WordNet, in *Proceedings of the Fourth International Conference on Language Resources and Evaluation (LREC 2004)* (Lisbon, Portugal, 2004), pp. 1083–1086

29. F Johansson, J Brynielsson, P Hörling, M Malm, C Mårtenson, S Truvé, M Rosell, Detecting emergent conflicts through web mining and visualization, in *Proceedings of the 2011 European Intelligence and Security Informatics Conference (EISIC 2011)* (Athens, Greece, 2011), pp. 346–353. doi:10.1109/EISIC.2011.21

30. J Brynielsson, S Nilsson, M Rosell, Feedback from social media during crisis management (in Swedish). Technical Report FOI-R--3756--SE, Swedish Defence Research Agency, Stockholm, Sweden, December 2013

14

Anticipating complex network vulnerabilities through abstraction-based analysis

Richard Colbaugh[1][*] and Kristin Glass[2]

Abstract

Large, complex networks are ubiquitous in nature and society, and there is great interest in developing rigorous, scalable methods for identifying and characterizing their vulnerabilities. This paper presents an approach for analyzing the dynamics of complex networks in which the network of interest is first abstracted to a much simpler, but mathematically equivalent, representation, the required analysis is performed on the abstraction, and analytic conclusions are then mapped back to the original network and interpreted there. We begin by identifying a broad and important class of complex networks which admit *vulnerability-preserving, finite state abstractions*, and develop efficient algorithms for computing these abstractions. We then propose a vulnerability analysis methodology which combines these finite state abstractions with formal analytics from theoretical computer science to yield a comprehensive vulnerability analysis process for networks of real-world scale and complexity. The potential of the proposed approach is illustrated via case studies involving a realistic electric power grid, a gene regulatory network, and a general class of social network dynamics.

Keywords: Complex networks, Finite state abstraction, Vulnerability analysis, Electric power grids, Biological networks, Social movements

Introduction

It is widely recognized that technological, biological, and social networks, while impressively robust in most circumstances, can fail catastrophically in response to focused attacks. Indeed, this combination of robustness and fragility appears to be an inherent property of complex, evolving networks ranging from the Internet and electric power grids to gene regulatory networks and financial markets e.g., [1-5]. As a consequence, there is significant interest in developing methods for reliably detecting and characterizing the vulnerabilities of these networks e.g., [6,7].

The challenges of vulnerability analysis are particularly daunting in the case of complex networks. Most such networks are large-scale "systems of systems", so that analysis methods must be computationally efficient. Additionally, because these networks perform reliably almost all of the time, standard techniques for finding vulnerabilities (e.g., computer simulations, "red

teaming") can be ineffective and, in any case, are not guaranteed to identify all vulnerabilities. These observations suggest that, in order to be practically useful, any method for analyzing vulnerabilities of complex networks should be *scalable*, to enable analysis of networks of real-world complexity, and *rigorous*, so that for instance it is guaranteed to find all vulnerabilities of a given class.

This paper presents a new approach to vulnerability analysis which possesses these properties. The proposed methodology is based upon *aggressive abstraction* – dramatically simplifying, property preserving abstraction of the network of interest [4]. Once an aggressive abstraction is derived, all required analysis is performed using the abstraction. Analytic conclusions are then mapped back to the original network and interpreted there; this mapping is possible because of the property preserving nature of the abstraction procedure.

Our focus is on dynamical systems with uncountable state spaces, as many complex networks are of this type. We begin by identifying a large and important class of dynamical networks which admit *vulnerability-preserving, finite state abstractions*, and develop efficient algorithms

---
* Correspondence: colbaugh@comcast.net
[1]Sandia National Laboratories, Albuquerque, NM 87111, USA
Full list of author information is available at the end of the article

for recognizing such networks and for computing their abstraction. We then offer a methodology which combines these finite state models with formal analytics from theoretical computer science [8] to provide a comprehensive vulnerability analysis process for large-scale networks. The potential utility of the proposed approach to vulnerability analysis is illustrated through case studies involving a realistic electric power grid, a gene regulatory network, and a general class of social network dynamics.

Preliminaries

This section introduces the class of network models to be considered in the paper and briefly summarizes some technical background that will be useful in our development.

The evolution to ensure robust performance in complex networks typically leads to systems that possess a "hybrid" structure, exhibiting both continuous and discrete dynamics [4]. More precisely, these networks often evolve to become *hybrid dynamical systems* – feedback interconnections of switching systems, which have discrete state sets, with systems whose dynamics evolve on continuous state spaces [9].

More quantitatively, consider the following definitions for hybrid dynamical system (HDS) models:

Definition 2.1: A *continuous-time HDS* is a control system

$$\sum\nolimits_{HDSct} \quad \begin{aligned} q+ &= h(q, k), \\ dx/dt &= f_q(x, u), \\ k &= p(x), \end{aligned}$$

where $q \in Q$ (with $|Q|$ finite) and $x \in X \subseteq \mathfrak{R}^n$ (with X bounded) are the states of the discrete and continuous systems that make up the HDS, $u \in \mathfrak{R}^m$ is the control input, h defines the discrete system dynamics, $\{f_q\}$ is a family of vector fields characterizing the continuous system dynamics, and p defines a partition of state space X into subsets with labels $k \in \{1, \ldots, K\}$.

Definition 2.2: A *discrete-time HDS* is a control system

$$\sum\nolimits_{HDSdt} \quad \begin{aligned} q+ &= h(q, k), \\ x+ &= f_q(x, u), \\ k &= p(x). \end{aligned}$$

We sometimes refer to an HDS using the symbol Σ_{HDS} if the nature of the continuous system (continuous- or discrete-time) is either unimportant or clear from the context.

The concept of finite state abstraction for an infinite state system is illustrated in Figure 1. Consider a complex network with states that evolve on a continuous space and an analysis question of interest. Such a situation is depicted at the bottom of Figure 1, where the

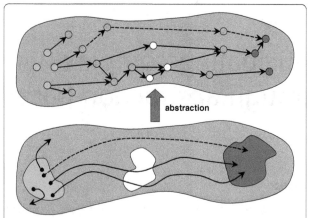

Figure 1 Finite state abstraction. Cartoon illustrates that the abstraction preserves network dynamics: trajectories of the infinite state system (curves in blue region at bottom) are mapped to equivalent finite state trajectories (sequences of state transitions at top).

continuous dynamics are shown as curves on a continuous state space (blue region), and the analysis question involves deciding whether states in the green region can evolve to the red region. Reachability questions of this sort are difficult to answer for generic complex networks. However, if it is possible to construct a finite state abstraction of the network which possesses equivalent dynamics, then the analysis task becomes much easier. To see this, observe from Figure 1 that a finite state abstraction of the original dynamics takes the form of a graph, where the states are graph vertices (nodes within the blue region at top) and feasible state transitions define the graph's directed edges. Reachability analysis is straightforward with a graph, and if the complex network and its abstraction have equivalent reachability properties then the much simpler graph analysis also characterizes the reachability of the original system.

Reachability assessment, while valuable, is typically not sufficient to answer real-world vulnerability analysis questions. For instance, suppose that the red region in Figure 1 is the set of failure states. It may be of interest to determine if all system trajectories which reach the red region first pass through the white "alerting" region, so there is warning of impending failure, or whether all trajectories which reach the red region subsequently return to the blue "normal" region, and thereby recover from failure. Addressing these more intricate questions requires that the analysis be conducted using a language which allows a nuanced description of, and reasoning about, network dynamics. We show in [4] that *linear temporal logic* (LTL) provides such a language, enabling quantitative specification of a broad range of complex network vulnerability problems. LTL extends propositional logic by including temporal operators, thereby allowing dynamical phenomena to be analyzed, and is similar to natural language and thus is easy to use [10].

As we wish to use LTL to analyze the dynamics of complex networks and we model these networks as HDS, we tailor our definition of LTL to be compatible with this setting:

Definition 2.3: The *syntax* of LTL consists of

- *atomic propositions* (q,k), where $q \in Q$ is an HDS discrete state and $k \in K$ is a label for a subset in the continuous system state space partition;
- *formulas* composed from atomic propositions using a grammar of Boolean ($\phi \vee \theta$, $\neg\phi$) and temporal ($\phi \mathcal{U}\theta$, $\bigcirc \phi$) operators.

The *semantics* of LTL follows from interpreting formulas on trajectories of HDS, that is, on sequences of (q, k) pairs: $(\mathbf{q}, \mathbf{k}) = (q_0, k_0), (q_1, k_1), \ldots, (q_T, k_T)$.

The Boolean operators $\vee$ and $\neg$ are disjunction and negation, as usual. The temporal operators $\mathcal{U}$ and $\bigcirc$ are read "until" and "next", respectively, with $\phi\mathcal{U}\theta$ specifying that ϕ must hold until θ holds and $\bigcirc \phi$ signifying that ϕ will be true at the next time instant (see [10] for a more thorough description).

Abstractions which preserve LTL also preserve all vulnerabilities expressible as LTL formulas; this property is stated more precisely in Section 4, where a formal definition is given for system vulnerability, and is also explained in [4]. Thus we seek an abstraction procedure which preserves LTL: given a system representation Σ_1, the procedure should generate a system abstraction Σ_2 which is such that $\{\Sigma_1 \mid= \phi\} \Leftrightarrow \{\Sigma_2 \mid= \phi\}$ for all LTL formulas ϕ (where $\mid=$ denotes formula satisfaction). Bisimulation is a powerful method for abstracting *finite* state systems to yield simpler finite state systems that are equivalent from the perspective of LTL [10]. However, the problem of constructing finite state bisimulations for continuous state systems is largely unexplored (but see the seminal work [11,12]). Indeed, one of the contributions of this paper is to develop a theoretically sound, practically implementable approach to obtaining finite state bisimulations for complex network models.

Bisimulation is typically defined for transition systems, so we first introduce this notion (see [10] for details):

Definition 2.4: A *transition system* is a four-tuple $T = (S, \to, Y, h)$ with state set S, transition relation $\to \subseteq S \times S$, output set Y, and output map $h: S \to Y$. T is *finite* if $|S|$ is finite.

Transition relation $\to$ defines admissible state transitions, so $(q, q') \in \to$, denoted $q \to q'$, if T can transition from q to q'.

Bisimilar transition systems share a common output set and have dynamics which are equivalent from the perspective of these outputs:

Definition 2.5: Transition systems $T_S = (S, \to_S, Y, h_S)$ and $T_P = (P, \to_P, Y, h_P)$ are *bisimilar* via relation $R \subseteq S \times P$ if:

- $s \sim p \Rightarrow h_S(s) = h_P(p)$ (R respects observations);
- $s \sim p$, $s \to_S s' \Rightarrow \exists\, p' \sim s'$ such that $p \to_P p'$ (T_P simulates T_S, denoted $T_S \angle T_P$);
- $p \sim s$, $p \to_P p' \Rightarrow \exists\, s' \sim p'$ such that $s \to_S s'$ ($T_P \angle T_S$),

where $\sim$ denotes equivalence under relation R.

A standard result from theoretical computer science e. g., [10] shows that bisimulation preserves LTL:

Proposition 2.1: If T_1 and T_2 are bisimilar transition systems and ϕ is an LTL formula then $\{T_1 \mid= \phi\} \Leftrightarrow \{T_2 \mid= \phi\}$.

The following statements offer an alternative definition for bisimulation, which is easily shown to be equivalent to the one presented in Definition 2.5 and is useful in the subsequent development:

Definition 2.6: A finite partition $\Phi: S \to P$ of the state space S of transition system $T = (S, \to, Y, h)$ naturally induces a *quotient transition system* $T/\sim = (P, \to_\sim, Y, h_\sim)$ of T provided that

- $\Phi(s) = \Phi(s')$ (denoted $s \sim s'$) $\Rightarrow h(s) = h(s')$;
- $h_\sim(p) = h(s)$ if $p = \Phi(s)$;
- $\to_\sim$ is defined so that $\Phi(s) \to_\sim \Phi(s')$ iff $s \to s'$.

Transition system T and its quotient $T/\sim$ are bisimilar if an additional condition holds:

Proposition 2.2: Suppose $T/\sim$ is defined as in Definition 2.6 and, in addition, $\Phi(s) \to_\sim \Phi(s') \Rightarrow \forall\, s'' \sim s\; \exists\, s''' \sim s'$ such that $s'' \to s'''$. Then T and $T/\sim$ are bisimilar.

Finally, we introduce a class of continuous state (control) systems which is important in applications.

Definition 2.7: The continuous-time system $dx/dt = f(x,u)$, with $f: \mathfrak{R}^n \times \mathfrak{R}^m \to \mathfrak{R}^n$, is *differentially flat* if there exists (flat) outputs $z \in \mathfrak{R}^m$ such that $z = H(x)$, $x = F_1(z, dz/dt, \ldots, d^r z/dt^r)$, and $u = F_2(z, dz/dt, \ldots, d^r z/dt^r)$ for some integer r and maps H, F_1, F_2.

Definition 2.8: The discrete-time system $x + = f(x,u)$ is *difference flat* (with memory k) if there exists (flat) outputs $z \in \mathfrak{R}^m$ such that $z = H(x)$, $x(t) = F_1(z(t), z(t + 1), \ldots, z(t + k - 1))$, and $u(t) = F_2(z(t), z(t + 1), \ldots, z(t + k - 1))$ for some maps H, F_1, F_2.

Background on flat systems may be found in [13]. Many real-world control systems are flat, including all controllable linear systems as well as all feedback linearizable systems. Perhaps more importantly, the complex, evolving networks underlying so much of advanced technology, biology, and social processes frequently possess flat subsystems.

Finite state abstraction

In this section we demonstrate that hybrid systems with (differentially or difference) flat continuous systems admit finite state bisimulations and present algorithms for constructing the bisimilar abstractions.

Consider an HDS of the form given in Definition 2.1 or 2.2. The following provides a transition system representation for the continuous system dynamics of HDS:

Definition 3.1: The *transition system model* T_{HDSc} for the continuous system portion of Σ_{HDS} is the collection $T_{HDSc} = \{T_q^k\}$, with one transition system $T_q^k = (X_q^k, \rightarrow_q^k, Y_q^k, h_q^k)$ specified for each (q, k) pair. Each T_q^k has bounded state space X_q^k, finite output set Y_q^k, an output map $h_q^k: X_q^k \rightarrow Y_q^k$ that defines a finite partition of X_q^k with labels $y \in Y_q^k$, and transition relation $\rightarrow_q^k$ reflecting the discrete- or continuous-time dynamics:

- for discrete-time continuous systems, $x \rightarrow_q^k x'$ iff $\exists u$ such that $x' = f_q(x,u)$ on subset k;
- for continuous-time continuous systems, $x \rightarrow_q^k x'$ iff there is a trajectory $x: [0, T] \rightarrow X_q^k$ of $dx/dt = f_q(x,u)$, a time $t' \in (0,T)$, and adjacent partitions of X_q^k labeled $y, y' \in Y_q^k$ such that $x(0) = x$, $x(T) = x'$, $x([0,t')) \subseteq y$, and $x((t',T]) \subseteq y'$.

We make the standard assumption that $k: X \rightarrow K$ partitions the HDS continuous system state space X into polytopes and that all HDS discrete system transitions are triggered by k transitions [9] (see Definitions 2.1 and 2.2).

Definition 3.1 allows Σ_{HDS} to be modeled as a feedback interconnection of two transition systems, one with continuous state space and one with finite state set:

Definition 3.2: The *transition system* T_{HDS} associated with the HDS given in Definition 2.1 or 2.2 is a feedback interconnection of 1.) the continuous system transition system $T_{HDSc} = \{T_q^k\}$ given in Definition 3.1 and 2.) the transition system associated with the HDS discrete system, given by $T_{HDSd} = (Q, \rightarrow_d, Q, id)$, where id is the identity map and $q \rightarrow_d q'$ iff $\exists k$ such that $q' = h(q, k)$. Thus $T_{HDS} = (Q \times X, \rightarrow_{HDS}, Q \times Y, h_{HDS})$, where $Q \times X = \cup_q (\cup_k \{q\} \times X_q^k)$, $Q \times Y = \cup_q (\cup_k \{q\} \times Y_q^k)$, and the definitions for $\rightarrow_{HDS}$ and h_{HDS} follow immediately from the transition relation and output map definitions specified for T_{HDSc} and T_{HDSd}.

Because the transition system T_{HDSd} corresponding to the HDS discrete system is already a finite state system, the main challenge in abstracting HDS to finite state systems is associated with finding finite state bisimulations

for the continuous systems $T_{HDSc} = \{T_q^k\}$. This is made explicit in the following

Theorem 1: If each transition system T_q^k associated with T_{HDS} is bisimilar to some finite quotient transition system $T_q^k/\sim = (Y_q^k, \rightarrow_\sim, Y_q^k, id)$ and the state space quotient partitions defined by the h_q^k satisfy a mild compatibility condition then T_{HDS} admits a finite bisimulation.

Proof: The proof is straightforward and is given in [4].

Theorem 1 shows that the key step in obtaining a finite state bisimulation for HDS T_{HDS}, and thus for Σ_{HDS}, is constructing bisimulations for the continuous state transition systems T_q^k. We therefore focus on this latter problem for the remainder of the section. Our first main result along these lines is for difference flat continuous systems:

Theorem 2: Given any finite partition $\pi: Z \rightarrow Y$ of the flat output space Z of a difference flat system, the associated transition system $T_F = (X, \rightarrow, Y, \pi \circ H)$ admits a bisimilar quotient $T_F/\sim$.

Proof: Consider the equivalence relation R that identifies state pairs (x, x') which generate identical sets of k-length output symbol sequences $y = y_0 y_1 \ldots y_{k-1}$, and the quotient system $T_F/\sim$ induced by R. R defines a finite partition of X (both $|Y|$ and k are finite), and $x \sim x' \Rightarrow \pi \circ H(x) = \pi \circ H(x')$ so that R respects observations. $T_F \angle T_F/\sim$ follows immediately from the definition of quotient systems. To see that $T_F/\sim \angle T_F$, note that flatness ensures *any* symbol string $y = y_k y_{k+1} \ldots$ is realizable by transition system T_F; thus $x \sim x'$ at time t implies that x and x' can transition to equivalent states at time $t + 1$. Therefore, from Definition 2.5, T_F and $T_F/\sim$ are bisimilar.

Remark 3.1: Efficient algorithms exist for checking if a given system is difference flat, so Theorem 2 provides a practically implementable means of identifying discrete-time continuous state systems which admit finite bisimulation [4].

Remark 3.2: The flat output trajectory completely defines the evolution of a difference flat system. As a consequence, because *any* finite partition of flat output space induces a finite bisimilar quotient for the flat system, this partition can be refined to yield any desired level of detail in the abstraction.

An analogous result holds for differentially flat HDS continuous systems. Our development of this result requires the following lemmas.

Lemma 3.1: A control system is differentially flat iff it is dynamic feedback linearizable.

Proof: The proof is given in [14].

Lemma 3.2: Control system Σ admits a finite bisimulation iff any representation of Σ obtained through coordinate transformation and/or invertible feedback also admits a finite bisimulation.

Proof: The proof is given in [12].

Lemmas 3.1 and 3.2 suggest the following procedure for constructing finite bisimulations for differentially flat systems: 1.) transform the flat system into a linear control system via feedback linearization, 2.) compute a finite bisimulation for the linear system, and 3.) map the bisimilar model back to the original system representation. As a result, we focus on building finite bisimulations for linear control systems.

In particular, the control system of interest is one "chain" of a Brunovsky normal form (BNF) system Σ_{BNF} [4]:

$$dx_1/dt = x_2,$$
$$dx_2/dt = x_3,$$
$$\ldots$$
$$dx_n/dt = u.$$

Concentrating on this system entails no loss of generality, as any controllable linear system can be modeled as a collection of these single chain systems, one for each input, and the decoupled nature of the chains ensures we can abstract each one independently and then "patch" the abstractions together to obtain an abstraction for the full system.

Consider the following partition of the (assumed bounded) state space $X \subseteq \mathfrak{R}^n$ of Σ_{BNF}:

Definition 3.3: *Partition π_ϵ is the map $\pi_\epsilon: X \to Y$ that partitions X into subsets $y_{is} = \{x \in X \mid x_1 \in [i\epsilon, (i + 1)\epsilon),$ sign$(x_2) = s_1, \ldots,$ sign$(x_n) = s_{n-1}\}$, where i is an integer and s is an $(n-1)$-vector of "signs" specifying a particular orthant of X.*

Note that π_ϵ partitions X into "slices" orthogonal to the x_1-axis.

We are now in a position to state

Theorem 3: The transition system $T_{BNF} = (X, \to, Y, \pi_\epsilon)$ associated with system Σ_{BNF} and partition π_ϵ admits a finite bisimilar quotient $T_{BNF}/\sim = (Y, \to_\sim, Y, id)$.

Proof: $T_{BNF}/\sim$ is finite because $|Y|$ is finite. Assume $\to_\sim$ is constructed so that $\pi_\epsilon(x) \to_\sim \pi_\epsilon(x') \Leftrightarrow x \to x'$, with the latter specified as in Definition 3.1. Then all the conditions of Definition 2.6 are satisfied, and from Proposition 2.2 we need only show $\pi_\epsilon(x) \to_\sim \pi_\epsilon(x') \Rightarrow \forall x'' \sim x \exists x''' \sim x'$ such that $x'' \to x'''$. This amounts to demonstrating that if x can be driven through face F of slice $\pi_\epsilon(x)$ then any x'' in that slice can be driven through F as well, which can be shown by checking this property for the system $x_1^{(n)} = u$ on each orthant of X (see e.g., [13] for a proof that system $x_1^{(n)} = u$ possesses this property).

Remark 3.3: The result given in Theorem 3 is most useful in situations where the control input u can be chosen large relative to the system "drift". Abstraction methods for applications in which control authority is limited are given in [4].

Next we turn to the task of *computing* finite bisimulations for HDS. We focus on constructing bisimulations for HDS continuous systems, as HDS discrete systems already possess finite state representations, and in particular on abstracting differentially flat continuous systems; the derivation of algorithms for difference flat continuous systems is analogous but simpler and is therefore omitted (see [4]).

Consider, without loss of generality (see Lemma 3.1), the problem of computing a finite state abstraction for continuous-time linear control system Σ_{lc}: $dx/dt = Ax + Bu$ (where A, B are matrices). The transition system associated with Σ_{lc} is $T_{lc} = (X, \to_{lc}, Y, h)$, with h: $X \to Y$ any finite, hypercubic partition of X and $\to_{lc}$ specified as in Definition 3.1. The finite state abstraction of interest is quotient system $T_{lc}/\sim = (Y, \to_{lc\sim}, Y, id)$. Observe that in order to obtain $T_{lc}/\sim$ it is only necessary to determine the set of admissible transition relations $\to_{lc\sim}$.

As most applications of interest involve large-scale systems, it is desirable to develop efficient algorithms for computing $\to_{lc\sim}$. We now introduce such a procedure. The algorithm decides whether a transition $y \to_{lc\sim} y'$ between two adjacent cells of the lattice y, y' is allowed, and is repeated for all candidate transitions of interest. We begin by summarizing a simple algorithm, based on computational linear system results given in [15], for deciding whether $y \to_{lc\sim} y'$ is admissible. Let k be the number of the coordinate axis orthogonal to the common face between y and y', V be the set of vertices shared by y and y', and a_k^T represent row k of A. Define $\Pi^k(w)$ to be the projection of vector w onto axis k, and suppose $y < y'$. Then y $\to_{lc\sim} y'$ iff $\Pi^k(Av_i + Bu) > 0$ for some $v_i \in V$ and $u \in U$. An algorithm which "operationalizes" this observation is

Algorithm 3.1:

If $y < y'$:

- If any element of row k of B is nonzero, $y \to_{lc\sim} y'$ is true. STOP.
- Repeat until $y \to_{lc\sim} y'$ is determined to be true or all vertices have been checked:

  - Select a vertex $v_i \in V$.
  - Compute the inner product $p = a_k^T v_i$.
  - If $p > 0$ then $y \to_{lc\sim} y'$ is true. STOP.

- If $y \to_{lc\sim} y'$ has not been found to be true it is false.

If $y > y'$: Algorithm is the same except that the comparison $p > 0$ is replaced by $p < 0$.

A difficulty with Algorithm 3.1 is that the number of vertices shared by two adjacent cells is 2^{n-1}, so that checking them becomes unmanageable even for moderately-sized systems. Interestingly, the algorithm can be modified so that feasibility of a transition can be tested by considering only a *single* well-chosen vertex, independent of the size of the model. The new algorithm is therefore extremely efficient and can be applied to very large systems. Let v_0 be the lowest vertex (in a component-wise sense) shared by y, y′ and let a_k^+ (a_k^-) be the sum of positive (negative) elements of row k of A, excluding the diagonal. We can now state

Algorithm 3.2 [4,16]:

If y < y′:

- If any element of row k of B is nonzero, $y \rightarrow_{lc\sim} y'$ is true. STOP.
- Compute the inner product $p = a_k^T v_0$.
- If $p + a_k^+ > 0$ then $y \rightarrow_{lc\sim} y'$ is true. STOP.
- Otherwise $y \rightarrow_{lc\sim} y'$ is false.

If y > y′: Algorithm is the same except that the comparison $p + a_k^+ > 0$ is replaced by $p + a_k^- < 0$.

A Matlab program which implements Algorithm 3.2 is presented in [4]. This program has been applied to systems with n = 10 000 state variables using desktop computers. Additionally, standard timing studies reveal that the computational cost of Algorithm 3.2 scales quadratically in the system state space dimension n (while Algorithm 3.1 scale exponentially in n), providing further support for the argument that this approach to abstraction can be applied to problems of real-world scale and complexity.

Vulnerability analysis

This section considers the *vulnerability assessment* problem: given a complex network and a class of failures of interest, does there exist an attack which causes the system to experience such failure? Other important vulnerability analysis tasks, including vulnerability exploitation and mitigation, are investigated in [4]. The proposed approach to vulnerability assessment leverages the finite state abstraction results derived in the preceding section. The basic idea is straightforward: given an HDS model for a network of interest and a class of failures of concern: 1.) construct a finite bisimulation for the HDS network model, 2.) conduct the vulnerability analysis on the system abstraction, and 3.) map the analysis results back to the original system model.

Observe that the proposed approach possesses desirable characteristics. For instance, the analytic process is scalable, because both the abstraction methodology [4] and the tools available for detecting vulnerabilities in finite state systems [e.g., 8] are scalable. Additionally, the analysis is rigorous. Because HDS vulnerabilities are expressible as LTL formulas, and bisimulation preserves LTL, the original complex network and its abstraction have identical vulnerabilities. Formal analysis tools such as model checking [8] can be structured to identify all vulnerabilities of the finite state abstraction, and bisimilarity then implies that the approach is guaranteed to find all vulnerabilities of the original network as well.

We now quantify the proposed approach to vulnerability assessment. It is supposed that the complex network

of interest can be modeled as an HDS, Σ_{HDS}, and that the network's desired or "normal" behavior can be characterized with an LTL formula φ; generalizing the situation to a set of LTL formulas $\{\phi_i\}$ is straightforward. Consider the following

Definition 4.1: Given an HDS Σ_{HDS} and an LTL encoding φ of the desired network behavior, the *vulnerability assessment problem* involves determining whether Σ_{HDS} can be made to violate φ.

The proposed vulnerability assessment method employs *bounded model checking* (BMC), a powerful technique for deciding whether a given finite state transition system satisfies a particular LTL specification over a finite, user-specified time horizon [8]. Briefly, BMC checks whether a finite transition system T satisfies an LTL specification φ on a time interval [0, k], denoted $T \mid =_k \phi$, in two steps: 1.) translate $T \mid =_k \phi$ to a proposition $[T, \phi]_k$ which is satisfied by, and only by, transition system trajectories that *violate* φ (this is always possible), and 2.) check if $[T, \phi]_k$ is satisfiable using a modern SAT solver [8]. Note that because modern SAT solvers are extremely powerful, this approach to model checking can be implemented with problems of real-world scale.

We are now in a position to state our vulnerability assessment algorithm. Let T_{HDS} denote the transition system associated with Σ_{HDS}, and consider the vulnerability assessment problem given in Definition 4.1. We have

Algorithm 4.1: Vulnerability assessment

1. Construct a finite bisimilar abstraction T for T_{HDS} using the results of Section 3.
2. Check satisfiability of $[T, \phi]_k$ using BMC:

- if $[T, \phi]_k$ is not satisfiable then T is not vulnerable and thus Σ_{HDS} is not vulnerable (on time horizon k);
- if $[T, \phi]_k$ is satisfiable then T, and therefore Σ_{HDS}, is vulnerable, and the SAT solver "witness" is an exploitation of the vulnerability.

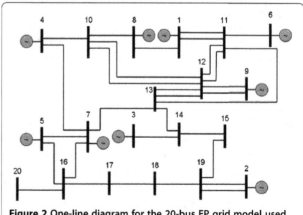

Figure 2 One-line diagram for the 20-bus EP grid model used in the vulnerability assessment case study.

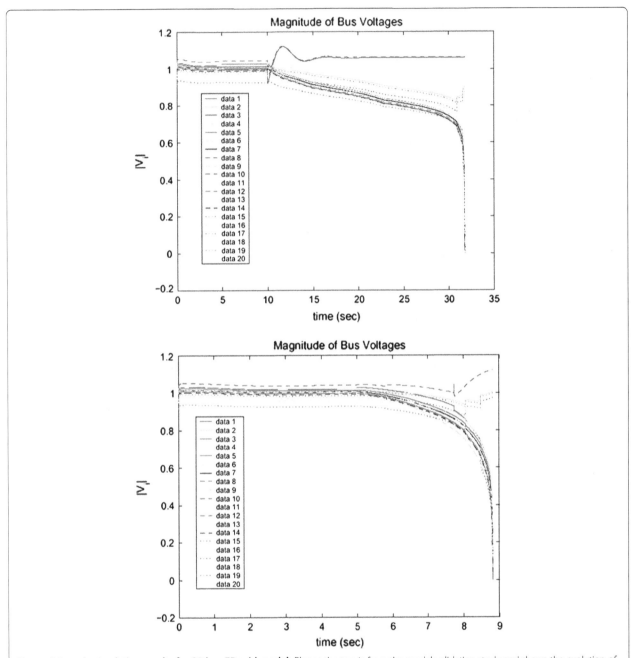

Figure 3 Sample simulation results for 20-bus EP grid model. Plot at the top is from the model validation study and shows the evolution of voltages at all 20 buses; these voltage time series are in good agreement with those observed in the corresponding cascading voltage collapse for the actual grid. Plot at bottom depicts voltage timec series which result from applying the vulnerability exploitation procedure designed using the proposed finite state abstraction methodology.

To illustrate the utility of the proposed approach to vulnerability assessment we apply the analytic method to an important complex network: an electric power (EP) grid. EP grids are naturally represented as HDS, with the continuous system modeling the generator and load dynamics as well as power flow constraints and the discrete system capturing protection logic switching and other "supervisory" behavior:

Definition 4.2: The *HDS power grid model* Σ_{EP} takes the form

$$\Sigma_{EP} \quad \begin{aligned} q+ &= h(q, \ k, \ v), \\ dx/dt &= f_q(x, \ y, \ u), \\ 0 &= g_q(x, \ y), \\ k &= p(x, \ y), \end{aligned}$$

where q and x are the discrete and continuous system states, v and u denote exogenous inputs, y is the vector of "algebraic variables", and all other terms are analogous to those introduced in Definition 2.1.

The continuous system portion of grid model Σ_{EP} is feedback linearizable [17], which implies the continuous system is differentially flat and consequently that Σ_{EP} admits a finite abstraction. Additionally, it can be shown that grid vulnerabilities are expressible as LTL formulas composed of atomic propositions which depend only on q and k [18]. Thus Algorithm 4.1 is directly applicable to power grids.

We now summarize the results of a vulnerability assessment for the 20bus grid shown in Figure 2. This grid provides a simple but useful representation of a real, national-scale EP system for which (proprietary) data are available to us [4]. The grid can be modeled as an HDS Σ_{EP} of the form given in Definition 4.2. The report [4] gives a Matlab encoding of the specific HDS model used in this study. Because the model Σ_{EP} corresponds to a real-world grid, the behaviors of the model and the actual grid can be compared. For example, the real grid recently experienced a large cascading voltage collapse, and data was collected for this event. We simulated this cascading outage (see Figure 3, top plot) and found close agreement between the behavior of the actual grid and the model Σ_{EP}. Observe that this result is encouraging given the well-known difficulties associated with reproducing such cascading dynamics with computer models (see, e.g., [17,18]).

Vulnerability assessment was performed using Algorithm 4.1. It was assumed that the grid's attacker wishes to drive the voltage at bus 11 to unacceptably low levels, so that the loads at this bus would not be served, and that the attacker has only limited grid access. In particular, we consider here a scenario in which the attacker can gain assess to the generator at bus 2 via cyber means [18]. Note that this class of vulnerabilities is interesting because the access point – the generator at bus 2 – is geographically remote from the target of the attack – the loads at bus 11.

The first step in the vulnerability assessment procedure specified in Algorithm 4.1 involves constructing a finite state bisimulation T for Σ_{EP}; this abstraction is computed using Algorithm 3.2. The second step in Algorithm 4.1 is to apply BMC to T to determine if it is possible to realize the attack objective, i.e., low voltage at bus 11, through admissible manipulation of the generator at bus 2. We employed NuSMV, an open source software tool for formal verification of finite state systems, for this analysis [19]. This vulnerability assessment reveals that it is possible for the attacker to realize the given objective via the assumed grid access, and gives a finite state "trace" of one means of exploiting the vulnerability. Using this trace, we synthesize an exploitation attack which is directly implementable with the HDS model Σ_{EP}. Sample simulation results are shown in Figure 3 (bottom plot). It can be seen from the bus voltage time series in Figure 3 that the attacker's goals can indeed be realized, in this case by

initiating a cascading voltage collapse which takes down bus 11 as well as most of the rest of the grid.

Discussion

This paper presents an approach for analyzing complex networks in which the network of interest is first abstracted to a much simpler, but mathematically equivalent, representation, the required analysis is performed using the abstraction, and analytic conclusions are then mapped back to the original network and interpreted there. We identify an important class of complex networks which admit vulnerability-preserving, finite state abstractions, provide efficient algorithms for computing these abstractions, and offer a vulnerability analysis methodology that combines finite state network representations with formal analytics to enable rigorous vulnerability analysis for networks of real-world scale and complexity. The considerable potential of the method is demonstrated through a case study involving a realistic electric power grid model.

We now demonstrate that the proposed approach to analyzing complex network dynamics can also be applied to biological and social systems. Consider first a biological example. Many aspects of the physiology of living organisms oscillate with a period of approximately 24 hours, corresponding to the duration of a day, and the molecular basis for this circadian rhythm has been quantified in several organisms. For instance, a useful model for the gene regulatory network responsible for circadian rhythm in *Drosophila melanogaster* (fruit fly) is [20]:

$$\frac{dM_P}{dt} = v_{sP}\frac{K_{IP}^n}{K_{IP}^n + C_N^n} - v_{mP}\frac{M_P}{K_{mP} + M_P} - k_d M_P,$$

$$\frac{dP_0}{dt} = k_{sP}M_P - V_{1P}\frac{P_0}{K_{1P} + P_0} + V_{2P}\frac{P_1}{K_{2P} + P_1} - k_d P_0,$$

$$\frac{dP_1}{dt} = V_{1P}\frac{P_0}{K_{1P} + P_0} - V_{2P}\frac{P_1}{K_{2P} + P_1} - V_{3P}\frac{P_0}{K_{3P} + P_1}$$
$$+ V_{4P}\frac{P_2}{K_{4P} + P_2} - k_d P_1,$$

$$\frac{dP_2}{dt} = V_{3P}\frac{P_1}{K_{3P} + P_1} - V_{4P}\frac{P_2}{K_{4P} + P_2} - k_3 P_2^2 + k_4 C$$
$$- v_{dP}\frac{P_2}{K_{dP} + P_2} - k_d P_2,$$

$$\frac{dC}{dt} = k_3 P_2^2 - k_4 C - k_1 C + k_2 C_N - k_{dC} C,$$

$$\frac{dC_N}{dt} = k_1 C - k_2 C_N - k_{dC} C,$$

where M_P, P_0, P_1, P_2, C, and C_N are state variables corresponding to the concentrations of the constituents of the circadian rhythm gene network, v_{sP} is an exogenous (control) input signal associated with the light–dark cycle of the environment, and all other terms are constant model parameters.

As is evident from Definition 2.7, a differentially flat system possesses (flat) outputs, equal in number to the number of inputs, which permit the system states and inputs to be recovered through algebraic manipulation of these outputs and their time derivatives. In the case of *Drosophila* circadian rhythm, C_N is one such flat output. To see this, note that C and its time derivatives can be obtained from the sixth equation through manipulation of C_N and its derivatives. These terms, in turn, permit P_2 (and its derivatives) to be obtained from the fifth equation, and continuing in this way up the "chain" of equations gives all of the states and the input v_{sP}. Thus the system states and input can be obtained from knowledge of C_N and its derivatives, proving that the above gene network model for *Drosophila* circadian rhythm is differentially flat. This, in turn, implies that the model admits a finite state bisimulation (Theorem 3).

We have constructed a finite state model for *Drosophila* using Algorithm 3.2, and then applied Algorithm 4.1 to this finite state representation to identify gene network vulnerabilities. More specifically, this methodology was employed to identify gene network parameters whose manipulation would quickly and efficiently reset the phase of Circadian rhythm. The parameters nominated by this analysis are:

- mRNA transcription rate;
- mRNA degradation rate;
- protein translation rate.

It is worth noting that these Circadian phase vulnerabilities are identical to the "control targets" obtained in [21] through a substantially more involved, computationally-intensive sensitivity analysis.

Consider next the phenomenon of social movements, that is, large, informal groupings of individuals and/or organizations focused on a particular issue, for instance of political, social, economic, or religious significance e.g., [22]. Given the importance of social movements and the desire to understand their emergence and growth, numerous mathematical representations have been proposed to characterize their dynamics. For example, [23] suggests a model in which each individual in a population of interest can be in one of three states – member (of the movement), potential member, and ex-member – and interactions between individuals can lead to transitions between these affiliation states (e.g., potential members can be persuaded to become members). In particular, [23] proposes the following model for social movement dynamics:

$$\sum\nolimits_{sm} \quad \begin{aligned} dP/dt &= \lambda - \beta PM + \delta_1 E, \\ dM/dt &= \beta PM - \delta_2 ME - \delta_3 M, \\ dE/dt &= \delta_2 ME + \delta_3 M - \delta_1 E, \end{aligned}$$

where P, M, and E denote the fractions of potential members, members, and ex-members in the population, Λ can be interpreted to be the system's input, and β, δ_1, δ_2, δ_3 are nonnegative constants related to the probabilities of individuals undergoing the various state transitions. It is worth noting that this model is shown in [23] to provide a good description for the growth of real-world social movements.

This model for social dynamics is differentially flat with flat output E. To see this, observe that M and its time derivatives can be obtained from the third equation through manipulation of E and its derivatives. These

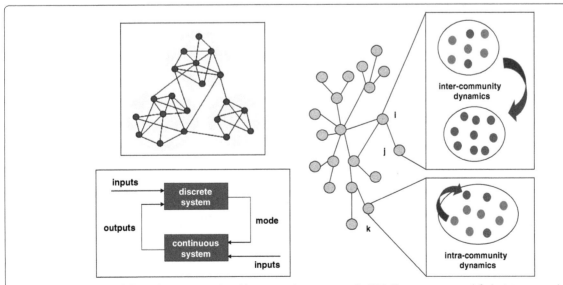

Figure 4 Modeling social dynamics on networks with community structure via HDS. The cartoon at top left depicts a network with three communities. The cartoon at right illustrates dynamics within a community k and between communities i and j. The schematic at bottom left shows the basic HDS feedback structure, in which the HDS discrete and continuous systems model the inter-community and intra-community dynamics, respectively.

terms, in turn, permit P (and its derivatives) to be obtained from the second equation. Finally, knowledge of P, M, E, and their derivatives allows the input Λ to be recovered from the first equation. Thus all of the system states as well as the input can be obtained from knowledge of E and its derivatives, which shows that the social movement model is differentially flat. This, in turn, implies that the model admits a finite state bisimilar abstraction (see Theorem 3).

We now consider the vulnerability of social movement dynamics. In order to make this analysis more interesting, the dynamics Σ_{sm} is extended to enable modeling of social movements propagation on networks with realistic topologies. More specifically, it is known that real-world social networks possess *community structure*, that is, the presence of densely connected groupings of individuals which have only relatively few links to other groups e.g., [22,23], and we are interested in modeling and analyzing social movement dynamics on these networks. One way to construct such a representation is to model movement dynamics as consisting of two components: 1.) *intra-community dynamics*, involving frequent interactions between individuals within the same community and the resulting gradual change in the concentrations of movement members, and 2.) *inter-community dynamics*, in which the movement jumps from one community to another, for instance because a movement member "visits" a new community.

It is natural to model these dynamics via HDS, with the continuous system representing intra-community dynamics via Σ_{sm}, or its finite state abstraction, the discrete system capturing the inter-community dynamics (e.g., using a simple switching rule), and the interplay between these dynamics being represented by the HDS feedback structure. A detailed description of the manner in which HDS models can be used to capture general social dynamics on networks with realistic topologies is given in [22], and the basic idea is illustrated in Figure 4.

We have constructed a finite state model for Σ_{sm} using Algorithm 3.2, and then connected these intra-community dynamics models together to represent the complete intra- and inter-community dynamics. We applied Algorithm 4.1 to this finite state representation to identify social movement vulnerabilities. More specifically, this methodology was employed to identify the characteristics of social movement dynamics which are most important for movement success. This analysis indicates that a key indicator of the ultimate success of a social movement is significant early dispersion of a movement across network communities; interestingly, this measure should be more predictive than the early volume of movement activity (which is a standard metric for predictive analysis of social dynamics).

Competing interests
The authors declare that they have no competing interests.

Author's contributions
RC and KG designed the research, RC developed the theoretical results, RC and KG developed the computational algorithms, and RC wrote the paper. All authors read and approved the final manuscript.

Acknowledgements
This work was supported by the U.S. Department of Defense and the Laboratory Directed Research and Development Program at Sandia National Laboratories. Sandia National Laboratories is a multi-program laboratory managed and operated by Sandia Corporation, a wholly owned subsidiary of Lockheed Martin Corporation, for the U.S. Department of Energy's National Nuclear Security Administration under contract DE-AC04-94AL85000.

Author details
¹Sandia National Laboratories, Albuquerque, NM 87111, USA. ²New Mexico Institute of Mining and Technology, Socorro, NM 87801, USA.

References
1. J. Carlson, J. Doyle, Complexity and Robustness. Proc. National Academy of Sciences USA **99**, 2538–2545 (2002)
2. J. Doyle, D. Alderson, L. Li, S. Low, M. Roughan, S. Shalunov, R. Tanaka, W. Willinger, The 'Robust Yet Fragile' Nature of the Internet. Proc. National Academy of Sciences USA **102**, 14497–14502 (2005)
3. P. Ormerod, R. Colbaugh, Cascades of Failure and Extinction in Evolving Complex Systems. J Artificial Societies and Social Simulation **9**, 4 (2006)
4. R. Colbaugh, K. Glass, G. Willard, *Analysis of Complex Networks Using Aggressive Abstraction*. SAND2008-7327 (Sandia National Laboratories, Albuquerque, NM, 2008). Additional file 1
5. R. LaViolette, K. Glass, R. Colbaugh, Deep Information from Limited Observation of 'Robust Yet Fragile' Systems. Physica A **388**, 3283–3287 (2009)
6. *National Infrastructure Protection Plan* (U.S. Department of Homeland Security, Washington DC, 2009)
7. H. Chen, C. Yang, M. Chau, S. Li (eds.), *Intelligence and Security Informatics* (Lecture Notes in Computer Science, Springer, Berlin, 2009)
8. E. Clarke, O. Grumberg, D. Peled, *Model Checking* (MIT Press, Cambridge, MA, 1999)
9. R. Majumdar, P. Tabuada (eds.), *Hybrid Systems: Computation and Control* (Lecture Notes in Computer Science, Springer, Berlin, 2009)
10. R. Milner, *Communication and Concurrency* (Prentice-Hall, NJ, 1989)
11. R. Alur, T. Henzinger, G. Lafferriere, G. Pappas, Discrete Abstractions of Hybrid Systems. Proc. IEEE **88**, 971–984 (2000)
12. P. Tabuada, G. Pappas, Linear Time Logic Control of Discrete-Time Linear Systems. IEEE Trans. Automatic Control **51**, 1862–1877 (2006)
13. P. Martin, R. Murray, P. Rouchon, (California Institute of Technology, Pasadena, CA, 2003)
14. E. Aranda-Bricaire, C. Moog, J. Pomet, A Linear Algebraic Framework for Dynamic Feedback Linearization. IEEE Trans. Automatic Control **40**, 127–132 (1995)
15. L. Habets, J. van Schuppen, A Control Problem for Affine Dynamical Systems on a Full-dimensional Polytope. Automatica **40**, 21–35 (2004)
16. J. Gardiner, R. Colbaugh, *Development of a Scalable Bisimulation Algorithm*, ICASA Technical Report (New Mexico Institute of Mining and Technology, Socorro, NM, 2006)
17. M. Ilic, J. Zaborszky, *Dynamics and Control of Large Electric Power Systems* (Wiley, NY, 2000)
18. J. Stamp, R. Colbaugh, R. Laviolette, A. McIntyre, B. Richardson, Impacts Analysis for Cyber Attack on Electric Power Systems, SAND2008-7300 (Sandia National Laboratories, Albuquerque, NM, 2008)
19. *NuSMV: a new symbolic model checker*. http://nusmv.fbk.eu, downloaded July 2007
20. J. Goncalves, T. Yi, (MTNS, Leuven, Belgium, 2004)

21. N. Bagheri, J. Stelling, F. Doyle, Circadian Phase Resetting via Single and Multiple Control Targets. PLoS Comput. Biol. **4**, e1000104 (2008)

22. R. Colbaugh, K. Glass, Proc. IEEE Multi-Conference on Systems and Control (Saint Petersburg, Russia, 2009)

23. P. Hedstrom, *Explaining the Growth Patterns of Social Movements*. Understanding Choice, Explaining Behavior (Oslo University Press, Oslo, Norway, 2006)

15

Factors influencing network risk judgments: a conceptual inquiry and exploratory analysis

Jennifer Cowley[1*], Frank L. Greitzer[2†] and Bronwyn Woods[1†]

Abstract

Effectively assessing and configuring security controls to minimize network risks requires human judgment. Little is known about what factors network professionals perceive to make judgments of network risk. The purpose of this research was to examine first, what factors are important to network risk judgments (Study 1) and second, how risky/safe each factor is judged (Study 2) by a sample of network professionals. In Study 1, a complete list of factors was generated using a focus group method and validated on a broader sample using a survey method with network professionals. Factors detailing the adversary and organizational network readiness were rated highly important. Study 2 investigated the level of riskiness for each factor that is described in a vignette-based factor scenario. The vignette provided context that was missing in Study 1. The highest riskiness ratings were of factors detailing the adversary and the lowest riskiness ratings detailed the organizational network readiness. A significant relationships existed in Study 2 between the level of agreement on each factor's rating across our sample of network professionals and the riskiness level each factor was judged. Factors detailing the adversary were highly agreed upon while factors detailing the organizational capability were less agreed upon. Computational risk models and network risk metrics ask professionals to perceive factors and judge overall network risk levels but no published research exists on what factors are important for network risk judgments. These empirical findings address this gap and factors used in models and metrics could be compared to factors generated herein. Future research and implications are discussed at the close of this paper.

Keywords: Perceived risk; Network risk judgments; Network risk; Network security

Introduction

An information system is a discrete set of information resources organized expressly for the collection, processing, maintenance, use, sharing, dissemination, or disposition of information [1]. All information systems, which we use interchangeably with the term networks, have inherent network-related risks that cannot be eliminated completely because of operational resource constraints. Risks, defined as "the possibility of loss, injury, or other adverse or unwelcome circumstance" [2], must then be prioritized based on the relative risk level and addressed according to the feasibility of mitigation strategies given both context and resource constraints. Network professionals must evaluate risk throughout the network lifecycle but

we focus on risk evaluation during network design and control configuration.

Within the U.S. Department of Defense (DoD) and civilian government networks, organizations must undergo a network certification process— i.e., ISO27000 series (information security standards published jointly by the International Organization for Standardization, ISO, and the International Electrotechnical Commission, IEC) and NIST 800 series [3])—to evaluate network risk. This process of certification involves a designated approving authority (DAA) who engages with the organization's information assurance (IA) officer to determine the organization's network risk level, based on risks identified and control configurations established to address those risks. Some risks are reduced, but not eliminated, through the implementation of various security controls—i.e., management, operational, and technical safeguards or countermeasures employed within an information system to protect the confidentiality, integrity, and availability of the system and its information (a listing of such controls is

*Correspondence: jcowley@cert.org
†Equal contributors
[1]Carnegie Mellon University Software Engineering Institute, CERT Division, 4500 Fifth Avenue, Pittsburgh, Pennsylvania 15213, USA
Full list of author information is available at the end of the article

found in [1]). Ultimately at the end of the certification process, the DAA certifies that the network, with certain controls implemented, meets an acceptable standardized level of network risk.

This network risk certification process, which requires the perception and judgment of network risk, is difficult to standardize across network professionals because in part, different people believe that different factors are important to judgments of risk ([4,5]). A factor is a perceived circumstance, event, influence, fact, etc. that is related to a particular outcome. Both risk perception and judgment can be influenced by network context ([6,7]), which we operationally define as perceivable factors physically and temporally surrounding an event or circumstance (e.g., the organizational policies, the types of adversaries targeting that organization, the types of adversaries, etc.). With respect to judgments of network risk, little is known about what factors are consistently important and unimportant to network professionals like the DAA and IA officers. Guidelines included in network risk metrics for assessing and assigning risk levels are often generic and not tailored to the conditions and contexts of a given network. Consequently during the decision process, individuals like the DAA may have to ignore certain network attributes not covered in the guidelines or ignore the guidelines altogether. Under circumstances where guidelines cannot be clearly applied, the DAA most likely relies on his/her own perceptual capabilities, work experiences, etc. to judge the network risk level, yet little prior research has investigated exactly what factors are actually being considered. Using a mixed-method approach [8] that combines qualitative and quantitative research methods to achieve study objectives, we attempted to identify and validate the factors people believe are most important to network risk judgments.

The challenges with judging network risk levels are due in part to the semantic complexity of the term itself. Underlying this semantic complexity is the lack of an agreed upon definition of risk from professionals in industry and academia ([6,9]). Consequently, risk miscommunications may arise [6] because interlocutors may have different semantic meanings of the term, risk. Risk is a psychological construct [10], an idea constructed in the human mind from the aggregation of dimensions or categories of abstract or tangible perceived phenomenon. The dimensions constituting network risk that we are familiar with include likelihood, vulnerability, resilience, impact, etc. but it is not clear whether network professionals all believe the same dimensions comprise network risk. Dimensions can be derived from perceived factors that include environmental information, past experiences, and other psychological phenomena such as attitudes and belief systems [6]. For example, a "likelihood" dimension of the network risk construct might be driven by perceived environmental factors and historical experience factors

indicating the "likelihood" of successful implementation of security controls prior to an attack. The risk research literature provides varying definitions of risk or perceived risk across different domains (e.g., [11-14]) but no consensus exists about the dimensions underlying risk in general or factors used to construct these dimensions ([6,15-21]). We conjecture that a relationship exists between how network risk is defined, what underlying dimensions are important to a network risk definition, and the relevant dimensional factors used in judgments of network risk. Investigating these dimensions and relevant factors might offer clues to how network risk is defined by network professionals. To our knowledge, no foundational research exists that documents the network risk dimensions and respective factors important to network professionals who design and secure networks. This is the impetus for our research.

We used an exploratory, mixed-method approach to identify what factors are important and unimportant for risk judgment in general (Study 1) and what factors are commonly and most consistently judged as more safe or more risky (Study 2) across our sample of network professionals. Because no prior research has identified network risk dimensions important to risk judgments in the context of a network, Study 2 was designed to address this. Prior research indicates that risk perception and judgment can be influenced by context ([6,7]). Therefore, we were interested in identifying robust dimensions and respective factors that are not susceptible to the effects of different contexts.

This paper is structured to review each study's objective, the method, the results and conclusions. We close this paper with an overall discussion that includes the implications of our findings, the limitations of our research and future directions.

Study 1: factors that impact network risk perception
Study purpose and research overview
The purpose of Study 1 was (a) to generate a comprehensive list of perceived factors that were relevant to judgments of network risk and (b) to determine which factors were considered most and least important to judgments of network risk. A focus group of cybersecurity professionals first generated a list of relevant factors, which were then validated with a broader sample of cybersecurity and network professionals using an online survey method.

Method
Participants
Focus Group Demographics. Five cybersecurity professionals plus one moderator comprised the focus group. All focus group members were employees at a single organization with a variety of cybersecurity expertise.

The self-reported expertise included acquisition support (1 participant), cyber threat and vulnerability analysis (1 participant), cyber enterprise and workforce management (1 participant), and enterprise threat/vulnerability management (2 participants). No other demographic information of this sample is permitted to be disclosed.

Survey Sampling and Demographics. The target population included cybersecurity and/or network professionals, who either designed, implemented, supported, and/or tested networks for security purposes or who trained individuals to do these functions. We used a snowball sampling technique [22], first soliciting colleagues at our institution for study participation; they subsequently invited others inside and outside our organization. The mean sample age ($n = 38$) was 47 years with a standard deviation (SD) of 10.3 years. The mean number of years worked in computer science professions was 13 ($SD = 9.7$), and the mean number of years in their current job was 9 ($SD = 7.7$). We did not require participants to report additional demographic information on the DHS sectors supported. Consequently, we had low response rates for this question and did not report on these questions.

Materials and procedure

Focus Group. During three sequential two-hour meetings spread over the course of a week, we conducted a moderated focus group using a brainstorming and consensus building technique [23] to identify all factors (at any granularity of detail) that impact network risk perception. We did not collect related information about why each factor was important, or why some factors had very specific language; we were just generating a comprehensive list. Focus group discussions about "why" a factor was provided often lead to desultory discussions and long debates about the validity of the factor so we discouraged those discussions. Each factor offered by each group member was then recorded on a single Post-it Note™ and organized taxonomically by the focus group on butcher paper using an affinity diagramming technique [24].

Online Survey. All factors generated in the focus group sessions, regardless of their granularity, were placed in an online survey to assess their validity on a broader sample of network professionals. The purpose of the online survey was to assess the consensus on the importance level of each factor. The survey was hosted by SurveyGizmo™, a browser-based survey design and deployment tool, and it comprised three survey subsections: informed consent, factor ratings, and demographics.

Informed consent was obtained in accordance with ethics guidelines for research with human subjects (Institutional Review Board approval HS12-571). After providing consent, participants read the online instructions and then rated each of the factors, presented in random order, one factor per survey page. Each factor was presented in a standardized sentence structure, bolded for quick identification (e.g., "Generally, how important is <factor> to your overall perception of network risk?"); no additional network information or context was provided. Participants were asked to adjust a slider to reflect a level of importance on a continuum between 0 (not at all important) and 100 (extremely important). If a participant could not understand the meaning of the factor or had no experience with it, this person was instructed to refrain from making a rating and to write "don't know" in a comments box below the factor. After rating all presented factors, participants could suggest additional factors.

Participants then answered demographics questions about (a) job title, (b) job-related expertise, current employer(s), (c) whether their current job supported the US government, military, private industry or whether he/she was a private consultant, and (d) which of the 18 DHS ISAC sector(s) he or she supports (e.g., healthcare, banking, energy). The order of the demographics questions was not randomized. Survey participants were financially compensated with a $15 gift card at the close of the survey.

Results

This section first discusses common distributions of ratings for each factor and then compares the factor means. All factors identified by the focus group and used in the online survey are listed in Additional file 1: Table SA-1, for quick reference.

Participants did not typically use the response scales consistently (e.g., some use the entire range of the response scale while others use a small portion) so we characterized these first. The mean importance ratings obtained from our 38 survey participants ranged from 38.8 to 83.5 on the 0 to 100-point scale. Three common distributions of factor ratings (for Factors 8, 5, and 51) are shown in Figure 1: unimodal, bimodal and multimodal. Factor 51 (The maturity of the organization's system capabilities for network defense), an example unimodal distribution, has a high level of agreement with most ratings clustered at the high level, indicating that this factor is very important to most participants. Factor 8 (whether the facility uses "SCADA" supervisory control and data acquisition systems) has a bimodal response distribution because scores were clustered around the low or less important end of the scale and around the high or more important end of the scale. Scores for Factor 5 (whether the network is for the military, government, or civilian sector) are distributed across the range of importance ratings. The Additional file 1: Table SA-2 lists all factors, rank-ordered in descending order according to mean importance ratings, and provides density plots of the rating distributions of each factor. Inspection of all density plots for each factor indicates that 27 factors have

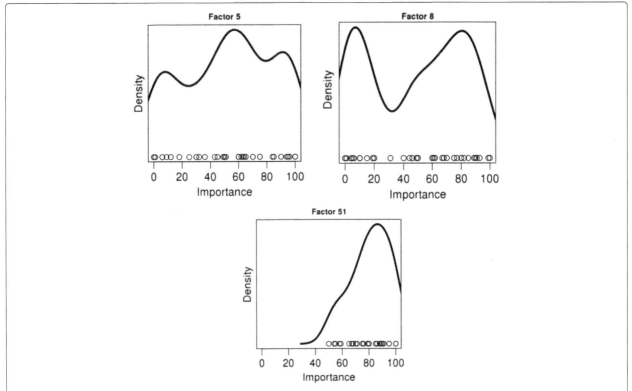

Figure 1 Representative density plots of importance ratings for three factors. Note: The y-axis is the density of responses, and the-x axis is the importance ratings given by participants. Each rating provided by a single participant is represented by a circle along the x-axis, and the curve is the estimated density or probability distribution of ratings for the population (Study 1).

roughly unimodal distributions, 16 factors have roughly bimodal distributions, and the remaining 26 factors have multimodal distributions.

Table 1 provides five factors with the highest mean importance ratings and five factors with the lowest mean importance ratings. The highest rated factors detailed the adversary capabilities and the complexity of the organization's network defense. For example, the factor with the highest mean importance rating was the adversary's knowledge about the organization's deployed network and security technologies (Factor 18, rank = 1). Other highly-rated factors include the skill of the adversary (Factor 31, rank = 3), how desirable the information on the network is to the adversary (Factor 63, rank = 6), whether the adversary has access to information needed to stage an attack (Factor 28, rank = 11), and whether the attack is persistent or casual (Factor 2, rank = 23).

The standard deviations (*SDs*) of the importance ratings (also shown in Additional file 1: Table SA-2) were computed to assess agreement across participants. Table 2 shows the five factors with the least inter-subject agreement (highest *SDs*) and the five with the most inter-subject agreement (lowest *SDs*). By comparing Tables 1 and 2, we note that three of the five factors with the most inter-subject agreement (Factors 18, 45, and 51) were also

deemed to be among the most important factors. We assessed whether a relationship existed between the level of importance of each factor (mean importance rating) and the agreement (*SDs*) and no linear relationship was found.

To determine whether dimensions emerged from our data, we used an affinity diagramming method to hierarchically classify the factors generated by the focus group. Three broad categories or dimensions emerged and were named by the research staff after reviewing each the underlying factors of each dimension (see Figure 2): (1) organization hosting the network, (2) threat/adversary, and (3) contractors (prime contractor, sub-contractors). Specific factors mapped to these dimensions were identified in Additional file 1: Table SA-1. An exploratory analysis revealed that of the ten highest-ranked factors, only one was associated with contractors (Factor 1), four were related to the adversary/threat (Factors 7, 18, 31, and 63), and five were associated with the organization (three of these five organizational factors are related to the network environment—Factors 23, 51, and 66). Also, of the ten factors with the lowest rankings, none were associated with the adversary/threat; five were associated with contractors and five with the organization (the low-ranking organizational factors are related to programmatic, policy, and workforce factors—none are associated with network

Table 1 The five least important and five most important factors rated across participants (Study 1, n = 38)

	Factor #	Mean	SD	Factor description
Least Important	30	38.8	29.5	The perceived organizational allegiance (purchases predominantly domestic brands of hardware/software versus purchases foreign brands)
	39	39.6	32.2	Different methods of paying the contractor (e.g., fixed price versus cost plus) to your perception of risk? Fixed price: Payment is a flat fee that must meet pre-determined list of requirements. Cost plus: Payment is not flat fee, but it scales over time to cover unforeseen costs of meeting predetermined requirements.
	49	40.6	30.5	The presence or absence of an organization's fear-driven responsiveness to threat
	44	41.8	30.5	The open- or closed-source protection technology used by your organization
	25	42.0	30.9	The recertification cycle (e.g., short versus long) as a constraint effecting the ability to secure the organization's network before an attack
Most Important	66	79.9	21.4	The complexity of the organization's systems and/or networks that makes it easy or difficult to secure
	45	80.5	13.7	The organization's response to threats (proactively planned for an attack versus reactively responded to an attack)
	31	80.8	23.3	The level of skill the adversary has (e.g., professional or amateur)
	51	81.1	14.3	The maturity of the organization's system capabilities for network defense
	18	83.5	17.4	The adversary's knowledge (e.g., high versus low knowledge) about the organization's deployed network and security technology

environment). Thus, factors associated with the adversary/threat and those associated with the organization's network environment appeared to be ranked high in importance; factors associated with contractors tend to be ranked lower in importance, as do other general organizational factors unrelated to the network environment. This is shown in Figure 3, which was generated to assess the relationship between dimensions and risk judgments. The bar chart in Figure 3 displays the percentages of factors in each of the three dimensions that were rated as high (top 1/3), medium (middle 1/3) and low (bottom 1/3) importance. The organization dimension was populated by the highest number of factors compared to the other two dimensions. The matrix in Figure 3 breaks down counts by dimension and level of importance. The highest rated factors (14) and most of the lowest rated factors (13) involved the organization. To assess whether there was a significant association between factor dimension and level of importance, a chi square test of association was conducted and found to be non-significant ($\chi^2(4) = 8.99, p = 0.06$).

Participants were asked whether any important factors needed to be added to our list and these were suggested:

- Does the organization support "doing the right thing" when the situation warrants?
- Morale of the IT, security, and general staff?

Table 2 Factors with the five highest and five lowest standard deviations of importance ratings (Study 1, n = 38)

	Factor #	SD	Mean	Factor
High SDs (Low Agreement)	8	34.0	48.3	Whether the facility uses SCADA systems
	5	32.4	53.3	Whether the network is for the military, government, or civilian sector
	39	32.2	39.6	The different methods of paying the contractor (e.g., fixed price versus cost plus) to your perception of risk?
	21	31.6	59.6	The information types that make up the network contents of your organization
	34	31.5	45.5	The ease (e.g., low versus high ease) of finding U.S.-born personnel instead of foreign-national personnel to fill network security positions within the organization
Low SDs (High Agreement)	45	13.7	80.5	The organization's response to threats (proactively planning for an attack versus reactively responding to an attack)
	51	14.3	81.1	The maturity of system capabilities for network defense
	18	17.4	83.5	The adversary's (level of) knowledge (e.g., high versus low) about the organization's deployed network and security technology
	11	19.3	78.8	Whether the organization has a disaster recovery plan
	12	19.3	70.7	The past performance of the organization's hired contractor

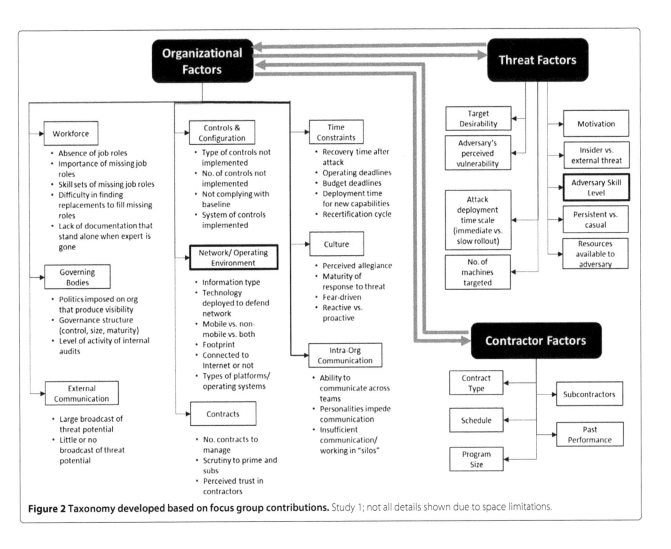

Figure 2 Taxonomy developed based on focus group contributions. Study 1; not all details shown due to space limitations.

- Access to historical intrusion/failure data
- Commitment to IT hygiene
- The presence or absence of a solid knowledge management system.

Discussion

A focus group of network security professionals generated a comprehensive list of factors considered relevant to network risk perception. Our survey results indicated that factors relating to the adversary or to the complexity of the organization's network defense were considered most important. We assessed whether a relationship existed between the level of importance (importance ratings) and the level of agreement SDs) amongst our sample participants. While a statistically significant linear relationship between SDs and mean ratings of all factors did not exist, the five most agreed-upon factors (lowest SDs) were also judged as relatively more important [mean ratings between 70.7 and 80.5]. Three emergent dimensions of factors were found (organization, adversary and contractors) in the absence of context.

The importance of each of our 69 factors was assessed but we could not ascertain whether each factor was safe or risky or whether context changes the emergent dimensions of factors. This became the impetus for the second study.

Study 2: context and network risk perception
Study purpose and research overview
We used a subset of factors from our original list of 69 factors and analyzed the degree of riskiness or safeness of each. Given the lack of contextual information related to each factor in Study 1, our subset of factors was analyzed using a vignette-based factor scenario method to provide context.

Method
Participants
The target population comprised network professionals versed in the practices of cybersecurity. As shown in Table 3, the 105 participants who completed the survey represented a variety of software engineering, IT

168

Information Security Management

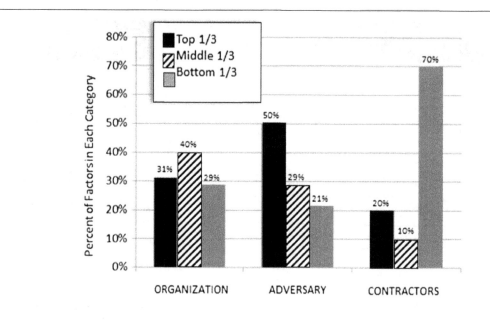

| | Factor Dimension | | | |
	ORGANIZATION	ADVERSARY	CONTRACTORS	Total
No. Ranked in Top 1/3	14 (31%)	7 (50%)	2 (20%)	23
No. Ranked in Middle 1/3	18 (40%)	4 (29%)	1 (10%)	23
No. Ranked in Bottom 1/3	13 (29%)	3 (21%)	7 (70%)	23
Total:	45	14	10	69

Figure 3 **Relationship between factor dimensions and importance ratings.** Percentages of factors in three factor dimensions that ranked in the top, middle, and bottom third in overall importance (Study 1).

management, and information security occupations. The overall mean number of years spent in the computer science professions was 9.6 (SD = 7.6) with a range between 1 and 36 years. We did require participants to report additional demographic information on the Department of Homeland Security (DHS) critical infrastructure sectors supported. The top five DHS sectors participants self-reported to support were Information technology (62), Academia (21), Communications (18), Banking & Finance (17), and Public health (11). Five supported the military, 15 supported the government and 11 were contractors.

Materials and procedures
Three vignettes were generated to represent different network contexts: Vignette 1 described a hospital network, Vignette 2 described a military network, and Vignette 3 described a software development firm network. The context of each vignette differed on attributes like the

history of the network and adversarial activity, how the network is manned, the type of information stored on that network and how the network is controlled and configured. Immediately after the participant read the vignette, he/she rated the overall network risk level using a slider (0 = low risk and 100 = high risk) and then offered a ranking (low, medium, or high network risk) according to the NIST SP800-30 guidance [3]. Then, ratings on individual factors were solicited. Originally, we designed the vignettes to depict factors using a few descriptive sentences to depict each factor, but in our survey beta testing, respondents believed that the factors were not the ones we originally intended. Instead, participants believed the main idea of each descriptive sentence was a single factor. Therefore, we obtained ratings for each sentence's main idea using a bipolar response scale between 0 = extremely safe and 100 = extremely risky. A rating of 50 was labeled neither safe nor risky.

Table 3 Frequencies of categories of self-reported job titles (Study 2, n=105)

Job category	Definition	Examples	Number of participants
Analyst	Analyst is a programmer, developer, implementer or other person who provides solutions to customer problems.	Applications security analyst, IT specialist, network systems specialist	34
Architect	Architect is a designer who develops system specifications and balances system-wide tradeoffs.	Network security architect, network architect	7
Engineer	Engineer is a senior developer with some design expertise.	Network engineer, information security engineer,	30
Manager	Manager is responsible for allocating resources to projects and meeting schedules.	Program manager, risk manager, sr. IT manager	12
Director	Director oversees a department or company.	Directory of engineering, director of research, director of IT, CSO	11
Other	"Other" includes students and non-IT-related positions.	Student, recreation assistant	11

SurveyGizmo™ hosted the online survey, which was divided into three sections: informed consent, vignette scenarios, and demographics (job title, the DHS critical infrastructure sectors supported, whether the person was working for the government, military, academia or in training). Informed consent was obtained in accordance with ethics guidelines for research with human subjects (Institutional Review Board approval HS12-571). After providing informed consent, each participant was randomly assigned to one of three vignettes using the survey randomizing tool. Each participant reviewed only one vignette. After reviewing a vignette and providing ratings, participants answered a set of un-randomized demographic questions and were awarded a $20 compensatory Amazon gift card.

Results
Exploratory data analysis of overall risk ratings and rankings
Figure 4 summarizes the vignette risk ratings and risk rankings. In the boxplot on the left, the x-axis represents the vignette number (1 = hospital network, 2 = military and 3 = software development firm) and the y-axis represents the risk ratings. The stacked bar chart on the right shows, for each of the vignettes on the x-axis, the frequency of participants that ranked the risk as either low, medium or high. As shown in the boxplot on the left, Vignette 2 had the highest mean risk rating denoted by the horizontal bar in the middle of the box; but the mean ratings were not significantly different. Though participants believed Vignettes 1 and 3 were relatively less risky, the stacked bar chart on the right of Figure 4 indicates

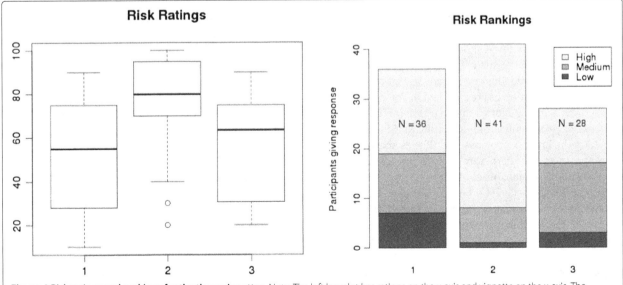

Figure 4 Risk ratings and rankings for the three vignettes. Note: The left boxplot has ratings on the y-axis and vignette on the x-axis. The stacked bar chart displays counts on the y-axis and vignette on the x-axis. The number of participants who read each vignette varied, as indicated by the labels on the bars (Study 2, n = 105).

that participants did not rank any of the vignettes as predominantly low-risk.

Factor grouping by risk impact

One of the goals of Study 2 was to determine which factors, described by certain contextual features, were perceived as risky or safe. We used Bonferroni corrected t-tests to identify factors affecting on risky/safe ratings (i.e., tests conducted against the null hypothesis that population risky/safe means were 50). Those factors with a corrected p-value above 0.05 were removed from further consideration. We then divided the remaining factors (those with mean ratings significantly different from 50) into four groups based on their median scores: VERY SAFE (median rating below 30) includes factors such as Machines are not connected to both the private network and the internet; SOMEWHAT SAFE (median rating between 30 and 45) includes factors such as The IT staff are fully trained; SOMEWHAT RISKY (median rating between 55 and 72) includes factors such as All patient records are digitized; and VERY RISKY (median rating above 72) includes factors such as Hackers in the past few weeks have been attacking various medical centers nationwide. The factors with the median ratings between 46 and 54 were not included in Table 4 because they were not significantly different from 50. Table 4 lists the factors in each of these groups, along with their median and mean risk scores, SDs, and vignettes to which they belong.

Table 5 displays the most agreed upon factors (lowest SDs) with respect to the risky/safe ratings and the least agreed upon (highest SDs). The values of SDs for these 85 factors, across all three dimensions, ranged from 10.2 to 24.4 (median = 18.05). To assess whether a relationship existed between the number of high vs. low standard deviations and the risky/safe ratings for those factors, we compared the risk levels assigned to factors that exhibited SDs below the median (high agreement among respondents) with those that exhibited SDs above the median (low agreement across respondents). For risk levels, we used the same categories shown above for Table 4: Safe (Rating < 45), Neutral (45 < Rating < 55), Risky (55 < Rating). Table 6 provides the 2 × 3 matrix of high/low agreement by safe/neutral/risky importance ratings. The resultant significant chi-square test of association ($\chi^2(2) = 7.06$, $p = 0.029$, $n = 85$) indicated that our study participants agreed more about factors that were judged as riskier, compared to those that relate to lower network risk.

Factor groupings based on correlation

One way to summarize the ratings data for each single vignette is to group the ratings into clusters of factors that vary together across participants. Then,

determine whether an underlying conceptual or semantic commonality exists amongst a group of factors that cluster; likened to a principal components analysis used with larger sample sizes. If commonalities exist, they may provide clues about 'agreed upon' underlying parameters or dimensions related to network risk judgments.

For each vignette independently, we computed the correlation matrix between all the factors (all pair-wise correlations). We used [1 − correlation] as a distance measure and performed hierarchical clustering with the Ward agglomeration method to divide the factors into groups that might be interpreted as dimensions of the perceived risk construct. We chose the number of clusters, k, for each scenario based on examining several heuristics. Other choices of k could be equally valid.

The resultant correlation matrices revealed clusters of factors for Vignettes 1 and 2 with relatively strong correlations within the group and low correlations between factors in different groups. Because no such relationships were observed in Vignette 3, it was not included in further analyses. While the groupings reflect statistical structure in the data, that structure does not always correspond to a semantic representation of single dimensions. When the majority of the constituent factors in a group shared a common semantic interpretation, we adopted this semantic interpretation as a label for a network risk construct dimension. Four labeled dimensions across the two vignettes emerged:

(a) *Information* factors related to the information stored on the network and the consequences of the information being compromised — inferred from Vignette 1 (hospital network)

(b) *Infrastructure* factors related to the infrastructure of the network and the compliance of the network with established protocols.)—inferred from Vignette 1 (hospital network)

(c) *Personnel Skill* factors related to the skill and training of network personnel — inferred from Vignette 2 (military network)

(d) *Adversary Skill* factors related to the skill, resources, and motivation of the adversary — inferred from Vignette 2 (military network).

Table 7 lists the factors (with associated mean risk ratings and SDs) in each of these emergent dimensions. Also shown in Table 7 (last column) is the risky/safe grouping (VS = Very Safe, SS = Somewhat Safe, SR = Somewhat Risky, and VR = Very Risky) to which the factor belongs (if any). We note that of the four dimensions of the perceived risk construct, the adversary skill dimension contains the highest percentage of risky (SR or VR)

Table 4 Factors organized by risky/safe ratings (Study 2)

Vignette	Median risk	Mean risk	SD	Factor
				Very safe (Median risk rating <30)
1	26.0	30.0	15.2	The hospital recently installed additional emergency electrical generators.
1	28.5	31.9	18.4	A disaster recovery plan has been implemented.
1	24.5	24.2	18.5	Machines are not connected to both the private network and the internet.
1	29.0	32.1	19.0	Results of the audit meet or exceed best practices for network configuration and maintenance.
1	25.0	32.8	20.8	The recovery effort from a natural disaster is expected to be rapid.
2	25.0	26.0	20.8	The network is a self-contained, segregated, and air-gapped network.
2	30.0	34.6	20.9	The IT staff man the network 24/7.
3	25.0	27.1	13.4	The networks are fully manned with very little employee turnover.
3	30.0	30.7	17.7	IT staff is highly trained in their area of expertise via outside training firms and local universities.
3	24.0	24.7	18.0	The chief strategy officer (CSO) has put in place a dedicated controls management team whose job is to make sure that the security controls implemented are the most effective ones possible whether or not they are required for compliance.
3	29.5	29.0	19.8	The CSO is passionate about security.
				Somewhat safe (Median risk rating between 30 and 45)
1	32.0	30.7	16.6	The personnel manning facilities are competent.
1	33.5	31.1	17.1	The IT department is adequately staffed.
1	42.0	36.5	18.0	IT had a yearly audit due to HIPAA requirements.
1	34.5	35.8	19.4	All digitized records are stored and processed on a private network.
2	35.0	36.7	15.9	An audit was recently passed.
2	35.0	35.1	18.4	The network is in full compliance with the DoD.
2	34.0	36.4	20.4	The IT staff are fully trained.
3	35.5	33.9	17.5	85% of these employees have been employees of the company for 15 years or more.
				Somewhat risky (Median risk rating between 55 and 72)
1	56.0	58.0	11.6	The recent legislation on the reformation of the national health care system
1	58.5	62.6	14.0	Various adversarial organizations have growing concerns over the lack of medical record privacy because of the legislation.
1	69.5	69.8	15.9	The type of data the hospital handles
1	65.5	64.6	16.2	All patient records are digitized.
1	70.0	66.8	16.6	End users have Windows machines.
1	65.0	68.2	17.3	It (the network) involves a large hospital.
1	59.5	63.1	17.4	The hacker's intent was to motivate another reformation of the national health care system.
2	70.0	68.5	20.2	The network is within a small geographical region near a war zone.
2	65.0	67.1	22.1	The network is heterogeneous with Windows, UNIX, and proprietary military operating systems.
3	68.5	66.5	10.2	The organization has 20 offices worldwide.
3	56.0	61.3	13.9	The software development firm has 13,000 employees.
3	70.0	71.5	14.1	Competition is fierce in the business intelligence domain.
3	60.0	63.8	14.2	Offices are located in North America, South America, Asia, Europe, and Australia.
3	72.0	73.8	14.9	It took a couple of years to recover from these two incidents.
3	70.0	74.2	17.8	Clients are from the government military and commercial sectors of 135 countries.
3	71.0	69.9	18.9	The intranet hosts a database of technical reports, proprietary design information, social collaboration tools, email servers, etc.

Table 4 Factors organized by risky/safe ratings (Study 2) *(Continued)*

				Very risky (Median risk rating >72)
1	76.0	74.9	18.1	A prolonged outage of digital recordkeeping could cause significant damage to the hospital's ability to serve its patients.
1	82.5	78.6	18.5	Release of patient care information puts the hospital in legal liability.
1	75.0	72.9	18.8	Hackers in the past few weeks have been attacking various medical centers nationwide.
1	74.5	73.2	19.1	These attacks in the past few weeks have leaked private patient care information on the internet.
1	75.0	74.4	20.0	These adversarial organizations are persistent and academically capable of executing an attack.
1	77.5	75.9	22.5	Release of patient care information damages the hospital's reputation.
1	75.0	70.6	24.0	Release of patient care information violates HIPAA regulations.
2	95.0	92.6	10.2	The primary adversary has excellent offensive cyber skills equal to or better than 90 existing nation states.
2	90.0	87.5	12.1	The primary adversary is well funded.
2	100.0	92.2	12.1	Malicious activity has been noted on the network in the past six months since wartime operations intensified in this region.
2	95.0	88.8	13.9	The adversary was likely trained by the U.S. government in the past two years.
2	95.0	87.7	14.8	The adversary is highly motivated.
2	90.0	86.2	14.9	The adversary is deeply interested in U.S. troop positioning.
2	80.0	78.8	16.4	The network has Windows systems.
2	85.0	83.1	16.9	The primary adversary is a nation state.
2	90.0	84.3	17.1	The network stores highly sensitive data related to enemy versus U.S. troop positioning and high-value target location information.
2	80.0	77.0	17.3	This network stores and processes time-sensitive intelligence information.
2	87.0	80.4	18.8	The information stored and processed on this network includes Top Secret SEI 5 Eyes NOFORN information.
2	77.0	69.9	24.1	This involves a classified military network.
3	77.5	82.5	12.6	Competitors have sophisticated well-funded espionage teams to steal competitive information.
3	75.0	77.9	14.8	Almost all employee machines have access to both the internet and intranet.

factors (90%), while the infrastructure dimension contains the highest percentage of safe (VS or SS) factors (60%).

Conclusion

As in Study 1, there tended to be higher agreement on the most risky factors. For example, of the 13 factors with the most agreement in ratings (lowest *SDs*), nine were judged as risky while two were rated neutral and one was rated safe. On the other hand, for the 16 least agreed upon factors (high *SDs*), no discernable differences were observed in risky/safe ratings. Moreover, factors that were associated with the adversary/threat tended to be rated as more risky in general. Of the 13 factors with the most agreement in ratings (lowest *SDs*), six involved descriptions of the adversary (five were rated as very risky and one was rated as somewhat risky). Factors relating to the organization's network infrastructure tended to be associated with lower risk as well. The semantic groupings, or dimensions, derived from inter-factor correlations have similar trending as discussed in the preceding paragraph. Of the

four emergent network risk dimensions (i.e., information, infrastructure, personnel skill and adversary skill), the highest proportion of the most risky factors comprised the adversary skill dimension (90%) while the highest proportion of the most safe factors comprise the infrastructure dimension (60%). Somewhat safe factors often comprise the personnel skill and infrastructure dimensions and somewhat risky factors span all four dimensions.

Overall discussion

Study 1 initially used a focus group method to produce a list of possible factors believed to influence network risk judgments and then used an online survey method to investigate the importance of these factors with a broader sample of network professionals. Study 1 did not ask participants how risky each factor was, just the level of importance. Study 2 extended the Study 1 findings by asking network professionals to review one of three vignettes and judge how risky or safe each factor was in the vignette. We understood that network risk judgments are difficult to

Table 5 Lowest 15 and highest 15 standard deviations of factor importance ratings (Study 2)

SD	Vignette	Median risk	Mean risk	Factor
				Low SDs (High Agreement)
10.2	2	95.0	92.6	The primary adversary has excellent offensive cyber skills equal to or better than 90 existing nation states.
10.2	3	68.5	66.5	The organization has 20 offices worldwide.
10.3	1	50.0	50.7	These adversarial organizations are not financially well funded.
10.9	1	50.0	45.2	Database is Linux based for large-scale processing and storage.
11.6	1	56.0	58.0	The recent legislation on the reformation of the national health care system.
12.1	2	90.0	87.5	The primary adversary is well funded.
12.1	2	100.0	92.2	Malicious activity has been noted on the network in the past six months since wartime operations intensified in this region.
12.6	3	77.5	82.5	Competitors have sophisticated well-funded espionage teams to steal competitive information.
13.4	3	25.0	27.1	The networks are fully manned with very little employee turnover.
13.9	2	95.0	88.8	The adversary was likely trained by the U.S. government in the past two years.
13.9	3	56.0	61.3	The software development firm has 13,000 employees.
14.0	1	58.5	62.6	Various adversarial organizations have growing concerns over the lack of medical record privacy because of the legislation.
14.1	3	70.0	71.5	Competition is fierce in the business intelligence domain.
14.2	3	60.0	63.8	The offices are located in North America, South America, Asia, Europe, and Australia.
14.4	1	50.0	48.2	Neither department has reported adversarial activity in the past that demonstrate a knowledge of the IT infrastructure.
				High SDs (Low Agreement)
20.9	2	30.0	34.6	The IT staff man the network 24/7.
20.9	3	36.5	38.1	These employees are divided into small, highly specialized teams working on one aspect of the network e.g., LDAP server teams, router teams.
21.4	1	50.0	45.4	Records are transferred from one hospital to another manually.
21.4	2	58.0	59.6	The network has various UNIX systems.
21.9	3	50.0	50.6	No targeted attacks in the past few years. Only non-targeted email scams
22.0	1	45.0	40.3	Recordkeeping could convert back to paper.
22.1	2	65.0	67.1	The network is heterogeneous with Windows, UNIX, and proprietary military operating systems.
22.3	2	42.0	41.6	Full recovery is expected to occur quickly.
22.5	1	77.5	75.9	Release of patient care information damages the hospital's reputation.
22.7	3	43.0	45.2	The company uses proprietary languages and tools that are very difficult to exploit.
22.9	2	47.0	48.1	The IT staff are supported by various stable vendor contractors.
24.0	1	75.0	70.6	Release of patient care information violates HIPAA regulations.
24.1	2	77.0	69.9	This involves a classified military network.
24.2	1	66.0	64.9	The back-end servers are unique and housed in a single data center on the hospital premises.
24.4	2	35.0	41.9	The systems running on the network use proprietary military operating systems.

make without contextual information so Study 2 provided contextual information that Study 1 lacked.

Study 2 was designed to help refine our understanding of the factors that were identified as important in Study 1. For example, factors relating to the adversary (knowledge/skill/capabilities) were considered highly important in Study1 and were also associated with higher levels of

network risk. Many of these factors detailing the adversary formed the adversary/threat dimension in Study 2. Also, in Study 1, factors detailing the organization were found to have different levels of importance. Study 2 helped us refine our understanding of the organizational factors that were and were not important. Specifically, factors relating to the organization's network infrastructure and

Table 6 Relationship between perceived risk level and agreement (Study 2)

	Safe	Neutral	Risky	*Totals*
Low Agreement (High SD)	17	10	14	41
High Agreement (Low SD)	9	6	26	41
Totals	26	16	40	82

its ability to defend against attacks were relatively more important than others in Study 1 and were associated with lower levels of network risk in Study 2. Both studies had two dimensions in common; threat/adversary and the organization. The two dimensions discovered in Study 2, information and personnel skill, were related to the subset of Study 1 organizational factors that seemed to have high variability in importance ratings. Hence, whether or not context was present, our sample of network professionals believed that dimensions of network risk should include both organizational network infrastructure (the preparedness for attack) and the threat/adversary (the attack). This provides some clues about the dimensions of network risk definitions that network professionals, rather than risk metric designers, endorse.

The finding that network risk judgments are strongly influenced by information about the adversary/threat is important because network certification generally neglects threat/adversary factors. For example, the NIST CVSS v2.10 metric focuses mainly on other factors associated with information, infrastructure, and personnel skill. One reason why the threat/adversary factors were both very important and risky to our study participants is that the existence of unknown, dangerous entities (i.e., the adversary) which cannot be easily perceived and controlled is anxiety provoking. While the factors we provided about the adversary were of known qualities (e.g., the adversary has excellent cyber offense skills, the adversary is highly motivated), the adversary still poses an uncomfortable uncertainty in network defense because one cannot predict when an attack will occur (and by whom), how the attack will be executed, and what the adversary wants. Prior research has indicated that people are generally uncomfortable with uncertainty and typically avoid it [25,26], and when uncertainty cannot be avoided, a fear response is invoked [27]. When fear increases, perceptions of risk also increase [28-30].

Implications
The importance of our results is that we used research methods from the social sciences to devise a list of factors that impact network risk judgments from network professionals. This information is important for risk metric designers who require metric users to subjectively interpret various factors as part of the metric output. Given little information is published on how certain factors were chosen for these network risk metrics, it is possible that

these factors were chosen according to the opinions of the risk metric designer rather than the opinions of network professionals. Factors that our sample agrees are more important to risk judgments may not be the factors the metric designer includes; which we detail in the subsequent paragraph. We make the argument herein that network risk is difficult for one person to accurately judge given the technical knowledge diversity required. Therefore, consensus on factors important to risk judgments from a sample of network professionals may inform risk metric designers. In addition, future research on network risk perception and judgment can build upon our findings.

The factors our sample agreed were risky and important to network risk judgments were not necessarily factors included in computed risk models like the NIST CVSS V2.10. For example, the CVSS V2.10 includes factors describing organizational and network readiness rather than the adversarial capabilities. While it could be argued that the NIST CVSS V2.10 metric assess vulnerabilities, the metric is being used for security risk management (http://www.first.org/cvss/cvss-guide). Our research identified drivers for high network risk levels that are missing or not well articulated in this NIST metric: From Study 1, "the adversary's knowledge about the organization's deployed network and security technology" and "the adversary's level of skill (professional vs. amateur)". The importance of these missing factors was confirmed in Study 2 when participants rated the adversary's skill and training as factors that greatly increase network risk levels. Other missing factors that we identified as contributing to risk perception were perceived adversarial motivation, success rate of the adversary exploitation in recent history, and the importance of the targeted data to be exploited. Factors that reliably increase or decrease perceived risk are likely to be important for an accurate computed risk model.

Limitations and future directions
A few limitations are worth mentioning that may have impacted our results. First, the target population in these two studies was difficult to persuade to participate in our studies. Network professionals familiar with adversarial techniques used to penetrate a network, may mistake the emailed survey links for a phishing campaign. Therefore, sampling was challenging, which was reflected in our low sample sizes and consequently, we were limited

Table 7 Emergent network risk dimensions and associated factors (Study 2)

Factor	Mean risk	SD	Risk group
INFORMATION DIMENSION: Features related to the information stored on the network, the adversaries who want that information, and the consequences of the information being compromised. [Vignette #1: Hospital network]			
Recordkeeping could convert back to paper.	40.6	21.8	
Hospital is in a metropolitan area.	56.6	16.1	
Various adversarial organizations have growing concerns over the lack of medical record privacy because of the legislation.	63.1	14.3	
The hacker's intent was to motivate another reformation of the national health care system.	63.1	18.0	SR
All patient records are digitized.	65.0	16.0	SR
It (the network) involves a large hospital.	68.4	17.4	SR
The type of data the hospital handles	68.9	5.9	SR
Release of patient care information violates HIPAA regulations.	71.9	24.1	VR
Hackers in the past few weeks have been attacking various medical centers nationwide.	72.4	9.3	VR
These attacks in the past few weeks have leaked private patient care information on the internet.	74.0	19.2	VR
These adversarial organizations are persistent and academically capable of executing an attack.	74.3	20.6	VR
A prolonged outage of digital recordkeeping could cause significant damage to the hospital's ability to serve its patients.	75.2	18.0	VR
Release of patient care information damages hospital's reputation.	76.2	22.6	
Release of patient care information puts the hospital in legal liability.	79.9	18.0	VR
INFRASTRUCTURE DIMENSION: Features related to the infrastructure of the network and the compliance of the network with established protocols. [Vignette #1: Hospital network]			
Machines are not connected to both the private network and the internet.	24.0	18.5	VS
The hospital recently installed additional emergency electrical generators.	29.6	15.6	VS
The personnel manning facilities are competent.	30.9	17.1	SS
The IT department is adequately staffed.	31.7	17.2	SS
A disaster recovery plan has been implemented.	32.0	18.8	VS
Results of the audit meet or exceed best practices for network configuration and maintenance.	32.0	19.6	VS
The recovery effort from a natural disaster is expected to be rapid.	32.3	21.2	VS
All digitized records are stored and processed on a private network.	36.0	19.9	SS
IT had a yearly audit due to HIPAA requirements.	36.6	18.5	SS
Database is Linux based for large-scale processing and storage.	44.8	11.1	
Records are transferred from one hospital to another manually.	45.3	20.6	
These adversarial organizations are not financially well funded.	50.6	10.2	
The recent legislation on the reformation of the national health care system	58.2	11.9	
Network is connected to programmable logic controllers (PLCs) for the medical equipment to receive test results and to manage and operate the machines. A PLC is a digital computer used for automating electromechanical processes.	59.7	17.4	
The back-end servers are unique and housed in a single data center on the hospital premises.	64.9	24.9	
PERSONNEL SKILL DIMENSION: Features related to the skill and training of network personnel. [Vignette #2: Military network]			
The network is a self-contained, segregated, and air-gapped network.	26.0	20.8	VS
The IT staff man the network 24/7.	34.6	20.9	VS
The network is in full compliance with the DoD.	35.1	18.4	SS
The IT staff are fully trained.	36.4	20.4	SS

Table 7 Emergent network risk dimensions and associated factors (Study 2) *(Continued)*

Factor	Mean risk	SD	Risk group
An audit was recently passed.	36.7	15.9	
The IT staff are well trained at various military schools.	39.2	19.3	
The military installation has a mature emergency operation plan (EOP) and continuity of operations plan (COOP) that comply with the Federal Emergency Management Agency (FEMA) recommendations.	41.0	19.3	
Full recovery is expected to occur quickly.	41.6	22.3	
The systems running on the network use proprietary military operating systems.	41.9	24.4	
The network is within a small geographical region near a war zone.	68.5	20.2	SR
ADVERSARY SKILL DIMENSION: Features related to the skill, resources, and motivation of the adversary. [Vignette #2: Military network]			
The network has various UNIX systems.	59.6	21.4	
The network is heterogeneous with Windows, UNIX, and proprietary military operating systems.	67.1	22.1	SR
The network has Windows systems.	78.8	16.4	VR
The primary adversary is a nation state.	83.1	16.9	VR
The adversary is deeply interested in U.S. troop positioning.	86.2	14.9	VR
The primary adversary is well funded.	87.5	12.1	VR
The adversary is highly motivated.	87.7	14.8	VR
The adversary was likely trained by the U.S. government in the past two years.	88.8	13.9	VR
Malicious activity has been noted on the network in the past six months since wartime operations intensified in this region.	92.2	12.1	VR
The primary adversary has excellent offensive cyber skills equal to or better than 90 existing nation states.	92.6	10.2	VR

in the types of statistical analyses we could conduct. For example, we wanted to relate the risky/safe ratings for each factor to the overall network risk rating of each vignette but the low sample sizes made that impossible. We also wished to assess group differences (military, private industry, government) but again, the sample sizes encumbered that effort. One way to reduce the time burden for study participation was to only require questions that were central to the study objective. Consequently, not all demographics questions were required in both studies, which resulted in low question response rates that could never characterize the sample.

Another limitation is that it is unclear whether our findings reflect the judgments of DAA and IA officers. The process of network certification described in our study may be of little relevance to the broader sample of individuals involved in network defense. The derived judgments and perceptions may not align with those of DAA and IA officers who conduct network certification in the public sector, especially military organizations (the relatively low representation of public sector respondents in Study 2 underscores this limitation). Similarly, construct dimensions derived in our data-driven approach may be a reflection of the views and experience of the participants in our study. While it was impractical for our studies to sample

exclusively from personnel responsible for configuring and certifying networks, future research should include validation studies to determine if our results are consistent with judgments obtained from individuals directly responsible for network certification.

In addition, future research should continue to flesh out which factors are significantly risky and safe in various network contexts and why. Our results were intended to serve as a foundation upon which future research and operations can be built. For example, network risk metrics in operations could improve the validity of network risk metrics by including some of our most agreed upon risky and safe factors. Researchers could investigate whether commonly agreed upon dimensions relate to factor perception and definitions of network risk.

Additional file

Additional file 1: Supplemental material for study 1.

Competing interests
The authors declare that they have no competing interests.

Authors' contributions
JC conceived, designed, and carried out the studies, oversaw analyses that were performed, and was the primary author of a technical report

documenting the studies. FG supported analyses that were performed, participated in interpreting results and implications of the work, and drafted the version of the manuscript for publication. BW conducted statistical analyses and helped to interpret results. All authors read and approved the final manuscript.

Acknowledgements
This material is based upon work funded and supported by the Department of Defense under Contract No. FA8721-05-C-0003 with Carnegie Mellon University for the operation of the Software Engineering Institute, a federally funded research and development center. References herein to any specific commercial product, process, or service by trade name, trade mark, manufacturer, or otherwise, does not necessarily constitute or imply its endorsement, recommendation, or favoring by Carnegie Mellon University or its Software Engineering Institute. No warranty. This Carnegie Mellon University and Software Engineering Institute material is furnished on an "AS-IS" basis. Carnegie Mellon University makes no warranties of any kind, either expressed or implied, as to any matter including, but not limited to, warranty of fitness for purpose or merchantability, exclusivity, or results obtained from use of the material. Carnegie Mellon University does not make any warranty of any kind with respect to freedom from patent, trademark, or copyright infringement. This material has been approved for public release and unlimited distribution. Carnegie Mellon® and CERT® are registered marks of Carnegie Mellon University. DM-0001925.

Author details
[1]Carnegie Mellon University Software Engineering Institute, CERT Division, 4500 Fifth Avenue, Pittsburgh, Pennsylvania 15213, USA. [2]PsyberAnalytix, 651 Big Sky Drive, Richland, Washington 99352, USA.

References
1. Joint Task Force Transformation Initiative, National Institute of Standards and Technology (NIST), *Security and Privacy Controls for Federal Information Systems and Organizations, NIST Special Publication 800-53, Revision 4*. (Washington, D.C., National Institute of Standards and Technology, 2013). http://nvlpubs.nist.gov/nistpubs/SpecialPublications/NIST.SP.800-53r4. pdf
2. Oxford English Dictionary (online). (Oxford/New York, Oxford University Press, 2014). risk, n. http://www.oed.com/view/Entry/166306?rskey= Z0aceK&result=1&isAdvanced=false (accessed November 17, 2014)
3. Joint Task Force Transformation Initiative, National Institute of Standards and Technology (NIST), *Guide for Conducting Risk Assessments (NIST Special Publication 800-30 Revision 1)*. (Washington, D.C., National Institute of Standards and Technology, 2012). http://csrc.nist.gov/publications/ nistpubs/800-30-rev1/sp800_30_r1.pdf
4. P Slovic, B Fischhoff, S Lichtenstein, in *Perilous progress: Managing the hazards of technology*, ed. by RW Kates, C Hohenemser, and JX Kasperson. *Characterizing perceived risk*. (Boulder: Westview, 1985), pp. 91–125
5. B Fischhoff, SR Watson, C Hope, Defining risk. Policy Sci. **17**, 123–139 (1984). doi:10.1007/BF00146924
6. B Fischhoff, in *Oxford Textbook of Public Health, Fifth Edition*. ed. by R Detels, R Beaglehole, MA Lansang, and M Gulliford. *Risk Perception and Communication*. (Oxford: Oxford University Press, Sage; 2009), pp. 940–952
7. EC Poulton, *Bias in Quantifying Judgments*. (East Sussex, UK: Laurence Erlbaum Associates, Ltd., 1989)
8. JW Creswell, *Mixed-method research: Introduction and application*. In C Ciznek (Ed.), *Handbook of educational policy*. (San Diego, CA: Academic Press, 1999), pp. 455–472
9. O Renn, Three decades of risk research: accomplishments and new challenges. J. Risk Res. **1**, 49–71 (1998). doi:10.1080/136698798377321
10. LJ Cronbach, PE Meehl, Construct validity in psychological tests. Psychol. Bull. **52**(4), 281–302 (1955)
11. T Aven, *Foundations of Risk Analysis: A Knowledge and Decision-Oriented Perspective*. (West Sussex, UK: John Wiley & Sons Ltd, 2003). ISBN 0-471-49548-4
12. LG Epstein, A definition of uncertainty aversion. Rev. Econ. Stud. **66**(3), 579–608 (1999)
13. WW Lowrance, *Of Acceptable Risk: Science and the Determination of Safety*. (Los Altos, CA: William Kaufmann, 1976)
14. A Pollatsek, A Tversky, A theory of risk. J. Math. Psychol. **7**(3), 540–553 (1970)
15. RA Bauer, *Consumer Behavior as Risk Taking*. In RE Karp (Ed.), *Issues in Marketing*. (New York: MSS Information Corporation, 1999), pp. 389–398. ISBN 0-8422-5165-0
16. AH Crespo, IR del Bosque, MMG de los Salmones Sanchez, The influence of perceived risk on internet shopping behavior: A multidimensional perspective. J. Risk Res. **12**(2), 259–277 (2009). doi:10.1080/13669870802497744
17. GR Dowling, Perceived risk: the concept and its measurement. Psychol. Mark. **3**(3), 193–210 (1986). doi:10.1002/mar.4220030307
18. HG Gemünden, Perceived risk and information search: a systematic meta-analysis of the empirical evidence. Int. J. Res. Market. **2**(2), 79–100 (1985)
19. YY Haimes, On the complex definition of risk: a systems-based approach. Risk Anal. **29**(12), 1647–1654 (2009). doi:10.1111/j.1539-6924.2009.01310.x
20. CA Ingene, MA Hughes, *Risk management by consumers*. In EC Hirschman (Ed.), *Research in Consumer Behavior, Vol. 1*. (Greenwich, CT: Emerald Group Publishing Limited, 1985), pp. 103–158
21. I Ross, Perceived risk and consumer behavior: a critical review. Adv. Consum. Res. **2**(1), 1–19 (1975)
22. P Biernacki, D Waldorf, Snowball sampling: problems and techniques of chain referral sampling. Sociol. Methods Res. **10**(2), 141–163 (1981). doi:10.1177/004912418101000205
23. DE Hartley, *Job Analysis at the Speed of Reality*. (Amherst, MA: Human Resource Development Press Inc., 1999)
24. H Beyer, K Holtzblatt, *Contextual design: defining customer-centered systems*. (Oxford, UK: Elsevier;1998)
25. G Hofstede, *Culture's Consequences: International Differences in Work-Related Values*, (Beverly Hills, CA: SAGE Publications, 1980)
26. PW Dorfman, JP Howell, in *Advances in International Comparative Management*. ed. by EG McGoun. *Dimensions of National Culture and Effective Leadership Patterns: Hofstede Revisited*. vol. 3 (Greenwich, CT: JAI Press, 1988), pp. 127–150
27. G Hofstede, *Culture's Consequences: Comparing Values, Behaviors, Institutions, and Organizations Across Nations, 2nd Edition*. (Thousand Oaks, CA: SAGE Publications, 2001)
28. B Fischhoff, et al., How safe is safe enough? a psychometric study of attitudes towards technological risks and benefits. Policy Sci. **9**, 127–152 (1978)
29. JS Lerner, RM Gonzalez, DA Small, B Fischhoff, Effects of fear and anger on perceived risks of terrorism a national field experiment. Psychol. Sci. **14**(2), 144–150 (2003)
30. P Slovic, E Peters, Risk perception and affect. Current directions in psychological science. **15**(6), 322–325 (2006)

Acoustic environment identification using unsupervised learning

Hafiz Malik[1]* and Hasan Mahmood[2]

Abstract

Acoustic environment leaves its characteristic signature in the audio recording captured in it. The acoustic environment signature can be modeled using acoustic reverberations and background noise. Acoustic reverberation depends on the geometry and composition of the recording location. The proposed scheme uses similarity in the estimated acoustic signature for acoustic environment identification (AEI). We describe a parametric model to realize acoustic reverberation, and a statistical framework based on maximum likelihood estimation is used to estimate the model parameters. The density-based clustering is used for automatic AEI using estimated acoustic parameters. Performance of the proposed framework is evaluated for two data sets consisting of hand-clapping and speech recordings made in a diverse set of acoustic environments using three microphones. Impact of the microphone type variation, frequency, and clustering accuracy and efficiency on the performance of the proposed method is investigated. Performance of the proposed method is also compared with the existing state-of-the-art (SoA) for AEI.

Introduction

In this digital age, technologies allow digital media to be produced, altered, manipulated, and shared in ways that were beyond the imagination a few years ago. This fact poses serious challenges to forensic science. Today, whether it be a viral video of *"pop corn with cell phone"* posted on youtube [1] or a set of *Iranian missile test images* release to international news media [2], we can no longer take the authenticity of media objects for granted. Digital technologies are the major contributing factor behind this *paradigm shift*. As digital technologies continue to evolve it will become increasingly important for the science of digital forensics to keep pace.

The past few years have witnessed significant advances in image forensics [3], on the other hand, techniques for digital audio forensics are relatively less developed. An overview of the existing audio forensics methods can be found in [4] and references. Existing audio forensics methods based on signal characteristics can be broadly divided into the following categories:

1. The electrical network frequency (ENF) based framework that verifies integrity by comparing the extracted ENF with the reference ENF datebase [5-8]. These methods are effective against *cut-and-paste* (CAP) attacks, but complex electro-physical requirements of ENF-based approaches [5] make them ineffective for recordings made using battery-powered devices.

2. Statistical pattern recognition based techniques [9-17] have been proposed for recording location and device identification. However, these methods are limited by their low accuracy and inability to uniquely map an audio recording to the source.

3. Model driven approaches [18-24] have been proposed to address limitations of statistical learning based methods. These methods use mathematical models to realize artifacts due to acoustic reverberations [18-22] and distortions due to microphone nonlinearities [23]. Performance of model driven approaches depends on accuracy of the assumed model and reliability of the model parameter estimation method used.

4. Time-domain analysis based methods [25-29] have also been proposed to determine authenticity of digital audio recordings by capturing traces of lossy compression using encoder frame offsets in time domain [25-27] or detecting traces of *"butt-splicing"* in the digital recording using higher-order time-differences and correlation analysis [28].

*Correspondence: hafiz@umich.edu
[1] Electrical and Computer Engineering Department, University of Michigan - Dearborn, Dearborn, MI 48128, USA
Full list of author information is available at the end of the article

5. Spectral analysis based techniques [24,30] have been proposed for good quality audio recordings. H. Farid in [24] modeled the splicing process as a nonlinear operation and used bispectral analysis framework to capture traces of audio splicing. Similarly, C. Grigoras [30] proposed audio forensics framework based on statistical analysis such as long-term average spectrum histogram (LTASH) to detect traces of audio (re)compression, assess compression generation, and discriminate between different audio compression algorithms.

The research in the field of audio forensics can be broadly divided into the following major focus areas: (i) speech recognition that aims at producing readable text from human speech, especially from ambiguous utterances, (ii) speaker verification that compares a known voice to an unknown voice to determine the identity of the unknown voice, (iv) speaker localization that uses acoustic environment features such as reverberations and background noise to determine speaker location and acoustic environment, and (iv) speaker identification that performs comparison of similarities and differences of elements of speech such as bandwidths, fundamental frequency, prosody, vowel formant trajectory, occlusive, fricatives, pitch striations, formant energy, breath patterns, nasal resonance, coupling, and any special speech pathology of the speaker. Audio forensics focuses not only the direct speaker verification but also the recording environment identification [16] which can be used to determine the underlying facts about the evidentiary recording and to provide authoritative answers to questions, such as [31]:

- Is an evidentiary recording *"original"* or was it created by splicing multiple recordings together?
- What are the types and locations of forgeries, if there are any, in an evidentiary recording?
- Was the evidentiary recording made at location L, as claimed?
- Is the auditory scene in the evidentiary recording original or was it digitally altered to deceive the listener?

The acoustic environment identification (AEI) therefore has a wide range of applications ranging from audio recording integrity authentication to real-time crime acoustic space localization/identification. For instance, consider a scenario where a police call center receives an emergency call from a victim being harassed or chased by an offender. Under such crime situations it is very common that the harassed persons are unable to provide any relevant information about their actual location. The acoustic signals in the audio recording can be used to determine the acoustic space (i.e. car, street, neighborhood, living room, bath room, bed room, kitchen, etc.)

of the crime scene. Similarly, for gun shooting cases, the sound of the firearms in the recording can be used to obtain important information about the crime scene such as weapon type.

The focus of this paper is acoustic environment identification (AEI) from evidentiary recording which has applications in the area of audio forensics, distant speech recognition, speaker localization. In the context of audio forensics, consider a test audio recording, obtained by *splicing* sections from one or multiple audio recordings made at different locations. When such spliced audio is used as evidence in the court of law its integrity must be verified. As doctored evidence can be used to fake the person, acoustic environment, event, auditory scene, acoustic environment, etc. in the evidentiary recording which might lead to serious consequence. It is therefore critical to authenticate the integrity of digital evidence.

This paper presents a model driven framework based on parametric modeling of late reverberations, parameter estimation using maximum likelihood estimation, and density-based clustering to determine where the recording was made. Motivation behind considering acoustic artifacts for AEI and audio forensic applications is that existing audio forensic analysis methods, e.g., ENF-based methods [5-8] and recording device identification based methods [11-14] cannot withstand *lossy compress attack*, e.g., MP3 compression. In our recent work [18,32], we have shown that acoustic reverberations can survive lossy compression attack, which is one of the motivations behind considering acoustic artifacts in an audio recording for AEI and digital audio forensic applications.

The major contribution of this paper is to develop a statistical framework for automatic AEI and its applications to digital audio forensics. Here, we exploit specific artifacts introduced at the time of recording to authenticate an audio recording and AEI, that is, to determine where the recording was made. Audio reverberation is caused by the persistence of sound after the source has terminated. This persistence is due to the multiple reflections from various surfaces in a room. As such, differences in a room's geometry and composition will lead to different amounts of reverberation time. There is significant literature on modeling and estimating audio reverberation (see, for example, [33]). We describe how to model and estimate audio reverberation – this approach is a variant of that described in [34]. In this paper, we have shown that reverberation can be reliably estimated. In addition, effectiveness of the proposed method is evaluated for recorded audio and speech datasets. Moreover, to achieve automatic recording environment identification, density-based clustering is used. Performance of the proposed framework has also been evaluated for microphone type, frequency, and clustering accuracy and efficiency. Effectiveness of the proposed scheme has also been evaluated using human speech recordings. Performance of the proposed method is also compared with the existing state-of-the-art (SoA) for AEI.

The rest of the paper is organized as follows: details of reverberation acoustic environment artifacts modeling and estimation are provided in Section 'Proposed method'; a brief overview of the density-based clustering is described in Section 'Automatic acoustic environment identification (AEI) using cluster analysis'; experimental results and performance analysis are provided in Section 'Experimental results'; and concluding remarks along with future research directions are discussed in Section 'Conclusion'.

Proposed method

Parametric modeling of acoustic environment artifacts

Consider a recorded response of an acoustic environment to an impulsive sound source "*a hand-clap*" shown in the Figure 1. It can be observed from Figure 1 that the recorded response can be divided into two non-overlapping segments: (i) strong early reflections (also known as early reverberations), and (ii) decaying reverberant tail or late reverberations. The early reflections are assumed to occur between the arrival of the *direct signal* and t_{ref} ms thereafter; whereas the late reverberations are occurring after t_{ref} ms, a typical value for $t_{ref} \in [50 - 100]$ ms [35]. Early reverberations depend on distance between the source and the receiver (e.g. microphone), directivity of source and receiver pair, etc. The late reverberations, on the other hand, depend on acoustic environment characteristics, e.g., enclosure geometry, surface area, surface material absorption coefficient, and so on. In this paper, We focus on late reverberations for the acoustic environment identification task.

We begin with a model for the late reverberations of acoustic activities in an acoustic environment (the dense reflections that follow the early reflections). The late reverberations are a result of multiple reflections, arriving at the receiver in *random order*, with successive reflections

being damped based on the arrival time, that is, reflection amplitude is damped to a greater degree if they arrive (at the receiver) later in time. The assumption of randomness is very important to the development of a statistical model used for reverberation modeling and estimation. It has been demonstrated [36] that when a burst of white noise is radiated into a test enclosure, the phase and amplitudes of the normal modes are random in the instant preceding the cessation of the sound. This generates random decaying output of the enclosure following sound cessation, even if repeated trials were conducted with the same source and receiver geometry.

To validate these claims, that is, (i) output of the enclosure following sound cessation is random, and (ii) decaying tails of the repeated trials are uncorrelated, we computed a cross-correlation function between two non-overlapping segments of same decaying tail. In addition, we also computed cross-correlation between two identical segments of two decaying tails of same "hand-clap" recorded at two different time instances. Shown in Figure 2 is the plot of cross-correlation function of two non-overlapping segments (35 msec. apart) of a decaying tail of same "hand-clap" recorded using microphone $Mic1$ in a restroom (a highly reverberant environment, E_5). And, shown in Figure 3 is the plot of cross-correlation function of two time-aligned segments of decaying tails of identical "*hand-clap*" recordings made at two different time instances with $Mic1$ in E_5 (i.e., by playing the same "hand-clap" recording twice).

It can be observed from Figures 1, 2 and 3 that the assumed model for late reverberations is reasonably accurate. Based on these observations, reverberant decaying tail envelope can modeled using an exponential with a single (deterministic) parameter, decay rate τ. As demonstrated in Figure 3 that late reverberations are uncorrelated, the reverberant or dense tail is therefore modeled using an exponentially damped uncorrelated noise sequence obeying Gaussian distribution. More specifically, the decay of an audio signal $x[n]$ is

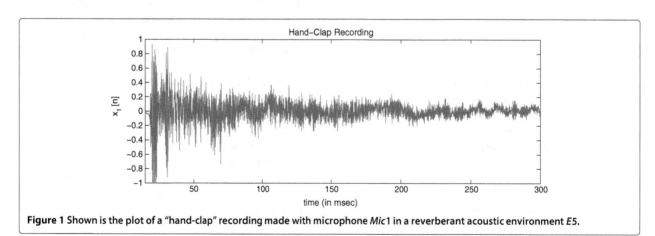

Figure 1 Shown is the plot of a "hand-clap" recording made with microphone *Mic*1 in a reverberant acoustic environment *E5*.

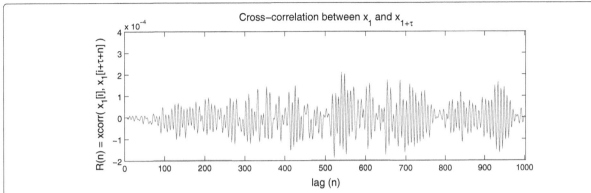

Figure 2 Shown is the plot of cross-correlation function between two non-overlapping segments (35 msec. apart) of decaying tail of a "hand-clap", recorded using microphone *Mic1* in a reverberant environment *E5*.

modeled with a multiplicative decay and additive noise (see Figure 4):

$$y[n] = d[n] x[n] + \eta[n], \tag{1}$$

where,

$$d[n] = \exp[-n/\tau]. \tag{2}$$

The decay parameter τ embodies the extent of the reverberation, and can be estimated using a maximum likelihood estimator.

It is important to mention that the proposed time-domain model does not include the direct sound or early reflections and it is accurate only during free decay, that is, when the sound source is not active. To capture traces of acoustic environment, decay rate of the reverberant tail is estimated from the exponentially decaying envelop.

Parameter estimation using maximum likelihood estimation

We assume that the signal $x[n]$ is a sequence of N independently and identically-distributed (*iid*) zero mean and normally distributed random variables with variance σ^2.

We also assume that this signal is uncorrelated to the noise $\eta[n]$ which is also a sequence of N *iid* zero mean and normally distributed random variables with variance $\sigma_\eta^2 = \rho \times \sigma^2$, where ρ is a real-valued positive constant representing the signal to noise ratio (SNR). With these assumptions, the observed signal $y[n]$ is a random variable with a probability density function given by:

$$P_{y[n]}(k) = \frac{1}{\sqrt{2\pi\sigma^2\gamma^2[n]}} \cdot \exp\left(-\frac{k^2}{2\sigma^2\gamma^2[n]}\right), \tag{3}$$

where

$$\gamma[n] = \sqrt{\exp(-2n/\tau) + \rho^{-1}}. \tag{4}$$

The likelihood function is then given by:

$$Ł(y, \sigma, \gamma) = \frac{1}{(2\pi\sigma^2)^{N/2} \prod_{k=0}^{N-1} \gamma(k)} \cdot \exp$$
$$\times \left(-\frac{1}{2\sigma^2} \sum_{k=0}^{N-1} \frac{y^2(k)}{\gamma^2(k)}\right). \tag{5}$$

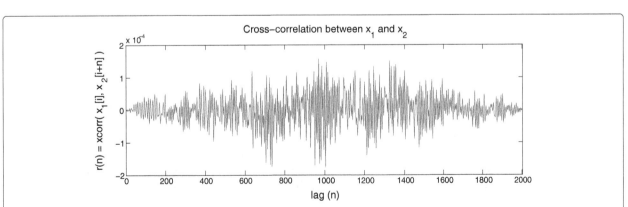

Figure 3 Shown is the plot of cross-correlation function between time-aligned segments of decaying tails of identical *"hand-clap"* recordings made at two different time instances using *Mic1* in *E5*.

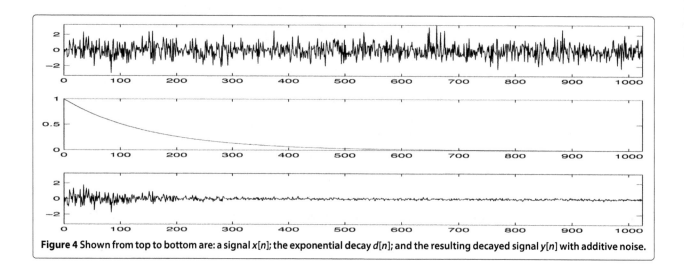

Figure 4 Shown from top to bottom are: a signal $x[n]$; the exponential decay $d[n]$; and the resulting decayed signal $y[n]$ with additive noise.

The log-likelihood function, $\ln(L(\cdot))$, is:

$$\mathcal{L}(y, \sigma, \gamma) = -\frac{N}{2} \ln(2\pi\sigma^2) - \sum_{k=0}^{N-1} \ln(\gamma(k))$$
$$- \frac{1}{2\sigma^2} \sum_{k=0}^{N-1} \frac{y^2(k)}{\gamma^2(k)}. \tag{6}$$

The decay parameter τ is estimated by maximizing the log-likelihood function $\mathcal{L}(\cdot)$. This is achieved by setting the partial derivatives of $\mathcal{L}(\cdot)$ equal to zero and solving for the desired τ. For the purpose of numerical stability, the maximization is performed on $\tilde{\tau} = \exp(-1/\tau)$ instead of τ.

$$\frac{\partial \mathcal{L}}{\partial \sigma} = -\frac{N}{\sigma} + \frac{1}{\rho\sigma} \sum_{k=0}^{N-1} \frac{1}{\gamma^2(k)} + \frac{1}{\sigma^3} \sum_{k=0}^{N-1} \frac{y^2(k)\tilde{\tau}^{2k}}{\gamma^4(k)} \tag{7}$$

$$\frac{\partial \mathcal{L}}{\partial \tilde{\tau}} = \sum_{k=0}^{N-1} \frac{k\tilde{\tau}^{2k-1}}{\gamma^2(k)} \left(\frac{y^2(k)}{\sigma^2 \gamma^2(k)} - 1 \right). \tag{8}$$

It can be observed from Eq. (7) and Eq. (8) that both the σ in Eq. (7) and $\tilde{\tau}$ in Eq. (8) cannot be solved for analytically. As such, an iterative non-linear minimization is required which is computationally inefficient and sometime does not convergence. To get around this issue, high signal to noise ratio (SNR) is assumed in the selected decaying tail region, i.e., $\sigma \gg \sigma_\eta$ or $0 < \rho \ll 1$. This is a realistic assumption, especially, when audio recording is made in a relatively quiet environment and/or it is pre-processed for speech enhancement. Experimental results presented here are based on audio recordings made in quiet acoustic environments and are pre-processed with a speech enhancement filter [37]. With moderate

SNR assumption, the Eq. (7) and Eq. (8) can be rewritten as:

$$\frac{\partial \mathcal{L}}{\partial \sigma} = -\frac{N}{\sigma} + \frac{1}{\sigma^3} \sum_{k=0}^{N-1} \frac{y^2(k)}{\tilde{\gamma}^2(k)} \tag{9}$$

$$\frac{\partial \mathcal{L}}{\partial \tilde{\tau}} = \sum_{k=0}^{N-1} \frac{k\tilde{\tau}^{2k-1}}{\tilde{\gamma}^2(k)} \left(\frac{y^2(k)}{\sigma^2 \tilde{\gamma}^2(k)} - 1 \right). \tag{10}$$

where,

$$\tilde{\gamma}[k] = \tilde{\tau}^k. \tag{11}$$

Although σ in Eq. (9) can be solved for analytically, $\tilde{\tau}$ in Eq. (10) still cannot. As such, an iterative non-linear minimization is required. This minimization consists of two primary steps, first to estimate σ and second to estimate $\tilde{\tau}$. In the first step σ is estimated by setting the partial derivative in Eq. (9) equal to zero and solving for σ, to yield:

$$\sigma^2 = \frac{1}{N} \sum_{k=0}^{N-1} \frac{y^2(k)}{\tilde{\gamma}^2(k)} = \frac{1}{N} \sum_{k=0}^{N-1} \frac{y^2(k)}{\tilde{\tau}^{2k}}. \tag{12}$$

This solution requires an estimates of σ_η and $\tilde{\tau}$. The $\tilde{\tau}$ is initially estimated using Schroeder's integration method [38]. In the second step, $\tilde{\tau}$ is estimated by maximizing the log-likelihood function $\mathcal{L}(\cdot)$ in Eq. (6). This is performed using a standard gradient descent optimization, where the derivative of the objective function is given by Eq. (10). These two steps are iteratively executed until the differences between consecutive estimates of σ and $\tilde{\tau}$ are less than a specified threshold. In practice, this optimization is quite efficient, converging after only a few iterations.

Automatic Acoustic Environment Identification (AEI) using cluster analysis

The similarity of the estimated acoustic reverberation parameters, τ and σ, from selected segments of a given audio recording can be used for both forensic analysis and acoustic environment identification (AEI). For example, a small (resp. large) distance in the estimated reverberation parameters from a test recording indicates relatively consistent (resp. inconsistent) acoustic environment. In addition, similarity in the estimated reverberation parameters from two different recordings indicates that these recordings were made in acoustically identical environments and vice versa.

Cluster analysis, *an unsupervised classification framework*, is used to determine acoustic environment similarity in the test audio recording using acoustic parameters. For automatic AEI, density based clustering is considered. More specifically, *Density-Based Spatial Clustering of Applications with Noise* (DBSCAN) [39,40], a density based clustering technique, is used to label audio recordings into acoustically similar groups (or clusters) based on estimated acoustic parameters. Motivation behind considering DBSCAN is that it can efficiently handle outliers in the data, it can find clusters of arbitrary (or non-convex) shapes, and it does not require prior knowledge of the number of clusters in the data. In addition, density-based clustering handles regions of varying densities more efficiently than commonly uses methods such as K-means, K-mediods, etc.

The DBSCAN uses center-based framework to estimate density for a particular point in the data set. More specifically, it counts the number of points in radius, ϵ, around point p. This center-based framework labels a given point, p, as (i) a *core point*, (ii) a *border point*, or (iii) a *noise point*. The core, border, and noise points are defined as:

- **Definition 1:** A point, p is a *core point* if $|\{x \mid d(x,p) \leq \epsilon\}| \geq MinPts$, where $MinPts$ denotes minimum number points and $d(x,p)$ denotes the Euclidian distance between of point x and p. The core points makes the interior of a cluster.
- **Definition 2:** A point, p is a *border point* if $|\{x \mid d(x,p) \leq \epsilon\}| < MinPts$ but is in the neighborhood of a core point.
- **Definition 3:** A point is a *noise point* if it is neither a core point nor a border point.

Given the definitions of core, border, and noise points the DBSCAN algorithm can be described as follows. Label data points as core, border, and noise points and remove noise points. Clustering is then performed by assigning same cluster label to any two core points that are within ϵ-distance. Likewise, any border point within ϵ-distance from a core point is also assigned the same cluster label as the core point.

Experimental results

To test effectiveness of the proposed framework, we analyzed simple recordings, e.g., hand-clap recordings and relatively complex recordings, e.g., speech recordings made in a diverse set of recording environments including small offices, a large office, hallway, staircase, restroom, atrium, and outdoor environments. These recordings were made using three microphones.

Dataset and experimental settings

Two datasets consisting of audio recordings are used for performance evaluation of the proposed method.

- The first dataset used for performance evaluation consists of 120 hand-clap recordings made using three microphones: (i) **Mic1: a built-in HP Compaq Laptop**, (ii) **Mic2: a built-in microphone in Apple's MacBook**, and (iii) **Mic3: a commercial grade external microphone**. These recordings were made in ten acoustically different environments: three *small offices* ($E1 - E3$), an *atrium* $E4$, a *restroom* $E5$, a *hallway* $E6$, two *outdoors* $E7$&$E8$, a *large office* $E9$, and *stairs* $E10$. The hand-clap recording (downloaded from http://www.freesound.org/samplesViewSingle.php?id=345) was played using a pair of commercial grade external speakers. In each recording environment three samples were made through each microphone while keeping the distance between a pair of speakers and the microphone same. These recording were made with mono audio channel and a sampling rate of 16000 samples per second.
- The second dataset used for performance evaluation of the proposed method consists of 60 speech recordings. We recorded human speech of three speakers (two males and a female) in four different recording environments: *outdoors* E_1; a *small office* (7' × 11' × 9') E_2; *stairs* E_3; and a *restroom* (15' × 11' × 9') E_4. In each recording environment, each speaker read five different texts (each consisting of couple of short sentences) while keeping the distance between the speaker and the microphone same, as a result, a total of 60 audio recordings were made using a commercial-grade external microphone.

Each recording was initially pre-processed with a speech enhancement filter [37]. For acoustic parameter estimation, decaying tails were manually selected from each clean recording. From the selected tails acoustic reverberation parameters, i.e., τ and σ were estimated using method discussed in 'Parameter estimation using maximum likelihood estimation'.

Clustering performance is evaluated using clustering *purity*, *efficiency*, and *Jaccard* scores [40]. These clustering assessment measures are defined as follows:

$$Purity = \frac{f_{11}}{f_{11} + f_{10}} \tag{13}$$

$$Efficiency = \frac{f_{11}}{f_{11} + f_{01}} \tag{14}$$

$$Jaccard = \frac{f_{11}}{f_{11} + f_{10} + f_{01}} \tag{15}$$

where f_{11} is the number of pairs that are labeled correctly, f_{10} is the number of pairs that are labeled together in the true data, but not in the predicted labels, and f_{01} is the number of pairs that are labeled together during clustering but are not in the true labels.

Automatic AEI: *hand-clap recording*

The goal of the first experiment is to tested performance of the proposed framework for AEI using hand-clap recordings. In this experiment, the reverberation parameters, τ and σ^2, were estimated from selected decaying tails in each of the recording in the first dataset using the method discussed in Section 'Parameter estimation using maximum likelihood estimation'. The decaying tails were manually selected. The noise floor criterion is used for manual tail selection, that is, tail on-set starts at the peak hand-clap energy level and ends at the position where it has decayed to the noise floor. Selected decaying tails are used to estimate reverberation parameters.

Shown in Figure 5 is the scatter plot of estimated reverberation parameters, τ (in msec) and variance σ^2 (in $\log \sigma^2$), from the hand-clap recordings made with Mic1 (the built-in HP Compaq Laptop). Shown in the left panel of Figure 5 is the true acoustic environment labels for the estimated parameters and shown in the right panel of Figure 5 is the predicted acoustic environment labels using DBSCAN-based clustering. We iteratively refined the clustering parameters to partition the input data into at least seven clusters. Shown in Figure 5 are the clustering results obtained with clustering parameters $\epsilon = 1.8$ and $MinPt = 3$.

The learned clustering parameters, $MinPts$ and ϵ, from recordings made with Mic1 are used for predicting cluster labels for recordings made using Mic2 and Mic3. Shown in the top panel of Figure 6 is the scatter plot of estimated parameters from hand-clap recordings made with Mic2 (built-in microphone on Apple's MacBook) along with true acoustic environments and shown in the bottom panel of Figure 6 is the predicted acoustic environment labels using DBSCAN-based clustering.

And, shown in the top panel of Figure 7 is the scatter plot of estimated parameters from hand-clap recordings

made with Mic3 (external microphone) along with true acoustic environments and shown in the bottom panel of Figure 7 is the predicted acoustic environment labels using DBSCAN-based clustering.

Following observations can be made from Figures 5, 6 and 7:

- It can be observed from Figure 5 that clustering process has accurately predicted environment labels (or cluster IDs (CIDs)) for all acoustic environments except small offices ($E1 - E3$) where it has predicted same environment label, e.g., *CID*1. As all three small offices are structurally identical and the only difference between them is their furniture settings therefore acoustic characteristics are these environments are expected to be very close, the true labels in the left panel of Figure 5 confirms it. In addition, it also indicates that Mic1 is relatively less sensitive to small variations in the acoustic environment therefore forensic analyst should be careful when using such microphones for audio forensic applications.

- Secondly, Figure 6 shows that clustering process has accurately predicted environment labels for acoustic environments $E1$, $E2$, $E3$ and $E10$; whereas, it has assigned two separate labels *CID*5 & *CID*6 to $E5$, same label *CID*4 to $E4$, $E7$ and $E8$, and same label *CID*7 to $E8$ and $E9$. It indicates that Mic2 is insensitive in less reverberant environments and it is relatively more sensitive to highly reverberant environments. Findings of Figure 6 also suggest that Mic2 is not a good choice to differentiate between acoustically similar environments such as outdoors and atrium, and large office and hallway.

- Thirdly, Figure 7 shows that clustering process has accurately predicted environment labels for all acoustic environments with two exceptions, that is, (i) two labels, e.g., *CID*7 & *CID*8, for $E6$, and (ii) miss classification of few data points of $E4$. In addition, clustering process has also assigned '*noise*' label to data points of acoustic environments $E3$, $E4$, $E6$ and $E10$. It can also be observed from Figure 7 that estimated parameters for Mic3 exhibit larger variance than the other two microphones used. The larger variance of Mic3 indicates that it exhibits relatively higher sensitivity (see Section 'Performance evaluation: *microphone variation*' for more discussion on microphone sensitivity).

- Finally, Figures 5, 6 and 7 indicate that Mic1 and Mic3 exhibit relatively higher accuracy than Mic2. We have also learned through extensive analysis that prediction performance of the proposed method can be improved by learning microphone dependent clustering parameters, that is, learning microphone

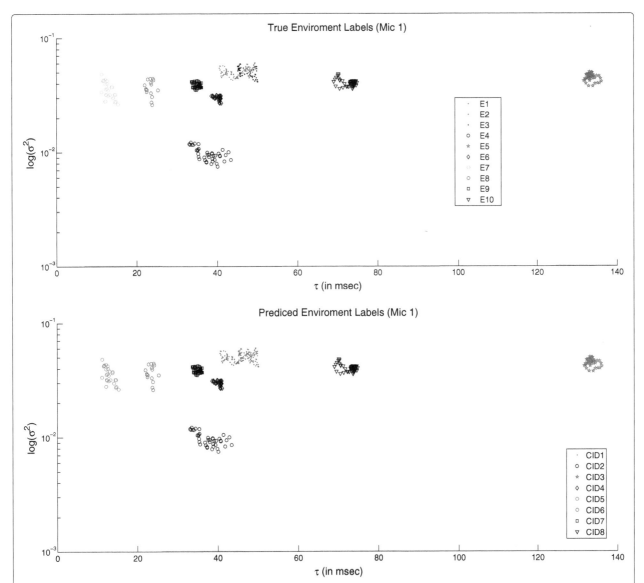

Figure 5 Shown in the top panel is the scatter plot of the estimated parameters from the hand-clap recordings made with Mic1 with true acoustic environment labels and shown in the bottom panel is the scatter plot of the estimated parameters with predicted environment labels.

specific clustering parameters and use them for environment prediction for recordings made.

To quantify microphone specific performance of the proposed method, AEI accuracy is measure is used. To this end, AEI accuracy is measured in terms of clustering purity, efficiently, and Jaccard scores defined in Equations (13-15). Shown in Table 1 is the microphone specific clustering performance.

It can be observed from Table 1 that Mic3 exhibits higher AEI accuracy than the other two microphones and Mic2 exhibits the lowest AEI accuracy than the other two microphones. Higher accuracy of Mic3 can be

attributed to it better sensitivity and lower sensitivity of Mic2 resulted in lower AEI accuracy.

Performance evaluation: *microphone variation*
The aim of the second experiment is to investigate the impact of microphone type on the accuracy of the estimated parameters. To this end, we compared reverberation parameters estimated from recordings made in a given acoustic environment simultaneously using all three microphones. We have observed through this analysis (it can also be observed from Figures 5, 6 and 7) that microphone sensitivity to an acoustic activity does influence estimated acoustic parameters. For example, estimated τ,

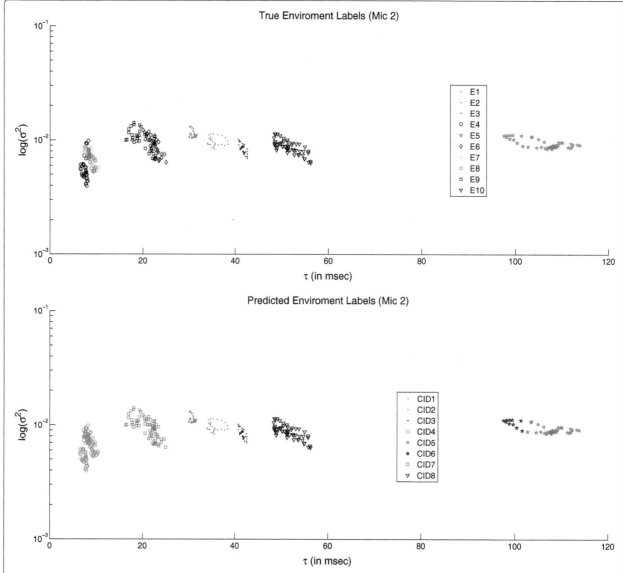

Figure 6 Shown in the top panel is the scatter plot of the estimated parameters from the hand-clap recordings made through Mic2 with true acoustic environment labels and shown in the bottom panel are the scatter plot of the estimated parameters with predicted environment labels.

for each acoustic environment, for Mic2 has significantly lower mean values, ($\mu_\tau = \frac{\sum_{i=1}^{n} \tau_i}{n}$), than μ_τ for Mic1 and Mic3. Similarly, μ_σ and standard deviation (std) of estimated σ^2, $\sigma_{\sigma^2} = \sqrt{(\frac{1}{n}\sum_{1}^{n}(\sigma_i^2 - \mu_{\sigma^2}))}$, where μ_{σ^2} is the mean value of sequence σ^2 of length n, for Mic2 is relatively larger than σ_{σ^2}s for remaining two microphones. To highlight this fact, we compared estimated parameters from recordings made in a given acoustic environment with all three microphones. Shown in Figure 8 are the scatter plots of the estimated τ and $\log(\sigma^2)$ for acoustic environment $E1$.

It can be observed from Figure 8 that the μ_τ and σ_τ for Mic3 is significantly larger than the μ_τ and σ_τ for

Mic2. Similarly, μ_{σ^2} value for Mic3 is also larger than the other two microphones. This observation can be explained using the fact that Mic3 is an external microphone, therefore, it is expected to exhibit better sensitive to acoustic activities and ambient noise than the built-in laptop microphones.

To investigate the microphone response variations further, we selected two acoustic environments: (i) a less reverberant environment (outdoors), and (ii) a highly reverberant environment (restroom). Shown in the left panel of Figure 9 are the scatter plots of the estimated τ and $\log(\sigma^2)$ for all three microphones for acoustic environments $E7$ and shown in the right panel are the scatter

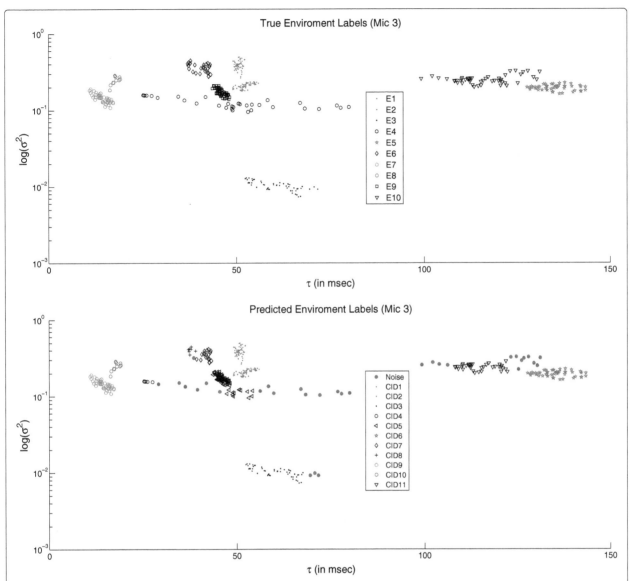

Figure 7 Shown in the top panel is the scatter plot of the estimated parameters from the hand-clap recordings made with Mic3 with true acoustic environment labels and shown in the bottom panel is the scatter plot of the estimated parameters with predicted environment labels.

Table 1 Shown AEI performances in terms of clustering accuracy for external, built-in HP, and built-in MacBook microphones

Microphone type	Purity score	Efficiency score	Jaccard score
Mic1: Built-in (HP)	75.17	75.17	60.22
Mic2: Built-in (MacBook)	73.64	71.80	58.22
Mic3: External	87.93	94.84	83.91

plots of the estimated parameters for all three microphones for acoustic environments $E5$.

Following observations can be made from Figures 8 and 9:

1. For external microphone: The μ_τ, μ_{σ^2}, σ_τ, and σ_{σ^2} for external microphone (as expected) is higher than the built-in microphones. This indicates that external exhibits relatively more sensitivity than the other two microphones.

2. For Mic1: The σ_τ and σ_{σ^2} for Mic1 is the lowest among all three microphones which makes it more suitable for forensics applications.

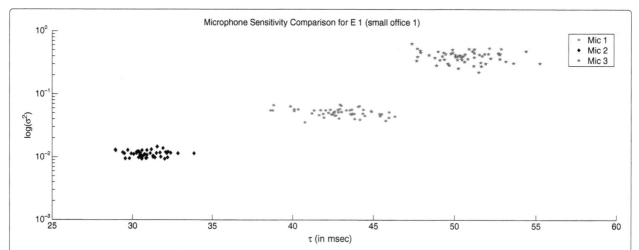

Figure 8 Shown is the scatter plots of the estimated parameters from the hand-clap recordings made with all microphones in the small-office 1.

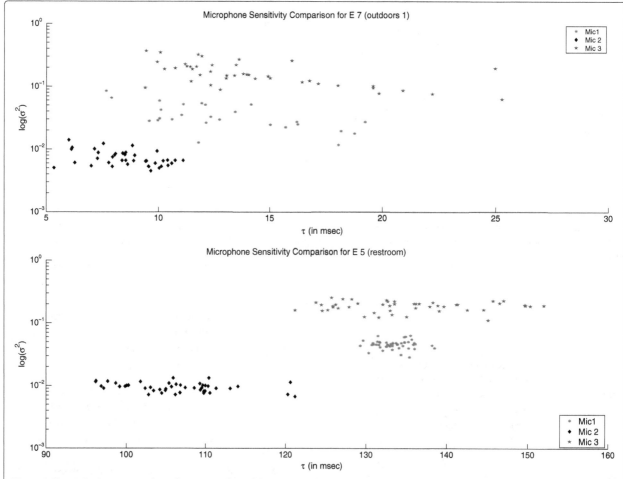

Figure 9 Shown in the top panel are the scatter plots of the estimated parameters from recordings made in acoustic environment *E7* and shown in the bottom panel are the scatter plots of the estimated parameters from recordings made environment *E5*.

3. For Mic2: The The μ_τ and μ_{σ^2} for Mic2 is lowest whereas variance is comparable to the external microphone for reverberant environments, e.g., $E1$ and $E5$.

To quantify variations in the estimated parameters, we computed mean and standard deviation (std) for each environment. Shown in Table 2 are the mean(std) of estimated parameters, τ and σ^2, for all microphones and all acoustic environments.

It can be observed from Table 2 that for all acoustic environments the μ_τ values of estimated τ for the external microphone and the built-in HP microphone are relatively close; whereas, the μ_τ for Mic2 are significantly lower than the other two microphones. This was a surprising observation, as recordings used were collected simultaneously using all three microphones, a small variation in the estimated parameters is understandable but a significant variation came as a surprise to us. Further investigation on recordings captured with Mic2 revealed that it has the lowest sensitivity among all three microphones used for data collection.

It can also be observed from Table 2 that the built-in MacBook microphone (Mic2) is relatively insensitive as compare to remaining two microphones. In addition, reli-ability of the estimated parameters decreases for complex acoustic structures such as atrium and stairs. This is due to the fact that due to low sensitivity Mic2 is unable to pick weak late reverberations and background noise which resulted in lower variance of the estimated parameters.

Finally, the external microphone is relatively more unreliable in complex environments than the built-in microphones which is reflected by a relatively large variance of the estimated τ for these environments. This is not a surprising observation as due to higher sensitivity, the Mic3 is expected to pick weak late reverberations mixed with background noise hence relatively higher variance of the estimated parameters.

In addition, as observed from Table 2 estimated τ is relatively higher for external microphone than the built-in microphones, this observation suggests that estimated reverberation parameter depends on microphone directivity and sensitivity. Therefore, for AEI and audio splicing detection performance microphones with superior directivity and sensitivity should be considered.

Impact of the frequency on estimated parameters

The goal of our third experiment is to investigate the impact of frequency on estimated parameters (e.g. τ and $\log(\sigma^2)$). To this end, each audio recording is decomposed

Table 2 Shown in third, fourth, and fifth columns are the mean(std) of estimated acoustic parameters from audio recordings made with the built-in HP, built-in MacBook, and external microphones, respectively

Environments		Microphones		
		Mic1: Built-in (HP)	Mic2: Built-in(MacBook)	Mic3: External
Small office1	τ mean(std)	42.95(1.46)	30.86(0.53)	50.68(0.74)
	σ_n mean(std)	0.05(0.004)	0.01(0.001)	0.39((0.052)
Small office2	τ mean(std)	47.93(0.99)	35.60(1.29)	52.50(1.7)
	σ mean(std)	0.05(0.004)	0.01(0.001)	0.21(0.017)
Small office3	τ mean(std)	47.40(1.82)	41.65(0.56)	60.60(5.37)
	σ mean(std)	0.05 (0.005)	0.01(0.001)	0.01(0.001)
Atrium	τ mean(std)	**37.75(2.77)**	**7.56(0.45)**	**49.38(15.24)**
	σ mean(std)	0.01(0.001)	0.01(0.002)	0.12(0.02)
Restroom	τ mean(std)	133.48(1.01)	106.28(4.41)	135.05(4.38)
	σ mean(std)	0.04(0.003)	0.01(0.001)	0.2(0.016)
Hallway	τ mean(std)	40.18(0.75)	22.33(1.22)	40.77(2.14)
	σ mean(std)	0.03(0.001)	0.01(0.002)	0.36(0.048)
Outdoors1	τ mean(std)	12.93(1.17)	8.58(0.92)	14.36(1.74)
	σ mean(std)	0.04(0.006)	0.01(0.001)	0.15(0.019)
Outdoors2	τ mean(std)	23.44(0.89)	8.81(0.54)	17.83 (0.92)
	σ mean(std)	0.04(0.006)	0.01(0.001)	0.25(0.031)
Large office	τ mean(std)	35.03(0.72)	19.84(2.12)	46.0 (1.11)
	σ mean(std)	0.04(0.002)	0.01(0.002)	0.17(0.018)
Stairs	τ mean(std)	**72.82(1.74)**	**51.73(2.42)**	**116.11 (7.51)**
	σ mean(std)	0.04(0.003)	0.01(0.001)	0.25(0.031)

Bold: Observations for these two environments exhibit relatively large variance.

into four subband signals with equal frequency bands, that is, $sb_1 : 0 \leq f_{sb1} \leq 2$ kHz, $sb_2 : 2001 < f_{sb2} \leq 4$ kHz, $sb_3 : 4001 < f_{sb3} \leq 6$ kHz, and $sb_4 : 8001 < f_{sb4} \leq 8$ kHz, using wavelet packet decomposition. Reverberation parameters are then estimated from each subband signal using method discussed in Section 'Parameter estimation using maximum likelihood estimation'. Estimated parameters from recordings made in environments $E1$, $E5$, and $E7$ with all three microphones are shown in Figure 10.

Following observations can be made from Figure 10:

1. *Irrespective of the microphone type or acoustic environment, the μ_{σ^2} decreases for higher subbands, i.e., sb_3 and sb_4.*
2. *For all microphones and all selected acoustic environments, the μ_{σ^2} for sb_1 and sb_2 (resp. sb_3 and sb_4) are relatively higher (resp. lower) than the μ_{σ^2} from original recordings.*
3. *For all microphones and for moderately-to-highly reverberant environments (e.g. $E5$ and $E1$), the μ_τ decreases for sb_3 and sb_4 and does not change for outdoors environment ($E7$). Whereas, for sb_1 and sb_2, the μ_τ do not change significantly (except Mic2 where μ_τ for sb_2 also decreases).*
4. *For all microphones and all environments, σ_τ for all subbands are larger than the σ_τ estimated from original recordings.* This not a surprising observation as τ estimated from subband signals is using roughly one-fourth of the samples of the original recordings which can be translated into relatively less reliable estimates than the original recording.

Automatic AEI: *human speech recording*
The goal of the fourth experiment to evaluate performance of the proposed framework using speech recordings. To this end, second dataset consisting of 60 speech recordings of three speakers (a female and two male speakers) made in four acoustically different environments: (i) outdoors; (ii) a small office; (iii) stairs; and (iv) a restroom, with a commercial grade external microphone.

Acoustic reverberation parameters are estimated from manually selected decaying tails from each clean recording using method discussed in 'Parameter estimation using maximum likelihood estimation'. The DBSCAN-based clustering method is used for automatic AEI using estimated acoustic reverberation parameters, i.e., τ and σ. Shown in Figure 11 are the scatter plots of estimated reverberation parameters τ in msec. and σ with predicted environment labels for all speakers in all four acoustic environments.

It can be observed from Figure 11 that the proposed framework is capable of correctly predicting environment labels for speech recordings with very high accuracy. In addition, for each acoustic environment, the estimated

τ exhibits relatively large spread compared with τ estimated from hand-clap recordings. Relatively large spread of the estimated τ for speech data can be attributed to the characterization of the speech signal and the decaying tail selection process. For example, in case of hand-clap recordings, decaying tail selection is very accurate as there is no overlapping from previous hand-clap instances, therefore, no interference, as a result reasonably consistent τ estimates from hand-clap recordings is expected. In case of speech recordings, on the other hand, for the voiced regions the previous phoneme utterance is likely to overlap with the following phoneme utterance, which causes interference in the selected decaying tails. Moreover, as the interference due to previous phoneme utterance is random in nature for real-world speech recordings. The τ estimated from decaying tails extracted from speech recordings is therefore expected to exhibit relatively larger spread than the hand-clap recordings, Figures 5, 6, 7, 8, 9, 10 and 11 support this argument.

Performance comparison with existing state-of-the-art
The aim of the final experiment to compare performance of the proposed framework with Hong's statistical learning-based method [18]. Speech recording dataset is used for this experiment.

For AEI using Hong's method, the reverberant component, $r(t)$, is extracted from each input speech signal using method discuss in the paper [18]. The resulting reverberant component is then pre-emphasized according to $r(t) = r(t) - p \times r(t-1)$ with $p = 0.97$. The estimated reverberant signal $r(t)$ is then decomposed into overlapping frames of length 25 ms with a frame shift of 10 ms, which resulted in 150 segments for each environment and a total of 600 segments for all four environments. For each segment, a Hamming window based 512-point DFT is computed, which is used to compute a 24-dimensional melspec coefficient vector. A 24-D *logarithmic melspec coefficient* (LMSC) vector is obtained by calculating the natural logarithm of the melspec coefficient vector; and a 24-D *mel-frequency cepstral coefficients* (MFCC) vector is obtained by computing DCT of the LMSC vector. For each segment, a 48-D feature vector is obtained by concatenating 24-D MFCC and 24-D LMSC vectors. The final 48-dimensional feature vector, averaged it over all frames is used for training and testing of the support vector machines (SVM) classifier.

For classification, a multi-class SVM trained with *radial basis kernel function* is used. The SVM tool downloaded from [41] was used for training and testing. To begin with, we randomly selected 50% of recordings from each category for training. The rest 50% are used to verify performance the proposed scheme. The optimal parameters for the classifier are determined using grid search

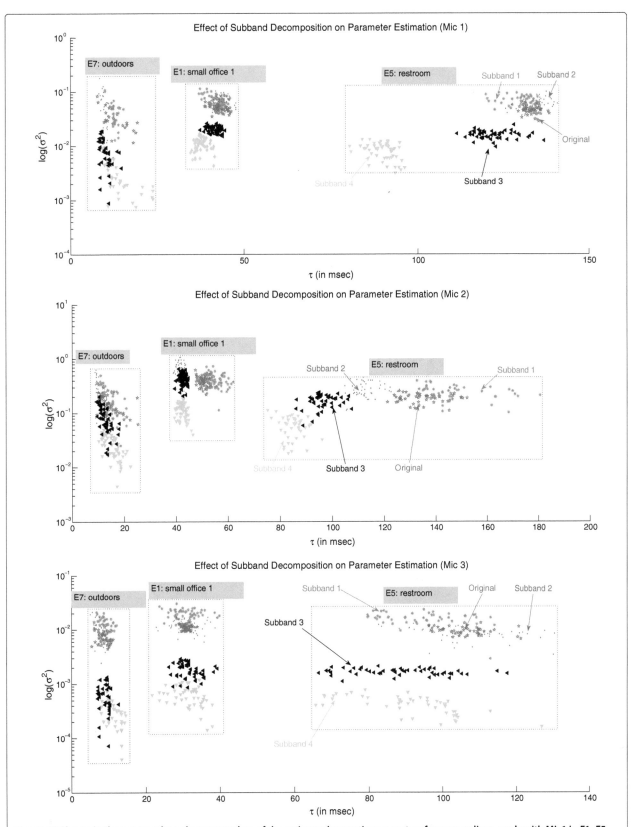

Figure 10 Shown in the top panel are the scatter plots of the estimated acoustic parameters from recordings made with Mic1 in *E*1, *E*5 and *E*7; shown in the middle panel are the scatter plots of the estimated parameters from recordings made with Mic2 in the selected environments; and, shown in the bottom panel are the scatter plots of the estimated parameters from recordings made with Mic3.

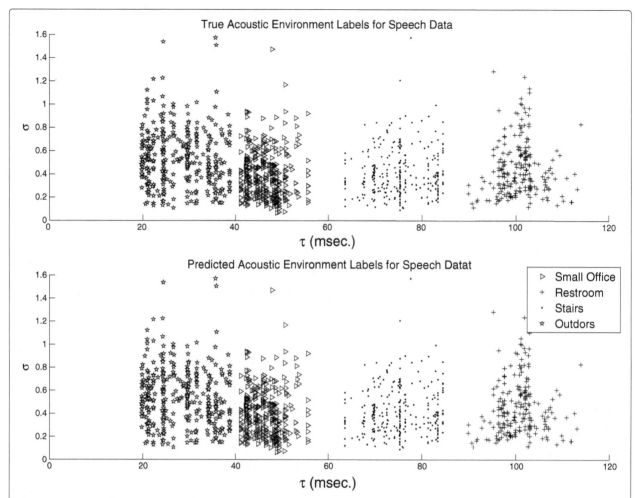

Figure 11 Shown in the top panel are the scatter plots of the estimated parameters from speech recordings with true acoustic environment labels and shown in the bottom panel are the scatter plots of the estimated parameters with predicted environment labels using DBSCAN-based clustering.

technique with five-fold cross-validation on training data. Shown in the Table 3 are the acoustic environment classification performance for Hong's method using speech dataset.

Shown in the Table 4 are the acoustic environment classification performance for the proposed method.

It can be observed from Table 3 Hong's learning-based method [18] achieves an average AEI accuracy around 94%; whereas the proposed scheme achieves perfect AEI accuracy, i.e., 100%, for the same dataset. This comparison indicates that the proposed scheme performs relatively better than the selected Hong's method. It is important to mention that the AEI results shown in Table 4 are obtained using manually selected decaying tails from speech recordings, whereas Hong's method does not require any user input for AEI. We have also observed

Table 3 Acoustic environment classification performance of the Hong's [18] scheme

True class	Predicted class label			
Label	Outdoors	Small of fice	Stairs	Restroom
Outdoors	88%	12%	0%	0%
Small of fice	10%	90%	0%	0%
Stairs	0%	0%	98%	2%
Restroom	0%	0%	1%	99%

Table 4 Classification performance of the proposed scheme

True class	Predicted class label			
Label	Outdoors	Small of fice	Stairs	Restroom
Outdoors	100%	0%	0%	0%
Small of fice	0%	100%	0%	0%
Stairs	0%	0%	100%	0%
Restroom	0%	0%	0%	100%

that when decaying tails are automatically selected using automatic tail selection method discussed in [42], AEI performance of the proposed method deteriorated around < 3%, which is still better than the Hong's method.

Conclusion

The acoustic environment identification (AEI) has a wide range of applications ranging from audio recording integrity authentication to real-time crime acoustic space localization/identification. For instance, consider a scenario where a police call center receives an emergency call from a victim being harassed or chased by an offender. Under such crime situations it is very common that the harassed persons are unable to provide any relevant information about their actual location. The acoustic signals in the audio recording can be used to determine the acoustic space (i.e. car, street, neighborhood, living room, bath room, bed room, kitchen, etc.) of the crime scene. Similarly, for gun shooting cases, the sound of the firearms in the recording can be used to obtain important information about the crime scene such as weapon type.

In this paper we proposed a statistical framework for automatic recording environment identification (AEI) using acoustic signature of an audio recording. Late reverberant tail is modeled using an exponentially damped uncorrelated noise sequence obeying Gaussian distribution, which is then used for acoustic signature estimation using maximum likelihood estimation framework. Similarity measure based on Euclidian distance is used to classify estimated reverberation parameters for AEI. Density-based clustering method DBSCAN is used for automatic AEI. Performance of the proposed method is evaluated using two datasets consisting of (i) hand-clap recordings and (ii) speech recordings. The audio recordings used for performance evaluation were collected in a diverse set of acoustic environments using commercial grade external and built-in microphones. Simulation results indicate that the proposed framework is efficient for most of the considered acoustic environments. We have also shown that accuracy and reliability of the proposed AEI depends on the microphone type (used to capture audio recording). Sensitivity of the proposed method to various frequency bands has also been evaluated. Performance comparison with Hong's statistical learning based method [18] indicates that the proposed method achieves relatively higher accuracy. We expect this approach to be a useful forensic tool when used in conjunction with other techniques that measure microphone characteristics, background noise, and compression artifacts.

Acknowledgments

This work was supported by the NPST program by the King Saud University under grant number 12-INF2634-02 and a grant from the National Science Foundation (CNS-1440929).

Author details

[1] Electrical and Computer Engineering Department, University of Michigan - Dearborn, Dearborn, MI 48128, USA. [2] Department of Electronics, Quaid-i-Azam University, Islamabad 45320, Pakistan.

References

1. Cellphone popcorn viral videos (2008). Avaliable on: http://www.wired.com/underwire/2008/06/cellphones-cant/
2. Iran 'Modifies' pictures of missile test (2008). Avaliable on: http://www.switched.com/2008/07/11/iran-photoshops-pictures-of-missile-test/
3. H Farid, A survey of image forgery detection. IEEE Signal Process. Mag. **2**(26), 16–25 (2009)
4. S Gupta, S Cho, CC Kuo, Current developments and future trends in audio authentication. IEEE Multimedia. **19**, 50–59 (2012)
5. C Grigoras, A Cooper, M Michalek, Forensic speech and audio analysis working group - best practice guidelines for ENF analysis in forensic authentication of digital evidence, in *European Network of Forensic Science Institutes*, (2009). http://www.cs.dartmouth.edu/~farid/dfd/index.php/publications/show/103
6. D Nicolalde, J Apolinario, Evaluating digital audio authenticity with spectral distances and ENF phase change, in *IEEE International Conference on Acoustics, Speech and Signal Processing (ICASSP'09)* (Taipei, Taiwan, 2009), pp. 1417–1420
7. C Grigoras, Applications of ENF criterion in forensic audio, video, computer and telecommunication analysis. Forensic Sci Int. **167**, 136–145 (2007)
8. C Grigoras, Application of ENF analysis method in authentication of digital audio and video recordings, in *Proceedings of the 123rd Convention of the Audio Engineering Society*, (New York, NY, 2007), p. 7273
9. H Hollien, *The Acoustics of Crime, The New Science of Forensic Phonetics*. (Plenum Publishing Corporation, New York, NY, ISBN-13: 978-0306434679, 1990)
10. H Hollien, *Forensic Voice Identification*. (Academic Press, Philadelphia, PA, ISBN-13: 978-0123526212, 2001)
11. D Garcia-Romero, C Espy-Wilson, Speech forensics: automatic acquisition device identification. J. Acoust. Soc. Am. **127**(3), 2044–2044 (2010)
12. D Garcia-Romero, C Espy-Wilson, Automatic acquisition device identification from speech recordings, in *Proceedings of the IEEE Int. Conference on Acoustics, Speech, and Signal Processing (ICASSP'10)* (Dallas TX, 2010), pp. 1806–1809
13. D Garcia-Romero, C Espy-Wilson, Automatic acquisition device identification from speech recordings. J. Acoustic Soc. Am. **124**(4), 2530–2530 (2009)
14. C Kraetzer, M Schott, J Dittmann, Unweighted fusion in microphone forensics using a decision tree and linear logistic regression models, in *Proceedings of the 11th ACM Multimedia and Security Workshop* (Princeton, NJ, 2009), pp. 49–56
15. C Kraetzer, A Oermann, J Dittmann, A Lang, Digital audio forensics: a first practical evaluation on microphone and environment classification, in *Proceedings of the 9th workshop on Multimedia and Security* (Dallas TX, 2007), pp. 63–74
16. A Oermann, A Lang, J Dittmann, Verifier-tuple for audio-forensic to determine speaker environment, in *Proceedings of the ACM Multimedia and Security Workshop 2005*, (New York, NY, 2005), pp. 57–62
17. R Buchholz, C Kraetzer, J Dittmann, Microphone classification using fourier coefficients, in *proceedings of 11th International Workshop on Information Hiding, Lecture Notes in Computer Science, Springer Berlin/Heidelberg Volume 5806/2009*, (Darmstadt, Germany, 2010), pp. 235–246
18. H Zhao, H Malik, Audio forensics using acoustic environment traces, in *Proceedings of the IEEE Statistical Signal Processing Workshop (SSP'12)* (MI Ann Arbor, 2012), pp. 373–376
19. H Malik, H Farid, Audio forensics from acoustic reverberation, in *Proceedings of the IEEE Int. Conference on Acoustics, Speech, and Signal Processing (ICASSP'10)* (Dallas, TX, 2010), pp. 1710–1713
20. S Ikram, H Malik, Digital audio forensics using background noise, in *Proceedings of IEEE Int. Conf. on Multimedia and Expo 2010* (Singapore, 2010), pp. 106–110

21. H Malik, H Zhao, Recording environment identification using acoustic reverberation, in *Proceedings of the IEEE Int. Conference on Acoustics, Speech, and Signal Processing (ICASSP'12)* (Kyoto, Japan, 2012), pp. 1833–1836

22. U Chaudhary, H Malik, Automatic recording environment identification using acoustic features, in *Proceedings of Audio Engineering Society 129th Convention 2010* (San Francisco, CA, 2010), p. 8254

23. H Malik, J Miller, Microphone identification using higher-order statistics, in *Proceedings of AES 46th Conference on Audio Forensics 2012* (Denver, CO, 2012), pp. 5–2

24. H Farid, *Detecting digital forgeries using bispectral analysis. Tech. rep., AIM-1657.* (Massachusetts Institute of Technology, 1999)

25. R Yang, Z Qu, J Huang, Detecting digital audio forgeries by checking frame offsets, in *Proceedings of the 10th ACM Workshop on Multimedia and Security (MM & Sec)'08,* (Oxford, UK, 2008), pp. 21–26

26. R Yang, Y Shi, J Huang, Defeating fake-quality, MP3, in *Proceedings of the 11th ACM Workshop on Multimedia and Security (MM & Sec)'09,* (Princeton, NJ, 2009), pp. 117–124

27. R Yang, Y Shi, J Huang, Detecting double compression of audio signal, in *Proceedings of SPIE Media Forensics and Security II 2010, Volume 7541,* (San Jose, CA, 2010)

28. A Cooper, Detecting butt-spliced edits in forensic digital audio recordings, in *Proceedings of Audio Engineering Society 39th Conf., Audio Forensics: Practices and Challenges,* (Hillerod, Denmark, 2010), pp. 1–1

29. S Hicsonmez, H Sencar, I Avcibas, Audio codec identification through payload sampling, in *IEEE Int. Workshop on Information Forensics and Security, (WIFS'11),* (Iguacu Falls, Brazil, 2011), pp. 1–6

30. C Grigoras, Statistical tools for multimedia forensics, in *Proceedings of Audio Engineering Society 39th Conf., Audio Forensics: Practices and Challenges,* (2010), pp. 27–32

31. H Zhao, H Malik, Audio recording location identification using acoustic environment signature. IEEE Trans. Inf. Forensics Secur. **8**(11), 1746–1759 (2013)

32. H Zhao, H Malik, Acoustic environment identification and its applications to audio forensics. IEEE Trans. Inf. Forensics Secur. **8**(11), 1746–1759 (2013)

33. R Ratnam, DL Jones, BC Wheeler, WD O'Brien Jr, CR Lansing, AS Feng, Blind estimation of reverberation time. J. Acoust. Soc. Am. **5**(114), 2877–2892 (2003)

34. H Lollmann, P Vary, Estimation of the reverberation time in noisy environments, in *Proceedings of International Workshop on Acoustic Echo and Noise Control* (Seattle, WA, 2008)

35. I Tashev, D Allred, Revereberation reduction for improved speech recognition, in *HSCMA* (Piscataway, NJ, 2005)

36. H Kuttruff, *Room Acoustics, 3rd edition.* (Elsevier, New York, 1991)

37. Y Lu, PC Loizou, A geometric approach to spectral subtraction. Speech Commun. **50**(6), 453–466 (2008)

38. M Schroeder, New method for measuring reverberation time. J. Acoust. Soc. Am. **3**(37), 409–412 (1965)

39. M Ester, HP Kriegel, J Sander, X Xu, A density-based algorithm for discovering clusters in large spatial databases with noise, in *Proceedings of Second International Conference on Knowledge Discovery and Data Mining (KDD-96),* (AAAI Press Portland, OR, 1996), pp. 226-231

40. PN Tan, M Steinback, V Kumar, *Introduction to Data Mining.* (Pearson Addison Wesley, Indianapolis, IN, ISBN-13: 978-0321321367, 2006)

41. C Chang, C Lin, Libsvm: a library for support vector machines (2012). [http://www.csie.ntu.edu.tw/cjin/libsvm]

42. H Malik, Audio recording location identification using acoustic environment signature. IEEE Trans. Inf. Forensics Secur. **8**(11), 1827–1837 (2013)

Security informatics research challenges for mitigating cyber friendly fire

Thomas E Carroll[1*], Frank L Greitzer[2] and Adam D Roberts[1]

Abstract

This paper addresses cognitive implications and research needs surrounding the problem of cyber friendly fire (FF). We define cyber FF as intentional offensive or defensive cyber/electronic actions intended to protect cyber systems against enemy forces or to attack enemy cyber systems, which unintentionally harms the mission effectiveness of friendly or neutral forces. We describe examples of cyber FF and discuss how it fits within a general conceptual framework for cyber security failures. Because it involves human failure, cyber FF may be considered to belong to a sub-class of cyber security failures characterized as unintentional insider threats. Cyber FF is closely related to combat friendly fire in that maintaining situation awareness (SA) is paramount to avoiding unintended consequences. Cyber SA concerns knowledge of a system's topology (connectedness and relationships of the nodes in a system), and critical knowledge elements such as the characteristics and vulnerabilities of the components that comprise the system and its nodes, the nature of the activities or work performed, and the available defensive and offensive countermeasures that may be applied to thwart network attacks. We describe a test bed designed to support empirical research on factors affecting cyber FF. Finally, we discuss mitigation strategies to combat cyber FF, including both training concepts and suggestions for decision aids and visualization approaches.

Introduction

Computer and network security are among the greatest challenges to maintaining effective information systems in public, private, and military organizations. In defining computer security, Landwehr [1] described three threats to Information systems: (1) the unauthorized disclosure of information, (2) the unauthorized modification of information, and (3) the unauthorized withholding of information (e.g., denial of service or DoS). Denning [2] referred to information warfare as a struggle between an offensive and a defensive player over an information resource, with outcomes that may affect availability or integrity of the resource. While much attention has been devoted to combating external threats such as worms, viruses, and DoS attacks, actions by insiders pose a significant threat to computer and network security. This insider threat, however, is not confined to "bad actors" that intentionally perform malicious acts against an information system. Just as unintended actions by friendly forces may impact

physical resources and security of friendly forces in military engagements, the actions of well-intentioned cyber defenders may result in harm to information resources and security. The focus of the present paper is on understanding and mitigating threats to intelligence and security informatics posed by cyber friendly fire.

While friendly fire (FF) is a familiar term, cyber FF is a relatively new concept for the information security community. An initial proposed definition of cyber FF, from Greitzer et al. [3], emphasizes three key characteristics:

- Cyber/electronic actions are performed intentionally,
- Actions are offensive or defensive,
- Actions result in inhibiting, damaging, or destroying friendly or neutral infrastructure or operations.

Andrews and Jabbour [4] provide the second:

The employment of friendly cyber defenses and weapons with the intent of either defending the blue cyber systems from attack from red or gray forces, or attacking the enemy to destroy or damage their people, equipment, or facilities, which results in unforeseen and unintentional damage to friendly cyber systems.

*Correspondence: Thomas.Carroll@pnnl.gov
[1] Pacific Northwest National Laboratory, P.O. Box 999, 99352 Richland, Washington, USA
Full list of author information is available at the end of the article

These definitions have many similarities: cyber FF is a consequence of offensive or defensive actions, the actions were performed with purpose, and the damage occurs to friendly or neutral cyber assets. Both definitions imply or overtly identify consequences of the action as unintentional. Furthermore, incidents that are born from accidents, negligence, carelessness, or malicious insiders are not friendly fire. From there, the definitions diverge. Greitzer et al. consider harm to both cyber systems and mission effectiveness, while Andrews and Jabbour focus only on systems. A recent Air Force chief scientist's report on technology horizons mentions the need for "a fundamental shift in emphases from 'cyber protection' to 'maintaining mission effectiveness' in the presence of cyber threats" [5]. Thus, mission effectiveness, and not only systems, is an appropriate focus for friendly fire incidents. In addition, we argue that cyber FF consequences may be felt well beyond cyber space [6]. Consider cyber physical systems that closely integrate physical, computational, and communication components to sense and effect changes in the real world. These systems are heavily employed in critical infrastructure to control and monitor processes. Adversely impacting the operation of these systems may result in large-scale power failures, toxic waste releases, or explosions that can have catastrophic consequences on the environment and life.

Given these considerations, a revised definition of cyber FF [6] is:

Cyber friendly fire is intentional offensive or defensive cyber/electronic actions intended to protect cyber systems against enemy forces or to attack enemy cyber systems, which unintentionally harms the mission effectiveness of friendly or neutral forces.

The following two examples illustrate cyber FF incidents that derive from defensive actions that unintentionally harm the organization's missions:

Illustrative Example 1. As a cost saving measure, Company XYZ has outsourced their corporate website and email to a hosting company. A hacker who has compromised and is now on the hosting company's infrastructure disrupts services by attempting to break into Company XYZ's resources. An administrator at Company XYZ notes the activity and quickly takes actions to protect company resources by blocking traffic from network addresses that are the source of the attack. As a direct consequence of these actions, Company XYZ employees lose access to their corporate website and email.

Illustrative Example 2. A current vulnerability to widely-deployed web serving software is being actively exploited. The vendor for the software has

issued a security patch. Company XYZ, who relies on the software as a critical component of their e-business platform, rapidly deploys the fix on their infrastructure. The patch introduces a problem into the software, causing transactions to fail and frustrating potential customers who are attempting to purchase the company's products.

The next examples illustrate defensive actions that unintentionally harm friendly assets, but do not constitute FF:

Illustrative Example 3. Company XYZ stores client personally identifiable information in a central database. The database is compromised by an adversary, who then actively engages in exfiltrating the sensitive data. Company XYZ administrators detect the extrusion of data and take action to stem the flow of data by severing the Internet connection until they can remediate and recover from the attack. The administrators fully comprehend that no client is able to access the company's services while disconnected, but the induced harm is far less than harm of continued data exfiltration.

Illustrative Example 4. A network administrator hastily writes a new firewall rule to block suspected malicious network traffic. He errors in composing the rule, but before he catches his mistake, he publishes the errant rule to production. The rule disrupts the operations of the company's web servers, which inhibits purchases, harming sales.

Cognitive approaches to cyber friendly fire research

The concept of cyber FF is similar in many respects to combat friendly fire [3], and like combat friendly fire, a fundamental cognitive issue lies in maintaining situation awareness (SA). In addition, cyber FF is closely related to some aspects of insider threat, especially when viewed within the broad framework of cyber security failures. This section provides some background and perspective on the cognitive foundations for cyber FF.

Cyber security failures and the unintentional insider threat

The domain of cyber security spans a broad spectrum of research and operational policies to address outsider cyber threats, insider threats, and other failures such as accidents or mishaps. Figure 1 provides a conceptual view of where cyber FF fits within this broader framework of cyber security failures.

Included in the framework is the familiar branch (shown in the black boxes) representing cyber attacks and exploits by malicious insiders, the latter representing the most highly studied insider threat research

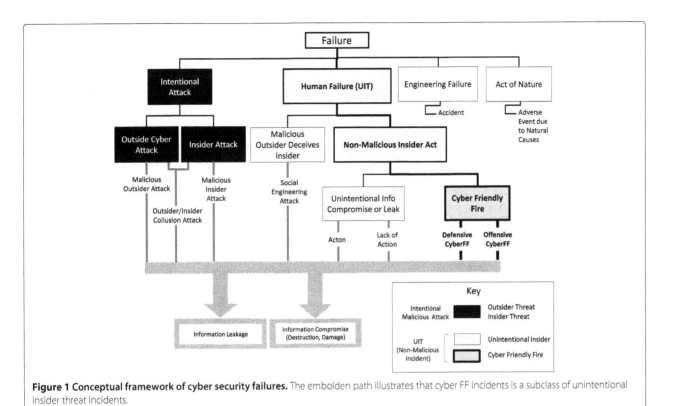

Figure 1 Conceptual framework of cyber security failures. The embolden path illustrates that cyber FF incidents is a subclass of unintentional insider threat incidents.

topic. Engineering failures that may be attributed to system/hardware/software vulnerabilities are represented in unfilled boxes. Of most interest for the present discussion are the branches of the hierarchy that relate to human failures that may be attributed to actions of insiders. The topic of unintentional insider threat (UIT) has been largely ignored until recent research by [7] that has provided a working definition of UIT:

An unintentional insider threat is (1) a current or former employee, contractor, or business partner (2) who has or had authorized access to an organization's network, system, or data and who, (3) through action or inaction without malicious intent, (4) unwittingly causes harm or substantially increases the probability of future serious harm to the confidentiality, integrity, or availability of the organization's resources or assets, including information, information systems, or financial systems

As pointed out in [7], UIT incidents share a common characteristic in which an organizational insider facilitates the actual or potential threat event. However, there is a distinction between the UIT cases that originate with actions performed by the internal, non-malicious member of the organization, versus UIT events that originate with an outside malicious agent (outside agent may recruit a malicious insider to participate in a collusion attack,

or outside agent may deceive a non-malicious insider to take actions that enable an attack). These various cases are depicted in separate branches of Figure 1. The research reported in [7] relates primarily to the light blue boxes in Figure 1, especially social engineering exploits, information leakage and information compromise. For these UIT cases, there are four main types of incidents, which are referred to in [7] as UIT threat vectors: (a) accidental disclosure (DISC), (b) attack enabled through use of malicious code such as malware or spyware (UIT-HACK), (c) improper disposal of physical records (PHYS), and (d) lost or stolen portable equipment (PORT).

We suggest that the cyber FF definition clearly fits within the above broad definition of UIT. However, UIT research to date has not considered the case of cyber friendly fire; for example, cyber friendly fire is not mentioned in [7] nor are any cases included in their discussion or taxonomic descriptions. This is not surprising since there is no repository of such cases to draw from. By the same token, our original work on cyber FF emphasized the differences between cyber FF and insider threat, maintaining that they are distinct cyber threats. This is true if one considers only malicious insider threats, but as we now argue, cyber FF should legitimately be considered as a special case of UIT.

Therefore, it is useful to examine UIT research and associated UIT mitigation strategies to identify possible approaches for addressing cyber FF. The area of greatest commonality between UIT and cyber FF is in human performance failures. As noted in [7]: "A major part of the UIT definition is the failure in human performance. While human errors can never be eliminated completely, they can be dramatically reduced through human error mitigation techniques. Such techniques should focus on system conditions that contributed to… the resulting errors and adverse outcomes." These remarks and associated suggestions for enhancing the decision maker's situation awareness and reducing human errors pertain just as strongly to cyber FF mitigation strategies as they do to UIT threat mitigation. For this reason, we may use the arguments and suggestions provided in [7] to provide high level organizational and human factors strategies for combating cyber FF.

Problems associated with organizational factors, such as work setting, management systems, and work planning, may impact employee performance. For example, job stress [8] and time pressure [9] negatively affect performance; heavy and prolonged workload can cause fatigue, which adversely affects performance [10]. Moreover, organizational factors that increase stress may in turn lead to human factors/cognitive impacts such as narrowing of attention (attending to fewer cues) [11,12] and reduced working memory capacity [13-15]. Cognitive factors associated with UIT susceptibility include attention deficits and poor situation awareness [16,17], lack of knowledge and memory failures [18-20], and high workload or stress that impairs performance or judgment [10,21]. Finally, external or organizational factors may affect an individual's emotional states, both normal and abnormal, which in turn can affect the human error rate and lead to UIT occurrences.

Cognitive systems perspective

The traditional approach in accounting for performance failures such as combat friendly fire/fratricide and the lesser-examined cyber FF is to regard these events as aberrations—failures of an individual or a system. As with most performance failures (errors), assigning blame to the individual(s) responsible for a cyber FF incident is not a sufficient mitigation strategy: there is typically no single cause of these errors that occur in the "fog of war". To understand the causes (and persistence) of cyber FF, it is necessary to consider the human factors, and it seems particularly relevant to address the problem from a cognitive systems/naturalistic decision making perspective (e.g., [22,23]). Thus, we should ask: *How did the individual perceive the situation? Why did the individual see the event that way? Why did the individual act in a way that turned out to be erroneous?*

A cognitive systems perspective leads us to consider research on SA and mental models. The SA scientific literature is substantial and no attempt is made here to report exhaustively on this topic. In short, the most accepted definition of SA is given by Endsley [16]: SA is the *perception* of the elements in the environment within a volume of time and space (Level 1 SA), the *comprehension* of their meaning (Level 2 SA), and the *projection* of their status into the future (Level 3 SA). Later work by McGuiness and Foy [24] added the *resolution* of the situation (Level 4 SA), which is deciding on a single course of action from a set of possible actions to achieve the required outcome to the situation.

SA depends on an accurate mental model [25]. Mental models have been described as well-defined, highly organized, and dynamic knowledge structures that are developed over time from experience (e.g., [26]). By representing organized "chunks" of information in the environment, mental models serve to reduce the information load that would otherwise overwhelm the ability of decision makers to attend, process, and integrate the large amount of information that is inherent in complex operational environments. Cues in the environment activate these mental models, which in turn guide the decision-making process. Appropriate and effective mental models enable experienced decision makers to correctly assess and interpret the current situation (Level 1 and Level 2 SA) as well as to select an appropriate action based on patterns (mental models) stored in their long-term memory [27].

Considering that a lack of SA is often a contributing factor to human errors in decision making, it is clear that a study of cyber FF should focus on factors that affect the cyber security officer's/system administrator's SA. What constitutes cyber SA?

Tadda and Salerno [28] mapped constructs of SA to more cyber-relevant network environments. A SA process model was constructed that has general applicability as well as specific relevance to cyber SA. The paper also suggested a set of metrics that may be useful in assessing the effectiveness of tools for supporting SA. Consistent with Tadda and Salerno's characterization of SA, our notion of cyber SA focuses on knowledge of a system's topology (connectedness and relationships of the nodes in a system), the characteristics and vulnerabilities of the components that comprise the system (and populate the nodes), the nature of the activities or work performed, and the available defensive (and offensive) countermeasures that may be applied to thwart network attacks. SA must also include an understanding of *why* each node exists, *what* it is doing, and the harm associated with disrupting that function as a response to attack. The trade-offs between accepting the ongoing risks of attack must be properly balanced against the damage done to the overall organization's mission, and the process of balancing those elements should motivate and guide the defender to select responses that minimize the total amount of harm.

More specifically, we may speculate on implications for cyber defense and cyber SA based on the notion of "digital SA"[a]. Given the complexity of cyber structures (particularly at the national scale of critical infrastructures such as the Internet or the electric power grid), it is necessary to take a "system of systems" perspective. In this view, there is never 100 percent certainty or complete knowledge, and it must be assumed that systems will be attacked (i.e., it is not possible to prevent all attacks with certainty). Thus, an appropriate cyber security strategy is *resiliency*, *i.e.*, the ability to anticipate, avoid, withstand, minimize, and recover from the effects of attacks (or for that matter, from the effects of natural disasters). To anticipate and avoid the effects of attacks or other adverse circumstances, a high level of SA is required. In particular, there is a critical need for operators to *anticipate* and *apply protocols* to avoid *cascade effects* in the network, thereby avoiding unintended consequences of defensive or offensive actions. The following types of knowledge (*critical knowledge units*) are required to invoke this anticipatory process:

- Knowledge of each enterprise, enterprise's network structure, and network component
- Knowledge of each computer system of interest in each enterprise/component
- Knowledge of each I/O port on each computer and how it is being used
- Record of traffic flow and volume on every I/O port
- Knowledge of the results of computing expected during the normal operation of each of the components in the network based on the current traffic flow and volume
- Knowledge of operating limits for each component, enabling the decision maker to project "faults" that may lead to shut-downs and cascade failures
- Knowledge of alternative corrective actions for such faults.

An additional consideration regarding the role of SA and cognitive models in cyber FF is the importance of Team SA: the degree to which each team member possesses the SA required for his or her responsibilities [16] and in particular, the extent to which team members possess the same SA on *shared* SA requirements [29,30]. Conflicts between goals and/or failures to coordinate goals among different members of the team are major underlying/root causes of many cyber FF incidents.

Given these considerations, a recommended approach is to capture the mental models that constitute the above types of knowledge, and then to tailor training approaches and tools to address associated cognitive factors.

Trends that make digital SA harder

Current trends challenge the abilities of individuals and teams to maintain digital SA; more particularly, changes in the roles and communications among cyber security professionals, as well as paradigmatic changes brought about by cloud and utility computing, have increased the difficulty of acquiring, understanding, and maintaining critical knowledge units necessary for effective defense and operation of the information and communications infrastructure. One trend is a growing separation between the roles of individuals responsible for cyber defense mission planning and the roles of individuals responsible for operating and defending the information and communications infrastructure. Missions are defined in terms of abstract resources and quality of service attributes, rather than actual systems and devices. For example, a mission in support of a business-to-business portal is defined in terms of number of concurrent users and user experience attributes, such as page response time. The requirements are translated into resource and location requirements (e.g., "ten web servers in the East Coast data center will be tasked"). In many cases, external third parties provide and operate the infrastructure. Under these circumstances, the mission planner may not be aware of what resources are allocated, the underlying network topology, or the geographical location of the resources. The operators and defenders are compartmentalized—and often isolated—from the mission planners, understand the resources and infrastructure but are unaware of the missions that the infrastructure is serving. Communication between mission planners, operators, and defenders is complicated—if it can occur at all (e.g., "need to know" restrictions)—because planners focus on the mission, while operators and defenders focus on resources. A second trend, offered by cloud and utility computing, employs dynamic resource allocations in response to changing demands and requirements. Dynamic resource management can quickly revise and relocate allocations, as well as change the purpose or criticality of systems—this changing operational landscape challenges the ability of cyber defenders to maintain an accurate accounting of system resources, assets, and vulnerabilities. The ability to acquire and maintain critical knowledge units that are needed to support effective SA for defending these types of enterprises exceeds the efforts of an individual or even a small team—it demands the support of an entire enterprise and its complement of third parties, an extremely difficult goal. Research is needed to flesh out requirements for information sharing and for automated tools, visualization support, and decision aids to ensure that defenders have the necessary knowledge and SA to protect their enterprise.

Mitigation approaches

In this section, we describe approaches and tools to mitigate cyber FF. Following research on organizational factors underlying human error, we first discuss organizational best practices (Section 'Organizational best practices') that are recommended to foster productive work environments, relieve stress, and reduce cognitive load. Next, in Section 'Training', we discuss relevant research on learning and cognition that may be applied to improve the effectiveness of training approaches in reducing the likelihood of cyber FF outcomes. In Section 'Effects of stress on performance', we discuss implications of this research for the design and development of tools to help enhance SA and decision making (for example, by promoting the acquisition and use of critical knowledge units elaborated in Section 'Cognitive systems perspective').

Organizational best practices

Following their discussion of possible organizational and human factors that contribute UIT, [7] described possible UIT mitigation strategies. Organizational best practices suggested in [7] that are most relevant to mitigating the incidence of cyber FF are those that help to reduce cognitive load, stress, and ultimately lead to lower risks of human errors:

- Review and improve management practices to align resources with tasks.
- Improve data flow by enhancing communication and maintaining accurate procedures.
- Maintain productive work setting by minimizing distractions.
- Implement effective work planning and control to reduce job pressure and manage time.
- Maintain employee readiness.
- Maintain staff values and attitudes that align with organizational mission and ethics.
- Implement security best practices throughout the organization.

Training

Conventional training, simulation-based training, and war gaming can each be utilized as parts of an integrated strategy to educate, raise awareness about cognitive biases and limitations, develop coping skills, and exercise skills designed to mitigate the environmental and situational factors that increase the likelihood of cyber FF. The goal of such training approaches is to provide the learner with experiences and instruction on cues, mental models, and actions that, with practice, will help establish a repertoire of well-learned concepts that can be executed under

stressful or in novel, uncertain conditions. To address training requirements and approaches to reduce cyber FF, it is useful to examine factors that impact cognition and human performance, particularly with regard to SA. Research has demonstrated a number of factors that impact performance; in the present context, effects of stress, overlearning, and issues relating to cognitive bias are particularly relevant. Greitzer and Andrews [31] review cognitive foundations and implications for training to mitigate combat friendly fire. Here we describe aspects of this research that are pertinent to training requirements for cyber FF.

Effects of stress on performance

Stress has strong effects on every aspect of cognition from attention to memory to judgment and decision making. Under stress, attention appears to channel or tunnel, reducing focus on peripheral information and centralizing focus on main tasks [32]. Originally observed by Kohn [33], this finding has been replicated often, first by seminal work from Easterbrook [34] demonstrating a restriction in the range of cues attended to under stress conditions (tunneling) and many other studies (see [35]). Research by Janis and Mann [36] suggests that peripheral stimuli are likely to be the first to be screened out or ignored, and that under stress, individuals may make decisions based on incomplete information. Similarly, Friedman and Mann [37] note that individuals under stress may fail to consider the full range of alternatives available, ignore long-term consequences, and make decisions based on oversimplifying assumptions—often referred to as heuristics. Research on the effects of stress on vigilance and sustained attention, particularly regarding effects of fatigue and sleep deprivation, shows that vigilance tends to be enhanced by moderate levels of arousal (stress), but sustained attention appears to decrease with fatigue and loss of sleep [38].

Overlearning

Several investigations have shown that tasks that are well-learned tend to be more resistant to the effects of stress than those that are less-well-learned. Extended practice leads to commitment of the knowledge to long term memory and easier retrieval, as well as automaticity and the proceduralization of tasks. These over-learned behaviors tend to require less attentional control and fewer mental resources [39,40], which facilitates enhanced performance and yields greater resistance to the negative effects of stress—i.e., overlearned behaviors are less likely to be forgotten and more easily recalled under stress. Van Overschelde and Healy [41] found that linking new facts learned under stress with preexisting knowledge sets helps to diminish the negative effect of stress. On the other hand, there is also a tendency for people under stress to "fall-back" to early-learned behavior [42-44]—even less efficient or more error prone behavior than more recently-learned strategies—possibly because the previously learned strategies or knowledge are more well-learned and more available than recently acquired knowledge.

Effects of stress on learning

Research suggests that high stress during instruction tends to degrade an individual's ability to learn. The research literature consistently demonstrates that elements of working memory are impaired, although the mechanisms behind these effects are poorly understood [35]. Stress appears to differentially affect working memory phases [45,46]. One instructional strategy to address stress effects is to use a phased approach with an initial learning phase under minimum stress, followed by gradual increasing exposure to stress more consistent with real-world conditions [31]. Similarly, stress inoculation training attempts to immunize an individual from reacting negatively to stress exposure. The method provides increasingly realistic pre-exposure to stress through training simulation; through successive approximations, the learner builds a sense of positive expectancy and outcome and a greater sense of mastery and confidence. This approach also helps to habituate the individual to anxiety-producing stimuli.

Team performance

Finally, it is important to consider group processes in this context. Research on team decision making indicates that effective teams are able to adapt and shift strategies under stress; therefore, team training procedures should teach teams to adapt to high stress conditions by improving their coordination strategies. Driskell, Salas, and Johnston [47] observed the common phenomenon of Easterbrook's attentional narrowing is also applicable to group processes. They demonstrated that stress can reduce group focus necessary to maintain proper coordination and SA—i.e., team members were more likely to shift to individualistic focus than maintaining a team focus.

Implications

Based on the brief foregoing discussion, we can summarize the challenges and needs for more effective training in general terms as well as more specifically focused on cyber defense and mitigation of cyber FF: training should incorporate stress situations and stress management techniques, development of realistic scenarios that systematically vary stress (e.g., as produced by varying cognitive workload through tempo of operations and density of attacks), and addressing challenges in preparing cyber warriors to overcome cognitive biases. The following factors should be included in designing training approaches:

- Training should provide extended practice, promoting more persistent memory and easier retrieval, and to encourage automaticity and the proceduralization of tasks to make them more resistant to the effects of stress.
- Training scenarios should include complex/dynamic threats that reflect the uncertainties of the real world—scenarios that force trainees to operate without perfect information and that incorporate surprises that challenge preconceptions or assumptions.
- Training scenarios should be designed to encourage the habit of testing one's assumptions to produce more adaptive, resilient cyber defense performance in the face of uncertainty.
- Training should enhance awareness of the effects of stress on cognitive performance—such as tunneling and flawed decision making strategies that ignore information—and coping strategies to moderate these effects. The training should be designed to make as explicit as possible what might happen to skill and knowledge under stress.
- Train awareness of cognitive biases and practices for managing these biases.
- Team training should focus on strategies for maintaining group cohesion and coordination, mitigating the tendency for team members to revert to an individual perspective and lose shared SA.
- Training should exercise the execution of cognitive tasks by both individuals and groups.

Tools

A key objective in the study of factors influencing cyber FF and mitigation strategies is to identify features of decision support tools with potential to reduce the occurrence of cyber FF. Our review of relevant research, as summarized in the foregoing discussion, strongly suggests that tools and visualizations to improve cyber SA are key ingredients of desired solutions. Important functions should include decision aids to support memory limitations, to counteract the negative effects of stress on performance (e.g., perceptual narrowing), and to avoid the negative consequences of cognitive biases on decisions.

Supporting memory limitations that reduce situation awareness

As stated earlier, support for the cyber analyst should strive to encourage proactive decision making processes that anticipate and apply protocols to avoid cascade effects in the network, and concurrently avoid unintended consequences of defensive or offensive actions. We identified a set of critical knowledge units required for enhanced SA and anticipatory decision making, including knowledge of components of the network, details of each computer system, I/O ports, traffic flow/volumes, and ability to project impacts of possible courses of action. Decision aids and/or visualization support is needed to alleviate memory lapses and limitations by providing readily accessible information on network topology and component assets/vulnerabilities—typically referred to as external representations or external memory by researchers advocating the study of "distributed cognition" in the broader context of the social and physical environment that must be interwoven with the decision maker's internal representations (also referred to as "situated cognition" [48,49]). Thus, a decision aid that displays critical knowledge units for components that are being considered for application of remedial actions may help to avoid cyber FF effects that impair system effectiveness. This concept is similar to what Tadda and Salerno [28] refer to as "Knowledge of Us" (data relevant to the importance of assets or capabilities of the enterprise)—hence, a process that identifies to the decision maker whether there is a potential or current impact to capabilities or assets used to perform a mission. Similarly, a tool may be envisioned that helps the decision maker understand and prioritize risks that may be computed for various possible alternative actions.

Mitigating cognitive biases

Gestalt psychology tells us that we tend to see what we expect to see. Expectancy effects can lead to such selective perception as well as biased decisions or responses to situations in the form of other cognitive biases like confirmation bias (the tendency to search for or interpret information in a way that confirms one's preconceptions) or irrational escalation (the tendency to make irrational decisions based upon rational decisions in the past). The impact of cognitive biases on decision performance—particularly response selection—is to foster decisions by individuals and teams that are based on prejudices or expectations that they have gained from information learned before they are in the response situation. Decision aids and visualizations are needed that help to reduce confirmation bias, irrational escalation, and other forms of impaired decision making. One possible form of decision support designed to counteract these biases is the use of the analysis of competing hypotheses (e.g., [50]). Other concepts that may serve as sources of ideas and strategies for the design of decision aids may be derived from problem solving techniques discussed by Jones in The Thinker's Toolkit [51].

Recommendations

Based on the foregoing discussion, we summarize the challenges and needs for more effective training and

decision support to improve cyber defense and mitigate cyber FF:

- Training recommendations

  - Develop realistic cyber war gaming scenarios that systematically vary stress (e.g., as produced by varying cognitive workload through tempo of operations and density of attacks)
  - Incorporate stress management techniques
  - Address challenges in preparing cyber warriors to overcome cognitive biases
  - Conduct experiments to assess effectiveness of different training approaches

- Information analysis and decision support recommendations

  - Conduct experiments to help identify effective features of decision support and information visualization tools. Will conventional training approaches to improve analytic process (e.g., analysis of alternative hypotheses, other decision making tools and strategies) be effective in the cyber domain? Our intuition suggests that the answer is "no" because of the massive data, extreme time constraints requiring near real-time responses, and the largely data-driven nature of the problem. New types of data preprocessing (triage) and visualization solutions will likely be needed to improve SA.
  - Perform cognitive engineering research to develop prospective information analysis and visual analytics solutions to enhance SA and decrease cyber FF.

Research test bed and preliminary studies

As concluded in Section 'Mitigation approaches', more research is needed to enhance our understanding of the factors underlying cyber FF and to explore and validate possible mitigation approaches and tools. Cognitive engineering research is needed to focus on determinants of SA deficiencies and human errors in working with tools aimed to support cyber security analyst perception and decision making processes.

Research in cyber FF should be founded upon scientific principles and empirical studies in human factors and cognitive engineering, such as seminal human factors work on SA by Endsley [16] and later by Tadda and Salerno [28], who mapped constructs of SA to more cyber-relevant network environments. The present paper has sought to define research questions and to lay a foundation for empirical investigations of factors contributing to the cyber FF phenomenon and impacts on performance of proposed mitigations that can be in the form of training/awareness or decision aids.

Along these lines, we conducted a preliminary study at PNNL to help address these research questions using the simulation capabilities of PNNL's Unclassified Security Test Range test bed. The purpose of the pilot study was to demonstrate feasibility of an experimental methodology to assess effectiveness of decision aids and visualizations for cyber security analysis. Because the experiment was limited to a very small number of participants, interpretation of results was speculative, but the design and implementation of the testbed itself serve to advance the research goals described here.

Unclassified security test range

The Unclassified Security Test Range consists of a combination of virtual and physical devices for testing, simulation, and evaluation. This closed network offers services found on a production network without the costs associated with duplicating a real environment. The idea is to duplicate enough of a real network to allow the test bed to appear realistic. In order to achieve this lofty goal, the virtual and physical environment is flexible and can be customized to represent different configurations based on requirements. With the proper configuration and orchestration of components, it is possible to create simulated environments that model Fortune 500 enterprises, and application and infrastructure service providers. The test range also has a room that is mocked up as an advanced "network operation center". Besides workstations provisioned with several large monitors, there were two large over head displays, allowing the projection of visualization such as network health and status. Observers can watch subjects from a vantage point, which is partially obscured from the participants view.

The test range creates virtual machines for user workstations and servers that interconnected using real networking switches, routers, and firewalls. Every virtual machine has at least two network interfaces, one for management and observation, and one or more for experiment network traffic. The test range features a unique simulation capability called ANTS. This software package simulates user behaviors: agents that are deployed on the virtual machines network have models or profiles of operator's use of real applications such as Microsoft Word, Outlook, and Internet Explorer. Application usage then generates the traffic found in normal networks. The advantage of this approach over others is its ability to create higher fidelity.

The test range has a network monitoring feature that provides the capability to monitor, log, and analyze all the traffic flowing through the network. Additionally, remote researchers and observers are provided a capability to view into the range.

Procedure

The test bed was configured to appear as an e-commerce website, a payment processor, and an "Internet" to ferret communication between e-commerce site and payment processor, and customers and malcontents to the e-commerce site. Participants were tasked with the role of network and security operations and were responsible for maintaining the operation of the e-commerce site. They were confronted with two types of events that interfered with customers assessing the website. The first event type, which manifested several times during the scenario, was a fault in the order-processing system that triggered the abnormal execution termination of the the order system. The second event was a Denial-of-Service (DoS) that originated from the payment processor partner. While a partner attacking appears exceptional, there have been cases in which attackers have exploited partner relationships and used compromised partners as stepping stones to further their compromise towards reaching their goals. The DoS attack consumed large quantities of resources, slowing customer access. Both events appear, at least at first glance, to be similar.

Participants were furnished with four widely available tools. The first is Big Brother (BB) system and network monitor. BB was configured to monitor various aspects of the system and network object attributes (e.g., CPU utilization, data rate, system event logs) and alerts when these object attributes exceed defined thresholds. BB supplies alert notifications in an easily understood panel. Figure 2 is a screen shot of the simulation's Big Brother network overview that is displaying "all conditions clear". The single alert informs the administrator that the system is unable to download updated malware/virus signatures. By design, the Test Range is isolated and constituent systems are unable to communicate with systems on the Internet. The second tool for monitoring is the Cisco ASA's ASDM panel (shown in Figure 3). The overview panel displays current network conditions, such as data rate and connection volume. Other ASDM panels display detailed network traffic traces and assist in traffic inspection. Half the participants was also furnished with EtherApe, a network monitor that displays network activity graphically. As depicted in Figure 4, the interface colorfully renders communication between systems by drawing a link between systems. The width of the link changes in proportion to the volume of traffic, i.e., the link width expands as traffic increases.

Participants

Participants were four PNNL network operations staff, solicited via email as study volunteers. The invitation

Figure 2 The Big Brother (BB) network and system monitor overview page. Each row is a network resource; each column is an indicator of a test result of the resource status. A green orb indicates healthy, while a red orb denotes a failed test.

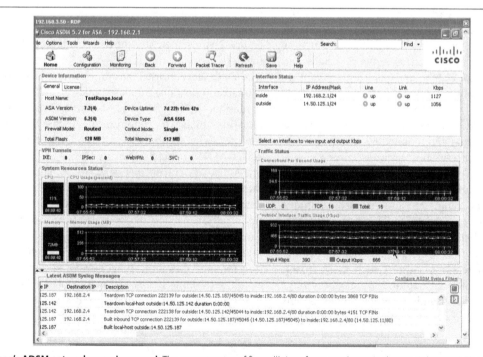

Figure 3 Cisco's ADSM network overview panel. The current status of firewall's interfaces are shown in the top right panel. The middle panels graph in real time resource utilization, connection rate, and data rate. Lastly, the bottom panel shows the device's system log messages.

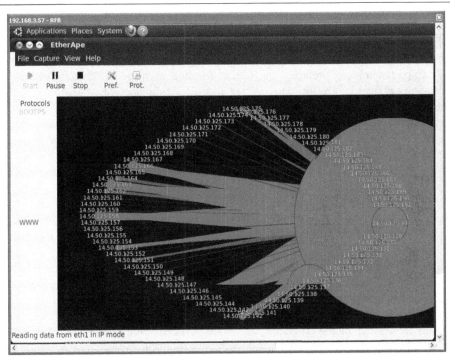

Figure 4 EtherApe network visualization tool. Rays indicate communicating systems; ray widths is proportional to data rates.

stated that they were invited to participate in several simulated scenarios as part of a study on network monitoring and security. The participants originate from different parts of PNNL and perform different job functions. Summarizing their jobs, two participants provide IT support for cyber security and national security research and development groups, another participant provides IT support for PNNL's various business applications, and the last performs a variety of tasks in support of general scientific computing. While every participant understood the concepts and skills necessary in performing the tasks at hand, only one had previous experience in operating in a small business climate as illustrated by the pilot study scenario. Examining the remaining three participants, two can be ranked as having intermediate level of experience and the last having little experience. All participants were familiar with the use of Big Brother network/system monitoring tool; in fact, all use it daily as part of their jobs. The experienced participant had some minimal level of exposure to the Cisco ASA and its ASDM overview page. No other participant had any prior experience. Finally, none of the participants had any exposure to EtherApe.

All participants were provided with BB and Cisco ASDM monitoring tools. Two participants were randomly selected (here identified as Participant 2 and Participant 4) and were furnished with EtherApe, which represented the "enhanced visualization" condition.

Results

To review, all participants had ready access to BB and Cisco ASDM monitoring tools; two were also provided with EtherApe as an additional visualization aid.

Participant 1 (without EtherApe) From our perch, it was not evident if the participant was choosing to use either Big Brother or the ASDM panel. During the first phase of the exercise, he relied on the alerts provided by the help desk before remediating problems. Due to a technical difficulty, the attack never reached a point to harm the ordering system. He did note the attack on the ASDM general overview panel and chose to ignore it.

Participant 2 (with EtherApe) This participant was hyper vigilant. Unfortunately, his choices and actions lead to cyber friendly fire. Nevertheless, his actions constitute cyber FF. He relied heavily on the ASDM overview display and noted problems nearly instantaneously. During the first phase, he reacted to the information by disabling the external interface of the ASA firewall device—in effect he chose to cut his network off from the Internet, thus committing textbook definition of cyber friendly fire. After we witnessed the participant act in this way twice, we informed the participant of the consequences. Unfortunately this was to no avail, as the participant disabled the external interface and was attempting to disable the internal interface during the DoS attack. If successful, he would no longer have remote access to administer the firewall.

Participant 3 (without EtherApe) The least experienced of the four participants, he preferred ASDM overview display over the Big Brother status display. He was methodical. In the first phase, he gathered available information before deciding on the course of restarting the ordering system. The deliberate approach was slow. While the participants 1 and 2 took under two minutes to note and correct the problem, it took him at least two minutes before taking corrective action. Four minutes passed before he realized the advent of the DoS attack and it took another three minutes before he decided to take any action.

Participant 4 (with Etherape) He was the most experienced of all the participants. While not part of his daily job function, he has served as a network operator in a part time job. During the exercise he was leaning back in his chair watching the EtherApe visualization or hunched over staring at the ASDM overview display. His response was rapid and in most cases remediated problems in under thirty seconds. Not once did we need to announce the occurrence of an event. He noted the DoS attack immediately from both the EtherApe and ASDM displays. He performed a packet trace and identified the source as the payment processor and that the attacking system was a critical component in processing payment transactions. He recognized that making changes to the firewall may cause harm later on; he would prefer contacting the partner first.

Discussion

It is not possible to draw generalizations from the small number of participants, particularly because of technical difficulties that affected performance of Participant 1 (and perhaps also because of existence of doubts about whether or not Participant 2 understood the instructions sufficiently to follow directions). Focus on results obtained for Participants 3 and 4 yields precious little data upon which to draw conclusions.

At a shallow level of analysis, we note that Participant 4 (who received the enhanced visualization condition) performed much better than Participant 3 (who did not receive the enhanced visualization condition). Besides the obvious conclusion that the experimental manipulation was effective, there are other possible explanations due to uncontrolled confounding factors: For example, Participant 4 had more experience than Participant 3. Because of time and budget constraints, we were unable to conduct a somewhat larger pilot study that could incorporate appropriate controls (such as a pretest-post-test design).

While we did not identify objectives related to training, some observations from the pilot study suggest training implications. Even when informed of the consequences of his choices, Participant 2 continued to engage in actions that resulted in cyber FF. This could have been a result of lack of experience with network and firewall operations, or possibly he missed the "message" communicated during the orientation session about the importance of maintaining business operations; or perhaps he believed that he was, in fact, taking the best course of action. In any case, this observation suggests that training approaches should be considered.

Because this was a pilot study, limitations and difficulties were not unexpected. Nevertheless, we still may conclude that the results at least suggest that one can demonstrate cyber FF performance differences that possibly can be related to the independent variable studied (visualization support); and perhaps more importantly for the present purposes, the Unclassified Cyber Test Range that we utilized at PNNL appears to be capable of supporting experimental studies of cyber FF. This point is important going forward, since it reinforces the recommended research strategy of conducting more controlled scientific studies of cyber SA and cyber FF in a high fidelity simulated environment.

Conclusions and recommendations that serve to inform future design of such experimental studies are:

- Access to a larger pool of participants is needed to allow for the possibility of statistically significant results. The observational methods employed, interview procedures, and the performance measures collected would readily apply to an expanded study with more participants.
- Participants should have a more relevant background and experience with the type of enterprise and network represented in the scenario. Participants should be fluent in the technical skills required to perform necessary actions. Experience ought to be controlled as a factor in the study.

Much more specific recommendations about the design and human factors of the Cyber Test Range were derived from observing the participants and obtaining feedback from the participants including deficiencies in software packages, monitor placement, choice of keyboard and mice, and the height of the overhead displays.

Conclusions and future direction

Cyber FF is one class of cyber security failures. Since it is based in human failure, we have argued that cyber FF belongs to a sub-class of cyber security failures that is characterized by unintentional insider threats. There is a tendency to regard such failures as aberrations that can be fixed with technological advances, such as technology solutions to improve SA, to increase accuracy in identifying targets, or to improve the precision of defensive or offensive actions. We have argued that a sound mitigation strategy, whether or not incorporating technological advancements, must be focused on identifying and accommodating the realities of human performance. Contributing factors attributed to cyber FF must be empirically studied along with the benefits of training, awareness, and tools meant to reduce the number and severity of incidents. To this end, we have described a preliminary study that we conducted that demonstrates cyber FF research in a controlled, isolated testbed environment. While results where speculative due to the small number of participants, it does demonstrate that experimentation in a testbed can advance the research goals described within.

Related research is ongoing: An advanced concept that is currently being pursued by PNNL cyber security research programs is the notion of Asymmetric Resilient Cybersecurity (ARC)[b], which is characterized by goals of standing up resilient and robust cyber infrastructure and network architectures that present a "moving target" to potential attackers in an attempt to overcome and hopefully reverse the current asymmetric state of affairs that favors the adversary. The goals and challenges of this program align with issues that we have articulated in our research on cyber FF, particularly in ways that can be seen as amplifying the cyber FF challenge: e.g., maintaining enterprise-wide SA when the network, systems, and components "move" continuously and dynamically. Moreover, ongoing research at PNNL seeks to develop and assess visualization and decision support tools that address cognitive limitations. Current research is developing Kritikos, a network resource identification, resource dependency discovery, and criticality assessment tool. Dependencies are identified by Self-Organizing Maps (SOM), a neural network machine learning algorithm, discovering repeated spatio-temporal patterns in IP Information Flow eXport (IPFIX) record sets. Patterns in time and space indicate usage; repeated observations of a pattern suggest a dependent relationship. The patterns allow a dependency-based network model to be generated. This model is a (disconnected) graph where vertices are resources and edges indicate dependent relationships. A business process/operations model annotated with indication of network resources and business criticality, assumptions not unusual for today's enterprises, can be fused with the network model, illuminating indirect resources. Furthermore, the relationship between business process and network resources can be used to assess the criticality of resources in terms of business objectives and requirements. Cyber FF research also directly meets essential needs of DOE cyber security as well as cyber

security programs within the DoD and the intelligence community.

The fundamental research goal is to develop a scientific understanding of the behavioral implications of cyber FF. Research is needed to extend our current understanding of cyber SA and to develop metrics and measures for cyber FF. The principal scientific research questions include: What are root causes of cyber FF? What are possible mitigating solutions, both human factors and technical/automated? We have examined relevant research and cognitive theory, and we have taken some initial steps toward investigating these research questions in empirical laboratory studies using realistic test scenarios in a cyber SA/FF testbed facility [52]. Continued empirical research is required to investigate the phenomenon and relevant contributing factors as well as mitigation strategies. A major objective should be to investigate approaches to and assessment of effectiveness of cyber FF mitigation strategies, such as training and decision aids/tools. Such research promises to advance the general field of cyber SA and inform other ongoing cyber security research. In addition, it is hoped that this research will facilitate the design and prototyping of automated or semi-automated systems (or decision aids) to increase cyber SA and eliminate or decrease cyber FF; this provides a foundation for development of commercial products that enhance system effectiveness and resiliency.

Endnotes

[a] The following discussion is based in part on an essay on situation awareness in Wikipedia: http://en.wikipedia.org/wiki/Situation_awareness.

[b] Information about PNNL's Asymmetric Resilient Cybersecurity (ARC) Lab Direct Research & Development Initiative can be found at: http://cybersecurity.pnnl.gov/arc.stm.

Acknowledgment

Portions of the research were also funded by PNNL's Asymmetric Resilient Cybersecurity (ARC) Laboratory Research & Development Initiative. The views expressed in this report are the opinions of the Authors, and do not represent official positions of the Pacific Northwest National Laboratory, the Department of Energy, or the Air Force Research Laboratory.

Author details

[1] Pacific Northwest National Laboratory, P.O. Box 999, 99352 Richland, Washington, USA. [2] PsyberAnalytix LLC, 99352 Richland, Washington, USA.

References

1. CE Landwehr, Formal models for computer security. ACM Comput. Surv. **13**(3), 247–278 (1981)
2. DE Denning, *Information Warfare and Security*. (ACM Press, New York, 1999)

3. FL Greitzer, SL Clements, TE Carroll, JD Fluckiger, Towards a research agenda for cyber friendly fire. Technical Report PNNL-18995, Pacific Northwest National Laboratory (2009)

4. DH Andrews, KT Jabbour, Mitigating cyber friendly fire: a sub-category of cyber mishaps. High Front. **7**(3), 5–8 (2011)

5. United States Air Force Chief Scientist (AF/ST), Report on Technology Horizons: A Vision for Air Force Science & Technology During 2010–2030 (2010). http://www.au.af.mil/au/awc/awcgate/af/tech_horizons_vol-1_may2010.pdf

6. FL Greitzer, TE Carroll, AD Roberts, Cyber friendly fire: Research challenges for security informatics, in *Proc. of the IEEE International Conference on Intelligence and Security Informatics (ISI 2013)* (IEEE, Piscataway, NJ, 2013), pp. 94–99

7. FL Greitzer, J Strozer, S Cohen, J Bergey, J Cowley, A Moore, D Mundie, Unintentional insider threat: contributing factors, observables, and mitigation strategies, in *Proc. of the 47th Hawai'i International Conference on System Sciences (HICCS-47)* (IEEE, Piscataway, NJ, 2014)

8. S Leka, A Griffiths, T Cox, *Work Organization & Stress: Systematic Problem Approaches for Employers, Managers and Trade Union Representatives,* Protecting Workers' Health Series No. 3. (World Health Organization, 2004). http://www.who.int/occupational_health/publications/pwh3rev.pdf, Accessed 7 Dec 2013

9. P Lehner, M-M Seyed-Solorforough, MF O'Connor, S Sak, T Mullin, Cognitive biases and time stress in team decision making. **27**(5), 698–703 (1997)

10. E Soetens, J Hueting, F Wauters, Traces of fatigue in an attention task. Bull. Psychonomic Soc. **30**(2), 97–100 (1992)

11. BK Houston, Noise, task difficulty, and Stroop color-word performance. J. Exp. Psychol. **82**(2), 403–404 (1969)

12. AF Stokes, K Kite, *Flight Stress: Stress, Fatigue, and Performance in Aviation.* (Gower Technical, Aldershot, 1994)

13. DR Davies, R Parasuraman, *The Psychology of Vigilance.* (Academic Press, London, 1982)

14. GRJ Hockey, Changes in operator efficiency as a function of environmental stress, fatigue and circadian rhythms, in *Handbook of Perception and Performance,* ed. by K Boff, L Kaufman, and JP Thomas, vol. 2 (Wiley, New York, 1986), pp. 1–44

15. PL Wachtel, Anxiety, attention, and coping with threat. J. Abnorm. Psychol. **73**(2), 137–143 (1968)

16. MR Endsley, Towards a theory of situation awareness in dynamic systems. Hum. Factors. **37**(1), 32–64 (1995)

17. MD Rodgers, RH Mogfor, B Strauch, Post hoc assessment of situation awareness in air traffic control incidents and major aircraft accidents, in *Situation Awareness Analysis and Measurement,* ed. by MR Endsley, DJ Garland (Lawrenece Erlbaum Associates, Mahway, 2000). pp. 73–112

18. R Dhamija, JD Tygar, M Hearst, Why phishing works, in *Proc. of the SIGCHI Conference on Human Factors in Computer Systems (CHI '06)* (ACM, New York, 2006), pp. 581–590

19. D Sharek, C Swofford, M Wogalter, Failure to recognize fake Internet popup warning messages, in *Proc. of the Human Factors and Ergonomics Society 52nd Annual Meeting* (Human Factors and Ergonomics Society, Santa Monica, CA, 2008), pp. 557–560

20. J-P Erkkilä, Why we fall for phishing, in *Proc. of the SIGCHI Conference on Human Factors in Computer Systems (CHI '11)* (ACM, New York, 2011)

21. SG Hart, CD Wickens, Workload assessment and predictions, in *MANPRINT: An Approach to Systems Integration,* ed. by HR Booher (Van Nostrand Reihold, New York, 1990), pp. 257–296

22. S Dekker, M Lützhöft, Correspondence, cognition and sensemaking: a radical empiricist view of situation awareness, in *A Cognitive Approach to Situation Awareness: Theory and Application,* ed. by Banbury S, Tremblay S (Ashgate, Burlington, 2004), pp. 22–41

23. KE Weick, *Sensemaking in Organizations,* Foundations for Organiztional Science. (SAGE Publications, Thousand Oaks, 1995)

24. B McGuiness, L Foy, A subjective measure of SA: the crew awareness rating scale (CARS), in *Proc. of the Human Performance, Situation Awareness and Automation Conference* (SA Technologies, Marietta, GA, 2000)

25. N Sarter, D Woods, Situation awareness: a critical ill-defined phenomenon. Int. J. Aviat. Psychol. **1**(1), 45–57 (1991)

26. SWJ Kozlowski, Training and developing adaptive teams: Theory, principles, and research, in *Making Decisions Under Stress: Implications for Individual and Team Training,* ed. by JA Cannon-Bowers, E Salas (America Psychological Association, Washington, DC, 1988)

27. D Serfaty, J MacMillan, EE Entin, EB Entin, The decision-making expertise of battle commanders, in *Naturalistic Decision-Making,* ed. by CE Zsambok, G Klein (Lawrence Erlbaum, New York, 1997)

28. GP Tadda, JS Salerno, Overview of cyber situation awareness, in *Cyber Situational Awareness: Issues and Research,* ed. by S Jajodia, P Liu, V Swarup, and C Wang (Springer, New York, 2010), pp. 15–35

29. MR Endsley, WM Jones, Situation awareness, information dominance, & information warfare. Technical Report AL/CF-TR-1997-0156, US Air Force Armstrong Laboratory (1997). http://www.dtic.mil/dtic/tr/fulltext/u2/a347166.pdf

30. MR Endsley, WM Jones, A model of inter- and intrateam situation awareness: implications for design, training, and measurement, in *New Trends in Cooperative Activities: Understanding System Dynamics in Complex Environments,* ed. by M McNeese, E Salas, and M Endsley (Human Factors and Ergonomics Society, Santa Monica, 2001)

31. FL Greitzer, DH Andrews, Training strategies to mitigate expectancy-induced response bias in combat identification: a research agenda, in *Human Factors Issues in Combat Identification,* ed. by DH Andrews, RP Herz, and MB Wolf (Ashgate, Farnham, UK, 2010)

32. J Kavanagh, Stress and performance: a review of the literature and its applicability to the military. Technical Report TR-192, RAND (2005)

33. H Kohn, Effects of variations of intensity of experimentally induced stress situations upon certain aspects of perception and performance. J. Genet. Psychol. **85**, 289–304 (1954)

34. JA Easterbrook, The effect of emotion on cue utilization and the organization of behavior. Psychol. Rev. **66**, 183–201 (1959)

35. MA Staal, Stress, cognition, and human performance: a literature review and conceptual framework. Technical Report NASA/TM-2004-212824, National Aeronautics and Space Administration (2004)

36. IL Janis, L Mann, *Decision Making.* (The Free Press, New York, 1977)

37. IA Friedman, L Mann, Coping patterns in adolescent decision-making: an Israeli-Australian comparison. J. Adolesc. **16**, 187–199 (1993)

38. DR Davies, GS Tune, *Human Vigilance Performance.* (Staples Press, London, 1970)

39. J Leavitt, Cognitive demands of skating and stick handling in ice hockey. Can. J. Appl. Sport. Sci. **4**, 46–55 (1979)

40. MD Smith, CJ Chamberlin, Effect of adding cognitively demanding tasks on soccer skill performance. Percept. Mot. Skill. **75**, 955–961 (1992)

41. JP Van Overschelde, AF Healy, Learning of nondomain facts in high- and low-knowledge domains. J. Exp. Psychol. Learn. Mem. Cognit. **27**, 1160–1171 (2001)

42. M Allnutt, Human factors: Basic principles, in *Pilot Error,* ed. by R Hurst, LR Hurst (Aronson, New York, 1982), pp. 1–22

43. RP Barthol, ND Ku, Regression under stress to first learned behavior. J. Abnorm. Soc. Psychol. **59**(1), 134–136 (1959)

44. RB Zajonc, Social facilitation. Science. **149**, 269–274 (1965)

45. S Kuhlmann, M Piel, OT Wolf, Impaired memory retrieval after psychosocial stress in healthy young men. J. Neurosci. **25**(11), 2977–2982 (2005)

46. S Kuhlmann, OT Wolf, Arousal and cortisol interact in modulating memory consolidation in healthy yound men. Behav. Neurosci. **120**(1), 217–223 (2006)

47. JE Driskell, E Salas, J Jonston, Does stress lead to a loss of team perspective? Group Dynam.: Theor. Res. Pract. **3**, 291–302 (1999)

48. DA Norman, *The Psychology of Everyday Things.* (Basic Books, New York, 1988)

49. J Hollan, E Hutchins, D Kirsh, Distributed cognition: toward a new foundation for human-computer interaction research. ACM Trans. Comput. Hum. Interact. **7**(2), 174–196 (2000)

50. RJ Heuer Jr, Analysis of competing hypotheses, in *Psychology of Intelligence Analysis* (Center for the Study of Intelligence, Central Intelligence Agency, Washington, D.C., 1999)

51. MD Jones, *The Thinker's Toolkit: Fourteen Powerful Techniques for Problem Solving.* (Three Rivers Press, New York, 1998)

52. FL Greitzer, TE Carroll, AD Roberts, Cyber friendly fire. Technical Report PNNL-20821, Pacific Northwest National Laboratory (2011)

Evasion-resistant network scan detection

Richard E Harang[1*] and Peter Mell[2]

Abstract

Popular network scan detection algorithms operate through evaluating external sources for unusual connection patterns and traffic rates. Research has revealed evasive tactics that enable full circumvention of existing approaches (specifically the widely cited Threshold Random Walk algorithm). To prevent use of these circumvention techniques, we propose a novel approach to network scan detection that evaluates the behavior of internal network nodes, and combine it with other established techniques of scan detection. By itself, our algorithm is an efficient, protocol-agnostic, completely unsupervised method that requires no a priori knowledge of the network being defended beyond which hosts are internal and which hosts are external to the network, and is capable of detecting network scanning attempts regardless of the rate of the scan (working even with connectionless protocols). We demonstrate the effectiveness of our method on both live data from an enterprise-scale network and on simulated scan data, finding a false positive rate of just 0.000034% with respect to the number of inbound flows. When combined with both Threshold Random Walk and simple rate-limiting detection, we achieve an overall detection rate of 94.44%.

Keywords: Intrusion detection systems; Network scanning; Algorithms; Experimentation; Measurement; Security

Introduction

Network scanning – an attempt to enumerate and/or fingerprint hosts and services on some victim network – is a common precursor to an attack, and often has utility in post-incident forensics. As discussed in [1], precisely quantifying what a 'scan' is can be difficult. This is particularly true when one considers parallelized scans (e.g. from a botnet), extremely slow scans attempting to evade detection, and the potential for non-hostile scans. We focus on detecting 'horizontal' scans from a single source that attempt to discover the active hosts on a network (e.g., "Ping scans") or a particular service across a network (e.g., scans for SSH services on port 22). This approach may apply to detecting scanning botnets as each contributing source can be detected individually. We do not detect 'vertical' scans that attempt to enumerate the services on a single host.

A highly effective and widely cited method for detecting scanners is the Threshold Random Walk (TRW) algorithm [2]. TRW can often detect single source scanning after only 4 or 5 connection attempts. Related approaches include [3] and [4]. While effective, these approaches suffer from two limitations: they can be circumvented through mixing probe attempts with accesses to known active hosts, and they cannot handle scans using stateless protocols. Simpler thresholding methods, such as those in [6-9], count probe frequency within some time window and can be circumvented by an attacker slowing down the scan rate.

Thus, there is thus a need for a complementary scan detection method that 1) cannot be circumvented through knowledge of existing hosts, 2) does not require stateful connections or additional information about the internal structure of the defended network, and 3) cannot be evaded by simple rate-limiting approaches. In this paper, we develop such an approach and then show how it can be combined with TRW and simple rate limiting to form a highly effective ensemble approach.

Our method draws on a related insight to that developed with TRW in [1]: since scanners do not know the internal structure of the network they are more likely to access inactive nodes. However, where TRW examines the number of legitimate and illegitimate targets with which each source communicates, we examine the number of sources communicating with each target. This conceptual inversion of the high-level TRW logic enables us to avoid many limitations of TRW (particularly the ability to evade TRW by connecting to operational servers), while retaining TRW's advantages in terms of rate-insensitivity and rapid detection.

* Correspondence: richard.e.harang.civ@mail.mil
[1]U.S. Army Research Laboratory, Adelphi, MD, USA
Full list of author information is available at the end of the article

We proceed as follows. In section 2, we present related work and our differentiation from it. In section 3, we present details of our scan detection methodology. Section 4 analyzes the algorithmic execution and memory complexities. Section 5 describes our experimental data, and section 6 provides the empirical results. We conclude in section 7.

Related work

A wide variety of scan detection methods have been surveyed in [2]. Perhaps the most influential and significant of those is that of [1], in which the TRW method is proposed. This approach is based on the observation that in the course of enumerating an unknown network, a scanner will generate a relatively large number of unsuccessful connections; legitimate traffic by contrast should generate unsuccessful traffic only rarely. By examining a ratio of successful to unsuccessful connections, robust and rapid identification of potential scanners can be achieved. A weakness of the algorithm is that a scanner can boost its successful connection count by accessing known good servers, enabling additional probing of unknown addresses prior to detection. If enough known good servers are probed first (e.g., 6 or 7 for the published TRW parameters), TRW will permanently classify the scanner as benign and will ignore any subsequent scanning activity [3]. TRW can be modified to avoid such permanent labelling, but this causes a significant increase in the computation and memory requirements [3], while still leaving open the ability for an attacker to delay being categorized as malicious by seeding scan activity with accesses to known servers. Another weakness is that TRW only operates on stateful protocols like TCP that clearly define a "failed" connection. This limitation is due to TRW classifying stateless communication as scan activity in situations where there is a lack of bi-directional communication [3].

TRW has been used as a building block for other work. The work of [4] describes enhancing TRW with a severity metric to distinguish reconnaissance scanning from peer-to-peer scanning. A ranking metric for a TRW-based method is also applied in [5] to detect inter-domain scans. The work of [6] examines a different extension of the TRW method in which the target thresholds for the likelihood ratio are sequentially adapted according to some user-defined acceptable risk for a bounded sequence, thus allowing the TRW method to converge to a decision in (almost surely) finite time. The work of [7] modifies TRW to allow for scan detection in network backbones where there is asymmetric routing. It considers the ratio of distinct IPs contacted to distinct ports contacted within a time window, and labels IP addresses that show a pronounced asymmetry in either direction (i.e., an extremely high number of IPs

contacted on just a few ports or an extremely large number of ports on a limited number of distinct IPs) as potential scanners.

The work of [8], similarly to TRW, uses a likelihood ratio test, however it focuses on comparing the empirical distribution of benign traffic with that of an assumed uniform distribution of scanning traffic. As noted in [1], an inaccurate empirical distribution may result in significant false positive results and an assumed uniform distribution of scanning traffic may present detection circumvention opportunities for attackers. Probabilistic methods are also used in [9] to construct a Bayesian belief network to detect anomalous packets that may be indicative of a scan and a correlation engine to attempt to collect these anomalous packets into sets that suggest scanning behavior. As in [8], the accuracy of this method depends in large part on the quality of the data used to build the statistical model that represents 'normal' traffic.

Other approaches include [10], in which the tools of social network analysis are applied to graphs constructed from netflow data to detect a wide range of intrusive behaviors, including scans. In [11], the RIPPER data mining tool is applied to a set of hand-crafted feature vectors in order to learn novel rules to classify network scans.

Simpler threshold based mechanisms (see, e.g., [12-15]), that simply tally connection attempts and alarm if the number of connections attempted by a single IP exceed some threshold within a certain period of time, have also been used. These can be effective for many types of scanning and were implemented in systems such as the Network Security Monitor [12] and Snort [13]. Later systems such as Bro [14] elaborated on this initial concept by also tracking failed connections in a side count for particular ports. Such techniques are lightweight and sufficiently effective on unsophisticated scanning activity that they continue to be widely used. More recent developments in this vein examine TCP flags attempting to find unusual sequences of flags, such as FIN flags being sent or received when no already established connection is present [15], or construct more elaborate feature vectors based on distinct IP counts of successful and unsuccessful connections [16].

Several methods address detecting groups of collaborating scanners, such as those coordinated through a botnet or other covert distributed system [17-20]. While our approach can detect individual scanners making up such a coordinated effort, we do not attempt to group detected scanners into collaborating groups.

Method

As stated previously, our method is designed to work with both stateful and stateless protocols in situations where knowledge of the currently active hosts is not available. It is also resistant to attackers deliberately accessing known active servers in order to perform a TRW camouflage attack [3]. The method is illustrated in Figure 1. First, we examine inbound flows (flows from internal to external hosts), and score each internal host on the basis of the number of unique external hosts that have contacted it (to associate higher scores with 'riskier' behavior, we take the inverse of this number; see annotations for W in Figure 1). Next, each external host is scored on the basis of the highest score obtained by any communicating partner (see annotations for S in Figure 1). Finally, to reduce false positives, we track the number of distinct connections that each external host creates (see annotations for C in Figure 1). Combining the S and C measures allow us to classify each external host as a scanner or benign host.

Formally, we construct a directed bipartite graph $G = (V,E)$ with $V = L \cup R$, all external hosts in L and all internal hosts in R. We let the edge (x,y) indicate that there exists observed traffic from x to y, and add only edges of the form $\{(x,y) : x \in L, y \in R\}$ (so that only "inbound" traffic is recorded). We then assign scores W_y, S_x, and C_x as:

$$W_y = 1/\#|x \in L : (x,y) \in E|$$

$$S_x = \sup_{y}\{W_y : (x,y) \in E\}$$

$$C_x = \#|y \in R : (x,y) \in E|$$

Where $\#|set|$ denotes the cardinality of *set*. The nodes with a high W are those that received communication attempts from a relatively low number of distinct

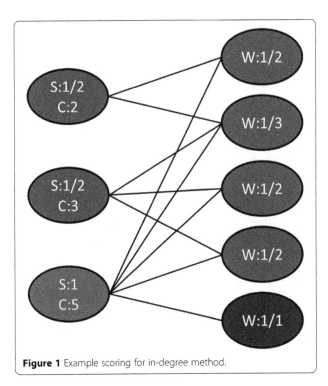

Figure 1 Example scoring for in-degree method.

hosts. The nodes with a high S are those that attempted to initiate connections to any such sparsely contacted hosts (the supremum of the edge connected W_y scores). And the nodes with a high C made many connections (without reference to the connectivity of the target).

Under the assumption that inactive hosts will receive far fewer inbound connection attempts than active hosts, and that scanners are disproportionately likely to attempt to both contact these inactive hosts and make a large number of connection attempts, it then follows that external nodes with high joint C and S scores are more likely to be scanners. If statistical information is known about the rate of incoming packets to active hosts, these scores may be used in a likelihood test similar to [1] or [8] to identify the probability that a particular external host is scanning. In the absence of this information, we may use unsupervised approaches such as thresholding or clustering to identify potential scanning nodes. A straightforward approach that does not require reliance upon strong distributional assumptions (e.g. normality of the distribution of contacts) is to choose some empirical quantile $\theta_s, \theta_c \in [0,1]$ and find thresholds α and β satisfying:

$$\alpha = \underset{i}{\operatorname{argmin}} P(S_x \leq i : x \in L) \geq \theta_s$$

$$\beta = \underset{t}{\operatorname{argmin}} P(C_x \leq t : x \in L) \geq \theta_c$$

where the probability measure P is obtained from the empirical distribution of S or C, as appropriate. We then designate an external host as a potential scanner if both $(S_x > \alpha)$ and $(C_x > \beta)$.

In Figure 1 we provide a simple worked example of the scoring method. We assume that the external IPs are the left partite component, and the internal IPs are the right partite component. The bottom-most external IP is a scanner, and the bottom-most internal IP is an inactive host. As the inactive host receives only a single connection from the scanner, it obtains a W score of 1; this is the largest across the W scores of the internal IPs connected to the scanner, so the scanner obtains an S score of 1. As the scanner contacts 5 internal IPs, it obtains a C score of 5.

Note that this method requires only directed flows from the L component to the R component in order to calculate the relevant scores. This feature allows the in-degree method to function in situations where asymmetric routing exists without any need for modification (c.f. [7], where the TRW approach required modification to function adequately under asymmetric routing conditions). We do not address this feature directly, but the experience of [7] suggests that direct deployment of the TRW method under asymmetric routing will be highly problematic.

Algorithm and execution complexity

This method can be implemented using a batch processing approach in time complexity O($m$log$m$) where m represents the number of flows but can achieve linear time with a slight variation. Most steps are O(m) while the calculations for α and β require O($m$log$m$) due to the requirement to sort two arrays containing S and C values respectively. If linear time complexity is needed, the calculations for α and β can be reused in subsequent batches provided that the time slices being evaluated are of the same length, or can be approximated through a number of on-line estimators [21]. The memory footprint required is at most O(m) provided one uses an in-place style sorting algorithm (e.g., in-place heapsort).

The algorithm is as follows:

1. Extract all flows whose source is in L and whose destination is in R in O(m) time.
2. Enumerate over all extracted flows to filter out those that do not connect distinct IP pairs. Use a hash table, LRHash, keyed by both IP addresses to determine if a flow connects distinct pairs. A single hash table lookup and insertion takes O(1). Since there are O(m) remaining flows, this operation takes O(m).
3. Enumerate over the set of flows with distinct IP pairs. For each flow, populate and update a hash table, RHash, by using the destination IP address as the key. For each processed flow, increment a count of source IPs communicating with the destination IP and update a variable containing the inverse of this value (the W metric). This uses O(m) time since there are O(m) flows and hash table lookups and updates are O(1).
4. Enumerate over the set of flows with distinct IP pairs. For each flow, populate and update a hash table, LHash, by using the source IP address as the key. For each processed flow, increment the count of destination IPs communicating with the source IP (this is the C metric) and append each destination IP to a list (one list for every hash key). This uses O(m) time since there are O(m) flows, hash table lookups and updates are O(1), and appending to a list is O(1).
5. Calculate the S metric for each source IP by accessing each key in LHash and traversing the local list to look up each destination IP in RHash. Assign S to be the largest W value found in the RHash lookups and store it in LHash. This takes O(m) to access each key, an amortized O(m) to traverse all destination IP lists, and O(1) for the RHash lookup. Overall this is O(m).
6. Calculate α in O($m$log$m$) by accessing each key in LHash, building a sorted array of the discovered S values, and extracting the value stored at the index ($\theta_S * length(list)$).

7. Calculate β in O($m$log$m$) by accessing each key in LHash, building a sorted array of discovered C values, and extracting the value stored at the index ($\theta_C * length(list)$).
8. Compare each source IP in LHash and its S and C values to α and β to identify the scanners in O(m) time.

This batch based algorithm can be executed with overlapping time windows since the linear execution option executes very quickly. The algorithm can then be run in small periodic increments (but still using large time windows), approximating an always-on online solution. A true online algorithm is more difficult to achieve because a single flow can change the S value in O(m) nodes in L. Even more problematic, a newly processed flow indicates that some amount of time has elapsed. Thus, previously process flows may need to drop out of the calculation for W, S, and C values for all nodes. Data structures to accommodate this are computationally expensive and so we suggest using linear complexity, continuously running, overlapping time window, batch jobs as a better solution.

Data

Our data sets consist of network flows, both live and simulated. Each flow contains source and destination IP addresses, port numbers, connection times, and TCP flags (used for TRW analysis).

Live data

Our live data was collected for 24 hours from a single network intrusion detection sensor. A total of 5,897,187 flows were observed, involving 454,510 distinct pairs of IP addresses. This data was known *a priori* to contain one port scan across a substantial portion of a class C subnet.

Due to the potentially sensitive nature of the live data, it has been anonymized in our results as follows:

1. Each distinct external class C subnet within the data has been replaced with a non-routable subnet selected uniformly at random from the set of non-routable subnets in 10.0.0.0/8.
2. Each distinct internal class C subnet within the data has been replaced with a non-routable subnet selected uniformly at random from 172.16.0.0/12.
3. Each final octet within each class C subnet (both internal and external) has been replaced with an octet selected uniformly at random from the range 1–255 (for the sake of simplicity we neglect the reduction in valid IP addresses caused by the assignment of gateway, network name, and broadcast addresses).
4. We do not report port information, other than noting whether source IP, destination IP, or both exhibit a fixed port during the reported scan.

Simulated data

To augment the live data, we simulate 3 scans by introducing appropriate flow records into the live data. We simulate an ICMP "ping" scan, a TCP SYN scan (with fixed source and destination ports), and a UDP scan (with fixed destination ports). Each simulated scan probes all 255 members of a class C subnet within the network perimeter from a spurious source IP address. Partial and rate-limited scans are simulated by subsampling some proportion of the full scans and distributing their event times uniformly over the duration of the flow being analyzed. Responses from active hosts to the simulated scanning packets were created as follows: ICMP packets generated no response; UDP packets generated either an ICMP Port Unreachable message, a mock UDP response packet, or no response (all with equal probability); TCP packets received an ACK for active hosts (followed by a final RST packet from the scanner). Inactive hosts created no response.

We note that our algorithm does not make use of subnetting information except at the presentation layer, and hence a very sparse scan across a class B subnet (for example, a single random IP within each class C subnet contained within the class B subnet) would yield the same results, however this renders the display of results less compact, and so is omitted for space.

Results

We first used our in-degree algorithm as a guide to discover novel scans within the live network data, as well as the scan known *a priori*, while examining the impact of various parameter settings. We then explore an ensemble scan detection solution by combining our algorithm with TRW and rate-based scanning. We show how TRW complements our approach by both approaches detecting different sets of scanning IPs. We furthermore show how pre-filtering our in-degree method with a rate-based scanning method can substantially reduce the false positive rate. We then compare our findings against a manual analysis of the same data. For our last data set, we investigate in-degree and TRW detection of the simulated scans injected into the live data. We conclude this section with an analysis of the difficultly of an attacker simultaneously circumventing both our in-degree approach and TRW.

In-degree method results on live network traffic

After the initial processing of live data as described above, 509 external hosts were identified as initiating connections with nodes within the portion of the network observed by the sensor. The S and C values were tabulated as described in section 3 and are presented in Figure 2 and Figure 3. Total counts that exceed joint thresholds of C and S are given in Table 1.

Marginal distributions of S and C suggest that the bulk of the data (89.2%) has an S score of 0.333 or less, and 83.3% of the data has a C score of 1 or less. The joint distribution indicates that there is a slight dependence between S and C, with approximately 2.0% (10/509) of the data having both $S > 0.333$ and $C > 1$ versus 1.8% if the scores were independent. The data having these values are highlighted in bold in Table 1 (bold italics indicates the presence of scans that were not detected by any combination of methods examined, as discussed below). At the other extreme, approximately 86.4% of our joint data falls into the lower bins in both dimensions (versus an expected value of 74.3% assuming independence). A permutation test yields a one-tailed p-value of 0.0178, indicating slight but significant correlation.

Detailed examination of the 10 external IPs in the bold cells in Table 1 indicated that 2 were false positives. One was determined to be the result of a web-based advertising network rotating through a pool of IP addresses serving auto-refreshing content to 4 otherwise idle hosts. The second was the result of network time protocol (NTP) traffic delivered to 2 otherwise inactive hosts. There was thus a .000034% false positive rate with respect to the number of original flows and .00044% with respect to distinct pairs of IP addresses. By either measure, the false positive rate is extremely low.

The remaining 8 were clearly identifiable as scan attempts, and confirmed to be such after examination by network analysts. Summaries of two of the most obvious scans, consisting of two external IP addresses directed traffic to 84 and 261 distinct IP addresses, respectively, are presented in Table 2 (scans 1 and 2) as well as a more subtle one (scan 3) discussed below. The TCP scan (scan 1) from Table 2 was known *a priori* to be in the data, and was successfully detected by our algorithm. While it is gratifying to note that these two scans were detected, it should be noted that these were rather obvious scans readily detected by even simple windowing methods. Scan 1 in Table 2 was perhaps somewhat rate limited, scanning just over 4 IP addresses per second; however, scan 2 in Table 2 made no attempts at subtlety, probing substantial portions of two class C subnets in less than 3 seconds.

Of perhaps greater interest are those scans that did attempt some degree of subtlety, presumably to evade traditional rate-based scan detection methods. Scan 3 in Table 2 shows a summary of one such scan detected in the live data by our method, in which just 7 IP addresses were scanned over the course of approximately 7.75 hours. Consultation with network analysts suggests that there is an extremely high likelihood that this traffic represents a deliberate attempt to evade rate-based portscan detection algorithms. Note that the ICMP protocol is not one that is supported by most stateful connection-based scanners [3],

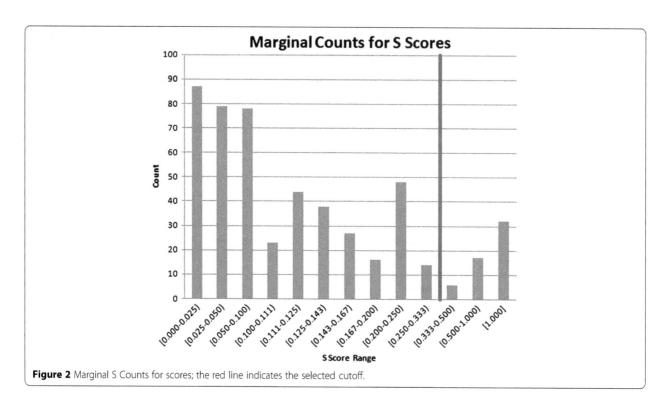

Figure 2 Marginal S Counts for scores; the red line indicates the selected cutoff.

and hence this scan would not have been detected by those methods.

Our results for the in-degree method alone are summarized in Table 3. This includes results for a 'filtered' version of in-degree where we use a rate-based detection scheme to filter out obvious scans (explained in more detail in section 6.2.2). We define a lateral scan as a scan in which a single target port was identical over all internal IP addresses scanned. We define a network enumeration scan as one in which either a portless protocol (i.e. ICMP) was used, or a single destination port per IP was contacted that varied from IP to IP in what appears

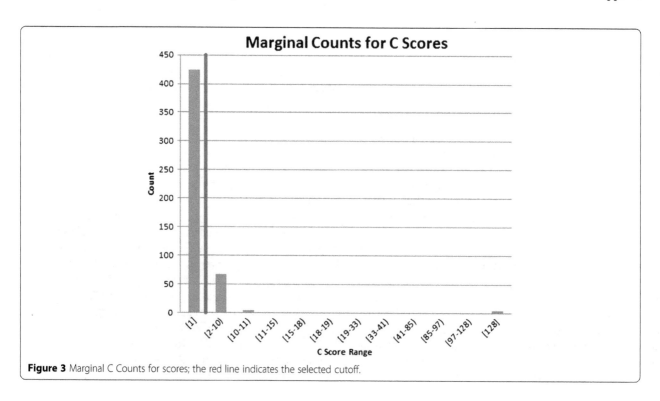

Figure 3 Marginal C Counts for scores; the red line indicates the selected cutoff.

Table 1 Cumulative counts greater than or equal to joint values of C and S

S score	C score						
	1	*2*	*10*	*18*	*85*	*97*	*128*
0.010	*509*	*85*	*17*	*10*	*6*	*5*	*4*
0.050	*343*	*54*	*17*	*10*	*6*	*5*	*4*
0.200	*117*	*40*	*15*	*9*	*6*	*5*	*4*
0.250	*69*	*17*	**2**	**2**	*1*	*0*	*0*
0.333	*55*	**10**	**2**	**2**	*1*	*0*	*0*
0.500	*49*	**7**	**2**	**2**	*1*	*0*	*0*
1.000	*32*	**7**	**2**	**2**	*1*	*0*	*0*

Bold font indicates that the S and C values were greater than or equal to the data-determined thresholds of 0.333 and 1.0, respectively; bold italics indicates the presence of scans at those S/C values that were not detected (see text for details). Note that these represent *cumulative* counts, and so, for example, the value of 10 for $S \geq 0.333$ and $C \geq 1$ includes all values below and to the right.

to be a largely random manner. We define a service enumeration scan as one where multiple connections were attempted to each internal IP across a fixed set of ports, with substantially the same set attempted for each such IP. We do not include false positives in the table but restate that 2 inactive hosts received legitimate traffic that resulted in a false positive result for both filtered and unfiltered methods.

Composition of methods on live data
We now explore how the in-degree method complements TRW detection and how rate-based detection methods can reduce in-degree false negatives.

TRW and in-degree method
The TRW algorithm was applied to the same data for comparison and the results are shown in Table 4. The data shows that the in-degree and TRW algorithms are strongly complementary, with very little overlap between the scans detected by the two methods. This suggests that our method successfully detects many scans that the TRW algorithm cannot (and vice versa).

Pre-filtering in-degree data with rate-based scanning
We next applied a simple rate-based detection scheme as a pre-filter to the in-degree algorithm (filtering out flows corresponding to detected scans) to obtain the results in Table 5. For this, we flagged an IP as a scanner if it completed more than 5 connections to distinct IP/port pairs within any 5-second window. Removing these scans before applying the in-degree method significantly enhanced the ability of the in-degree method to detect the remaining scanners; it did not improve the detection rate of the TRW algorithm. As all three scans removed by rate-limiting were UDP scans, and the TRW algorithm is not capable of detecting UDP scans in the absence of a network state oracle of some form, the removal of these scans did not alter the information available to the TRW algorithm or its performance. Three scans were detected and filtered in this way. These three scanned large portions of the network, increasing the number of connections to internal IPs, and thus lowered their W scores. In 6 cases these obvious scans lowered the S scores of other scanners (for the unfiltered in-degree instance), interfering with the ability of the in-degree method to detect them. Service enumeration scans (as defined above) were particularly vulnerable to this problem.

Table 5 then represents our most important result. Of the 36 known scans in our dataset, the tri-algorithm approach detected 34 of them. 3 were detected solely by the rate limiting approach. 13 were detected solely by TRW. 12 were detected solely by the in-degree algorithm. 6 were detected by both TRW and the in-degree algorithm. The overall detection rate for the tri-algorithm approach was then 94.44%. This compares to individual detection rates of just 50.00% for in-degree,

Table 2 Scan detected from live traffic

Field	Value(s) – scan 1	Value(s) – scan 2	Value(s) – scan 3
Scan duration	6 minutes, 7 seconds	2.8 seconds	7 hours, 48 minutes
Protocol	TCP	ICMP and TCP	ICMP
Flags	SYN or SYN-ACK	SYN or SYN-ACK (TCP only)	N/A
Source IP (anonymized)	10.141.12.103	10.97.54.7	10.60.88.39
Source ports	Constant	Varied between 4 values	N/A
Destination IPs (anonymized)	84 within 172.40.102.0/24	29 within 172.198.57.0/24	7 within 172.198.57.0/24
		110 within 172.45.99.0/24	
		122 within 172.110.117.0/24	
Destination ports	Constant	Constant (when TCP)	N/A
Packets transmitted	3 per contact	6 (ICMP) or 1 (TCP) per contact	1 or 3 per contact
Total bytes transmitted	186 per contact	420 (ICMP) or 62 (TCP) per contact	70 bytes per packet
Data bytes transmitted	24 per contact	48 (ICMP) or 8 (TCP) per contact	8 bytes per packet

Table 3 Detection counts by class of scan

Type	Detected (unfiltered)	Detected (filtered)	Not detected
Lateral port (TCP)	6	9	0
Lateral port (UDP)	0	0	3
Network enumeration (any)	2	5	0
Service enumeration	0	4	2
Totals	8	18	5

Table 5 Cross-tabulation of TRW and filtered in-degree detections

In-degree (pre-filtered)	TRW		
	Detected	Not detected	Total
Detected	6	12	18
Not detected	13	5*	18
Total	19	17	36

*3 of these 5 were detected by the rate-limiting scan detection algorithm and removed.

52.78% for TRW, and 8.33% for rate-limiting. The dramatic increase in the overall detection rate highlights the complementary nature of these three algorithms.

Manual analysis

We performed a manual analysis of the inbound traffic subset of the 5.9 million flow records identified above, using a variety of internal analysis and aggregation tools, as well as direct examination of the flows. This required significant analyst effort and thus is a completely infeasible method for routine scan detection. Our analysis revealed the 2 scans not detected by any automated detection method, both contained within the darker shaded cells in Table 1. These two appeared to be service enumeration scans, resulting in higher S scores for each scanned host as multiple services were requested. Note that as this was a manual analysis, we cannot rule out the possibility of additional false negatives. Reducing the threshold for S to 0.250 would have successfully detected both such scans at the cost of an additional 5 false positives (we also note that proposed modification to the TRW described in [3] would have enabled the TRW method to detect them). 25 external hosts also delivered a single contact to nodes which had not received any other traffic. While these cannot be ruled out as extremely slow scan attempts, they were determined to be most likely the result of misdirected traffic.

Simulated data

Simulated data was included in the raw data as described above in an attempt to precisely quantify the effect of scan size on the likelihood of detection. Values for α and β were selected as described above, using values of 0.75 for θ in both cases. Scans were directed at a single moderately populated subnet with 119 active IP addresses

Table 4 Cross-tabulation of TRW and in-degree detections

In-degree	TRW		
	Detected	Not detected	Total
Detected	2	6	8
Not detected	17	11	28
Total	19	17	36

out of the space of 254 possible ones (excluding standard gateway and broadcast addresses). For each trial, the indicated number of probes were directed to random addresses in the subnet, and the in-degree algorithm run without further refinement. In all cases, the cutoff for C was 2 (preventing detection of scans consisting of a single probe) and the cutoff for S was 0.333. Scans were reliably detected with as few as 4 IPs scanned per attempt, and in no case did a single scan of 5 or more scanned IPs escape detection. Despite the creation of additional connections that could potentially have reduced the S score of some hosts as described above, our inclusion of simulated scans did not alter the detection rates for any of the scans detected in our initial analysis; we therefore only report the detection results for the additional, simulated scans. Results are shown in Figure 4.

As successful connections are only defined for TCP connections, the TRW method was applied only to the simulated TCP scans. Results are given in Figure 4. While the TRW method did successfully identify the majority of simulated scans as the number of probes per IP address approached 10, the success rate was markedly less than that of the in-degree method. The TRW results for probes 1–5 were expected as the construction of TRW requires a sufficient history of failed probes in order to be able to alert on a scan. The deficiency of TRW when compared to in-degree for probes 6–10 reflects the fact that probes to active services (prevalent in this subnet) can camouflage scanning activity against TRW detection. Conversely, in the operational data in section 6.2, scans generally involved a large number of probes per scan, resulting in a much higher TRW performance.

Circumvention analysis

While the in-degree method shows excellent performance when detecting random scans on the basis of low in-degree count, our false negative and rate-limited scan results point out a potential evasion technique: generating multiple connections to each host from distinct IP addresses in order to artificially decrease the S scores. Preliminary work has shown that under modest assumptions, it is not difficult to construct a 'chaff' set of connections from a set of scanning IP addresses that will

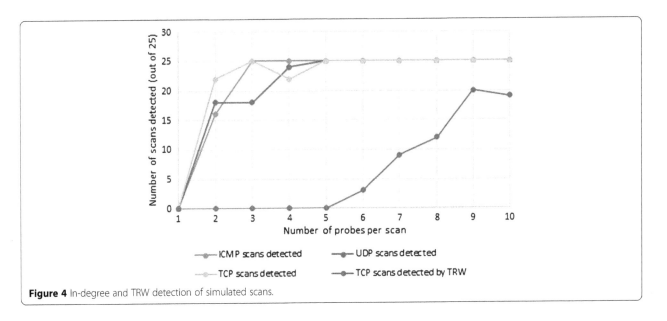

Figure 4 In-degree and TRW detection of simulated scans.

reduce the S scores sufficiently to avoid detection under this method, while simultaneously maintaining a low enough rate to evade rate-based intrusion detection systems. As shown above, however, the TRW method of [1] forms an excellent complementary method to ours (for TCP based scans) such that it will be difficult for an adversary to avoid both detectors simultaneously. The TRW method and its variants can be evaded by maintaining a sufficiently high ratio of successful to unsuccessful connections [1,3] while our method ultimately forces a potential attacker to create numerous unsuccessful connections to evade detection. In order to simultaneously maintain both a non-alerting TRW score and a non-alerting S score, the total number of connections that the attacker must therefore create per inactive IP address probed to avoid detection increases significantly. However, note that there are no limits on the rate at which any feasible covert scanning may be accomplished. By reintroducing rate-based detection methods, which limit the total rate of connections regardless of status, the combination of these three methods places limits on the total rate at which new IPs can be scanned without detection. In future work, we will investigate the synthesis of the three methods and theoretical limits on the potential for covert attacker scanning rates.

Conclusions

We have presented a novel approach to scan detection that operates in a complementary fashion to the Threshold Random Walk (TRW) method of [1]. Instead of just providing another scan detection methodology, our approach detects previously unmitigated TRW circumvention activity as well as activity that operates using connectionless protocols. Our novel method has a low time complexity,

and has been applied to real-world network data both alone and in conjunction with the TRW and rate-limiting scan detection methods. The in-degree method is shown to detect scans not identified by the TRW method, and to do so with increased accuracy when the data is pre-processed to remove scans detected by a simple rate-limiting method. Further application to randomly generated scans have shown that – under the assumption that target IPs are picked at random from the available addresses in the subnet, and the subnet in question is not completely allocated – the in-degree method is extremely effective at picking out novel scans. While doing this, the in-degree method maintains a very low false positive rate.

We combined in-degree method with TRW and simple rate limiting to form a highly effective ensemble algorithm. Since TRW and in-degree work using distinct data sets (internal node behavior versus external node behavior), the combination makes it extremely difficult for scanners to operate without detection and mitigates known circumvention approaches. Deliberately connecting to know active hosts prior to probing unknown addresses to circumvent TRW is likely to be detected by in-degree and 'chaff' connections designed to circumvent in-degree are likely to be detected by TRW.

Abbreviations
ICMP: Internet Control Message Protocol; IP: Internet Protocol; SSH: Secure Shell; TCP: Transmission Control Protocol; TRW: Threshold Random Walk; UDP: User Datagram Protocol.

Competing interests
The authors declare that they have no competing interests.

Authors' contributions
PM and RH jointly conceived the initial version of the in-degree algorithm. PM developed an efficient implementation of the in-degree method in Python. RH performed the experimentation. Both authors contributed equally

to writing and data analysis. Both authors read and approved the final manuscript.

Acknowledgments

This research was sponsored by the U.S. Army Research Labs and the National Institute of Standards and Technology (NIST). It was partially accomplished under Army Contract Number W911QX-07-F-0023. The views and conclusions contained in this document are those of the authors, and should not be interpreted as representing the official policies, either expressed or implied, of the Army Research Laboratory, NIST, or the U.S. Government. The U.S. Government is authorized to reproduce and distribute reprints for Government purposes, notwithstanding any copyright notation hereon. The authors would like to thank Harold Booth of NIST for assisting with the initial formulation of the in-degree concept.

Author details

[1]U.S. Army Research Laboratory, Adelphi, MD, USA. [2]National Institute of Standards and Technology, Gaithersburg, Maryland, USA.

References

1. J Jung, V Paxson, AW Berger, H Balakrishnan, *"Fast portscan detection using sequential hypothesis testing,"*. IEEE Symposium on Security and Privacy, 2004, pp. 211–225
2. M Bhuyan, DK Bhattacharyya, JK Kalita, "Surveying Port Scans and Their Detection Methodologies". Comput J **54**(10), 1565–1581 (2011)
3. P Mell, R Harang, "Limitations to Threshold Random Walk and Mitigating Enhancements,", in *First IEEE Conference on Communications and Network Security (submitted)*, 2013
4. V Falletta, F Ricciato, "Detecting scanners: empirical assessment on a 3G network". Int J Network Secur **9**(2), 143–155 (2009)
5. L. Aniello, G. Lodi and R. Baldoni, "Inter-domain stealthy port scan detection through complex event processing,," Proceedings of the 13th European Workshop on Dependable Computing. (ACM, Pisa Italy, 2011)
6. X Chen, *"New Sequential Methods for Detecting Portscanners," arXiv preprint, 1204(1935)*, 2012
7. A Sridharan, T Ye, S Bhattacharyya, *Connectionless port scan detection on the backbone*. Performance, Computing, and Communications Conference, 2006
8. C Leckie, R Kotagiri, *A probabilistic approach to detecting network scans*. Network Operations and Management Symposium, 2002, pp. 359–372
9. S Staniford, JA Hoagland, JM McAlerney, Practical automated detection of stealthy portscans. J Comput Secur **10**(1/2), 105–136 (2002)
10. Q Ding, N Katenka, P Barford, E Kolaczyk, M Crovella, *Intrusion as (anti) social communication: characterization and detection*. Proceedings of the 18th ACM SIGKDD international conference on Knowledge discovery and data mining, 2012, pp. 886–894
11. GJ Simon, H Xiong, E Eilertson, V Kumar, *Scan detection: A data mining approach*. Proceedings of the Sixth SIAM International Conference on Data Mining, 2006, pp. 118–129
12. LT Heberlein, GV Dias, KN Levitt, B Mukherjee, J Wood, D Wolber, *A network security monitor*. IEEE Computer Society Symposium on Research in Security and Privacy, 1990, pp. 296–304
13. M Roesch, *Snort – lightweight intrusion detection for networks*. Proceedings of the 13th USENIX conference on System administration, 1999, pp. 229–238
14. V Paxson, Bro: a system for detecting network intruders in real-time. Comput Netw **31**(23), 2435–2463 (1999)
15. M Dabbagh, AJ Ghandour, K Fawaz, WE Hajj, H Hajj, *Slow port scanning detection*. 7th International Conference on Information Assurance and Security, 2011, pp. 228–233
16. M Alsaleh, PCV Oorschot, *"Network scan detection with LQS: a lightweight, quick and stateful algorithm"*. Proceedings of the 6th ACM Symposium on Information, Computer and Communications Security, 2011
17. C Gates, *"Coordinated scan detection"*. Proceedings of the 16th Annual Network and Distributed System Security Symposium, 2009
18. R Baldoni, GAD Luna, L Querzoni, *"Collaborative Detection of Coordinated Port Scans"*. Midlab Technical Report, 2012
19. M Kang, J Caballero, D Song, *"Distributed evasive scan techniques and countermeasures,"*. Detection of Intrusions and Malware, and Vulnerability Assessment, 2007, pp. 157–174
20. Y Zhang, B Bhargava, Allocation Schemes, Architectures, and Policies for Collaborative Port Scanning Attacks. J Emerg Technol Web Intell **3**(2), 154–167 (2011)
21. M Greenwald, S Khanna, Space-efficient online computation of quantile summaries. ACM SIGMOD Record **30**(2), 58–66 (2001)

Permissions

The contributors of this book come from diverse backgrounds, making this book a truly international effort. This book will bring forth new frontiers with its revolutionizing research information and detailed analysis of the nascent developments around the world.

We would like to thank all the contributing authors for lending their expertise to make the book truly unique. They have played a crucial role in the development of this book. Without their invaluable contributions this book wouldn't have been possible. They have made vital efforts to compile up to date information on the varied aspects of this subject to make this book a valuable addition to the collection of many professionals and students.

This book was conceptualized with the vision of imparting up-to-date information and advanced data in this field. To ensure the same, a matchless editorial board was set up. Every individual on the board went through rigorous rounds of assessment to prove their worth. After which they invested a large part of their time researching and compiling the most relevant data for our readers.

The editorial board has been involved in producing this book since its inception. They have spent rigorous hours researching and exploring the diverse topics which have resulted in the successful publishing of this book. They have passed on their knowledge of decades through this book. To expedite this challenging task, the publisher supported the team at every step. A small team of assistant editors was also appointed to further simplify the editing procedure and attain best results for the readers.

Apart from the editorial board, the designing team has also invested a significant amount of their time in understanding the subject and creating the most relevant covers. They scrutinized every image to scout for the most suitable representation of the subject and create an appropriate cover for the book.

The publishing team has been an ardent support to the editorial, designing and production team. Their endless efforts to recruit the best for this project, has resulted in the accomplishment of this book. They are a veteran in the field of academics and their pool of knowledge is as vast as their experience in printing. Their expertise and guidance has proved useful at every step. Their uncompromising quality standards have made this book an exceptional effort. Their encouragement from time to time has been an inspiration for everyone.

The publisher and the editorial board hope that this book will prove to be a valuable piece of knowledge for researchers, students, practitioners and scholars across the globe.

List of Contributors

Kristin Glass
Institute for Complex Additive Systems Analysis, New Mexico Institute of Mining and Technology, Socorro, USA

Richard Colbaugh
Analytics and Cryptography Department, Sandia National Laboratories, Albuquerque, USA

Nitesh Bharosa
Delft University of Technology, Jaffalaan 5, 2628BX, Delft, The Netherlands

JinKyu Lee
Spears School of Business, Oklahoma State University, 317 North Hall, 700 N. Greenwood Ave, Tulsa, OK 74106, USA

Marijn Janssen
Delft University of Technology, Jaffalaan 5, 2628BX, Delft, The Netherlands

H Raghav Rao
Management Science and Systems, University at Buffalo, 325C Jacobs Mgmt Center, Amherst, NY 14260, USA9 Department of GSM, Sogang University, Seoul, Korea

Craig M Vineyard
Sandia National Laboratories, Albuquerque, NM, USA

Stephen J Verzi
Sandia National Laboratories, Albuquerque, NM, USA

Michael L Bernard
Sandia National Laboratories, Albuquerque, NM, USA

Shawn E Taylor
Sandia National Laboratories, Albuquerque, NM, USA

Irene Dubicka
Sandia National Laboratories, Albuquerque, NM, USA

Thomas P Caudell
Department of Electrical and Computer Engineering, University of New Mexico, Albuquerque, NM, USA

Kshanti Greene
Management Sciences, Inc., Albuquerque, NM, USA

Dan Thomsen
SIFT, LLC, Minneapolis, MN, USA

Pietro Michelucci
Strategic Analysis, Inc., Washington, DC, USA

Yue Zhang
Predictive Technology Laboratory, Department of Systems and Information Engineering, University of Virginia, Charlottesville, Virginia, USA

Donald E Brown
Predictive Technology Laboratory, Department of Systems and Information Engineering, University of Virginia, Charlottesville, Virginia, USA

Carlo Morselli
School of Criminology, Université de Montréal, C.P. 6128, succursale Centre-ville, Montreal, QC H3C-3 J7, Canada

Victor Hugo Masias
Faculty of Economics and Business, Universidad Diego Portales, Manuel Rodríguez Sur 253, 8370057, Santiago de, Chile
Department of Management Control, University of Chile, Diagonal Paraguay 257, 8330015, Santiago de, Chile

Fernando Crespo
Universidad de Valparaíso, Brigadier de La Cruz 1050, 8900183, Santiago de, Chile

Sigifredo Laengle
Department of Management Control, University of Chile, Diagonal Paraguay 257, 8330015, Santiago de, Chile

Rachel A Hegemann
Department of Mathematics, University of California Los Angeles, 520 Portola Plaza, Los Angeles CA, USA

Erik A Lewis
Department of Mathematics, University of California Los Angeles, 520 Portola Plaza, Los Angeles CA, USA

Andrea L Bertozzi
Department of Mathematics, University of California Los Angeles, 520 Portola Plaza, Los Angeles CA, USA

Paul T Bartone
Center for Technology & National Security Policy, National Defense University, Ft. McNair, Washington, DC 20319-5062, USA

Lorraine Bowman-Grieve
School of Psychology, University of Lincoln, Lincoln, UK

Richard Berk
Department of Statistics, Department of Criminology, University of Pennsylvania, Philadelphia, USA

Laura A McNamara
Sandia National Laboratories, PO Box 5800, MS 0519, Albuquerque, NM 87185-0519, USA

Victor Benjamin
MIS Department, University of Arizona, Tucson, AZ, USA

Wingyan Chung
Department of Decision and Info Sciences, Stetson University, DeLand, FL, USA

Ahmed Abbasi
McIntire School of Commerce, University of Virginia, Charlottesville, VA, USA

Joshua Chuang
HC Analytics, Tucson, AZ, USA

Catherine A Larson
MIS Department, University of Arizona, Tucson, AZ, USA

Hsinchun Chen
MIS Department, University of Arizona, Tucson, AZ, USA

Jacob R Scanlon
Predictive Technology Laboratory, Department of Systems and Information Engineering, University of Virginia, Charlottesville VA, USA

Matthew S Gerber
Predictive Technology Laboratory, Department of Systems and Information Engineering, University of Virginia, Charlottesville VA, USA

Rasmus Rosenqvist Petersen
The Maersk Mc-Kinney Moeller Institute, University of Southern Denmark, Odense, Denmark

Uffe Kock Wiil
The Maersk Mc-Kinney Moeller Institute, University of Southern Denmark, Odense, Denmark

Joel Brynielsson
FOI Swedish Defence Research Agency, Stockholm, Sweden
KTH Royal Institute of Technology, Stockholm, Sweden

Fredrik Johansson
FOI Swedish Defence Research Agency, Stockholm, Sweden

Carl Jonsson
Avanti Communications Group plc, London, UK

Anders Westling
Ericsson, Stockholm, Sweden

Richard Colbaugh
Sandia National Laboratories, Albuquerque, NM 87111, USA

Kristin Glass
New Mexico Institute of Mining and Technology, Socorro, NM 87801, USA

Jennifer Cowley
Carnegie Mellon University Software Engineering Institute, CERT Division, 4500 Fifth Avenue, Pittsburgh, Pennsylvania 15213, USA

Frank L. Greitzer
PsyberAnalytix, 651 Big Sky Drive, Richland, Washington 99352, USA

Bronwyn Woods
Carnegie Mellon University Software Engineering Institute, CERT Division, 4500 Fifth Avenue, Pittsburgh, Pennsylvania 15213, USA

Hafiz Malik
Electrical and Computer Engineering Department, University of Michigan - Dearborn, Dearborn, MI 48128, USA

Hasan Mahmood
Department of Electronics, Quaid-i-Azam University, Islamabad 45320, Pakistan

Thomas E Carroll
Pacific Northwest National Laboratory, P.O. Box 999, 99352 Richland, Washington, USA

Frank L Greitzer
PsyberAnalytix LLC, 99352 Richland, Washington, USA

Adam D Roberts
Pacific Northwest National Laboratory, P.O. Box 999, 99352 Richland, Washington, USA

Richard E Harang
U.S. Army Research Laboratory, Adelphi, MD, USA

Peter Mell
National Institute of Standards and Technology, Gaithersburg, Maryland, USA

Printed in the USA
CPSIA information can be obtained
at www.ICGtesting.com
JSHW052023301024
72690JS00004B/144